Parliament House, Westminster Hall, and the Abbey,
From an engraving by Heliar, 1647

the Abby

CONFESSING
THE FAITH

CONFESSING
THE FAITH

A reader's guide to the
Westminster Confession of Faith

Chad Van Dixhoorn

THE BANNER OF TRUTH TRUST

THE BANNER OF TRUTH TRUST

The Grey House, 3 Murrayfield Road, Edinburgh, EH12 6EL, UK
P.O. Box 621, Carlisle, PA 17013, USA

❧

© Chad Van Dixhoorn 2014

First published 2014
Reprinted 2014
Reprinted 2016

❧

ISBN:
Print: 978-1-84871-404-5
EPUB: 978-1-84871-405-2
Kindle: 978-1-84871-406-9

❧

Typeset in Adobe Garamond Pro 10.5/13.5 pt at
The Banner of Truth Trust, Edinburgh
Printed in the USA by
Versa Press Inc.,
East Peoria, IL

❧

In this book the author cites from the King James Version (KJV), New
International Version (NIV), American Standard Version (ASV), English
Standard Version (ESV), New American Standard Version (NASB),
and offers his own translations where warranted.

Fight the good fight of the faith.
Take hold of the eternal life to which you were called and about
which you made the good confession
in the presence of many witnesses.
1 Timothy 6:12

For Victoria, Caroline, Ashley, Peter and Charlotte.
May each of you make a good confession
before many witnesses.

CONTENTS

FOREWORD

ECENT years have witnessed a growing interest in what is
increasingly known as 'confessional Christianity'. This is a most
encouraging development because the term generally refers to
a Christianity which takes doctrine seriously. 'Confessional Christians'
are those who believe that the Bible actually teaches things about God
which apply in all times and in all places to all people. Doctrine is not
simply a description of religious psychology—how the Christian thinks
or feels about God—but rather a description of who God is and how he
has acted. That more Christians are prepared to self-consciously identify
with such a conception of Christianity is grounds for gratitude and joy.

Nevertheless, there is more to truly *confessional* Christianity than
mere belief in the importance of doctrine. In fact, I have a suspicion that
today's 'confessional Christianity' is simply a reiteration of what used to
be called simply 'conservative' Christianity: a Christianity which believes
in the non-negotiability of ten or twelve basic points of doctrine, usually
embodied in a congregation's doctrinal statement.

Confessional Christianity is more than that. Confessional Christianity is marked by two things: an elaborate confession of faith which
goes beyond the ten or twelve points necessary for a basic Christian
profession of faith; and a church structure which provides for elders,
accountability and indeed ongoing pedagogy. Confessional Christians,
therefore, are not simply committed to doctrine; they are committed to
a particular way of life within the context of the church. If the 'confessional Christianity' which is currently so popular is to service and indeed
mature and thrive, it needs to become confessional Christianity in the
more traditional, ecclesial sense.

Confessionally Reformed Christians tend to look to one of two sets
of documents for their doctrinal statements: the Three Forms of Unity

(the Heidelberg Catechism, the Belgic Confession, and the Canons of Dordt) and the Westminster Standards (The Confession, the Larger and Shorter Catechisms). Reformed churches with origins in Germany and the Netherlands tend to hold to the former, those with Scottish Presbyterian roots to the latter. There is little difference in doctrine between the two, with both providing solid and thorough expositions of the faith.

Given all that, this book is an excellent contribution to the literature on confessional Christianity and will, I trust, be of immense help in further educating confessional Christians in their faith. 'World authority', like 'expert', is a much over-used hyperbole these days, when any Hollywood star with a passport is regarded as competent to comment on world affairs. Yet in the case of Chad Van Dixhoorn and the Westminster Confession, the title is most apt. As editor of the Minutes of the Westminster assembly, Chad has spent more time and devoted more attention to the minutiae of the Confession than anyone else has ever done, excepting perhaps the Westminster delegates themselves. There is no safer or more learned guide to the Confession.

Chad is also a churchman and pastor. Scholarship is one thing; the ability to deploy that scholarship for the benefit of the church is quite another. Chad does both with aplomb. This book is learned but it is also accessible, the fruit of immense and intense study but also of a deep love for God's people.

In short, this guide is a true gem. It deserves to be the standard reference book for any pastor seeking to use the Westminster Standards in his ministry. It should be the first volume for which any Sunday School teacher reaches when asked to do a class on the Confession. It should be the constant companion of all elders. Indeed, it should be on the bookshelves of anyone interested in learning more deeply about the riches of the Reformed and Presbyterian faith. Enjoy—and learn.

CARL R. TRUEMAN
Paul Woolley Professor of Church History,
Westminster Theological Seminary
Pastor, Cornerstone Presbyterian Church,
Ambler, Pennsylvania
February 2014

PREFACE

I was taught that a preface needs to announce what a book is about, offer an excuse for writing it, and make a case for reading it.

This book is a biblical discussion of thirty-three doctrinal topics. It takes the form of a reader's guide to a statement of faith issued more than three and a half centuries ago—a confession which has since that time been in constant and widespread use in the Christian church, and has come to be known as the Westminster Confession of Faith.

I engaged in this study because I expected that it would be instructive to me and I hoped that it could be useful to others too. I chose to write on this particular confession of faith because I have found that I can identify very closely with its teaching and because I have learned something of the historical and theological ecosystems in which it developed. I should also confess, because it will be obvious to my colleagues, that this is the kind of book that historians write when they wish to further a knowledge of God without running the risk of writing their own systematic theology.

In commending this classic creed and commenting on it I am not writing without sympathy for modern conversations in theology. But I am writing as an historian and as a Christian who is deeply appreciative of the power and majesty of some classic statements of faith. For those two reasons—a commitment to history and a conviction about truth—this commentary contains doxology and exhortation. I was not sure how a creedal statement synthesized by Puritans and sympathetically elaborated by a confessing Christian could not end up infused with praise for God and application for the Christian life.

Whether this commentary was worth writing, readers will have to judge for themselves. But the confession itself is worthy of consideration and can more than make up for any deficiencies in the commentary. The Westminster Confession of Faith is a summary of biblical doctrine. But it is more than that. It is a creed, and one from which all evangelical Christians will derive much benefit if it is carefully studied. This is a text rich in theology, offering a wealth of biblical and doctrinal reflection. It is not flawless. Nonetheless it is very good. And I consider its age to be more of a benefit than a liability; it is good to study texts which remind us that Christianity was not invented last Tuesday.

Convinced of its merits, I am offering a fresh look at an historic statement of faith that has proved its usefulness over time. Admittedly, commentaries on confessions constitute a genre of theological literature that is not widely celebrated in the Christian community. For many years confessional theology was reduced to an eddy within mainstream evangelicalism. On the whole we have preferred brief statements of faith and the briefer the better. That said, there may be a growing recognition that doctrinal minimalism could be the Achilles heel of evangelicalism.

In my mind, the typical evangelical 'creed' is in fact too small, and not sufficiently theological. It should not be enough for the evangelical movement to enjoy buoyant moments in the political sphere. We must be able to analyse and respond to powerful currents within our culture that undermine the church and the Christian faith. One part of our response must be to deepen the faith of leaders and laity in evangelical churches. As I see it, the church needs to experiment with theological maximalism in place of its current minimalism if we are to maintain a faithful witness to Christ in our generation. A dozen doctrinal points on a website is probably inadequate for the church's thriving, for its mission not only to *evangelize* but also to *teach* the nations. This creed from Westminster holds out a large faith for us to own, a welcome view of the triune God and his work, and an unusually robust statement of the gospel of Christ. I hope readers will consider carefully the commentary, but especially the confession, and discover that the good news this book celebrates is not too good to be true.

Suggestions for reading this book

Similar to the successful study of any subject, learning theology does not just 'happen'. It requires a plan. One possible plan for reading this book, and thus for learning some Christian doctrine, is to read a section each day. As readers will notice, almost every chapter has been divided into bite-sized portions of roughly equal length that take approximately ten to twelve minutes to read aloud, perhaps less if read silently. Individuals, families, or educators who prefer ready-made discussion questions may be interested to know that a study guide is in preparation. It will direct readers to the confession, the commentary, and the Scriptures, and will offer questions of personal application.

I hope that this text will be used by college and seminary students needing a new lens through which to view classical Christian theology, and by elders- and deacons-in-training in Reformed churches. But I am especially hopeful that church members, including younger people, will be exposed to this confession. Students study Shakespeare, biology, and business theory. They should be able to tackle a Christian confession. And arguably, the most demanding part of this book may be its preface. So if you have made it this far, you might as well finish it.

CHAD VAN DIXHOORN
Reformed Theological Seminary
Washington, DC
31 October 2013

ACKNOWLEDGEMENTS

I
F there is any strength to this collection of comments on the Westminster Confession of Faith it is owed to those who exercised much
patience in hearing and reading my reflections over the past fifteen
years. Craig Troxel and the elders and members of Calvary Orthodox
Presbyterian Church in Glenside, Pennsylvania first gave me the opportunity to think aloud on the confession while a seminary student. Ten
years later, Ian Hamilton and Peter Leverton were willing to grant me
the opportunity to share my more developed thoughts with the members of Cambridge Presbyterian Church during post-doctoral studies. A
few years ago Grace Presbyterian Church in Vienna, Virginia, began to
receive yet another iteration of lectures on the confession.

In the transition process from lecture to book, Pierre Du Plessis,
Richard Gaffin IV, Elizabeth Flanagan, and Mike Warner read many or
all of these pages, making useful suggestions; my eldest daughter Victoria
helped double-check many scriptural references; my mother hunted for
grammatical mistakes. Colin Roworth, at the Banner of Truth Trust in
Edinburgh, kindly flagged irritating inconsistencies in the commentary. Mark Garcia prepared a scripture index with a generous head-start
from John Bower; Jennifer Redd developed a helpful subject index with
a timely grant from Reformed Theological Seminary's Randall Fund.
My wife Emily, who is also my greatest encouragement, made valuable
observations along the way and is in the process of producing a study
guide, which I eagerly anticipate, based upon this commentary. Together
they have paved a better path for future readers.

A further feedback loop has been provided by the theological com-
munities which I serve. I have received assessment of this material from
seminary students (and from fellow ministers posing as students) at the

Ministerial Training Institute of the Orthodox Presbyterian Church, at Puritan Reformed Theological Seminary in Grand Rapids, and at Reformed Theological Seminary in Washington, DC. Comments from Paul Jeon, Matthew Judd, Mike Law and Peter Wallace led to further clarifications, and questions from Scott R. Clark, Richard Gaffin, Jr., and Robert Letham led to longer footnotes. This is a sturdier book because of them.

The most extensive assessment came from five additional friends and colleagues: Peter Lee, whose office is down the hall at Reformed Theological Seminary in DC; then Mark Garcia and Rowland Ward, old friends serving congregations in Pennsylvania and Australia, respectively; and finally, in Edinburgh and South Ayrshire, Jonathan Watson, the very capable editor of the Banner of Truth Trust, and Dr Graham Keith, who ably served as copy editor for the Banner. These men have invested enormous time and energy in reading and commenting on the whole of this text. For their poking and prodding I am profoundly grateful.

INTRODUCTION

The Westminster assembly (1643-1653)

Two years prior to the gathering of an assembly of theologians in Westminster Abbey (from whence the Westminster Confession of Faith derives its name), a prominent pastor named Edmund Calamy urged the House of Commons to reform the Church of England. This was no nostalgic look back to the Edenic days of England's boy-king, the evangelical and Reformed Edward VI. On the contrary, Calamy urged Parliament to 'reform the Reformation itself'. It was not until 1643 that Calamy's modern reformation took shape in the calling of what proved to be the last of the great post-Reformation synods.

It is easier to announce a maxim than it is to live it. This was certainly true for the one hundred and twenty theologians of the Westminster assembly, for they had to decide how to reform the church and its doctrinal standards. The Westminster assembly was summoned by the English Parliament during its bloody civil war with King Charles I in the early 1640s. The synod's remit was to propose to Parliament any corrections which might need to be made to the existing structures, worship, and teaching of the church. In other words, the gathering was tasked with doing what Puritans within the church had long dreamed of doing. There were also those outside the English church who longed for reform, namely the Scottish Presbyterians. Left with the lingering, bitter taste of English interference in their church affairs, they had become convinced that only a major reform in the church to the south could safeguard the core teachings of their church in the north.

On a national and local level, the Westminster assembly was instrumental in purging the English church of many appalling preachers and filling it with less appalling ones. On the international stage, it attempted to revise, and eventually rewrote, texts for the churches of England and Wales, Scotland and Ireland. It drafted directions for church government, published a guide for public worship, issued statements on doctrine, corresponded with foreign churches, authored two catechisms, and wrote a new confession of faith.

Really, Edmund Calamy and his colleagues should have been very pleased, but they were not. The task of revising or writing a document such as a directory or confession looked easier than it really was. While individual ministers could state their own understanding of the Bible, it was much harder to come to agreement as a group. Then (as now) there were too many architects wanting reform and too few builders who could actually effect it. The experience was frustrating, leaving Calamy to mourn that 'noe man knows what this reformation is. This is a sin & misery'.

The Westminster Confession of Faith (1646)

In 1644 Edmund Calamy was in despair but by 1646 the assembly had managed to finish its landmark confession. The end product was worth celebrating then and still is today. Indeed the assembly's statement of faith is a truly remarkable text in the history of Christianity, and all who peruse its pages will find a sure-footed summary of truth for life.

The Westminster Confession is a summary of Christian theology in the Reformation tradition. It digests more than thirty distinct truths of Scripture, each topic originally entitled an 'Article' of faith, in imitation of the Thirty-nine Articles of the Church of England. It is probably because the confession was intended to replace the Thirty-nine Articles that it is written in the voice of a third person and not the voice of the first person: its pages declare what the Bible teaches rather than declaring what the saints believe the Bible to teach. Like the Thirty-nine Articles, it presents orthodoxy more authoritatively than personally.

Nonetheless, for those who embrace the Christian story and the meaning of that story as it is told here, this confession does declare what the saints believe; once believed it becomes personal. The confession's opening pages rejoice in the wonder of God's revelation of himself in the world and in the Word. Whole paragraphs linger over the fullness and clarity of the Scriptures, and show marked deference to the authority and finality of the Bible's sixty-six books. With devotion and delight, the confession goes on to consider the God who reveals himself in all his perfections. With reverence and awe the Westminster divines strive to say what can be said of the God who is one and the God who is three. The glories of the eternal God occupy some lines; the 'most loving, gracious' and 'merciful' character of God occupies others.

Readers will quickly see that, chapter by chapter, the Westminster Confession of Faith traces the great history of our redemption: the grim realities of the fall, God's gracious covenants with man, the stunning announcement of salvation, and our sure hope of eternal life—all these are sketched out in bold but considered strokes. It is because of the clarity of this gospel presentation in all of its parts that the Westminster Confession of Faith finds itself in the first rank of great Christian creeds. It is valued by Reformed Congregationalists, Baptists, Methodists, and Episcopalians, and treasured by Presbyterians. Perhaps it is the wisest of creeds in its teaching and the finest in its doctrinal expression. Certainly it is a reliable guide to the Scriptures, which are the only reliable guide to God. In fact users will find that reflection on the chapters of the confession often leads to the study of the words of Scripture. Few other exercises can provide such rich returns on one's investment in time.

Viewing the text as a whole, the Westminster Confession of Faith enjoys three great strengths. The first lies in the coherence and clarity of its carefully focused chapters, each of them organized around a major doctrinal or biblical theme. Writing at the end of the long Reformation, the members of the Westminster assembly (1643–1653) were eager to harvest the best biblical exegesis of the Reformers, the most useful doctrinal structures of the medieval theologians, and the most enduring insights of the church fathers. The members of the assembly read widely from all three of these groups and invested enormous time and energy in synthesizing their findings into this 12,000-word document. They also reflected personally on the wider implications of these doctrines and attempted to thoughtfully live out the theology they confessed. In this confession we see the fruit of their labours.

The second distinguishing feature of this confession is its use as a guide to readers of the Bible. The confession offers paragraphs written for the sole purpose of helping Christians to understand scriptural words and phrases. The assembly also offered 2,500 'proof-texts' in support of the confession's teaching. For those with the patience to investigate the biblical basis for Christian doctrine, a study of this declaration of faith and its supporting passages of Scripture will yield rich dividends. But patience is essential, for there are no explanations attached to the passages that are cited by the assembly. Scholars will recognize that these texts function as footnotes not only to scriptural passages but also to a Reformed understanding of those passages which we can access in books written at or before the time of the assembly. However most of us do not have access to these old books, and thus understanding these scriptural references requires careful reflection, prayer, and even meditation before the light that these verses shone on our forefathers can shine on us too. Nonetheless, properly employed, this is an asset on which diligent readers can build.

The third major advantage of this confession is that it deals not only with fundamental doctrines that are obvious, but also with some fundamental doctrines that are difficult. Many of the topics raised in this confession of faith have deterred the faint-hearted, such as the problem of evil, the divine decrees, and the freedom or bondage of the will. The assembly offers careful sketches on each subject as well as clear counterpoints to associated errors; both new initiates to Christianity and seasoned theologians will find these outlines helpful.

The assembly's confession is clear, offers a good guide to the Bible, and provides a useful treatment of difficult doctrines. Nonetheless, it is not as crisp a treatment of Christian doctrine as it could be. This is due, in part, to the fact that any attempt to treat doctrinal subjects as isolated areas of theology is open to border disputes between those topics. How can one round out a doctrine of justification and not say something about the atonement or saving faith? In the end the Westminster assembly was more dedicated to discussing each topic thoroughly than to crafting a confession concisely.

However, readers not only wonder about redundancy. They sometimes also query the confession's specificity. Why is it not enough to speak simply about being 'saved' or being 'in Christ'? Why must the confession also define 'justification' and 'imputation' and 'forgiveness'? If I am to be candid, it seems to me that one reason for the specificity of the confession has to do with the simple pleasure of its authors. Thoughtful Christians sometimes develop an appetite for God that can become an insatiable desire to discover fresh reasons for doxology. As it happens, the Scriptures provide this kind of food for thought and praise because component parts of doctrines, and not simply large clusters of Christian truth, are presented in the Bible for our attention and meditation. We are told to rejoice in the details of his saving plan and in the distinct blessings we receive from God and his gospel. Serious students in Christ's school become instinctively equipped to enjoy every brush stroke on the canvas of God's revelation of redemption, and not simply the final effect that the Master has produced.

The other reason why we see a careful attention to precise terminology in this confession is that labelling can promote learning. We see this in chemistry or grammar. We see this in theology too. Take the doctrine of justification as an example. The Scriptures tell us about a true righteousness being credited to those who do not deserve it and a free gift of forgiveness purchased for sinners. Sometimes the Scriptures tether this credited righteousness to justification, sometimes they tie forgiveness to justification. The authors of this confession, like many Bible readers before and after them, noted these frequent associations of words and ideas and, in this case, concluded that 'justification' must be the Bible's umbrella term for credited righteousness and divine forgiveness, two distinct but united aspects of the one doctrine of justification.

Now having discovered such detail after careful study of the Scriptures, it is hardly possible for an attentive Christian to be content only to speak of 'justification in general' or 'the word justification as it was understood in the Greek world'. No, since biblical authors give specific content to doctrine and to words, responsible biblical study requires that this content be identified, explained, and confessed. This is what the Westminster Confession of Faith does in all of its chapters: it introduces doctrinal ideas, outlines how they are parsed and associated in the Bible, and helps the reader confess these doctrines in a thoughtful way.

The text of the confession

That is not to say that the Westminster assembly got it all right, and this commentary does, from time to time, first state the assembly's own perspective on an issue and then argue against it. This commentary also discusses some American amendments to the confession carried out in four stages, with significant revisions taking place in 1788, followed by other changes in 1887, 1903 and 1936.

The late eighteenth-century revisions affected confessional chapters 20.4, 23.3 and 31.2 and reflected a changed perspective on the relationship between the church and the state. The eighteenth-century revisions also included changing Larger Catechism answer 109, which originally prohibited 'tolerating a false religion', a proscription no longer tenable in the American State, and changing a word in answer 142, which had originally prohibited 'depopulations', a ban which was embarrassing given the ongoing European settlement of territory once belonging to native Americans.

A late nineteenth-century revision merely relaxed the church's rules in chapter 24.4 about remarriage to a close relative of a deceased spouse. The early twentieth-century revisions, by contrast, were extensive. The Presbyterian Church in the USA rewrote chapter 16.7 on the good works of unbelievers, it removed the last sentence of chapter 22.3 and thus softened the requirements for taking oaths, it helpfully rewrote chapter 25.6, and removed a reference to the Pope of Rome as the antichrist, and it added two new chapters, one on the Holy Spirit and the other on the love of God and missions. The addition of two new chapters and the revisions to chapter 16.7 were changes leaning towards an Arminian, rather than a distinctively Reformed, presentation of doctrine.

Breaking away from the main Presbyterian Church in the United States in 1936, the Orthodox Presbyterian Church (OPC) determined to retain all revisions prior to 1903, and reject most of those proposed in 1903. It did approve the 1903 change to chapter 22.3, and while it rejected the rewritten chapter 25.6 of 1903, the OPC did agree with the removal of the reference to the Pope as antichrist. The Presbyterian Church in America (PCA) has adopted the 1936 text as their own, and other confessional Presbyterian bodies allow their church officers to use the same text, or to make the same conscientious exceptions to the original text.

In order to aid readers unfamiliar with older English, I have reprinted in a parallel column the *Modern English Study Version of the Westminster Confession of Faith*, © 1993 The Committee on Christian Education of the OPC, gratefully acknowledging the committee's kind permission to use their text. This text has no constitutional authority in the OPC, but it can, nonetheless, be useful for those who are seeking to grasp the general meaning of the original text. The Banner of Truth has made no changes to this modern study version except to standardize spelling according to current British norms.

Actual interpretation of a text should use the most reliable version available. The primary text of the confession printed in this commentary is a (gratefully acknowledged) version of John Bower's critical edition of the assembly's 1640s text, complete with scriptural proof-texts, and painstakingly reconstructed text in his book, *The Westminster Confession of Faith: A Critical Text and Introduction* (Grand Rapids, expected 2014). I believe that the series of critical editions of assembly texts being edited by John are the best to date and unlikely to be surpassed by subsequent scholars. The confessional text as it appears here is Dr Bower's own work in which only the spelling and capitalization of the critical text is standardized for ecclesiastical use. The Banner of Truth has made no changes to Dr Bower's text except to further standardize capitalization. John Bower, in setting this text, has updated spelling and archaic forms (thus 'farre' is rendered as 'far', and 'doth' as 'does'). The original punctuation, quirky and awkward as it may be, is useful for interpretation and has been retained. For a lack of a better title, I have termed it the 'Historic Text', and it is set alongside the modern version in parallel columns throughout. Superscript references to Scripture proofs in the Historic Text follow the traditional pattern of the confession, and thus do not include 'j' or 'v' (neither of which was considered a distinct letter from 'i' or 'u').

In this book I primarily comment on the historic text (the left column), but also comment on the revisions to the original edition, as accepted by the OPC in 1936 (the right column). Where these revised lines or paragraphs occur in chapters 20.4, 22.3, 23.3, 24.4, 25.6 and 31.2, they are set beside the original text of the confession in a centred parallel column. The text of the American revisions of 1788 is taken from *The Constitution of the Presbyterian Church in the United States of America* (Philadelphia, 1789). I have modernized the spelling and capitalization of the 1789 text, but not punctuation. As the

1788 revisions did not include proofs of Scripture, I have supplied proof-texts for these revisions from the OPC's current edition of its confession of faith. All retained confessional revisions subsequent to 1788 constitute only the removal of phrases, and thus do not require the citation of particular editions.

This commentary

Any claim to originality in this commentary lies principally in two main areas, both of them historical in nature. First, this is an attempt to expound one late Reformation text and not Reformed theology generally conceived. This is not a book intended to reflect the author's own theological interests or preferred emphases. It is a study of the Westminster Confession of Faith, and for that reason the chapter on creation does not address evolution and the chapter on marriage does not discuss feminism. As it happens, many historical facts, much redemptive history, and many connections between doctrines interest me and occupy my energies as a minister or as a historian. Nonetheless, they are not discussed in the confession, and are thus not pursued here.

It is because I attempt to be sensitive to the historical context and the creative process behind the Westminster Confession of Faith that I do not make much of the order of its chapters. The arrangement of the chapters themselves is logical, not loose and disjointed. It is usually easy to see why one chapter follows or is grouped with another. Nonetheless, it is not the case that any one chapter derives its content from another, or that there is a single doctrine upon which all the others are built like an inverted pyramid. Undoubtedly some theologians, especially in the twentieth century, have pursued one or another theological idea in such a way that it has determined every other idea. However, theologians in the seventeenth century attempted to deduce both a doctrine's content and its significance through a process of biblical exegesis. I have sought to understand this text in that light.

The second related characteristic of this commentary is its attempt to enrich and inform the interpretation of the text of the confession by reflecting on the portions of Scripture cited by the Westminster assembly. After each phrase and chapter of the confession was drafted, the assembly debated and then approved a series of scriptural passages in support of that doctrine. Later, the gathering was required by Parliament to provide references to Scripture alongside the confession. The assembly did so reluctantly as it had no opportunity to explain, by a mere citation of a text, the exegesis of that text. But once the assembly's members accepted the task, they chose supporting passages of Scripture carefully, refining the list of scriptural passages approved in their earlier debates. In attempting to use these biblical texts to understand confessional phrases, this book, again, strives to be both an historical and a textual study. Of course modern editions of the confession sometimes employ alternative proof-texts which sometimes offer even better biblical support to the assembly's own doctrines. Nonetheless, as they offer no insight into the assembly's own thinking, I do not refer to them here.

Since the assembly did not explain how each text was to be interpreted, I have endeavoured to construe biblical passages in ways agreeable to interpretations prevalent in and prior to the seventeenth century. My use of scriptural passages rests on my knowledge of the assembly's texts and debates, the writings of assembly members, and that of contemporary and prior exegetes. When in doubt I checked these sources for plausibility, and I hope that other students of the history of exegesis will be able to concur with my use and expositions of these texts.

A note regarding the third printing

I am grateful for the initial reception given to *Confessing the Faith*. I have made about a dozen and a half minor changes to the text of the book, the most substantive being the addition of a few lines on p. 223. I also include quotation marks on p. 25, for in re-reading a text by Augustine I discovered that a favourite line from his editor had over time become my own. For proper attribution, see Augustine, *On Christian teaching*, trans. R. P. H. Green (Oxford, 1999), p. xii.

ABBREVIATIONS

WCF   Westminster Confession of Faith (1646)

WLC   Westminster Larger Catechism (1647)

WSC   Westminster Shorter Catechism (1647)

RCF   Revised Confession of Faith (1788, 1887, 1903, or 1936)

OED   Oxford English Dictionary

FOUNDATIONS

CHAPTER 1:

OF THE HOLY SCRIPTURE

Historic Text

1.1 Although the light of nature and the works of creation and providence do so far manifest the goodness, wisdom, and power of God, as to leave men unexcusable;[a] yet are they not sufficient to give that knowledge of God and of his will, which is necessary unto salvation.[b] Therefore it pleased the Lord, at sundry times, and in divers manners, to reveal himself, and to declare that his will unto his church;[c] and afterwards, for the better preserving and propagating of the truth, and for the more sure establishment and comfort of the church against the corruption of the flesh, and the malice of Satan and of the world; to commit the same wholly unto writing:[d] which makes the Holy Scripture to be most necessary;[e] those former ways of God's revealing his will unto his people being now ceased.[f]

Modern Version

1.1 Although the light of nature and the works of creation and providence manifest the goodness, wisdom, and power of God, to such an extent that men are without excuse, yet they are not sufficient to give that knowledge of God and of his will which is necessary for salvation. Therefore it pleased the Lord, at various times and in diverse ways, to reveal himself and to declare his will to his church; and afterward—for the better preserving and propagating of the truth, and for the more sure establishment and comfort of the church against the corruption of the flesh and the malice of Satan and of the world—to commit this revelation wholly to writing. Therefore the Holy Scripture is most necessary, God's former ways of revealing his will to his people having ceased.

Scripture Proofs

1.1 [a] Rom. 2:14,15; Rom. 1:19,20; Psa. 19:1-3; Rom. 1:32, with Rom. 2:1. [b] 1 Cor. 1:21; 1 Cor. 2:13,14. [c] Heb. 1:1. [d] Prov. 22:19-21; Luke 1:3,4; Rom. 15:4; Matt. 4:4,7,10; Isa. 8:19,20. [e] 2 Tim. 3:15; 2 Pet. 1:19. [f] Heb. 1:1,2.

General revelation: conscience, creation, and providence

The opening chapter of the Westminster Confession of Faith begins with
the doctrine of Holy Scripture. The opening sentence does not. Instead,
this historic statement of doctrine begins by reminding us that God has
revealed himself to all people, even to those without a Bible. The confession mentions that this general revelation comes to us in two forms.
There is 'the light of nature', by which is meant the divine imprint which
is left on each of us by our Maker. That is, we are made in God's image
and even though we are fallen creatures, God's image remains stamped
upon us. And there are 'the works of creation and providence.' The world
that we see and the world about which we read tell us of our Creator and
Provider, the one who once made and now upholds all things.

These forms of general revelation, both the one inside us and the one
around us, are astonishing in what they declare. They should be valued
highly by every person; for they 'manifest' or show forth 'the goodness'
of God, his 'wisdom' and his 'power'. It is the unexpected beauty and
intricacy of this revelation which leaves us breathless at times, as we view
the world around us. It is this revelation which leads Christians to prayer
and praise; for it reveals the true God, rather than offering a vague sense
that there is some kind of a god.

Here, unmistakably, the confession is following the trail laid down
by the Apostle Paul in Romans 1-2 (see esp. *Rom.* 1:19, 20, 32; 2:1, 14, 15;
cf. Psa. 19:1-3). In those chapters the apostle both reminds us of this general revelation and tells us that it leaves every person without an excuse
before God. For this reason, both in our evangelism and in our defence
of the faith, we should always remember that Christians should never
be trying to prove the existence of God to unbelievers. We are reminding unbelievers of what they already know. Every person has been stung
with a knowledge of God; there is an Existence about which they may be
intensely aware, or which they may consciously or subconsciously suppress. But every person knows enough about God that they ought never
to stop searching for him.

Special revelation: the Word of God

This general revelation has limits. As the confession reminds us, 'they are not sufficient to give that knowledge of God, and of his will, which is necessary unto salvation.' Human wisdom has its boundaries, as Paul reminded the Corinthians repeatedly (*e.g., 1 Cor.* 1:21; 2:13, 14). This is especially true when it comes to the gospel. The most thoughtful or meditative person will not find true hope by looking within, and no explorer will ever find the way to eternal life merely by travelling through this wide creation.

Therefore, since the real objective of Christian theology, and of this confession, is to show the way *to* life and the way *to live* life, this chapter goes on to tell us about God's spoken revelation. Quoting from the author of the letter to the Hebrews, the confession reminds us that 'it pleased the Lord, at sundry (or various) times, and in divers manners (or different ways), to reveal himself'.

Above all, it is the purpose of Scripture to reveal God. It is his self-revelation, for it is not only the case that he himself is the one who reveals, but it is also the case that what he reveals is his own self. No other subject than God himself could be worthy of such a book. And yet the comprehensiveness of biblical revelation and the extent to which it moulds a Christian's view of all things mean that sometimes we lose sight of the central purpose and message of the Bible. So great is the magnitude and impact of God's self-disclosure and all that it entails that we can sometimes lose the epicentre for the aftershocks. And so this confession reminds us of the obvious: this is the book about God.

Although the coherence of this book lies in God himself, who is its central theme, it also 'pleased the Lord' to reveal in the Scriptures 'his will unto his church'—which is to say, his will regarding salvation. This revelation of the road to a life with God has come to men and women through conversations with God, visions and dreams, and visits by angels. It came once from the very hand of God on the two tablets of stone which contained the Ten Commandments. And as the writer to the Hebrews reminds us, it came most often through God's prophets (*Heb.* 1:1).

Nonetheless, for our generous God, even this was not enough! In his goodness and wisdom God used his great power to commit his revelation of himself into a written form. He gave us the Bible. There are many reasons why God should have done this, but among them are the reasons mentioned in the confession. God wanted 'better to preserve and propagate his truth'. And he wished firmly to establish the church against three untiring opponents: 'the corruption of our own flesh, the malice of Satan, and the malice of the world'. You may remember how Isaiah called the Israelites to God's Word when the world called them to experiment with witches or wizards (*Isa.* 8:19, 20), and how our Lord used Scripture to refute Satan himself (*Matt.* 4:4, 7, 10). The Word of God is intended to give us certainty (*Prov.* 22:19-21; *Luke* 1:3, 4) and comfort (*Rom.* 15:4) even against our worst enemies. How much more should we use it in our day-to-day struggles and trials!

Little wonder then that we are reminded here just how necessary this revelation from God is. It is 'most necessary'. What else could it be? After all, it reveals a 'knowledge of God' and a knowledge of what is 'necessary for salvation' (*cf. 2 Tim.* 3:15), and since it is useful for building up the church and defending us from our enemies, the Scriptures are necessary for the good spiritual health of Christian people, and necessary for the very existence of the church and its doctrine.

The Bible is also necessary because God no longer reveals himself by dreams and visions and prophets. Those vehicles of revelation are no longer needed and they no longer function. William Gouge, a Puritan patriarch at the Westminster assembly, argued that 'pretence of new light and immediate inspiration in these daies, is a meer pretence'.[1] Francis Cheynell complained of people in his day who too quickly gave a platform to anyone who had persuaded himself that he had some spiritual interpretation of the Word by 'inspiration, suggestion' or 'assistance of the Holy Ghost'.[2] And George Walker, yet another member of the

---

[1] William Gouge, *A Learned and Very Useful Commentary on the Whole Epistle to the Hebrewes* (London, 1655), part 4, p. 77. Daniel Featley, in a book against Anabaptists, declared that 'none now pray by immediate inspiration'. Featley, *Dippers Dip't* (London, 1647), p. 89.

[2] Francis Cheynell, *The Rise, Growth, and Danger of Socinianisme* (London, 1643), p. 61.

assembly who wrote on the topic, had hard words for weak men who told ladies to marry them because of some 'pretence of inspiration and divine revelation'.[1] Whether out of laziness or desperation, men should not try to push a woman a little closer to a wedding because 'God had said' they were meant for each other.

As Peter reminds us, we now have what we can consider to be a 'more sure word' from God than spoken or private utterances—we have a written word which contains prophecy (*2 Pet.* 1:19) and much more. The letter to the Hebrews reminds us of the same: Christ spoke himself and his apostles spoke on his behalf (*Heb.* 1:1, 2). What we need to know has been preserved for us. Of course God reveals himself to us in the preaching of his Word and in the administration of the sacraments. However, these ways of revelation are measured against this final and definitive word from God that we find in the Bible alone.

It remains to be said that we owe a great debt to God for these gifts of revelation. How thankful we can be that men and women and children who do not have a Bible do have a conscience! How grateful we are as we go about our day's work or study that the very heavens declare the glory of God (*Psa.* 19:1-3)! And how much we owe to God simply because he gave his church his Word! We sometimes feel a need to reveal something about ourselves for our own sakes. God did not need to reveal himself for his own sake. He did it for us.

Let us praise him for his Word by centring our worship every week around the singing, reading and preaching of that Word which, through Jesus Christ, gives us life and hope and eternal rest.

---

[1] George Walker, *The History of the Creation as It Was Written by Moses* (London, 1641), p. 206.

Historic Text	*Modern Version*
1.2 Under the name of Holy Scripture, or the Word of God written; are now contained all the books of the Old and New Testament, which are these:	**1.2** Under the name of Holy Scripture, or the written Word of God, are all the books of the Old and New Testaments, namely:

OF THE OLD TESTAMENT

Genesis	2 Chronicles	Daniel
Exodus	Ezra	Hosea
Leviticus	Nehemiah	Joel
Numbers	Esther	Amos
Deuteronomy	Job	Obadiah
Joshua	Psalms	Jonah
Judges	Proverbs	Micah
Ruth	Ecclesiastes	Nahum
1 Samuel	Song of Solomon	Habakkuk
2 Samuel	Isaiah	Zephaniah
1 Kings	Jeremiah	Haggai
2 Kings	Lamentations	Zechariah
1 Chronicles	Ezekiel	Malachi

OF THE NEW TESTAMENT

The Gospels according to	2 Corinthians	The Epistle to the Hebrews
Matthew	Galatians	The Epistle of
Mark	Ephesians	James
Luke	Philippians	The first and second
John	Colossians	Epistles of Peter
The Acts of the Apostles	1 Thessalonians	The first, second, and third
Paul's Epistles to the	2 Thessalonians	Epistles of John
Romans	1 Timothy	The Epistle of Jude
1 Corinthians	2 Timothy	The Revelation of John
	To Titus	
	To Philemon	

All which are given by inspiration of God, to be the rule of faith and life.ᵍ

All these are given by inspiration of God to be the rule of faith and life.

1.3 The books commonly called Apocrypha, not being of divine inspiration, are no part of the canon of the Scripture; and therefore are of no authority in the church of God, nor to be any otherwise approved, or made use of, than other human writings.ʰ

1.3. The books commonly called the Apocrypha, because they are not divinely inspired, are not part of the canon of Scripture, and therefore are of no authority in the church of God and are not to be approved, or made use of, in any manner different from other human writings.

Scripture Proofs

1.2 ᵍ Luke 16:29,31; Eph. 2:20; Rev. 22:18,19; 2 Tim. 3:16.
1.3 ʰ Luke 24:27,44; Rom. 3:2; 2 Pet. 1:21.

Holy Scripture

The first paragraph of the Westminster Confession of Faith's first chapter reminds us that God's revelation of himself is most necessary for Christians, especially the Word of God, first spoken and later written.[1] These next two paragraphs discuss this written Word, informing us what Scripture is and what it is not.

Scripture is, in the first place, holy. It is sanctified, set apart from all other writings in the world. Other books contain history, poetry, and great wisdom. Other books contain great truths that are worthy of study, imitation and meditation. But there is no book like the Holy Scripture, and that is because this alone is the written Word of God. Of course no book could be written without the talents and insights that God gives to his creatures. Yet only the Holy Scripture is owned by God as his own writing.

A complete canon

That writing takes the form of a small library of sixty-six books, divided into two parts. Thirty-nine of these books are found in the Old Testament, written before the time of Christ's birth, and twenty-seven are

[1] By the 'Word of God written' the assembly is distinguishing the written Scriptures from either spoken revelation, or, less likely in this context, from Jesus Christ as the Word of God.

found in the New Testament, written after the time of Christ's death and glorious resurrection.

These books are summarized in a variety of ways in Scripture. For example, the Old Testament is sometimes simply called the Law and the Prophets (*Luke* 16:16), or Moses and the Prophets (*Luke* 16:29, 31).[1] The list of books presented in the confession is a detailed one—the one found in the table of contents in today's Protestant Bibles, and it includes all the books that are common to Christian Bibles around the world.

Protestants understand that these books are not an anthology of works collected from a greater corpus, a mere selection from a wider number of God's writings. On the contrary, this is the total number of the books that are inspired by God and preserved for his church. For that reason, we do well to take the warning at the close of the book of Revelation and apply it to the whole of God's revelation, for who are we to add to it or take away from it? (*Rev.* 22:18, 19; see also *Deut.* 4:2).

An inspired book

In speaking about 'inspired' books, the confession picks up the wording of Paul's second letter to Timothy, which states that 'all Scripture is God-breathed' (*2 Tim.* 3:16). Sometimes Christians speak of inspired authors of the Bible. And of course it is true, as Peter says, that holy men of old who wrote the Bible 'spoke . . . as they were carried along by the Holy Spirit' (*2 Pet.* 1:21). Certainly it is the case that Scripture is not of private origination and did not come by the mere will of man. We need to emphasize these things, and yet at the same time we need to be sure that we do not lose sight of the fact that it is the Bible itself that is inspired. This book, this Scripture alone resides with God's breath of life in it. It is perhaps for this reason that the letter to the Hebrews says that 'God's word is living and active' (*Heb.* 4:12) and Peter says that the 'word of God' is 'living and enduring' (*1 Pet.* 1:23).

If this is God's Word, then little wonder that it is to be our rule of faith and of life. Here we learn who and how to worship, who and

---

[1] The Westminster assembly also considered Ephesians 2:20 and its reference to 'apostles and prophets' to refer to old and new covenant revelation. It seems more likely that it refers to New Testament apostles and prophets.

how to trust for our salvation and all of our needs, and how to live our lives. It is for this reason that the whole Bible should be read frequently by all Christians, and should be at the centre of the Christian church. Those who ignore the Holy Scripture are doomed to stumble into ever deepening darkness. Those who embrace this Scripture, believe what it promises, and walk by its precepts, will never be without a guide or a light, and they will find their way to their Father's home.

Apocrypha

In discussing the books of the Bible we also need to say that for a variety of (ultimately inadequate) reasons, some have added to these sixty-six books other ancient writings. These books are sometimes called secondary or deutero-canonical books, later additions often imprecisely defined by the churches which use them, including the Roman Catholic and Eastern Orthodox churches. They were not part of the writings of Moses, the Prophets and Psalms, as Luke summarizes the Old Testament canon (*e.g., Luke* 24:27, 44); they are not part of the 'oracles of God', a phrase Paul uses to describe the Old Testament in his letter to the Romans. Indeed even today they are set apart in a special section in many printed Bibles.

Additionally, some of these books hid their true date and authorship under false names or false titles—so many in fact that the entire corpus of additional books is often called the 'Apocrypha' (or 'hidden things'). These books do not carry divine authority, and are thus not part of the list, or catalogue or canon of Scripture. The confession insists here that they are not to be recommended as anything but ancient human writings. This was a strong statement by the Westminster divines contradicting the teaching of the Church of England, since its Thirty-nine Articles recommend the Apocrypha as particularly useful for 'example of life and instruction of manners', while adding that these books cannot 'establish any doctrine'. But to say this is to misunderstand the relationship between Christian doctrine and Christian living. Our life must flow from our faith. Christian piety should be a reflection of Christian theology and, if the Apocrypha cannot be useful for establishing doctrine, we should not elevate it as a guide for the Christian life.

It is wiser by far to use the Apocrypha as we would any other ancient book. And it is wisest of all to treasure the Holy Scripture that God has given, to heed its authority, to give it our heart's approval, and to make use of it more than any human writing.

Historic Text

1.4 The authority of the Holy Scripture, for which it ought to be believed and obeyed, depends not upon the testimony of any man, or church; but wholly upon God (who is truth itself) the author thereof: and therefore it is to be received, because it is the Word of God.[i]

1.5 We may be moved and induced by the testimony of the church to an high and reverent esteem of the Holy Scripture.[k] And the heavenliness of the matter, the efficacy of the doctrine, the majesty of the style, the consent of all the parts, the scope of the whole (which is, to give all glory to God,) the full discovery it makes of the only way of man's salvation, the many other incomparable excellencies, and the entire perfection thereof, are arguments whereby it does abundantly evidence itself to be the Word of God: yet notwithstanding, our full persuasion and assurance of the infallible truth, and divine authority thereof, is from the inward work of the Holy Spirit bearing witness by and with the Word, in our hearts.[l]

Modern Version

1.4 The authority of the Holy Scripture, because of which it ought to be believed and obeyed, does not depend upon the testimony of any man or church, but entirely upon God, its author (who is truth itself); therefore it is to be received, because it is the Word of God.

1.5 We may be moved and induced by the testimony of the church to a high and reverent esteem for the Holy Scripture. The heavenly character of its content, the efficacy of its doctrine, the majesty of its style, the agreement of all its parts, the scope of the whole (which is to give all glory to God), the full disclosure it makes of the only way of man's salvation, its many other incomparable excellencies, and its entire perfection, are arguments by which it gives abundant evidence that it is the Word of God. Nevertheless, our full persuasion and assurance of its infallible truth and divine authority is from the inward work of the Holy Spirit bearing witness by and with the Word in our hearts.

Scripture Proofs

1.4 [i] 2 Pet. 1:19,21; 2 Tim. 3:16; 1 John 5:9; 1 Thess. 2:13.

1.5 [k] 1 Tim. 3:15; [l] 1 John 2:20,27; John 16:13,14; 1 Cor. 2:10-12; Isa. 59:21.

God's Word

The confession begins by explaining why revelation, and especially written revelation, is necessary for God's people. It goes on to explain how the Bible is unique and holy because it is God-breathed, or inspired. In paragraphs four and five the discussion turns to the authority of Scripture, and the way in which Christians recognize that authority.

Paragraph 4 begins by reminding us that we need an adequate reason to obey and believe Holy Scripture. We must not obey the Bible simply because of the influence of other people, no matter how wise or impressive they might be as human beings. Nor is it a sure enough reason to trust the Scripture because told to do so by a church (although the Roman Catholic Church would seriously disagree with this statement!)

The only authority sufficient to command our commitment to Scripture is God himself—the one who does not lie, and who is in fact, truth itself (*John* 1:14; 14:6). This has always been the case, and yet as Peter explained to his readers in his Second Epistle, the God who has always spoken truly has now offered his people an even 'more sure word', or a 'word more fully confirmed'. That is not to say that we should have more confidence in the New Testament than the Old. Peter carefully guards against this kind of misunderstanding by looking at the phenomenon of prophecy. In prior times, God's message did not come by the mere will of the prophet. On the contrary, 'holy men of God spoke as they were moved by the Holy Spirit' (*2 Pet.* 1:19, 21). This is true of written revelation as well, and Peter makes the link himself, telling us that this is how we are to view Scripture (*2 Pet.* 1:20). So what is Peter saying? Peter's point is that New Testament revelation is on a par with the Old when it comes to authority, but even better than the Old when it comes to clarity.

The apostle's point about authority—which is the main point discussed in this section of the confession—can be applied to his own letter: although we are reading the second letter of Peter, we are also reading a letter from God. God is the author of Scripture—a point that Paul makes with equal clarity in a letter to Timothy. In fact, there we are told that 'all Scripture is God-breathed' (*2 Tim.* 3:16). It is in this context that we are told that Scripture is 'profitable' or 'useful' for us. Since this is a word from God, we are to take it as doctrine designed for our instruction; it is the divine authority of the Bible that calls us to use this book in such a way that we will be reproved and corrected by its teaching.

We receive this book because it is God's. Of course we do! After all, as the Apostle John points out, we routinely accept the word and witness of other people. And 'if we receive the testimony of men, the testimony of God' is only greater (*1 John* 5:9). This was the perspective of the Thessalonians. When they realized that Paul and his company were bringing them a word from heaven, they 'received it not as the word of men, but as it is in truth, the word of God' (*1 Thess.* 2:13).

Our persuasion and assurance

We trust Scripture because it is God's Word. But how do we know that it is God's Word? Certainly one encouragement to see it as such is the testimony of the Christian church throughout the ages. Although the church is not the edifice itself, 'the church of the living God' is, as Paul teaches Timothy, 'a pillar and buttress of truth' (*1 Tim.* 3:15). The witness over the ages from great churches and great churchmen to the reliability and authority of Scripture can certainly give us a 'high and reverent esteem of the Holy Scripture'. Today too, people are often drawn to read and trust the Scriptures because of the encouragement of a local church or a member of it.

An even clearer testimony to the authority of Scripture is Scripture itself. Its focus is heavenward, like no other book. Its teaching transforms. Its prose and poetry have moved men and women for thousands of years. And readers old and new continue to marvel at the weight and density of this book, and the way in which the various parts of the Bible inform and illumine each other. And this is only the beginning! Is there any other book that has so perfectly achieved its purpose of giving all glory to God? Is there another place where we can learn all that we need to know about the one way of salvation? Really, there are so many incomparable excellencies to which we could point, such overwhelming evidence of perfection, that we can only conclude that the Bible 'abundantly evidence[s] itself to be the Word of God'. In a very real sense, we can say that Holy Scripture is self-authenticating.

And 'yet notwithstanding' the unique characteristics, effects and message of Scripture itself, a Christian's full persuasion and assurance of the infallible truth and divine authority of God's Word is actually 'from the inward work of the Holy Spirit'. It is the Spirit who bears 'witness by and with the Word in our hearts'. He speaks to us through the Word.

The close association of Spirit and Word was evident long ago to the prophet Isaiah, who explained how the Spirit abides with God's Word in the speech of God's people, from generation to generation (*Isa.* 59:21). And when the Apostle John considered the 'unction' or 'anointing' of the Holy One, who is Christ, it is clear that this anointing is the Holy Spirit. This is significant because John goes on to link this anointing or Christian knowledge with discernment of the truth, including the truth which he was writing at that moment (*1 John* 2:20, 27; *cf.* 2:21, 26).

John points out in his epistles and his Gospel that the Spirit of truth guides Christians to see, hear and receive God's truth (*e.g., John* 16:13, 14). Paul puts it another way in 1 Corinthians 2, where he reminds us that the Spirit was given to us to reveal the deep things of God. Indeed, 'we have received, not the spirit of the world, but the Spirit who is from God'—for the precise reason 'that we might know' God and his gifts (*1 Cor.* 2:10-12).

We were created to recognize truth, a gift that was misused, and then left tattered after the fall of humanity. However, God in his mercy has given us his Spirit who testifies to us as we read his Word that this is his revelation, his gift to us. The same Spirit who helps us to see Jesus as our Saviour and Lord is the one who helps us to grasp the Word of life, recognizing its authority, and trusting its promises.

It is just as Jesus said regarding the good shepherd. He speaks, and his sheep know his voice (*John* 10:11-16). Praise God that he continues to speak through Scripture, and that we are enabled to hear the voice of our good shepherd. For it is in Holy Scripture that we wonderfully discover 'the things freely given to us by God' (*1 Cor.* 2:12).

Historic Text	*Modern Version*
1.6 The whole counsel of God concerning all things necessary for his own glory, man's salvation, faith, and life, is either expressly set down in Scripture, or by good and necessary consequence may be deduced from Scripture: unto which nothing at any time is to be added, whether by new revelations of the Spirit, or traditions of men.^m Nevertheless we acknowledge the inward illumination of the Spirit of God to be necessary for the saving understanding of such things as are revealed in the Word:ⁿ and that there are some circumstances concerning the worship of God, and government of the church, common to human actions and societies, which are to be ordered by the light of nature and Christian prudence, according to the general rules of the Word, which are always to be observed.^o	**1.6** The whole counsel of God concerning all things necessary for his own glory and man's salvation, faith, and life, is either expressly stated in Scripture or by good and necessary inference may be deduced from Scripture, unto which nothing at any time is to be added, whether by new revelations of the Spirit or by traditions of men. Nevertheless, we acknowledge that the inward illumination of the Spirit of God is necessary for the saving understanding of such things as are revealed in the Word. We also acknowledge that there are some circumstances concerning the worship of God and the government of the church—circumstances common to human activities and societies—which are to be ordered by the light of nature and Christian prudence, according to the general rules of the Word, which are always to be observed.

Scripture Proofs

   1.6   ^m 2 Tim. 3:15-17; Gal. 1:8,9; 2 Thess. 2:2.   ⁿ John 6:45; 1 Cor. 2:9,10,12. ^o 1 Cor. 11:13,14; 1 Cor. 14:26,40.

Scripture sufficient

Chapter 1, paragraph 6, states the doctrine of the sufficiency of Scripture. The idea is that if you want to know what will 'thoroughly equip' you for salvation, for faith, or for life, you will find it in Scripture (*2 Tim.* 3:15-17). If you want to know what God considers essential for his own glory, you will find it in the Bible. In fact 'the whole counsel [or plan] of God' concerning all these necessary things is revealed in God's Word.

These teachings are often expressly set down in Scripture. What could be plainer than God's teaching that 'In the beginning God created the heavens and the earth' (*Gen.* 1:1)? What could be clearer than the assertion of Scripture that 'there is one God and one mediator between God and men, the man Christ Jesus' (*1 Tim.* 2:5)? What can give more comfort than the promise that 'neither height nor depth, nor anything else in all creation, will be able to separate us from the love of God that is in Christ Jesus our Lord' (*Rom.* 8:30)? What could be more sure than Jesus' promise that 'the Holy Spirit, whom the Father will send in my name, will teach you all things and will remind you of everything I have said to you' (*John* 14:26)? Scripture surely sets down what we need to know, and does so with great clarity.

The sufficiency of Scripture applies to all matters pertaining to our salvation. We need go nowhere else—we cannot go anywhere else—to find the way of salvation. This applies too for all matters of faith—all Christian doctrine is to be derived from the Bible alone. And the Scriptures are sufficient for life too, by which the Westminster assembly means that the Bible contains the law of God as well as all the general principles to which we need to adhere to live before the face of God. The sufficiency of Scripture for life does not deny that we need constant and extensive information and supplies from the created world in order to live. Of course we do. Scripture is sufficient in the sense that no further special revelation from God is needed to guide us through life other than the revelation graciously available to us in the Bible.

Good and necessary consequence

Nonetheless, we sometimes need to work out or deduce Christian doctrines from Scripture. We need to thoughtfully and carefully meditate on Scripture and compare its different passages. When we do that, we shall find some truths that inevitably flow from the Scripture. George Gillespie, a member of the assembly, notes that we work out from the Scriptures who should come to the Lord's table and who should be baptized, even though the Bible does not mention either explicitly.[1]

God often reveals his will to us in principles and we must not modify, ignore or go beyond them. In other words, the Christian church is to heed what is expressly set down in Scripture, and equally it is to dedicate itself to what can be deduced by good and necessary consequence. And then the church is to stop.

---

[1] For the examples of the Lord's supper and baptism, see George Gillespie, *A Treatise of Miscellany Questions* (Edinburgh, 1649), pp. 243-44.

The Scriptures are sufficient to teach us the whole counsel of God for all things that we need to know, and at no time are we to add to them. If someone suggests that they have a new revelation of the Spirit, we are not to be rattled; in fact we can ignore it (2 *Thess.* 2:2). If someone says that there are traditions about God's glory, or about salvation, or faith, or the Christian life which we need to follow, we are not to listen to them.

In making this point, the authors of the confession refer to Paul's letter to the Galatian churches, in which he tells them to ignore even 'an angel from heaven' should he come to them with another gospel (*Gal.* 1:6-9). The teaching of Christ and his apostles is sufficient for us. Their explanation of Christianity is definitive. There is no need for further good news about salvation: the news we have could not get any better. There is no need for further doctrine: all that we need to know for the Christian faith is found in the Bible in such richness that we could mine the Scripture for our whole lives and not even begin to exhaust its treasures. There is no need for further revelation on the Christian life. From here to heaven, all that we need for every step of our pilgrimage is found in the sixty-six books of the Bible.

Qualifier 1: we need the Spirit

There are only two important things that we need to add to this by way of qualification and explanation.

First, we do not need new revelations of the Spirit, but that does not mean that we do not need the Spirit, or that he has finished his work! On the contrary, we readily 'acknowledge the inward illumination of the Spirit of God' as absolutely 'necessary for the saving understanding of such things as are revealed in the Word'. No new truths are conveyed by the Spirit today—rather, he opens our minds to see the truths which have always been in the Scriptures, although perhaps not previously noticed by the church.

To put things in a different way, the Bible is sufficient for all our needs, but our needs are very great—for in sad fact, our sin and foolishness have left us blind and deaf to the reading and hearing of God's Word. As Paul explained to the Corinthians, our eyes do not see and our ears do not hear 'what God has prepared for those who love him'. For that reason it is also true that the salvation which God has prepared does not enter 'into the heart of man'. It is the unanimous witness of the prophets and apostles that if we are going to hear the gospel savingly, we need God's Spirit to shine into the darkness of our hearts. And so how grateful ought we to be that God in his astounding mercy does just this! He reveals his truth 'to us by his Spirit: for the Spirit searches all things'—certainly all things concerning our salvation, faith and life as well as so much more, 'even the deep things of God' (see *1 Cor.* 2:9-12). We need to be taught by God (*John* 6:45).

Qualifier 2: worship and government

The second thing we need to say is that the perfect sufficiency of the Scriptures extends to all of life, including the church's worship and the church's government. Nonetheless, 'there are some circumstances concerning the worship of God, and government of the church' which are not determined by the Word.

This needs to be stated clearly. There is nothing regarding salvation, Christian doctrine, or the Christian life which is not determined by the Word of God. And even the ordering of the church and Christian prayer and praise are in a great measure directed by God—Scripture is sufficient for worship and government too!

But in worship and government God does require us to use the light of nature and Christian prudence (see 1.1 above). The very light of nature can tell us some things about the worship of God (see by analogy what Paul says in *1 Cor.* 11:13, 14). Surely we do not need special revelation to tell us that God will not be amused if we chat with a friend during prayer. And Christian prudence suggests that we find a place of worship where we shall stay dry in the rain and warm in the cold. As Paul told the Corinthians more than once, we need to do all things decently, orderly and sensibly, giving thought to each person's edification (*1 Cor.* 14:26, 40).

Some things are simply 'common to human actions and societies'. God tells us we must worship him. Yet, whether a congregation meets for one service of four hours or four services of one hour is a matter of circumstance—we simply need to agree on it, so that we will worship together, however long or however often we meet. God shows us that we ought to have more than one elder in a church. However, we are not told if we are to have three or five or twelve. That depends on his provision and our wisdom.

What remains untouchable are the 'general rules of the Word, which are always to be observed'. Let us give thanks for the gift of general rules, and pray for the wisdom to follow them rightly. In doing so we shall find great reward.

⟡

Historic Text

1.7 All things in Scripture are not alike plain in themselves, nor alike clear unto all:[p] yet those things which are necessary to be known, believed, and observed for salvation, are so clearly propounded and opened in some place of Scripture or other, that not only the learned, but the unlearned, in a due use of the ordinary means, may attain unto a sufficient understanding of them.[q]

1.8 The Old Testament in Hebrew (which was the native language of the people of God of old,) and the New Testament in Greek, (which at the time of the writing of it was most generally known to the nations) being immediately inspired by God, and by his singular care and providence kept pure in all ages, are therefore authentic;[r] so as, in all controversies of religion, the church is finally to appeal unto them.[s] But, because these original tongues are not known to all the people of God, who have right unto, and interest in the Scriptures, and are commanded, in the fear of God, to read and search

Modern Version

1.7 Not all things in Scripture are equally plain in themselves or equally clear to all; yet those things which are necessary to be known, believed, and observed for salvation are so clearly stated and explained in one place or another in Scripture, that not only the educated but also the uneducated may gain a sufficient understanding of them by a proper use of the ordinary means.

1.8 The Old Testament in Hebrew (which was the native language of the people of God of old) and the New Testament in Greek (which at the time it was written was the language most generally known to the nations), being directly inspired by God and by his unique care and providence kept pure in all ages, are therefore authoritative, so that in all controversies of religion the church is finally to appeal to them. But, because these original languages are not understood by all the people of God, who have a right to, and a vital interest in, the Scriptures and are commanded to read and search them in the fear of them,^t therefore they are to be translated into the vulgar language of every nation unto which they come,^u that the Word of God dwelling plentifully in all, they may worship him in an acceptable manner;^w and, through patience and comfort of the Scriptures, may have hope.^x

God, therefore the Scriptures are to be translated into the common language of every nation to which they come; so that, the Word of God dwelling abundantly in all, they may worship him in an acceptable manner and by perseverance and the encouragement of the Scriptures may have hope.

Scripture Proofs

1.7   ^p 2 Pet. 3:16;   ^q Psa. 119:105,130.

1.8   ^r Matt. 5:18.   ^s Isa. 8:20; Acts 15:15; John 5:39,46.   ^t John 5:39.   ^u 1 Cor. 14:6,9,11,12,24,27,28.   ^w Col. 3:16.   ^x Rom. 15:4.

The clarity of Scripture

The first chapter of the Westminster Confession of Faith has made statements about the necessity of Scripture, the canon of Scripture, the authority of Scripture and the sufficiency of Scripture. Here we are told about the clarity of Scripture and about texts and translations of Scripture.

Paragraph 7 begins by explaining that Bible reading is not always easy. On the one hand, certain parts of Scripture are harder to read than others. The Apostle Peter himself made the astonishing admission that 'some things' written by a fellow apostle were 'hard to understand' (*2 Pet.* 3:16). Actually any reader of the Bible, including one who has read the Bible for many years, knows that 'all things in Scripture are not alike plain in themselves'.

On the other hand, one cannot fail to notice that we all read the Bible at different levels and so, as the confession puts it, the Scripture is not 'alike clear unto all'. Some Christians understand the Bible better than other Christians. We are not all teachers. And we are not all seasoned saints. In fact some people have just entered the Bible for the first time. Some things they have seen, but do not yet understand. There are many doors which they have not yet entered, many corners they have yet to explore.

Given that certain portions of the Bible are demanding, especially for some people, it is important to be humble as we approach the Bible and listen to those who teach it. We must not reject an interpretation of the Bible simply because it is challenging to understand, either for us, or for everyone. On the contrary, we should remember that this is God's revelation of himself, and we should not expect that everything revealed about the triune God will be easy for humans to grasp. Mapping the high points of the Bible is tiring work.

Nonetheless, what a grave mistake it would be to think that everything in the Bible was beyond us! It is not for nothing that the psalmist says once and again that God's Word is a light (*Psa.* 119:105, 130). How right the Westminster assembly was to say that 'those things which are necessary to be known, believed, and observed for salvation' are not beyond our grasp. Every aspect of the gospel is 'clearly propounded, and opened in some place of Scripture or other'. If you are reading Ecclesiastes and you end up confused about eternal life, then by all means turn to the Gospels, to Ephesians, or to Romans! In Romans you can read that 'all have sinned and fall short of the glory of God'. In Ephesians you can read that 'by grace you are saved, through faith'. That salvation 'is not of ourselves—it is a gift of God'. And in the Gospels we hear Jesus say, 'No man has greater love than this, that he lays down his life for his friends.' And then we see what he means.

Truly, 'not only the learned, but the unlearned' can understand these things and, we might add, explain them to others. Our responsibility is to use the Word of God properly—reading it carefully and listening to it prayerfully. That is to say, we can expect the Holy Spirit's blessing, especially if we do not neglect the ordinary means by which he teaches his people. For the Spirit delights in using the preaching of the Word, the emblems of the gospel provided in baptism and the Lord's supper, and his own answers to prayer to help us understand Scripture.

Texts and translations of Scripture

Paragraph 8 takes this discussion of the Bible in a different direction, first providing us with comment on the text of the Bible. Most of the inspired Old Testament, apart from a few chapters, is in Hebrew, and most of the New Testament, apart from a few words, is in Greek.

The wonderful thing is that God, who directs all of human history, preserved the ancient Hebrew and Greek texts of the Bible as he preserved no other. No other ancient texts survive in such great number and in such good form as do the biblical texts. For example, when this confession was written in the 1640s, the first-century books and letters which might have been possible contenders for inclusion in the New Testament either existed in fragments only or were missing entirely. The fact that late-dated copies of works like the Epistle of Barnabas or the Shepherd of Hermas were finally located at the turn of the twentieth century only emphasizes further the contrast between the preservation of New Testament books and other early pious literature.[1]

Thus, no other book in the world shows God's 'singular care and providence'—only the Scriptures. It is not the case that every ancient scribe who ever copied a portion of the Bible was kept from error. God's providence and this text's purity are more a comment on the survival rates of manuscripts than on textual exactitude. Nevertheless we have such a carefully maintained Old Testament textual tradition, and such a large number of ancient New Testament manuscripts, that we can determine the text of the Bible and believe it with such confidence that we can actually discuss its jots and tittles, the smallest letters and pen strokes (*Matt.* 5:18). The Bible we have is authentic.

Since we have an authentic Bible, it is to its law and testimony that we must appeal, as did Isaiah (*Isa.* 8:20). We want to ensure that our views agree with the Scriptures, as was the aim in the first council of the church, recorded in Acts 15 (see verse 15). As Jesus told the religious leaders of his day, we need to both search the Scriptures and believe them (*John* 5:39, 46).

It is only sensible to add that if we are wise, it is to the Hebrew and Greek text of the Bible that we should appeal in any controversy in religion. Where else could we turn? What else could command our attention by its authority? It was the experience and then the verdict of the Westminster assembly that those engaged in deciding controversies should usually know Hebrew and Greek, and this is the main reason

---

[1] The Didache was not rediscovered until 1873. The entirety of the Epistle of Clement was only discovered in the late nineteenth century. The Epistle of Polycarp has not survived in any one early manuscript and can only be pieced together from Greek and Latin manuscripts. The major part of the Greek text of the Epistle of Barnabas was not recovered until the nineteenth century.

why these languages are required to be learned in solid Christian seminaries or training colleges for ministers.

Even so, as paragraph 7 quickly re-iterates, the Scriptures clearly point the way of salvation for all and sundry. Searching and believing are for everyone (*John* 5:39, 46), and that assumes that we shall all be able to read the Bible, or understand it being read—even without a working knowledge of Hebrew and Greek. In answer to ever-developing languages and the ongoing mission of the church, we are to translate the Bible into every common language. It is not often that the Westminster assembly spoke of the 'rights' of Christians. But the men gathered there were convinced that every child of God has an equal right to hear his or her Father's voice. Every child of God has an interest, has something invested, in hearing and reading God's Word. And every person under heaven has a duty to read and search the Scriptures.

This insistence on translation of the biblical text seems to capture one idea behind Paul's corrections to Corinthian worship, for he tells them not to communicate in languages that no one can understand (*1 Cor.* 14:6, 9, 11, 12, 24, 27, 28). Hence we translate the Bible so that the Word of God will dwell 'richly' or 'plentifully in all' (*Col.* 3:16). Only then will we 'worship him in an acceptable manner'. Only then will the words of the Apostle Paul at the end of Romans ring true for all Christians: the things written in old times 'were written for our learning, that we through patience and comfort of the scriptures might have hope' (*Rom.* 15:4).

Historic Text	*Modern Version*
1.9 The infallible rule of interpretation of Scripture is the Scripture itself: and therefore, when there is a question about the true and full sense of any Scripture (which is not manifold, but one) it must be searched and known by other places that speak more clearly.[y]	**1.9** The infallible rule of interpretation of Scripture is the Scripture itself. Therefore, when there is a question about the true and full meaning of any Scripture (which is not manifold, but one), that meaning must be searched out and ascertained by other places that speak more clearly.

1.10 The supreme judge by which all controversies of religion are to be determined, and all decrees of councils, opinions of ancient writers, doctrines of men, and private spirits, are to be examined; and, in whose sentence we are to rest; can be no other but the Holy Spirit speaking in the Scripture.[z]

1.10 The supreme judge by whom all controversies of religion are to be settled and all decrees of councils, opinions of ancient writers, doctrines of men, and claims to private revelations are to be examined, can be only the Holy Spirit speaking in the Scripture. With his decision we are to be satisfied.

Scripture Proofs

   1.9 [y] 2 Pet. 1:20,21; Acts 15:15,16.

   1.10 [z] Matt. 22:29,31; Eph. 2:20, with Acts 28:25.

The infallible rule

Chapter 1, paragraph 9 of the confession tells us that the most important resource to help us understand the Bible is the Bible itself. In some sense, this is a very familiar rule, for we should approach any book in the world in this way. If we are trying to understand any statement by any author we need to read it in context. This is especially true if we encounter trouble in understanding a book. We assume that an author is trying to make sense and we try to see that sense when we read someone's book.

This is a very good rule of interpretation for the writings of men and women, even though human beings are not always consistent and do not always make sense. This is an infallible rule of interpretation for the Word of God. The significance of this rule is found in the fact that God is the author of every book in Scripture. Remember what Peter tells us, that 'holy men of God spoke as they were moved by the Holy Ghost' (*2 Pet.* 1:20, 21). And with the Holy Spirit there is perfect consistency; with him all things make sense and cohere.

This is an important point for us to remember. Roman Catholics, 'with the exaggeration that often accompanies an important insight', tell us that we *need* the church to understand the Bible. Various cults tell us we need their literature. The truth is that while good guidance can be helpful in reading the Scriptures, the Scriptures themselves are clear in addressing every significant subject about which they speak. Therefore nothing must be more foundational than the Scriptures in our interpretation of them, and in our endeavour to establish doctrine.

In that sense we can and must stand by Scripture alone, *sola scriptura*. When there is a question about the 'true' meaning or the 'full sense of any Scripture', we need to compare Scripture with Scripture. In fact we see this procedure in the Bible itself, where the writers of inspired Scripture insist on referring to other books in the Bible. We see this again in the first council of Jerusalem, where the apostles and elders compare a battery of Old Testament texts to understand the place of the Gentiles in the early church (*Acts* 15:15-18).

And so, if we wish to search out Scripture truly, and in its fullest sense, we need to read the whole of the Bible and know it well. By doing so we shall know those places where the light of the truth shines most clearly, and then we can use those statements to understand portions of the Bible that are less clear to us, or to everyone. In that way also we shall come to an interpretation of each part of Scripture that agrees with every other part of Scripture, ensuring that we have come to an understanding of the Bible, and not a misunderstanding.

Before we leave paragraph 9, we should also note the confession's passing comment that there are not many true and full senses of Scripture, but one. In the medieval church interpreters came to believe that it was their responsibility to find four meanings to every biblical text. This fourfold exegesis, or *quadriga*, referred to the original meaning, a comparative meaning (which they called allegory), a moral meaning, and a heavenly meaning. Sometimes this fourfold interpretation led to a responsible treatment of Scripture. After all, some texts do have a historical meaning which is only understood properly through other passages. That same text might have moral applications and might even relate to the coming of Christ or to heaven itself. Sometimes, therefore, in the hands of the best medieval teachers, the fourfold exegesis could lead to a better interpretation of God's Word. Unfortunately at other times this fourfold interpretation fell into the hands of less capable men and proved profoundly unhelpful. People read interpretations into the Bible rather than deriving them from the Bible. The *quadriga* could lead to some very strange interpretations indeed!

With the Reformation there came a stress on the literal meaning of the text and the unity of that meaning, with the Reformers assigning only one primary grammatical and historical sense to each passage according to its literary classification or genre. For the assembly's members, the interpretation of every text started here.

Nonetheless, in agreement with the saner medieval theologians, most Reformation and post-Reformation theologians did recognize that a passage in the Bible could point beyond itself. This is obviously true when the grammatical genre and historical purpose of the text made this explicit: books of the Bible use language that is figurative, prophetic or apocalyptic; authors and speakers employ allegory and parable. But it is also true that all parts of the Bible are in conversation with other parts, speaking together about the divine Author and his actions. While urging respect for authorial diversity and intent within the Bible, the Westminster assembly carefully book-ended paragraph 9 with reminders that no part of the canon of Scripture can be read in isolation from the rest. God ultimately intended sixty-six books to be read as *one* book.

The supreme judge

Paragraph 10 concludes this chapter. Here the assembly repeats and expands an important point mentioned in paragraph 8; that is to say, that the Holy Scripture is the 'supreme judge' of all spiritual truths, great and small. One reason why people err, as our Lord said to the Sadducees long ago, is that they do 'not know the Scriptures nor the power of God' (*Matt.* 22:29). We need to plunder the Scriptures, for it is in them that the Holy Spirit speaks to us, as Paul tells his detractors in Acts 28:25, and it is in them that the church finds its one foundation, as it reflects on God's revelation through prophets, apostles, and most of all, Jesus Christ himself (*Eph.* 2:20).

Ask yourself: are there 'controversies of religion' that need to be settled? Then there is only one standard that is necessary for us to use, one court to which every Christian and church must appeal. Are there 'decrees of councils' that need to be evaluated? Then there is only one canon by which these councils and their decrees—including the decisions of the Westminster assembly and this confession of faith—can be authoritatively considered right or wrong. Have you or your friends encountered weighty 'opinions of ancient writers'? There is only one balance in which they can be weighed. Do we meet the 'doctrines of men' in conversation, in reading, and in preaching? There is only one light by which they can be examined. Are there 'private spirits' or personal opinions in the church? Then there is only one way in which they are to be judged. There is one 'sentence' in which 'we are to rest'. And that 'can be no other but the Holy Spirit speaking in the Scripture'.

CHAPTER 2:

OF GOD, AND OF THE HOLY TRINITY

Historic Text

2.1 There is but one only,[a] living, and true God:[b] who is infinite in being and perfection,[c] a most pure spirit,[d] invisible,[e] without body, parts,[f] or passions,[g] immutable,[h] immense,[i] eternal,[k] incomprehensible,[l] almighty,[m] most wise,[n] most holy,[o] most free,[p] most absolute,[q] working all things according to the counsel of his own immutable and most righteous will,[r] for his own glory;[s] most loving,[t] gracious, merciful, long-suffering, abundant in goodness and truth, forgiving iniquity, transgression, and sin;[u] the rewarder of them that diligently seek him;[w] and withal, most just and terrible in his judgments,[x] hating all sin,[y] and who will by no means clear the guilty.[z]

Modern Version

2.1 There is only one living and true God, who is infinite in being and perfection. He is a most pure spirit, invisible, with neither body, parts, nor passive properties. He is unchangeable, boundless, eternal, and incomprehensible. He is almighty, most wise, most holy, most free, and most absolute. He works all things according to the counsel of his own unchangeable and most righteous will, for his own glory. He is most loving, gracious, merciful, long-suffering, abundant in goodness and truth, forgiving iniquity, transgression, and sin, and he is the rewarder of those who diligently seek him. He is also most just and terrifying in his judgments, hating all sin, and will by no means acquit the guilty.

Scripture Proofs

2.1 [a] Deut. 6:4; 1 Cor. 8:4,6. [b] 1 Thess. 1:9; Jer. 10:10. [c] Job 11:7-9; Job 26:14. [d] John 4:24. [e] 1 Tim. 1:17. [f] Deut. 4:15,16; John 4:24, with Luke 24:39. [g] Acts 14:11,15. [h] James 1:17; Mal. 3:6. [i] 1 Kings 8:27; Jer. 23:23,24. [k] Psa. 90:2; 1 Tim. 1:17. [l] Psa. 145:3. [m] Gen. 17:1; Rev. 4:8. [n] Rom. 16:27. [o] Isa. 6:3; Rev. 4:8. [p] Psa. 115:3. [q] Exod. 3:14. [r] Eph. 1:11. [s] Prov. 16:4; Rom. 11:36. [t] 1 John 4:8,16. [u] Exod. 34:6,7. [w] Heb. 11:6. [x] Neh. 9:32,33. [y] Psa. 5:5,6. [z] Nah. 1:2,3; Exod. 34:7.

One God, no limit

If God has revealed himself to us, as the first chapter of this confession teaches, it makes sense to ask who God is. That is the focus of this second chapter, which offers dozens of descriptive words and phrases for the God of the Bible.

We can of course ask a question about *who* God is, but Scripture often first answers the question, *how many* gods are there? The most basic creed of the Old Testament is the cry, 'Hear, O Israel: The LORD our God, the LORD is one' (*Deut.* 6:4). We need to remind ourselves of this because there are many things that are wrongly valued as gods (*1 Cor.* 8:4-6), while the truth is that there is only one God who is both 'living' and 'true', as Jeremiah told the Israelites and Paul told the Thessalonians (*Jer.* 10:10; *1 Thess.* 1:9).

But while God is limited in number, he is unlimited in his being and in all his perfections. Job and his friends were wrong about many things, but at least all of them understood that the depths of the divine Being cannot be sounded by any mere man; we can hardly even grasp 'the outer fringes of his works' (*Job* 26:14; cf. *Job* 11:7-9).

The God who is Spirit

One reason for our struggle to comprehend God is that in his being, 'God is Spirit', as Jesus told the Samaritan woman at the well (*John* 4:24). Among other things, this entails that we understand God as one who is invisible—indeed, Paul praises him as the one who is 'eternal, immortal', and 'invisible' (*1 Tim.* 1:17). It is because God is not constrained by a human body with its different parts that God forbade forging idols in his image (*Deut.* 4:15, 16). After all, as Jesus reminded his disciples after his resurrection, 'a spirit does not have flesh and bones' (*Luke* 24:39; cf. *John* 4:24).

Creator and creature

But even angels are spirits, and so we have to say much more about God in order to properly distinguish him from his creatures. For there are many things that God is that his creatures are not. It is because the true God is so different from us that Paul and Barnabas were horrified when a crowd at Lystra attempted to worship them. The two urged the crowd to see that they were men of like passions, that is, they had a similar nature with comparable defective impulses, to each person in the crowd (*Acts* 14:11-15). By implication, they were saying that this could hardly be true of God!

How right they were to draw distinctions between the Creator and his creatures! God is 'immutable', he 'does not change like shifting shadows' (*James* 1:17)—indeed, the prophet Malachi once noted, God does not change at all (*Mal.* 3:6). God is 'immense'; he fills all things, and is everywhere present. We cannot hide from God, and there is no place for God to hide—the universe testifies to him—he fills it from one end to the other (*1 Kings* 8:27; *Jer.* 23:23, 24). He is the 'King of ages', which is only to say that he is 'eternal' (*1 Tim.* 1:17); and what is true of space is also true of time: God is 'from everlasting to everlasting' (*Psa.* 90:2). No wonder the Psalmist asks how we can fathom this kind of greatness (*Psa.* 145:3). Even though we say that we know all these things about God, how can we search out what these categories really mean when applied to God? God is knowable—he has revealed himself. But there are such vast limits to our knowledge that we also admit that in a profound sense God is 'incomprehensible'.

Even here, we are only making a beginning, for there is so much more to say. From Genesis to Revelation, God is adored as 'almighty' (*e.g., Gen.* 17:1; *Rev.* 4:8). Before the church the apostle praises the vastness of God's wisdom (*Rom.* 16:27). Before the throne of heaven, beasts and angels praise the perfection of his holiness (*Isa.* 6:3; *Rev.* 4:8). God is truly the one who is 'almighty, most wise, most holy', and, as Psalm 115 reminds the nations, 'most free', doing all that he pleases (*Psa.* 115:3). And that is because God is 'absolute'; he is who he is, as he once told a frightened Moses at the burning bush (*Exod.* 3:14).

The works of God

In all these characteristics we are seeking not only to describe something about God as he is, in and of himself, but also to praise him for how he expresses his character to the world he has made. He is the one who works all things 'according to the counsel of his own immutable and most righteous will', as the confession paraphrases Paul's words in Ephesians 1:11, and 'for his own glory', as it paraphrases Romans 11 (*Rom.* 11:36; *cf. Prov.* 16:4).

His own people know him as 'most loving'. Members of the Westminster assembly did. Studying the day-to-day references to God in the ordinary writings of the assembly, and not merely the major confessional and churchly texts which they produced, we must be impressed by the fact that the assembly's various references to the love and mercy of God far outstrip any other adjectives or descriptions of God's character offered by these post-Reformation pastors and theologians.[1] Of infinitely greater significance, the Apostle John has taught us to say that 'God is love' (*1 John* 4:8, 16). And God himself announced to Moses that he is 'gracious, merciful, long-suffering, abundant in goodness and truth, forgiving iniquity, transgression, and sin' (*Exod.* 34:6, 7).

This is good news for sinners, which is what we all are. And yet while Scripture tells us that our God 'rewards those who seek him' (*Heb.* 11:6), it was right for Nehemiah to confess that God in his justice can also be awesome—in the sense of terrifying—to those who disobey him (*Neh.* 9:32-33). God hates sin, as Psalm 5 bluntly puts it (*Psa.* 5:5, 6). It is because of his perfect justice and hatred of sin that God warns us once and again that he 'does not leave the guilty unpunished' (*Exod.* 34:7; *Nahum* 1:2, 3).

In speaking of God's justice and mercy, of his power and his wisdom, indeed of all his attributes, we do not for a moment think that we are able to 'define' God, in any limiting sense. If these paragraphs were pages, or if all the world were print, we could never hope to catalogue the perfections of our triune God. What we do want to do is to rejoice in God's character with as much depth as we are able, so that we may better reflect his image, give him much glory, and enjoy him forever.

---

[1] For the assembly's miscellaneous writings, see C. Van Dixhoorn, ed., *The Minutes and Papers of the Westminster Assembly, 1643-1652* (Oxford, 2012), vol. 5.

Historic Text

2.2 God has all life,[a] glory,[b] goodness,[c] blessedness,[d] in, and of himself; and is alone in, and unto himself all-sufficient, not standing in need of any creatures which he has made,[e] nor deriving any glory from them,[f] but only manifesting his own glory, in, by, unto, and upon them: he is the alone fountain of all being, of whom, through whom, and to whom are all things;[g] and, has most sovereign dominion over them, to do by them, for them, or upon them whatsoever himself pleases.[h] In his sight all things are open and manifest,[i] his knowledge is infinite, infallible, and independent upon the creature,[k] so as nothing is to him contingent, or uncertain.[l] He is most holy in all his counsels, in all his works, and in all his commands.[m] To him is due from angels and men, and every other creature, whatsoever worship, service, or obedience he is pleased to require of them.[n]

Modern Version

2.2 God has all life, glory, goodness, and blessedness in and of himself. He alone is all-sufficient, in and to himself, not standing in need of any creatures which he has made, nor deriving any glory from them, but rather manifesting his own glory in, by, to, and on them. He alone is the fountain of all being, of whom, through whom, and to whom are all things. He has absolute sovereignty over them, to do by them, for them, or upon them whatever he pleases. In his sight all things are open and manifest; his knowledge is infinite, infallible, and independent of his creatures; so that nothing to him is contingent or uncertain. He is most holy in all his counsels, in all his works, and in all his commands. To him is due from angels and men, and every other creature, whatever worship, service, or obedience he is pleased to require of them.

Scripture Proofs

2.2 [a] John 5:26. [b] Acts 7:2. [c] Psa. 119:68. [d] 1 Tim. 6:15; Rom. 9:5. [e] Acts 17:24,25. [f] Job 22:2,3. [g] Rom. 11:36. [h] Rev. 4:11; 1 Tim. 6:15; Dan. 4:25,35. [i] Heb. 4:13. [k] Rom. 11:33,34; Psa. 147:5. [l] Acts 15:18; Ezek. 11:5. [m] Psa. 145:17; Rom. 7:12. [n] Rev. 5:12-14.

God in himself

The first paragraph of this chapter encourages us to behold our God, and to consider his character; to wonder at 'the depth of the wisdom and knowledge of God.' We can echo the considered exclamations of the Apostle Paul at the end of Romans 11, who praised God for his 'unsearchable judgments', confessing that his 'ways are past finding out.'

This second paragraph of chapter 2 continues in doxology as it considers God's 'aseity', or absolute independence from all things. As Jesus tells us, God has life 'in himself' (*John* 5:26). As Paul adds, no one can know God's mind or be his counsellor. Therefore, no one can add anything to who God is. For 'who has ever given to God, that God should repay him?' (*Rom.* 11:35; see 11:33-36).

As you can see, every effort is taken in this section of the confession to show that God does not need us, or owe us anything. This is hardly a startling statement for those who have read the whole of the Bible or who are students of the created world. If anything is clear, it is that 'God has all life' in and of himself. All glory and goodness and blessedness reside in God alone, as martyrs, poets and apostles testify (*Acts* 7:2; *Psa.* 119:68; *1 Tim.* 6:15; *Rom.* 9:5). Naturally, God does not need anything other than himself. When he was alone, before the creation of the universe, he was 'all-sufficient'. He stood in no 'need of any creatures which he had made'. He did not need them to sustain his life, to increase his glory, to disclose his goodness or to add to his blessedness. God has not changed, and the same is true today.

God does not need us for anything. In fact the exact opposite is true. Take God's glory as a case study. As Paul explained to the people of Athens, God does not command our worship because he needs something from us (*Acts* 17:24-25). Surely one of Job's friends was having a moment of clarity when he argued that God does not benefit from us (*Job* 22:2-3), or from any of the wonderful creatures he has made—not from the blazing stars glittering in the night, nor from whales frolicking in the seas, nor from flowering lilies arrayed in all their splendour, nor from men and women at the height of their wisdom, strength and beauty. God's glory comes from himself. And God is infinite in all of his perfections, including his glory. To speak of God increasing in glory may be, in a very real sense, to speak nonsense. At the very least we should acknowledge that when saints and angels 'give' glory to God, we ascribe glory, not add glory, to him.

The reality is that God actually 'manifests' or shows his glory through us as he puts us on display for himself to enjoy. In the same way, God reveals his glory in us, leaving us to wonder at the one who made us. And in his supreme goodness, God even gives glory to us, permitting us the honour of honours, the privilege of reflecting his image, undeserving though we are and always have been.

God and us

Nonetheless, if we follow the Westminster divines in this paragraph, or indeed, if we follow the Apostle Paul in Romans 11, we shall see that we are not only to reflect on God's absolute independence and incomparable greatness. We are also to see what that means for God's creatures in our utter dependence.

That is what the confession means when it states that God 'is the alone fountain of all being'. God is not only the supreme being. He is also the one through whom all others have their being. All things are 'of' God, all things are 'through' God. He made all things and he upholds all things by his mighty power. And so all things are to be oriented 'to' God (*Rom.* 11:36).

The fact that God is the fountain of all things, and that all things are to be oriented to him, has consequences for the world. The greatest of these consequences is that God 'has most sovereign dominion over' us. No matter who or what we are talking about, it is always true that God can 'do by them, for them, or upon them whatsoever himself pleases'. He is 'the only Ruler, the King of kings and Lord of lords' (*1 Tim.* 6:15). This was something Nebuchadnezzar had to learn the hard way. It was only after he was driven from society and treated like an animal that he finally came to see that there was one who was 'Most High' and that 'among the inhabitants of the earth' there is no one who 'can stay his hand or say to him, "What have you done?"' (*Dan.* 4:25, 35). This was something which creatures and elders in heaven know instinctively. This is why they proclaim him to be worthy of glory, honour and power: God has 'created all things' and by his will they exist (*Rev.* 4:11).

This paragraph ends by referring to God's pleasure. God is able to do what will please him because he sees all and knows all. In God's sight 'all things are open and manifest'—they are clearly open to his view. As the writer to the Hebrews says so plainly, 'Nothing in all creation is hidden from God's sight. Everything is uncovered and laid bare before the eyes of him to whom we must give account' (*Heb.* 4:13). God's 'knowledge is infinite' and because of this it is 'infallible'. The 'infinite' knowledge of God can account for all possible variables and eventualities.

His knowledge is 'independent' of his creatures and all that may happen to them or all that they may do. There are depths to the riches of God's wisdom and knowledge that we shall never reach. His judgments really are unsearchable and his paths are beyond our tracing (*Rom.* 11:33, 34). This must be the case if God's 'understanding is infinite', as the psalmist says it is (*Psa.* 147:5). If God's understanding is infinite, it is not idle philosophical speculation to say that 'nothing is to him contingent,[1] or uncertain'. Indeed, as the Holy Spirit told Ezekiel, and Ezekiel told Israel's leaders, God even knows what goes through our minds (*Ezek.* 11:5). If we properly understand the God who has revealed himself to us in the Scriptures, then we shall also understand that God knows the end from the beginning (*Acts* 15:17, 18), for he planned it all to his pleasure.

God knows what things will please him because he knows all things; he also knows what will please him because he knows himself. He is holy, and thus his ways will be holy. How good it is for God's people to say with all their hearts and with all the Scriptures, 'He is most holy in all his counsels, in all his works, and in all his commands' (see, *e.g.*, *Psa.* 145:17; *Rom.* 7:12).

With such a God, how could we not recognize that 'To him is due from angels and men'—in fact from all his creatures—the 'worship, service, or obedience he is pleased to require of them'? Is that not exactly what we see in John's vision of heaven (*Rev.* 5:12-14)? If so, then we must prepare ourselves to worship him in heaven, serving him here with our hearts and minds and voices and gifts. By God's grace let us go from this reflection about God and endeavour to give him the obedience that he has been pleased to require of us.

---

[1] Dependent on something not yet certain.

Historic Text	*Modern Version*
2.3 In the unity of the Godhead there be three persons, of one substance, power, and eternity; God the Father, God the Son, and God the Holy Ghost.° The Father is of none, neither begotten, nor proceeding: The Son is eternally begotten of the Father:ᵖ the Holy Ghost eternally proceeding from the Father and the Son.۹	**2.3** In the unity of the Godhead there are three persons, of one substance, power, and eternity: God the Father, God the Son, and God the Holy Spirit. The Father is of none, neither begotten nor proceeding; the Son is eternally begotten of the Father; the Holy Spirit eternally proceeds from the Father and the Son.

Scripture Proofs

   2.3   ° 1 John 5:7; Matt. 3:16,17; Matt. 28:19; 2 Cor. 13:14.   ᵖ John 1:14,18.
۹ John 15:26; Gal. 4:6.

One and three

Previous paragraphs examined God's perfections, his independence from the world and our dependence on him. Here in this final paragraph of chapter 2 we find a series of statements about God as one and God as three.

The Bible has much to say about the unity and oneness of God. We hear this throughout the Old Testament, but also in the New Testament, for when Paul is reminding us that there is only one mediator between God and man, he also points out that 'there is one God' (*1 Tim.* 2:5). Indeed this truth is so basic, James says, that even the devils do not deny it (*James* 2:19).

However, the remarkable fact is that in the unity that is God, there are 'three persons'. God's unity is like none other, for it is a tri-unity, or trinity. These three are one in the most profound sense. It is because they are one, that when we behold the glory of the Son we find ourselves beholding the glory of the Father; the one cannot help but reveal and declare the other (*John* 1:14, 18).

They are one in the way in which they illumine each other. They are also one in their eternity, always having existed with one another. There was never a time when they did not live together in love, and peace, and glory, abounding in every perfection and in all fullness. Likewise they are one in their 'power'. The three powerfully act as one and are equal and unsurpassed in their power. As one God, they are unified in their 'substance'. Here we are grasping for words! We are only trying to say that the three really are one God. First, there is 'God the Father'; second, there is 'God the Son'; third, there is God the Holy Spirit or 'Holy Ghost'.

The Westminster divines were trying to make clear in as few words as possible that the Father, the Son and the Spirit are God; and this is just what the Bible teaches. When Paul is outlining the problem with paganism and idol worship, he reminds the Corinthians that 'to us there is but one God, the Father, of whom are all things, and we in him' (*1 Cor.* 8:6). When John is marvelling at the incarnation of the Son of God, he tells us first that 'in the beginning was the Word'. Not only was the Word in the beginning, not only was the Word 'with God'—the reality is that the Word *is* God (*John* 1:1). And when, in a sad chapter of church history, the Apostle Peter told Ananias and Sapphira that their pretended generosity was really a sham, he first told them that they had 'lied to the Holy Spirit'; he then clarified what he meant: they had 'not lied unto men, but unto God' (*Acts* 5:3, 4). These apostles are not disagreeing with each other. And they are offering more than dramatic figures of speech. They are pointing, piece by piece, to one triune reality.

Truly this is a remarkable testimony. It is hard to know how well, or how often, it was understood by Old Testament saints. It was certainly understood by the apostles themselves, which is why the Apostle Paul blessed the Corinthians in the name of the triune God, offering to them the 'grace of the Lord Jesus Christ, and the love of God, and the fellowship of the Holy Spirit' (*2 Cor.* 13:14). But although the apostles understood this doctrine, others have not. Everyone agrees that the revelation of one God who is three persons is hard to understand and impossible to fully explain.

Nonetheless because of the demanding nature of the doctrine, and because some do not accept the authority of the Bible, there are people who have thought that God is not truly three persons. These people do not read the Bible carefully and prayerfully, and they reduce our triune God to a Grade B movie without enough actors. God acts or appears as the Father one moment, they say, as the Son at another, or as the Spirit at yet another.

There are many problems with this view, called Modalism or Sabellianism, but chief among them is the fact that God revealed himself as Father and Son and Spirit simultaneously in events such as the baptism of Jesus. In God's infinite wisdom he recorded and revealed this event for us. In Matthew 3 we are told with great clarity that the Father declared from heaven his approval of his Son, even as the Holy Spirit came upon him like a dove as it descended from the sky. Here all three members of the Trinity revealed themselves in one way or another, not in a series of events, not as modes of being, but in one grand and unforgettable public display in the history of redemption (*Matt.* 3:16, 17).

We also insist that the three are truly distinct and different because, as the confession reminds us, they do different things. This is summarized so well by Jesus in John 15:26, where our Lord promised, 'When the Counsellor comes, whom I will send to you from the Father, the Spirit of truth who goes out from the Father, he will testify about me'. Putting the pieces together, here and elsewhere, we see that 'the Father is of none'. He is not 'begotten'. He does not proceed, or is not sent, from anyone else. But he does eternally and divinely beget the Son—by which we only understand that he is in some way always a Father to the Son. And he sends the Spirit. The Son also sends the Spirit, for Christ says that he will send the Counsellor, his Holy Spirit (*John* 16:7). But the Son is different from the Father because he is 'eternally begotten'—by which we only understand that he is in some way always a Son to the Father. And the Spirit is different from both. He is the executor of the will of the Father and the Son; he knows the mind of God, as Paul says in Romans 8. And in equal power and eternity with the Father and the Son, he is sent to put their will into action. As Paul puts it, 'God sent forth the Spirit of his Son' (*Gal.* 4:6).

Ultimately we are to remember that the three are distinct and that they are one because when the disciples are told to baptize, they are told to do it in the name—of course God's name—but then three names are given. The movement from singular to plural is significant. So too is the fact that they are explicitly told to 'teach all nations, baptizing them in the name of the Father, and of the Son, and of the Holy Ghost' (*Matt.* 28:19).

This is a doctrine which has implications for all of life. It is the one-ness of God the Spirit, God the Son and God the Father that the Apostle Paul invokes when he is calling the Ephesian Christians to unity. For 'there is one body, and one Spirit, even as ye are called in one hope of your calling; one Lord, one faith, one baptism, one God and Father of all, who is above all, and through all, and in you all' (*Eph.* 4:4-6).[1]

In order that we might grasp this truth better, and celebrate it together, let us gather often to worship, in unity, the only true God—praying that the Father, by the grace of his Son, would bless us by his Holy Spirit.

---

[1] The Westminster assembly cited 1 John 5:7 as additional support for the doctrine of the Trinity. This text is neither necessary, nor, given its weak manuscript history, persuasive.

THE DECREES OF GOD

CHAPTER 3:

OF GOD'S ETERNAL DECREE

Historic Text	*Modern Version*
3.1 God from all eternity did, by the most wise and holy counsel of his own will, freely, and unchangeably ordain whatsoever comes to pass:[a] yet so as thereby neither is God the author of sin,[b] nor is violence offered to the will of the creatures, nor is the liberty or contingency of second causes taken away, but rather established.[c]	**3.1** God, from all eternity, did—by the most wise and holy counsel of his own will—freely and unchangeably ordain whatever comes to pass. Yet he ordered all things in such a way that he is not the author of sin, nor does he force his creatures to act against their wills; neither is the liberty or contingency of second causes taken away, but rather established.
3.2 Although God knows whatsoever may, or can come to pass upon all supposed conditions,[d] yet has he not decreed anything because he foresaw it as future, or as that which would come to pass upon such conditions.[e]	**3.2** Although God knows whatever may or can come to pass under all conceivable conditions, yet he has not decreed anything because he foresaw it as future or as that which would come to pass under such conditions.

Scripture Proofs

3.1 [a] Eph. 1:11; Rom. 11:33; Heb. 6:17; Rom. 9:15,18. [b] James 1:13,17; 1 John 1:5. [c] Acts 2:23; Matt. 17:12; Acts 4:27,28; John 19:11; Prov. 16:33.

3.2 [d] Acts 15:18; 1 Sam. 23:11,12; Matt. 11:21,23. [e] Rom. 9:11,13,16,18.

An eternal, wise and holy plan

This chapter speaks of God's eternal counsel or plan. Here we learn the things that God positively 'ordains' or decrees. In later chapters, specifically 5 and 6, we shall discover what God 'permits'.

Our God has ordained, or ordered, 'whatsoever comes to pass'. All that happens in time and eternity is according to the will of the one who 'made' both. All things exist for God's pleasure, and God finds pleasure when all things go according to his plan.

This plan of the eternal God was settled from 'all eternity'. And from the beginning, God's plan or counsel for the ordering of all things is 'most wise and holy'. What else could it be, since God is the one who planned it? God's ordering of all things is wise and holy because, as Paul says in his letter to the Ephesians, God works 'all things after the counsel of *his* own will' (*Eph.* 1:11), and no one influences God. He decides all things 'freely' (see Paul's discussion of election in Romans 9, especially his comments in verses 15 and 18). And God's ordering of all things is wise and holy because God is himself most wise and holy. The depths of the riches of the wisdom and knowledge of God are truly unsearchable (*Rom.* 11:33).

God's plan is eternal. So, too, God's plan is unchangeable, as the letter to the Hebrews states (*Heb.* 6:17). God formed his plan in all eternity; it is perfect; and God himself does not change. Almost needless to say, God does not allow anyone else to change his counsel without his consent or against his will.

Three qualifiers

God did 'unchangeably ordain whatsoever comes to pass', but this comprehensive statement requires three qualifying fences lest we should wander in directions that would prove dangerous. The first fence keeps out the idea that God could ever be the 'author of sin'. He is the author of life, as Peter preached after Pentecost (*Acts* 3:15), and the author of salvation and of faith, as the writer to the Hebrews tells us (*Heb.* 2:10; 12:2). But in spite of the fact that he 'unchangeably ordains whatsoever comes to pass', including great calamities (*Isa.* 45:7), he is not the cause of sin. The Westminster divines actually issued a special paper on this very theme, because a preacher in their own day had drifted into error on this point.[1]

---

[1] Van Dixhoorn, ed., *The Minutes and Papers of the Westminster Assembly*, vol. 5, pp. 224-7, Document 80.

Certainly these are deep waters, and we admit that we only splash in the shallows of theology. After all, Jesus said to Pilate that the governor would have no power to crucify him unless it were given to him from above (*John* 19:11). And we know from all of Scripture that it was the plan of the triune God to send a Saviour who would die on a cross. But this does not mean that God was the author of the evil that was Pilate's. He was no more at fault for what Pilate and the soldiers did than he was for what Adam did in the garden. We must remember that it is not only true that 'God cannot be tempted by evil', but it is also true, as James goes on to say, that God 'does not tempt anyone' (*James* 1:13).

Now the declaration that God ordains all things, and yet does not command sin, leaves many questions unanswered. But as we push toward the outer limits of what we can understand of God and his ways, it is important to always remember what we do know. And what we do know is that God is holy. We must recall the mature utterance of the Apostle John, who writes that 'God is light; in him there is no darkness at all' (*1 John* 1:5). There could hardly be any follower of Jesus more qualified to say so than a witness of the transfiguration of Jesus, and the one who would one day receive a revelation of God on a lonely island.

The second fence is almost as important as the first. And the point is that we need to remember that God's ordaining of whatsoever comes to pass does not do 'violence' to the will of men and women. To invert Proverbs 16:33, 'every decision is from the Lord', but 'the lot' is still cast into our own laps. God is sovereign, but in a very real way we are free, and in every way we are responsible for our actions.

This truth can be overheard as we listen to Jesus talking about the way in which people did what they wanted with John the Baptist (*Matt.* 17:12). We hear it again when we listen to the Apostle Peter preaching at Pentecost to a vast crowd containing so many who approved of Jesus' crucifixion. Consider how the apostle could stand up and acknowledge that Jesus was 'handed over' to them 'by God's set purpose and foreknowledge'. And yet, Peter could say with equal authority that they were 'wicked men' who put Jesus 'to death by nailing him to the cross' (*Acts* 2:23; *cf. Acts* 4:27, 28). We are not puppets. The honest truth is that we sin freely—we sin willingly, and we know it. This too deserves a prominent place in our doctrine of the divine decrees.

The third protective fence is that God's plan still employs real secondary causes. In other words, God has decided the end from the beginning, but the middle still matters. It still matters because God not only decides what will happen in the end, but how it will happen. Consider how God decided to save sinners. When he decided to save sinners, he specifically decided to save sinners *by Jesus Christ*. After that decision had been made, Jesus Christ really did need to be born and to suffer for our salvation. These happenings between God's plan in eternity and our salvation in time and space are crucial. The reality and necessity of such events are not removed by God's decree, nor is the reality of these 'middle events' or 'secondary causes' in any way diminished.

The important thing to remember now is that the liberty or freedom of these causes is real; the contingency or possibility of these events is not taken away, a point that is effectively identical with that made before. All events—even those events which we see as secondary causes—are also part of God's decree, and so God's decree establishes these causes and events too.

The God who is free

The second paragraph in chapter 3 leaves off developing an outline of our liberty (the subject of a later chapter) and returns to discuss God once more. Here we are reminded that God knows all things. He sees, with a clear-eyed vision of all that is on or below the surface of life, and all that is to come. Indeed, God has known all things 'from the beginning of the world' (*Acts* 15:18).

However, God does not only know all that *has* happened and *will* happen. He also knows all that *could* happen (what used to be called 'middle knowledge'). We see this plainly in biblical narrative. Take the example of David, who once posed a series of questions to the Lord, first about Saul, and then about some townspeople. David queried whether they would hand him over to Saul if the king demanded it. This line of questioning was not too hard for God, because, unfathomable as it is for us to contemplate, there is no scenario which God does not already know (*1 Sam.* 23:11, 12; see also *Matt.* 11:21-23).

And yet, although God knows 'whatsoever may or can come to pass upon all supposed conditions', this does not influence his plan or decisions. What comes to pass comes to pass because he decides so. Stated differently, God has not 'decreed anything' merely 'because he foresaw it as future'. For example, he does not save you because he knew that you would respond positively to the gospel. We love him only 'because he first loved us', as John says (*1 John* 4:19). Nor does God decide to do something merely because he knows what will 'come to pass upon' certain 'conditions'. Though God knows every possible conditional, every possible 'if . . . then' statement, these conditionals do not influence him. He makes his decisions apart from them. The knowledge of God does not bind him. We serve the God who is entirely free.

The decree of God has been the subject of too much debate in the history of the church. The reality is that the parties in these disputes are often much closer to one another than they admit. The happy truth is that those who dispute the absolute lordship of God check their arguments at the door when they enter their closets to pray. The sad truth is that those who defend a doctrine of divine sovereignty often complain when things do not go their own way, forgetting that their grumbling is against God.

It may be hard for us to accept that God can say, 'Jacob I loved, but Esau I hated' even 'before the twins were born or had done anything good or bad'. We may even be surprised that God says in his Word, 'I will have mercy on whom I have mercy, and I will have compassion on whom I have compassion.' We may even wonder, as Paul half-expected his readers to do so long ago, 'Why does God still blame us? For who resists his will?' But let us push these imprudent thoughts aside and ask ourselves two questions also found in Paul's theological tract to the Romans: 'Who are [we] to talk back to God?' And 'Shall what is formed say to him who formed it, "Why did you make me like this?"' (*Rom.* 9:11-20). Let us then entrust ourselves to the one whose counsel is most wise and most holy—the one who does all things well.

❦

Historic Text

3.3 By the decree of God, for the manifestation of his glory, some men and angels[f] are predestinated unto everlasting life, and others foreordained to everlasting death.[g]

3.4 These angels and men thus predestinated and foreordained, are particularly, and unchangeably designed, and their number is so certain, and definite, that it cannot be either increased, or diminished.[h]

3.5 Those of mankind that are predestinated unto life, God, before the foundation of the world was laid, according to his eternal and immutable purpose, and the secret counsel and good pleasure of his will, has chosen, in Christ, unto everlasting glory,[i] out of his mere free grace and love, without any foresight of faith, or good works, or perseverance in either of them, or any other thing in the creature, as conditions, or causes moving him thereunto:[k] and all, to the praise of his glorious grace.[l]

Modern Version

3.3 By God's decree, for the manifestation of his glory, some men and angels are predestined to everlasting life, and others are foreordained to everlasting death.

3.4 These angels and men, thus predestined and foreordained, are individually and unchangeably designated, and their number is so certain and definite that it cannot be either increased or decreased.

3.5 Those people who are predestined to life, God—before the foundation of the world was laid, according to his eternal and unchangeable purpose and the secret counsel and good pleasure of his will—has chosen in Christ to everlasting glory. He chose them out of his free grace and love alone, not because he foresaw faith, or good works, or perseverance in either of these, or anything else in the creature, as conditions or causes moving him to do this; and all to the praise of his glorious grace.

Scripture Proofs

3.3 [f] 1 Tim. 5:21; Matt. 25:41. [g] Rom. 9:22,23; Eph. 1:5,6; Prov. 16:4.

3.4 [h] 2 Tim. 2:19; John 13:18.

3.5 [i] Eph. 1:4,9,11; Rom. 8:30; 2 Tim. 1:9; 1 Thess. 5:9. [k] Rom. 9:11,13,16; Eph. 1:4,9. [l] Eph. 1:6,12.

Destinies of life and death

Every serious Bible reader can see that God has a plan for every person he has made; it is also the case, as paragraph 3 reminds us, that he has a plan for every angel. The Bible discusses this less often, but not less clearly. Some he considers his elect, or chosen ones (*1 Tim.* 5:21); others he has cursed, leaving them with the fires of hell, rather than a home in heaven (*Matt.* 25:41).

For both men and angels, God has predestined some to everlasting life, while others are 'foreordained to everlasting death'. For some, God shows patience, 'in order to make known the riches of his glory for vessels of mercy' (*Rom.* 9:22). These are predestined, as Paul told the Ephesians, 'for adoption through Jesus Christ' (*Eph.* 1:5, 6). For others, for those who die in their sins, God reserves some purpose—indeed, 'the LORD has made everything for its purpose, even the wicked for the day of trouble' (*Prov.* 16:4).

Sometimes we wonder why God destines some for heaven and others for hell. Why do some see God in his mercy and others, ultimately, only in his wrath? We may perhaps never be able to give these questions a sufficient answer and we need to recognize that in addressing this subject we are hardly ploughing unbroken ground. Discussion about predestination has been in progress since the time of the apostles. Nonetheless, it is helpful to remember three things.

First, we all have earned the wages of sin and if we have looked unblinkingly at our wicked hearts, we know what should be coming to us on the judgment day. We shall never understand divine punishment until we have an understanding of our own depravity with its wider implications as well as an accurate portrait of the comprehensive purity of God. Few who question God's decrees have the patience to investigate the character of his holiness or the nature of our sin.

Second, the greatest marvel is not God's judgment, but that at the end of our day we discover that our Master planned in eternity a mercy for us that we do not deserve. Recall the conclusion of one of Jesus' parables, where the owner of the vineyard is criticized for injustice, and he responds with a question that exposes the critics' jealousy of his generosity. Certainly it would not be wrong to put this question in the mouth of God himself: 'Am I not allowed to do what I choose with what belongs to me? Or do you begrudge my generosity?' (*Matt.* 20:8; see also *Rom.* 9:14, 15).

Third, we must heed the opening line in this third paragraph of chapter 3 of the confession which reminds us that when God determines the destiny of his creatures he does this, as he does all things, for his own glory, because he is God (*Rom.* 9:23).

A certain number

As we would expect with one who does all things well, God does not change his plan over time. There is a certain number of angels and men, predestined and foreordained, for eternal life and death, and once decided, that number is immune to mathematical addition or subtraction. Paul reminds Timothy that 'the Lord knows those who are his' and, we might add, those who are not (2 Tim. 2:19). Of course Paul is only echoing what Jesus says himself, when he states, 'I know whom I have chosen' (John 13:18).

It may appear that even these brief statements are leaning towards one side of the story, giving more emphasis to election than reprobation. This is correct. The Westminster assembly selected passages of Scripture to support the theology of these statements, and the emphasis of these passages is on the assurance that God's plan gives to God's people. However, this selection of verses, and this emphasis, are not arbitrary. These verses reflect the dominant emphasis of Scripture itself, which celebrates the selection of God's own people more than his passing by a rebel people whom he does not plan to save. The main point in this section, following a main point of the Bible itself, is that God never sets his love on someone only to abandon him or her later. Our salvation is secure.

A secret counsel

In the fifth paragraph of this chapter, our attention is focused firmly on those who are predestined to life. In a medley of passages taken from the first chapter of Ephesians we are taught that God's plan for our salvation was drawn up 'before the foundation of the world was laid'. This was done 'according to the purpose' of God's will, which is at once 'eternal and immutable', or unchangeable (Eph. 1:4, 9, 11). This counsel is of course secret; we cannot penetrate the sovereign pleasure of God in making his decisions, but we trust that it is good.

In Christ alone

What we do know is that God's plan for us is firmly rooted 'in Christ'. God does choose each one of us, not in a mass, but individually, personally. But God chose all of us as his children *in Christ*—he is the chosen one of God, the foreordained one, and we are saved as we are united to him. In one way or another, this is what Paul says to the Ephesians, to Timothy, and to the Thessalonians. We are 'predestined . . . through Jesus Christ' (*Eph.* 1:5), his purpose for us is 'set forth in Christ' (*Eph.* 1:9), his grace is given us 'in Christ Jesus before the ages began' (*2 Tim.* 1:9). In short, 'God has not destined us for wrath, but to obtain salvation through our Lord Jesus Christ' (*1 Thess.* 5:9). And all of this is not only done for God's glory, but for our own—'for those God predestines, he also calls, and those whom he calls, he also justifies, and those whom he justifies, he also glorifies' (*Rom.* 8:30). God had our crown in view long before our creation.

Free grace, not foreseen faith

All of this flows out of God's sheer, 'free grace', a grace which is tinged—no, saturated with his love. Of course, the Lord sees all things. But he did not peer into the future in order to find sparks of faith that he could fan into flame. To think that we can do something that will make God then choose us is to construct a façade in the hope that God will add a real structure behind it. He did not predestine us to salvation because he predicted our good works, or knew we would persevere in the Christian life. There is nothing in us that motivated his choice. He set no conditions which he needed to foresee before he would choose us. All such notions need to be deconstructed before we can advance in the school of grace. There was no human cause that set God in motion towards our salvation.

We can be sure of this because of what we are told in the classic biblical chapters on the divine decrees, Romans 9 and Ephesians 1. In Romans Paul explains that nothing that could have been done by either of the twins would have led to God's election of Jacob and not Esau. God wanted his purpose to stand because of his call, not because of their future works (*Rom.* 9:11). Why did God love Jacob? Not because of human will or exertion, but because of God's own mercy (*Rom.* 9:13, 16). In Ephesians, a similar point is made, but from a different angle. There we are told that we were chosen so that we could *become* holy and blameless, not because we naturally would be. There too we are reminded again that there is a mystery to God's will—a reality that we should take seriously and humbly (*Eph.* 1:4, 9; see also 2:10).

Ultimately the last word on the subject of election has to be about God himself, recalling with Paul that the doctrine of divine election is all 'to the praise of his glorious grace' (*Eph.* 1:6). God chose us so that we 'might be to the praise of his glory' (*Eph.* 1:12; see also *1 Pet.* 2:9). And so, whenever we are called to present the precious truth of predestination, let us do so in a way that will elevate God in our minds, as we are mindful to humble ourselves in his sight.

Historic Text	***Modern Version***
3.6 As God has appointed the elect unto glory; so has he, by the eternal and most free purpose of his will, foreordained all the means thereunto.[m] Wherefore they who are elected, being fallen in Adam, are redeemed by Christ,[n] are effectually called unto faith in Christ, by his Spirit working in due season, are justified, adopted, sanctified,[o] and kept by his power through faith unto salvation.[p] Neither are any other redeemed by Christ, effectually called, justified, adopted, sanctified and saved; but the elect only.[q]	**3.6** As God has appointed the elect to glory, so he has—by the eternal and most free purpose of his will—foreordained all the means to that end. Therefore, his chosen ones, all of them being fallen in Adam, are redeemed by Christ and are effectually called to faith in Christ by his Spirit working in due season. They are justified, adopted, sanctified, and kept by his power, through faith, unto salvation. No others are redeemed by Christ, effectually called, justified, adopted, sanctified, and saved, except the elect only.

Scripture Proofs

3.6 [m] 1 Pet. 1:2; Eph. 1:4,5; Eph. 2:10; 2 Thess. 2:13. [n] 1 Thess. 5:9,10; Titus 2:14. [o] Rom. 8:30; Eph. 1:5; 2 Thess. 2:13. [p] 1 Pet. 1:5. [q] John 17:9; Rom. 8:28-39; John 6:64,65; John 10:26; John 8:47; 1 John 2:19.

Appointed for glory

The opening sentence of this sixth paragraph tells us two things. First, God has a people, the elect, and he has determined that they will be glorified—that is, he 'has appointed the elect unto glory'. His decree has eschatology, the end, in view. Second, God has not only appointed that his elect will meet him in glory but, 'by the eternal and most free purpose of his will', he has also decided how his entirely unreliable people will keep that appointment with him. When God appoints the elect to glory, both ends and means are important.

Thus, when we think of election, we must talk of more than eternal life. We also need to discuss the way to life, because we shall not reach the end of our journey happily any way we please. For example, Peter says that we are 'chosen', but he links this fact with another: God's chosen ones are all to experience 'the sanctifying work of the Holy Spirit' (*1 Pet.* 1:2; *cf. 2 Thess.* 2:13). We are chosen and predestined, Paul says, but this election will be tethered to a life of good works and increasing holiness within the context of our life in the family of God (*Eph.* 1:4, 5; 2:10). God decides to save and sanctify us, but not without suffering and learning, not without preaching and prayer. Perhaps it does not matter how you come to your church on a Sunday—no doubt there are many ways to get there. But it matters a great deal how we come to heaven; for God has one plan of redemption, which is the only way to glory.

'By Christ' and 'in Christ'

In the remainder of this section, we are given a preview of the way in which God brings his elect to glory, the means of redemption that are more fully retold in chapters 6 to 17 of this confession of faith. In the story of redemption, there are two people that feature most prominently. The first is Adam, in whom all are horribly fallen, both the elect and the non-elect. The second is Christ, by whom God's elect are wonderfully redeemed. When we think about the means that God has appointed for our redemption, the most important thing to remember is the person and work of Jesus Christ, who is the way, the truth and the life. God destined us to 'obtain salvation through our Lord Jesus Christ' (*1 Thess.* 5:9, 10). In fact, it is 'by', 'with' and 'in Christ' that all saving blessings flow.

We also need to understand that Christians were not redeemed in eternity when God chose us. There is a difference between God choosing to redeem us and his actual accomplishment of that work. Our redemption was accomplished in time and space by our Lord Jesus Christ 2,000 years ago when he shed his blood and gave his life in our place. It is he who 'gave himself for us, that he might redeem us from all iniquity', as Paul once told Titus (*Titus* 2:14).

The Holy Spirit's work

We have no hope of salvation so long as we are outside of Christ. We need to be effectually called to Christ 'by his Spirit working in due season'. And it is hardly surprising to learn that this calling will be effectual—no call to Christ from his Spirit could ever go unheard, ignored or resisted. God always makes his Spirit's call to salvation an effective and successful one. And as he calls us, he also gives us confidence in him. Faith in Christ is yet another free gift from God. Trust in the gospel is not about our developing a religious faith that will please God. It is about the Spirit who works faith in us. And it is through Spirit-worked faith that we are 'justified' in Christ, 'adopted' in Christ, and 'sanctified' in Christ. In fact, we are 'kept' by the Holy Spirit and guarded by God's 'power' 'through faith unto salvation' (*1 Pet.* 1:5).

The idea of God's electing love is not an abstract doctrinal structure built by early-modern theological architects. It is a glorious component part of the self-contained system of salvation revealed in the Scripture. After all, are we not told in Romans that those 'whom [God] did predestinate, them he also called: and whom he called, them he also justified' (*Rom.* 8:30)? Did not Peter write that we are 'elect according to the foreknowledge of God the Father, through sanctification of the Spirit' (*1 Pet.* 1:2)? Is it not true that God has 'predestinated us unto the adoption of children by Jesus Christ . . . according to the good pleasure of his will' (*Eph.* 1:5)?

A blessed hope, a solemn reality

God's predestinating choice is good news for those who are fallen in Adam. Because God has ordained every step of our salvation we can have 'that blessed hope' of 'the glorious appearing of the great God and our Saviour Jesus Christ'. It is because God has given us a Saviour, who gives us his Spirit, who gives us the gift of saving faith, that we can have the hope and confidence that we shall be 'kept by the power of God through faith unto salvation' (*1 Pet.* 1:5). This is good, clear news, but it still casts a shadow, for there is another reality. The truth is that 'neither are any other redeemed by Christ, effectually called, justified, adopted, sanctified and saved, but the elect only'. God will not save everyone.

This hard truth is particularly emphasized in the writings of the Apostle John. He shows how Christ our mediator intercedes for his people, but not all people (*John* 17:9). When Jesus discussed Judas, he reminded his people that there are some who never really come to him; indeed, the very ability to come to him is a gift in the Father's hand (*John* 6:64, 65). The fact is that some will not follow the Shepherd because they are not his sheep (*John* 10:26). They don't hear him because they 'are not of God' (*John* 8:47). Sometimes they will even leave the church, but they will do so because they were never really part of it (*1 John* 2:19).

As Paul notes at the end of Romans 8, it is a wonderful fact that God works all things for good; it is a solemn fact that this is true only for those who love him. We have confidence that if God has given us his own Son, then he will give the best answers to our every prayer and give us all things that we truly need. We find comfort that an accuser cannot condemn us when Christ makes intercession for us. But all of these blessings are for God's elect only (*Rom.* 8:28-39, esp. 33).

Undoubtedly, we ought to think clearly about election, for it is a doctrine taught clearly in Scripture. But while we need to be thoughtful about these realities, our thinking should as much as possible conform to the pattern of Scripture. Let us note that the doctrine of election, or predestination, is repeatedly and primarily mentioned in Scripture in order to give God the glory in the salvation of his people—stressing that we love him because he first loved us. This is designed to keep us humble in the Christian life.

And let us note that election is also mentioned in Scripture to give Christians assurance, to help us grasp that the God who does not change his mind will never change his mind about us, sinners though we are. It is God's decree that nothing 'shall be able to separate us from the love of God, which is in Christ Jesus our Lord' (*Rom.* 8:39). Only God knows the reasons, the details, and the glories of his divine plan. It is for us to focus on the ordinary means of our salvation, and for us to rejoice in God's grace, his initiative, and his persevering love.

Historic Text	*Modern Version*
3.7 The rest of mankind God was pleased, according to the unsearchable counsel of his own will, whereby he extends, or withholds mercy, as he pleases, for the glory of his sovereign power over his creatures, to pass by; and, to ordain them to dishonour and wrath, for their sin, to the praise of his glorious justice.^r	**3.7** The rest of mankind God was pleased—according to the unsearchable counsel of his own will, whereby he extends or withholds mercy as he pleases—for the glory of his sovereign power over his creatures, to pass by; and to ordain them to dishonour and wrath for their sin, to the praise of his glorious justice.
3.8 The doctrine of this high mystery of predestination is to be handled with special prudence and care,^s that men attending the will of God revealed in his Word, and yielding obedience thereunto, may, from the certainty of their effectual vocation, be assured of their eternal election.^t So shall this doctrine afford matter of praise, reverence, and admiration of God,^u and of humility, diligence, and abundant consolation to all that sincerely obey the gospel.^w	**3.8.** The doctrine of this high mystery of predestination is to be handled with special prudence and care, so that men, taking heed to the will of God revealed in his Word and yielding obedience to it, may—from the certainty of their effectual calling—be assured of their eternal election. Thus, this doctrine shall provide reason for praise, reverence, and admiration of God; and for humility, diligence, and abundant consolation to all who sincerely obey the gospel.

Scripture Proofs

   3.7 ʳ Matt. 11:25,26; Rom. 9:17,18,21,22; 2 Tim. 2:19,20; Jude v. 4; 1 Pet. 2:8.
   3.8 ˢ Rom. 9:20; Rom. 11:33; Deut. 29:29. ᵗ 2 Pet. 1:10. ᵘ Eph. 1:6; Rom. 11:33.
ʷ Rom. 11:5,6,20; 2 Pet. 1:10; Rom. 8:33; Luke 10:20.

Passed by

Paragraph 7 sums up and restates some of the sombre realities begun earlier in the chapter. Whereas God elected some 'to the praise of his glorious grace' (*Eph.* 2:6), he was 'pleased' to do something different with 'the rest of mankind'.[1] But even before being told what God had planned for the rest of mankind, we are reminded that this is what *God* decided to do. And in case it should not be obvious to everyone that God does what

---

[1] Paragraphs 6 and 7, when read together, clarify that even subtle forms of seventeenth-century hypothetical universalism are excluded in chapter 3 considered as a whole.

he alone pleases, we are reminded again that this act of choosing some and not others is 'according to the unsearchable counsel of his own will'.

This may be hard for us, but remember that the Son of God actually gave thanks that his Father 'hid' important truths 'from the wise and prudent', and did so because this was his Father's 'good pleasure' (*Matt.* 11:25, 26). The reality is that in a great house some vessels are designed for honour, some for dishonour (*2 Tim.* 2:19, 20). The same is true in God's world. Some people are marked out for condemnation, Jude says, and 'they are godless men, who change the grace of our God into a licence for immorality and deny Jesus Christ our only Sovereign and Lord' (*Jude* 4).

Ultimately we cannot know who all these people are in this life, for we always have hope, and we know that the Lord is intent on saving many of the worst of sinners. Nonetheless we also know, as Peter tells us, that there are people who are appointed to stumble over the rock of our salvation (*1 Pet.* 2:8).

Unbelievers and confused believers consider this to be Reformed megalomania, but it is simply the teaching of Scripture. As Paul makes clear in Romans 9, whether persons or whole nations are in view, God 'extends or withholds mercy, as he pleases for the glory of his sovereign power over his creatures' (see *Rom.* 9:17, 18, 21, 22). And it is his choice to save some sinners, and 'to pass by' others—actually, 'to ordain them to dishonour and wrath, for their sin, to the praise of his glorious justice'. And this is justice, for sin does deserve wrath.

This high mystery

It needs to be said at the close of this discussion, as at the beginning, that predestination is at the deep end of theological waters. We must never avoid the subject for this reason alone. And yet there are always some who dive in without reserve, and so the Westminster assembly stated that the doctrine needs to be discussed with caution. As the final paragraph in this chapter reminds us, this is a 'high mystery', and needs to 'be handled with special prudence and care'. Both shepherds and sheep need to remember that God has revealed this doctrine of election primarily to teach us about himself. Children are not to answer back to their parents; much less are we to 'answer back to God' (*Rom.* 9:20). It is precisely here that we are called to ponder 'the depth of the riches and wisdom and knowledge of God' (*Rom.* 11:33).

Consider too how God did not merely make salvation a possibility for all people (as our Arminian brethren teach), but a reality for his chosen people (as our Reformed fathers taught). That is to say, God did not build a wide bridge part-way to heaven. No, in Jesus Christ he built a secure bridge all the way to heaven. Bless God that all 'those whom he did predestinate, them he also called: and whom he called, them he also justified: and whom he justified, them he also glorified' (*Rom* 8:30). It is our duty to consider the doctrine of election to be one more item 'to the praise of his grace' (*Eph.* 1:6) and to join the Apostle Paul in exclaiming, 'How unsearchable are his judgments and how inscrutable his ways' (*Rom.* 11:33)! It is our task as men and women to attend to 'the will of God revealed in his Word'. After all, as Deuteronomy 29:29 states, 'The secret things belong to the LORD our God, but the things revealed belong to us and to our children'. If you would like to 'make your calling and election sure', as Peter urges (*2 Pet.* 1:10), then trust in Jesus Christ. Yield obedience to God's Word (*Rom.* 11:33).

It is entirely appropriate to end this reflection on election with a consideration of our own election by the grace of God, for we could easily have drifted along in unbelief, if it were not for his merciful intrusion into our lives (*e.g., Rom.* 11:5-20). The doctrine of election proves to be invaluable material for doxology when we remember that no one can 'bring any charge against God's elect' that will be heard in the court of God's kingdom (*Rom.* 8:33). It is for this reason that we 'rejoice that [our] names are written in heaven' (*Luke* 10:20). When we remember this, then, as this confession states, 'this doctrine' will 'afford matter of praise, reverence, and admiration of God, and of humility, diligence, and abundant consolation to all that sincerely obey the gospel'.

CHAPTER 4:

OF CREATION

Historic Text

4.1 It pleased God the Father, Son, and Holy Ghost,[a] for the manifestation of the glory of his eternal power, wisdom, and goodness,[b] in the beginning, to create, or make of nothing, the world, and all things therein, whether visible or invisible, in the space of six days; and all very good.[c]

Modern Version

4.1 It pleased God the Father, Son, and Holy Spirit, for the manifestation of the glory of his eternal power, wisdom, and goodness, in the beginning, to create—or make out of nothing—the world and everything in it, whether visible or invisible, in the space of six days, and all very good.

Scripture Proofs

4.1 [a] Heb. 1:2; John 1:2,3; Gen. 1:2; Job 26:13; Job 33:4. [b] Rom. 1:20; Jer. 10:12; Psa. 104:24; Psa. 33:5,6. [c] Gen 1:1-31; Heb. 11:3; Col. 1:16; Acts 17:24.

Creation as the work of the triune God

God's decrees, discussed in the previous chapter, are worked out in creation and providence. This chapter discusses the former, the next chapter the latter.

Creation is the powerful work of the triune God, and we see in Scripture that each person of the Trinity is involved in the work of creation. The letter to the Hebrews begins by telling us that God (clearly speaking about the Father) made the world by his Son (*Heb.* 1:2). One way in which the Gospel of John announces the divinity of Christ is to remind us that 'all things were made by him; and without him was not any thing made that was made' (*John* 1:2, 3). And as a gigantic thunderstorm was brewing, the young Elihu could not only call Job to see God's hand of providence, but to remember the creative power of the Spirit of God, the same Spirit mentioned in the opening lines of the Bible (*Job* 33:4; *Gen.* 1:2; perhaps also *Job* 26:13).

Creation preaches God's glory

As with all that our triune God does, his creative work is executed for the manifestation, or display, of his glory. This is a point that is often brought home with force in the Bible, and is singled out especially for the attention of those who profess not to believe in God. Paul tells us in Romans 1 that the creation shows the 'eternal power' of God to all people, believers and unbelievers alike (*Rom.* 1:20). The prophet Jeremiah rebuked the Israelites for their idol worship, and called them to take note of the God 'who made the earth by his power, who established the world by his wisdom, and by his understanding stretched out the heavens' (*Jer.* 10:12). Although this creation does not provide the good news of the gospel, it does provide us with material for preaching repentance to those who ignore God's testimony, and for defending the faith against those who deny his existence.

But the glorious message of creation is not intended for unbelievers alone. The psalms also extol God's full power and 'wisdom', and they remind us that the earth, even in its fallen state, provides abundant testimony of God's faithfulness or 'goodness' (*Psa.* 33:5; cf. *Psa.* 104:24). As the psalms of Scripture show us, this created world supplies us with endless material for songs of praise to God's glory.

All things of nothing

What creation does not tell us, but what we believe as an article of faith, based on the sure testimony of God's Word, is *how* this world came to be. Creation points to a Creator, but only the Bible tells us about the beginning—that moment when the God of eternity created time itself, and this world, out of nothing.

In saying that God created the world 'of nothing', the authors of this confession are not forgetting the creation of human beings, where created material was used. Rather, they are echoing the wonder of Genesis 1, where we are told repeatedly that God simply spoke. God spoke and there was a line where earth and sky met; God spoke, and mountain ranges reared while oceans crashed into their places; God spoke, and galaxies were scattered; God spoke and ants and elephants appeared on the plains. It is not by observation, but, as the writer to the Hebrews tells us, it is 'by faith we understand that the universe was created by the word of God, so that what is seen was not made out of things that are visible' (*Heb.* 11:3).

Visible and invisible

In our rejoicing over creation we most often focus on what we see, for this is what our senses absorb from day to day and this is what we find most useful in instructing our children and confronting our sceptics. But the confession picks up on Paul's comment to the Colossians, where he states that by Christ 'all things were created, in heaven and on earth, visible and invisible' (*Col.* 1:16). No less spectacular than prairie sunsets, tropical beaches, and thundering waterfalls are the things we cannot see. While men and women are marvellous in many ways, what are human beings and mighty nations when compared to the 'thrones or dominions or rulers or authorities' that we cannot see? What is man that God is mindful of us, when empires of angels serve him?

This created world is a sampling and a foretaste of all that we shall see one day. And if this world in its fallenness speaks so clearly of our God, we can eagerly wonder about the world that awaits us. God is the 'Lord of heaven and earth' (*Acts* 17:24), and perhaps the fact that Scripture puts it in that order is no accident (see also *Gen.* 1:1 and *Col.* 1:16). It might not be easy to point to the invisible in order to inspire awe for God in our family, or to resolve the doubts of an atheist. And yet it seems completely possible that the powers and principalities which we cannot see are more magnificent than anything in the world we know. Surely the invisible creations of God provide more material for praise than we commonly allow, even if they have limited pedagogical and apologetic uses.

In the space of six days, and all very good

Finally, we are told that this world was made 'in the space of six days; and all very good'. Some of the members of the assembly preferred to state that a little more precisely, saying that God made the world in six twenty-four hour days. But it has always been hard to consider how long a day is, and what a day means, without the presence of a sun or moon.

In the end, for some reason, the Westminster assembly decided not to elaborate on the words of Scripture. In spite of the way in which some members specified in their own writings how long those days were, the assembly instead chose to highlight the conclusion of Scripture: that all of God's creation was 'very good'. The excellence of creation was God's own declaration as he looked on the creation of light. It was good. It was what he thought of day and night, and then land and sea. They were good. When God made the solar system on the fourth day, he said it again: 'It is good.' This was the pronouncement on each part of God's work, and when he saw the whole, he announced that it was very good (*Gen.* 1). This is to be our judgment too. As we see the visible creation and sing of the invisible, let us give Father, Son and Holy Spirit all the glory for his eternal power, wisdom and goodness.

Historic Text	*Modern Version*
4.2. After God had made all other creatures, he created man, male and female,[d] with reasonable and immortal souls,[e] endued with knowledge, righteousness and true holiness, after his own image;[f] having the law of God written in their hearts,[g] and power to fulfill it:[h] and yet, under a possibility of transgressing, being left to the liberty of their own will, which was subject unto change.[i] Beside this law written in their hearts, they received a command, not to eat of the tree of the knowledge of good and evil, which while they kept, they were happy in their communion with God,[k] and had dominion over the creatures.[l]	**4.2.** After God had made everything else, he created mankind. He made them male and female, with rational and immortal souls, endowed with knowledge, righteousness, and true holiness, after his own image. They had the law of God written in their hearts and had power to fulfill it. They were, however, under a possibility of transgressing, being left to the liberty of their own will, which was subject to change. In addition to this law written in their hearts, they received a command not to eat of the tree of the knowledge of good and evil. As long as they obeyed this command, they were happy in their communion with God and had dominion over the creatures.

Scripture Proofs

4.2 [d] Gen. 1:27. [e] Gen. 2:7, with Eccles. 12:7, and Luke 23:43, and Matt. 10:28. [f] Gen. 1:26; Col. 3:10; Eph. 4:24. [g] Rom. 2:14,15. [h] Eccles. 7:29. [i] Gen. 3:6; Eccles. 7:29. [k] Gen. 2:17; Gen. 3:8-11,23. [l] Gen. 1:26,28.

Creator and creature

In this second paragraph on the subject of creation we are reminded first that we are made by God as one part of the rest of his world. There will always be a humbling distinction between the Creator and the creation; this is not a difference in degree, but a difference in kind. We are creatures. Though we are the final and crowning work of God's creation, we are created out of the mud of the earth that God made.

Male and female

Still, when we think of the creation of man, we need to remember that the pinnacle of creation is not one, but two. 'God created man' 'male and female' (*Gen.* 1:27). The high point is not a human being, but a pair of them. We know from elsewhere in Scripture that it is not in God's providence for every adult to be married, and that unique good, sometimes greater good, can be done by those who live and labour without the responsibility of a spouse or family. The Apostle Paul comes to mind as a prominent example. And yet we also need to see that marriage is good, and that the apex of creation is not a man, but a couple. Together, not alone, they would fill and have dominion over the earth.

Reason and immortality

Part of what sets men and women apart from other creatures is the fact that we are endowed with reason. The age of reason and the romantic period both began on day six. Our Maker blessed us with the (admittedly under-used) faculty to think before we speak; he blessed us with the ability to love, and not simply to lust.

We are different again, in that we have immortal souls; a life like, but also unlike animals (*Gen.* 2:7). Perhaps there will be dogs in the new creation, possibly even cats. But since Scripture does not mention these creatures having eternal souls, we have no reason to expect our own dear Fido or our neighbour's Tabby will greet us; for when any creature in this world passes away, it passes forever—except for man. When we die, our spirits return to the God who gave them to us (*Eccles.* 12:7). The most savage animal will turn to dust, but a savage man will have to answer to the one who made heaven and hell (*Matt.* 10:28). It is a grave reality that the death of a human being is not the death of his soul. This is also our hope, for we know that even the worst man, in the last hour of his life, can call out in repentance and faith and be told, 'Today you will be with me in paradise' (*Luke* 23:43).

The image of God

Human reason and immortality set us apart from all other creatures, but nothing so distinguishes us, in every sense of the word, as the fact that we are made in the image of God. Doubtless this is a doctrine at once wonderful and difficult to grasp—after all, this is *God's* image that we are speaking about. And yet it is the clear teaching of the Scriptures, for as the triune God reveals our creation, he records his decision to 'make man in our image' (*Gen.* 1:26).

It is because we are made in the image of God that we find such interest in mankind. When we are studying man we are studying the image of God himself, and thus we indirectly learn of God. Christians cannot do anthropology without in some way doing theology. But it is also because of this image that the fall of man is so horrific. We see in Adam and Eve's rebellion not only the crowning part of creation dissatisfied with its crown, but the very image of God rebelling against God himself.

We must be clear that as a defining aspect of our creation, the image of God in us is not erased by the fall. The image of God is not a property that can be abstracted from us; to ask what aspect of humanity contains the image of God is to make a mistake. Understood in its plainest terms, the language of Genesis 1 states that man in his entirety is the image of God.

Nonetheless it is also the case that at least three dimensions of this image are mentioned in one place or another in the Scriptures as the assembly's proofs illustrate. Genesis 1 mentions that humanity was made in God's likeness, immediately after which we are told that men and women are to exercise dominion over the creatures of this world (*Gen.* 1:26). Colossians 3 mentions that Christians are being remade in the image of God, and special mention is made that we are being renewed in knowledge (*Col.* 3:10). Ephesians 4 tells us that the new man in Christ is 'created after the likeness of God', and that means, at the very least, a creation 'in true righteousness and holiness' (*Eph.* 4:24).

In picking up these themes the assembly is probably not setting up 'dominion', 'knowledge', 'righteousness', and 'holiness' as a complete catalogue of ways in which man images God's glory, although the confession and both catechisms give them unique prominence. These things are simply brought into view because they are aspects of the image of God that are severely tarnished in the fall, and restored in the sanctifying work of the Spirit. This is a doctrine which has implications for the way in which we live, as James notes in his Epistle (*James* 3:9). It speaks today for those who would end the lives of unborn children, avoid the company of people from another race, argue for the superiority of one gender over another, or care about chimps more than children. The image of God is important for ethics: it is as much an equalizer among humans as it is an 'elevator' over all other creatures.

The law in our hearts

Much more can be said about the creation of mankind, but surely we must mention that God has given us a conscience. The second chapter of Romans is one reference point for those considering the human conscience. There Scripture teaches us that God's law is written on our hearts (*Rom.* 2:14, 15). Before the fall of Adam and Eve into sin, this knowledge was perfect and extensive. After the fall, that knowledge remains, but like every facet of our being, it is impaired to different degrees.

Before the fall there was also an ability to keep this law, for we were made 'upright': the tragedy that Genesis records, and upon which the writer of Ecclesiastes reflects, is that Adam ended up being more interested in his own schemes than God's precepts (*Gen.* 3:6; *Eccles.* 7:29). There was from the beginning the possibility of transgression. We were made perfect, but able to 'change' for the worse.

The law about the tree

Famously, God did not only put laws in our hearts: he gave at least one law that was not intuitive at all—he told Adam and Eve that there was a fruit tree that they could not enjoy, 'the tree of the knowledge of good and evil' (see *Gen.* 2:17; 3:8-11, 23). We do not know how long our first parents heeded this injunction, but we can be sure that while they did, they enjoyed fellowship with God, in whose likeness they were made, and ruled over all the animals that God had created (see these themes in *Gen.* 1:26, 28). Mankind was to find joy in imitating God and serving as stewards of his world. So long as they honoured God, they enjoyed those blessings. The problems started when they did not.

CHAPTER 5:

OF PROVIDENCE

Historic Text

5.1 God the great Creator of all things does uphold,[a] direct, dispose, and govern all creatures, actions, and things,[b] from the greatest even to the least,[c] by his most wise and holy providence,[d] according to his infallible foreknowledge,[e] and the free, and immutable counsel of his own will,[f] to the praise of the glory of his wisdom, power, justice, goodness, and mercy.[g]

Modern Version

5.1 God—the great Creator of all things—upholds, directs, disposes, and governs all creatures, actions, and things, from the greatest even to the least. He exercises this most wise and holy providence according to his infallible foreknowledge and the free and unchangeable counsel of his own will, to the praise of the glory of his wisdom, power, justice, goodness, and mercy.

Scripture Proofs

5.1   [a] Heb. 1:3.   [b] Dan. 4:34,35; Psa. 135:6; Acts 17:25,26,28; Job, chapters 38-41.   [c] Matt. 10:29-31.   [d] Prov. 15:3; Psa. 104:24; Psa. 145:17.   [e] Acts 15:18; Psa. 94:8-11.   [f] Eph. 1:11; Psa. 33:10,11.   [g] Isa. 63:14; Eph. 3:10; Rom. 9:17; Gen 45:7; Psa. 145:7.

The extent of God's providence

The first three chapters of the confession remind us that both the world around us and the Bible that has been given to us reveal that there is a true God who has decreed all things. From there the confession goes on to tell us how God executes those decrees. The previous chapter outlined how God created all things: he spoke, and there they were. In this chapter, and from this point forward in the confession, we shall see how 'God the great Creator' providentially upholds all things, or, as the letter to the Hebrews says, how 'he sustains all things by his powerful word' (*Heb.* 1:3).

As we would expect from a God who has decreed and created all things, God's upholding of creation is not a basic maintenance programme. He 'directs, disposes and governs' his creation—all of his creatures, all their actions, and all of those parts of creation that cannot act. This comes as no surprise for those who are familiar with almost any part of the Bible. Is not this all-encompassing control of nations portrayed so vividly in the dreams sent to King Nebuchadnezzar and explained by the prophet Daniel (*Dan.* 4)? Is not providence the wonder for which the psalmist praises the Lord, the Lord who 'does whatever pleases him, in the heavens and on the earth, in the seas and all their depths' (*Psa.* 135:6)? Certainly this is the precise point Paul preaches to sceptics in Athens, reminding them that 'God gives all men life and breath and everything else' and 'determines the times set for them and the exact places where they should live' (*Acts* 17:25-28). And this perfect providence is the message God communicated to a very quiet Job after he foolishly demanded an interview with his Maker (*Job* 38-41).

We may forget this sometimes when we complain about our smaller problems or forget to praise God for our smaller blessings. But the fact remains, as Jesus reminded his disciples, that all things are under God's control, 'from the greatest even to the least'. All things are under God's direction, even the sparrow sadly dropping from the sky; even the hair sadly dropping from our heads (*Matt.* 10:29-31).

The goodness of providence

All things are in God's hands, but this would bring little comfort to God's people if we ever ceased to remember that these are good hands. All providence is God's 'most wise and holy providence'. We can trust him, and know that he is right. Of course, this providence is 'most wise and holy' (*cf. Prov.* 15:3; *Psa.* 104:24; 145:17) because it is in perfect harmony with God's 'infallible foreknowledge' (*cf. Acts* 15:18; *Psa.* 94:8-11), and 'the free, and immutable counsel of his own will' (*cf. Eph.* 1:11). As the psalmist reminds us elsewhere, 'the plans of the Lord stand firm forever, the purposes of his heart through all generations' (*Psa.* 33:11).

The glory of God's providence

It is comforting news that we can trust God's providence. The reason Jesus spoke of his care for the sparrow was to assure us of his care for us. This is comforting news, but by far the most important news is that God's providence works for the praise of his own glory among his people on earth and among the powers of heaven itself (see *Eph.* 3:10). And as we reflect on the wisdom of God's works and the holiness of God's ways we shall see that he is especially directing 'all creatures, actions, and things' so that we may learn to glorify him on earth for what he does from his heaven. If we do want God to increase and us to decrease, then we shall do well to meditate upon his providence, his hand upon our own lives, and his work in his saints of old.

Just think of the prophet Isaiah, who learned to acknowledge the glory of God's wisdom by watching the way in which God keeps a horse running free without stumbling, or a herd of cattle plodding home without confusion (*Isa.* 63:13, 14). Recall Joseph, who extolled the glory of God's power when reflecting on how the Lord took a sad attempt to destroy one brother and used it to save a whole family (*Gen.* 45:7). Consider Paul, who wondered at the glory of God's justice in punishing Pharaoh, and his goodness in saving selfish Israelites (*Rom.* 9:17). And never forget the psalmist, who knew for himself the glory of God's mercy, and therefore sang of his 'abundant goodness' (*Psa.* 145:7).

And how abundant is that goodness and mercy! The remarkable thing is that God not only counts every hair on our heads but every sin in our lives; and yet in his 'wisdom' and 'power', and with a sacrificial 'justice', he shows us the splendour of his providence in providing us with his Son.

Historic Text	Modern Version
5.2 Although, in relation to the fore-knowledge and decree of God, the first cause, all things come to pass immutably, and infallibly:[h] yet, by the same providence, he orders them to fall out, according to the nature of second	**5.2** Although—in relation to the fore-knowledge and decree of God, the first cause—all things come to pass unchangeably and infallibly; yet, by the same providence, he orders them to occur according to the nature of second

causes, either necessarily, freely, or contingently.[i]

5.3 God, in his ordinary providence makes use of means,[k] yet is free to work without,[l] above,[m] and against them at his pleasure.[n]

causes, either necessarily, freely, or contingently.

5.3 In his ordinary providence, God makes use of means, yet he is free to work without, above, and against them as he pleases.

Scripture Proofs
5.2 [h] Acts 2:23; [i] Gen. 8:22; Jer. 31:35; Exod. 21:13, with Deut. 19:5; 1 Kings 22:28,34; Isa. 10:6,7.

5.3 [k] Acts 27:31,44; Isa. 55:10,11; Hos. 2:21,22. [l] Hos. 1:7; Matt. 4:4; Job 34:20. [m] Rom. 4:19-21. [n] 2 Kings 6:6; Dan. 3:27.

The first cause

God's perfect providence (his arrangement and care of all things in time) is the working out of his perfect predestination (his planning and ordering of all things in eternity). And so, as paragraph 2 of chapter 5 states, from the perspective of 'the foreknowledge and decree of God', 'all things come to pass immutably' [or unchangeably] 'and infallibly' [without error or failure].

We can find to our chagrin that the supervisor on a building site sometimes uses an architect's plan more as a suggested guideline than as a blueprint to follow in every detail. But in God's world, he is both architect and supervisor, and no detail will be changed as his plan 'comes to pass'. As Peter reminded the crowds of Jerusalem, this foreknowledge and decree extend to all things, and even the capture and execution of God's own Son was according to 'God's set purpose and foreknowledge' (*Acts* 2:23). God is the 'first cause'; he is the executor of his own will.

Second causes: necessary, free, contingent

God needs no one else to help him. If he had wished, God could have planned to continuously create every action and event, each movement and thought in the history of the world. In other words, he could have remained the only cause of all effects. And yet God did not do that. In his wise providence he chose to govern a world with patterns and regularities (*e.g., Gen.* 8:22) where some events or actions cause other events or actions.

God ordered all things to happen 'according' to what we could call 'the nature of secondary causes'. From our perspective, these causes and their effects appear in a variety of types. Some causes appear necessary, some free, some contingent—all of which are illustrated within Scripture itself.

First, as Jeremiah reminds us, God has given the sun for light by day, and the moon and the stars for light by night. These are the necessary means or causes for the illumination of our world, so long as it continues (*Jer.* 31:35).

Second, as Exodus 21 or Deuteronomy 19 remind us, if a man innocently killed another in Israel, he had some freedom of means to preserve his life, some ways to cause his chance of survival to increase: he could run to one of the cities of refuge (compare *Exod.* 21:13 with *Deut.* 19:5).

Third, we can remember the words of Micaiah the prophet, who told King Ahab that he would die in battle. As Micaiah explained to those around him, the contingency of Ahab's death would be the means to establish either the truthfulness or the falsehood of Micaiah's claim to speak in God's name. If the king should die, then the prophet would be speaking the truth (*1 Kings* 22:28, 34). If not, he would be a liar.

It is important to understand that God had definitively decreed how each of these three events would turn out. But he also decided that the functioning of the solar system would be a necessary cause of the earth's light, that men would be saved or lost by their choice of a city of refuge (a free cause), and that Micaiah's integrity as a prophet would depend on Ahab's death (a contingent cause).

And of course, God can do all of this with or without the concurrence or knowledge of people. Actually it was one of Isaiah's messages to Assyria, that God can make armies his instruments, using them to perform tasks that are far from a commander's own intentions (*Isa.* 10:6, 7).

Ordinary and less ordinary providence

Ordinarily, God uses various 'means' to effect his sovereign will. Whether he sends rain to the earth or preachers to his people, his purposes are achieved through a variety of ways (*Isa.* 55:10). He is the one who makes the sky and earth conspire together to produce the grain, wine and oil we enjoy (*Hos.* 2:21, 22). Ordinarily God uses ordinary means, and it is because he knew this that the Apostle Paul told those on board a sinking ship that they would be saved, provided they remained on board until the ship began to break up—but then they needed to swim, or to grab broken pieces of the ship if they were to make it to shore (*Acts* 27).

Nonetheless, God is not restricted to 'ordinary providence'. He can, and sometimes does, overturn all standard assumptions about his work in the world. God is 'free' in his work, as paragraph 3 reminds us, and we see this in the pages of sacred history. He 'is free to work' outside of normal parameters. He could have calmed the storm if it had been his will, or miraculously transported Paul's ship and its passengers to the other side of the Mediterranean Sea. He can sweep away mighty warriors without the aid of human hands (*Job* 34:20), for he is not tied to ordinary means. Our Lord himself testified to this in passing when he was both hungry and tempted and yet, in a multi-layered message, told Satan that we do not live by bread alone (*Matt.* 4:4). God can provide for human needs however he sees fit; that is to say, God can work 'without' any secondary means whatever. Miracles are part of God's providence too.

God can also work 'above' normal means. That is to say, he can stretch standard limitations and subvert conventional assumptions. He could take aged Sarah, and give her a child long after she should have lost the ability to bear children (*Rom.* 4:19, 20). God can work 'against' normal means as well. Thus in Elisha's day he caused an iron axe head to float on water (2 *Kings* 6:6), and in Daniel's day he caused three men to be untouched even by the smell of fire in a furnace so hot that it killed those coming near it (*Dan.* 3:27). And what more shall I say? For time would fail me to tell of Gideon and his fleece, of Barak and the storm that attacked his enemies, of Samson with the gates of a city upon his shoulders, of prophets who 'subdued kingdoms', who 'stopped the mouths of lions', and who witnessed 'women receiving their dead raised to life again' (*Heb.* 11:32-35).

Yet there *is* one more thing to say. All of God's good decisions— whether to use ordinary means, extraordinary means, or nothing at all— whatever he does in his most wise and holy providence, is done according to his own 'pleasure'. And with that divine pleasure God's people must learn to be content, because we take Abraham's ancient question to be our ancient creed: 'Shall not the judge of all the earth do right?' (*Gen.* 18:25).

Historic Text

5.4 The almighty power, unsearchable wisdom, and infinite goodness of God so far manifest themselves in his providence, that it extends itself even to the first fall, and all other sins of angels and men;[o] and that not by a bare permission,[p] but such as has joined with it a most wise and powerful bounding,[q] and otherwise ordering, and governing of them, in a manifold dispensation, to his own holy ends:[r] yet so, as the sinfulness thereof proceeds only from the creature, and not from God, who being most holy and righteous, neither is, nor can be the author or approver of sin.[s]

Modern Version

5.4 The almighty power, unsearchable wisdom, and infinite goodness of God manifest themselves so completely in his providence that it extends even to the first fall and all other sins of angels and men—not by a bare permission, but by a permission which has joined with it a most wise and powerful limiting, and otherwise ordering and governing of them in a varied administration, for his own holy purposes. However, the sinfulness comes from the creatures alone and not from God, who, because he is most holy and righteous, neither is nor can be the author or approver of sin.

Scripture Proofs

5.4 [o] Rom. 11:32-34; 2 Sam. 24:1, with 1 Chron. 21:1; 1 Kings 22:22,23; 1 Chron. 10:4,13,14; 2 Sam. 16:10; Acts 2:23, Acts 4:27,28. [p] Acts 14:16. [q] Psa. 76:10; 2 Kings 19:28. [r] Gen. 50:20; Isa. 10:6,7,12. [s] James 1:13,14,17; 1 John 2:16; Psa. 50:21.

The fall, and the sins of angels and men

At the close of Romans 11, the Apostle Paul is full of praise for the 'ways', the 'wisdom', and the 'mercy' of God. Unexpectedly, this doxology forms the conclusion to a lengthy discussion about divine predestination and providence; about sin, salvation and damnation. The members of the Westminster assembly took the matter of Paul's conclusion and made it their introduction. They lauded the 'almighty power, unsearchable wisdom, and infinite goodness of God', and they did so because they too were discussing predestination and providence, as well as sin, salvation, and damnation.

The main point of this paragraph is to prove that (and then to explain how) God 'manifests' or shows forth his power, wisdom, and goodness 'in his providence'. This includes his providential working in 'the first fall', and then after the fall, in 'all other sins of angels and men'. That this solemn truth must be believed seems obvious enough. If God really does ordain and then govern all things, he must have ordained and governed Satan's rebellion in heaven and Adam and Eve's rebellion on earth. And yet if this sounds too speculative as a general idea about the first fall, one has only to look at the specific details of God's providence regarding the sins of angels and men.

The previous paragraph in the confession reminded us that God uses means to do his will. As it happens, God, in his wisdom, recorded examples of his 'behind-the-scenes' workings, including his management of some extraordinarily evil events. Recall, for example, that sad story in 1 Chronicles, where an old adversary provoked proud King David to number the troops of Israel (*1 Chron.* 21:1). Here we see an evil angel prompting a saint to sin. And yet 2 Samuel 24:1 reveals that this was God's will, and we can quickly see that God used Satan's deceitful ideas and David's sins in order to punish the people of Israel for their own wickedness. To us it may seem complicated—so many layers in David's apparently straightforward command to carry out a census. To God it is all part of a perfect plan.

Other examples abound, and this confession points to a few of them in its Scripture texts (*1 King*s 22:22, 23; *1 Chron.* 10:4, 13, 14; *Acts* 2:23), but perhaps none is as poignant as the one mentioned by the persecuted church in Jerusalem. In the midst of their sufferings, they remembered in prayer that even God the Father's 'holy child Jesus', the 'anointed' one, also suffered under Herod and Pilate and the Gentiles—but these enemies of the Saviour did only what God's 'hand' and 'counsel determined before to be done' (*Acts* 4:27, 28).

God's permission

So we understand that our holy God has revealed to us in his holy Word that he uses even sin and sinners for his own ends. But how does he do this? Is he associated with sin by giving it his 'bare permission'? By setting up a world that could sin, and then allowing sin to happen? After all, Paul and Barnabas once told a crowd at Lystra that 'in the past' God had 'let all nations go their own way' (*Acts* 14:16). Did God simply not interfere, and in that way permit sin to happen?

The answer to that must be no. God permits sin, but it is the sort of permission that is 'joined with . . . a most wise and powerful bounding' or limiting. God rules over sin and sinners. God decides the extent to which sin will reign and the extent to which it will be restrained in his world, and in the life of every man, woman and child. Certainly this is a great mystery to us as it surely was to the psalmist, when he calls attention to the fact that even 'the wrath of man' can praise God, and the remainder of that wrath God can restrain (*Psa.* 76:10).

So these sins are ordered and governed by God in a 'manifold dispensation'. That is to say, God sometimes limits our sin (*2 Kings* 19:28), and sometimes permits sin in a varied, complex administration or arrangement, and always according 'to his own holy ends'. This is just the message that Joseph was trying to teach his once treacherous, but later repentant brothers: 'You intended to harm me', he said, 'but God intended it for good to accomplish what is now being done, the saving of many lives' (*Gen.* 50:20). As God used evil men to save the people of Israel early in their history, in a similar way God would use evil nations to punish his people later in their history, as the prophets often reminded the Israelites (*e.g., Isa.* 10:6, 7, 12).

The holiness and innocence of God

So God governs all things, even sin. He does so for his most holy ends. And thanks be to him, one of his purposes is to save us when we sin or suffer, and another is to chastise us when we stray. But however we understand divine providence over sin, we must realize that the actual sinfulness of people and of situations proceeds 'only from the creature', never from the creator. God is most holy, God is most righteous. He was not, is not, and will not be the author of sin. And he did not, does not, and will never approve of sin.

This is a fact which Scripture does not explain, but which it does state with unqualified precision and clarity. Of course, it says this indirectly whenever it mentions that God is holy or righteous; when we are reminded that God is not like us: he notices sin and he will do something about it (*Psa.* 50:21). But James makes this point most explicit when he admonishes those who are tempted, warning them never to say, 'God is tempting me.' The reason why we must not say this of God, James explains, is that 'God cannot be tempted by evil, nor does he tempt anyone' (*James* 1:13). John affirms the same truth when he writes that 'all that is in the world, the lust of the flesh, and the lust of the eyes, and the pride of life, is not of the Father, but is of the world' (*1 John* 2:16).

True, in some way God permits sin and governs it, and there is much about this that we do not understand. But the dismal reality, as James also makes clear, is that 'every man is tempted, when he is drawn away of his own lust, and enticed' (*James* 1:14). This is just what happened to Satan, and then Eve, and then our forefather Adam. How this all began, we shall never know. But we know where it led: to the death of God's Son on the cross. Just think of that. Some say that God's permission of the first sin is a great mystery, and so it is. But it is a small mystery indeed when compared with the real wonder of God's providence—that he would provide his only Son to bear our sin and suffer our punishment. When we consider this holy end of God's providence, then we shall just begin to understand 'the almighty power, unsearchable wisdom, and infinite goodness of God'.

Historic Text	*Modern Version*
5.5 The most wise, righteous, and gracious God does oftentimes leave for a season his own children to manifold temptations, and the corruption of their own hearts, to chastise them for their former sins, or to discover unto them the hidden strength of corruption, and deceitfulness of their hearts, that they may be humbled;ᶜ and, to raise them to a more close and constant dependence for their support upon himself, and to make them more watchful against all future occasions of sin, and for sundry other just and holy ends.ᵘ	**5.5** The most wise, righteous, and gracious God often leaves his own children, for a time, to manifold temptations and to the corruption of their own hearts. He does this to chastise them for their past sins, to humble them by making them aware of the hidden strength of the corruption and deceitfulness of their hearts, and then to raise them to a closer, more constant dependence upon himself for their support, to make them more watchful against all future occasions for sinning, and to fulfill various other just and holy purposes.

5.6 As for those wicked and ungodly men whom God, as a righteous judge, for former sins does blind and harden,[w] from them he not only withholds his grace, whereby they might have been enlightened in their understandings, and wrought upon in their hearts;[x] but, sometimes also withdraws the gifts which they had,[y] and exposes them to such objects as their corruption makes occasions of sin;[z] and withal, gives them over to their own lusts, the temptations of the world, and the power of Satan:[a] whereby it comes to pass that they harden themselves, even under those means, which God uses for the softening of others.[b]

5.7 As the providence of God does in general, reach to all creatures; so after a most special manner, it takes care of his church, and disposes all things to the good thereof.[c]

5.6 As for those wicked and ungodly men whom God, as a righteous judge, blinds and hardens because of their past sins, God withholds his grace, by which their minds might have been enlightened and their hearts affected. He also sometimes takes away the gifts which they had, and exposes them to such things as their corrupt nature makes into occasions for sinning. Moreover, he gives them over to their own lusts, the temptations of the world, and the power of Satan, by which they harden themselves even under the same means which God uses to soften others.

5.7 As, in general, the providence of God reaches to all creatures, so, in a very special way, it cares for his church and disposes all things for its good.

Scripture Proofs

5.5 [t] 2 Chron. 32:25,26,31; 2 Sam. 24:1. [u] 2 Cor. 12:7-9; Psa. 73:1-28; Psa. 77:1-12; Mark 14:66-72, with John 21:15-17.

5.6 [w] Rom. 1:24,26,28; Rom. 11:7,8. [x] Deut. 29:4. [y] Matt. 13:12; Matt. 25:29. [z] Deut. 2:30; 2 Kings 8:12,13. [a] Psa. 81:11,12; 2 Thess. 2:10-12. [b] Exod. 7:3, with Exod. 8:15,32; 2 Cor. 2:15,16; Isa. 8:14; 1 Pet. 2:7,8; Isa. 6:9,10, with Acts 28:26,27.

5.7 [c] 1 Tim. 4:10; Amos 9:8,9; Rom. 8:28; Isa. 43:3-5,14.

Evil for good

As the Westminster Confession of Faith develops an outline of the doctrine of divine providence, it reminds us that God directs all things, that he uses different means to work his wise purposes, and that he even uses sin and sinners to do his holy will. In these three final paragraphs of chapter 5 we are reminded that God actually uses sin and suffering for his people's good, that he uses surprising blessings for the just punishment of the wicked, and that he works all things for the special good of his church.

Paragraph 5 is primarily pastoral in its concern. It seeks to explain to us why a God who is 'most wise, righteous, and gracious' would not infrequently leave us in sin or suffering. Why is it that the one who will tempt no man leaves us to temptations? How is it that the one who is holy will leave us with the corruption of our own hearts? Why does a loving Father chastise his own dear children 'for their former sins', as he did with David (*1 Sam.* 24:1)? In short, what is the reason for God revealing unto us the often 'hidden strength of corruption, and deceitfulness' of our own hearts?

As we might expect from the one who is God himself, there is no single reason for this exposure to suffering and to our own sin. God uses it to humble us. He did so for the proud people of Jerusalem and their king, Hezekiah, so long ago. As 2 Chronicles records, 'God left him to test him and to know everything that was in his heart' (*2 Chron.* 32:31). He also exposes us to temptation and to the spiritual decay of our own hearts in order 'to raise [us] to a more close and constant dependence for [our] support upon himself'. He uses these sad times 'to make [us] more watchful against all future occasions of sin'. In fact he will do all that it takes to keep us walking close to himself and far from sin 'and for sundry other just and holy ends', some only known to himself.

And so God sent Paul a thorn in the flesh to trouble him, 'lest he should be exalted beyond all measure' by the gifts and graces given to him (*2 Cor.* 12:7-9). He brought the author of Psalm 73 low so that he would properly value the ways and worship of God (*cf. Psa.* 77:1-12). He used Peter's sad denial of his Lord and friend to once-and-for-all rid the apostle of his recurring self-confidence (*Mark* 14:66-72) and to make him a more loving shepherd to the Great Shepherd's sheep (*John* 21:15-17).

Good for evil

God can work evil for good, but he also withholds good and, in a sense, even works good for evil. That is the sad but true message of paragraph six. There are 'wicked and ungodly men' whom God will righteously judge for their 'former sins'; that is, sins that they have already committed. In fact, he will 'blind and harden' them.[1] The Bible uses these very words in Romans 11:7, 8 and Deuteronomy 2:30, and it teaches this very truth in Romans 1. There are those who do 'not like to retain God in their knowledge'. As a result 'God gave them over to a reprobate mind' and to all those tragic actions of which a twisted and fallen mind dreams (*Rom.* 1:24-28). All God's works are ultimately good, but when he removes his restraining hands from unrepentant sinners, as he sometimes does, evil increases.

As with all of God's providence, this is no 'bare permission'. Of course it is true that Moses once told those gathered about him that 'the LORD has not given you a mind that understands, or eyes that see, or ears that hear' (*Deut.* 29:4). But it is not merely the case that God withholds his grace—a grace which might have shone light into blind understandings and worked to soften hard hearts. No, God 'sometimes also withdraws the gifts which they had'—which is the punch line of more than one of Jesus' parables, in which the gifts or possessions of unrepentant people are taken from them (*Matt.* 13:12; 25:29). God sometimes also exposes sinners to the sorts of things that only worsen existing vice, making new occasions for sin. Thus Deuteronomy records how God deliberately led his people near the pagan King Sihon's territory—an action which led Sihon into the further sin of forbidding the needy Israelites water, even though they promised to be good customers and pay for every drink (*Deut.* 2:30). And 2 Kings records how God told the diabolical Hazael that he would be king over Syria, leading to the murder of his master and a later massacre of Israelites (*2 Kings* 8:12, 13).

In sum, God gives sinners 'over to their own lusts, the temptations of the world, and the power of Satan', whether they be pagan rulers, unrepentant sinners or his own chosen people (see *Exod.* 7:3; 8:15, 32; *2 Thess.* 2:10-12; *Psa.* 81:11, 12). And so 'it comes to pass that they harden themselves, even under those means which God uses for the softening of

---

[1] Assembly member Anthony Burgess suggests that in considering God's work in 'hardening' hearts we need to steer clear of two extremes: (1) That idea that God actually caused Pharaoh to sin, or that (2) God simply waited for the king to destroy himself with his own sin. Burgess goes beyond these typical limiting comments to suggest that God hardened Pharaoh by removing from him his divine 'mollifying' or restraining grace that keeps sinners from descending into the worst of their depravity. Burgess, *A Treatise of Original Sin* (London, 1658), p. 290.

others'. How sad this fact is, and yet how sure we are that it is true. The same event, action or position can be used by one for their own good and by another for their destruction. One Pharaoh's predicament was used to help God's people; another Pharaoh used his power to harden his heart and harm God's people (*Gen.* 45-50; *Exod.* 1-15). 'To the one' an apostolic ministry is the smell of death; 'to the other', the fragrance of life (*2 Cor.* 2:15, 16).

Above all, consider the words of Isaiah; for he reminds us that 'The LORD Almighty' will be 'a sanctuary' for some, but for others 'he will be a stone that causes men to stumble and a rock that makes them fall'. Of course Isaiah was speaking of no one less than Jesus, as the Apostle Peter confirmed (*Isa.* 8:13, 14; *1 Pet.* 2:7, 8). And in this rejection too, God is sovereign, the Holy Spirit is active, and yet we are responsible for our own damnation—just as Isaiah again predicted, and as the Apostle Paul confirmed (*Isa.* 6:9, 10; *Acts* 28:26, 27).

The church

In leaving this subject let us remember that 'the providence of God does, in general, reach to all creatures', sometimes blessing undeserving individuals, and sometimes cursing deserving individuals. But let us also remember that 'after a most special manner', God 'takes care of his church, and disposes all things to the good thereof'. Even when he chastises his people, shaking them like grain in a sieve, he is only ridding them of the chaff (*Amos* 9:8, 9). This is our comfort, and has been the comfort of God's people for all generations. As the Lord told Isaiah, 'I am the LORD, your God, the Holy One of Israel, your Saviour . . . Do not be afraid, for I am with you' (*Isa.* 43:3, 5). Whatever Paul fully intends with the assertion that he makes in 1 Timothy 4:10, it is clear that God cares 'especially' for 'those who believe'. And as God has assured us in Paul's letter to the Romans, 'we know that in all things God works for the good of those who love him, who have been called according to his purpose' (*Rom.* 8:28). Do you love God? Then you can be most sure that his holy, wise, and perfect providence will work for your good and his glory.

SIN AND THE SAVIOUR

CHAPTER 6:

OF THE FALL OF MAN, OF SIN, AND OF THE PUNISHMENT THEREOF

Historic Text

6.1 Our first parents being seduced by the subtlety and temptation of Satan, sinned, in eating the forbidden fruit.[a] This their sin, God was pleased, according to his wise and holy counsel to permit, having purposed to order it to his own glory.[b]

6.2 By this sin they fell from their original righteousness and communion with God,[c] and so became dead in sin,[d] and wholly defiled in all the faculties and parts of soul and body.[e]

Modern Version

6.1 Our first parents, being seduced by the subtlety and temptation of Satan, sinned in eating the forbidden fruit. God was pleased to permit this sin of theirs, according to his wise and holy counsel, because his purpose was, through it, to glorify himself.

6.2 By this sin they fell from their original righteousness and communion with God, and so became dead in sin and wholly defiled in all the parts and faculties of soul and body.

Scripture Proofs

   6.1 [a] Gen. 3:13; 2 Cor. 11:3. [b] Rom. 11:32.

   6.2 [c] Gen. 3:6-8; Eccles. 7:29; Rom. 3:23. [d] Gen. 2:17; Eph. 2:1. [e] Titus 1:15; Gen. 6:5; Jer. 17:9; Rom. 3:10-19.

The fall

Chapter 6 of the confession tells us the sad story of the fall of man, and then details the grim realities of sin and of punishment. It does so because this story is our story. It is *our* first parents that were seduced by the depths of Satan's subtlety, deceived by the one who was wise as a serpent. Actually, he took the shape of a serpent, and tempted Adam and Eve to eat the fruit that God had forbidden them to eat. The confession can outline these events in brief, bold strokes because the details are supplied in Genesis 3. There we are told that the first people knew God's law. There we are told that one of God's creatures contradicted the Maker of heaven and earth. There we are told that the woman and the man listened, looked—and then plunged into sin.

Given all that we know of the goodness of God and the perfect fairness of all his commands, this is a shocking event, and not one that we could ever have expected. And yet this is a story worth repeating. The temptation of Satan and the fall of man explain all that is to follow in human and biblical history. The temptation of Satan and the fall of man are important for us all since our 'minds' also 'may somehow be led astray from' a 'sincere and pure devotion to Christ' (2 Cor. 11:3).

The fall is a shocking event to us, but it was not to God. He knew it was coming because he 'was pleased, according to his wise and holy counsel', to permit Satan's smooth propaganda and Adam and Eve's rebellion. He allowed our first parents to sin because he was going to work it all for his glory. As the letter to the Romans reminds us, one part of his glory that he wanted to display is his mercy. 'God bound all men over to disobedience so that he may have mercy on them all' (*Rom.* 11:32). It is perhaps the first irony, and arguably the greatest irony in history, that the creator planned to use Satan's supposed subtlety to display 'the depths of the riches of the wisdom and knowledge of God' (*Rom.* 11:33).

Fallenness

Men and women will only know the greatness of God's plan at the end of time, but they can see the effects of sin in rapid order. As paragraph 2 points out, 'by this sin they fell from their original righteousness'. They were no longer holy. They now fell short of God's glory not only in their humanness, but in a twisted fallenness (*Rom.* 3:23). They could no longer have 'communion with God'. The Genesis account tells how they now fled from God when he came near them. They hid from the one who came to seek them out (*Gen.* 3:8).

To run from God, to hide from God—how tragic and foolish! Having given their ears to Satan, they could no longer hear their God without fear. They were made upright, as Ecclesiastes reminds us, but now they would go about cringing (*Eccles.* 7:29). All their instincts were now twisted. Never again would the ordinary men or women or children of this world be wise as they were created to be. They fell, and the glory of God departed from the human race (*Rom.* 3:23).

Death

These first movements in the garden were a grim overture to all the misery that was to follow. As we listen to the Word of God we hear that all people would now enter life already 'dead in transgressions and sins' (*Eph.* 2:1). We are not merely weakened, weary or sick. This is a cancer we cannot cure; a walking death, a plight from which we cannot help ourselves. It is spiritual death and it is more. When a murderer is caught after an act of atrocity by the lynch-mob, we can say that he is a dead man even though he is not yet swinging from a tree. How much more true is this when a sinner falls into the hands of a powerful and just judge.

Furthermore, as God had warned when he issued his law, this spiritual death began a physical death. On the day that Adam and Eve foolishly ate of the tree of the knowledge of good and evil, they died, in a very real sense (*Gen.* 2:17). It was a slow death, yes. But death and decay now entered their bodies and minds, and it was inevitable from that moment they would one day become dust again.

This walking death and decay in sin showed itself in the defilement of all our parts and faculties. All our powers, abilities, qualities, capacities are infected by sin. This penetration of sin is true of our bodily, physical existence. We abuse our own bodies by the things we do and the places we go. And when God permits strength in one person, it is used to wreak havoc with the weakness of another person. And so it is that we use our feet and hands, our memories and mouths not to praise God, but to abuse others.

A sad conspiracy

This penetration of sin is also true of the intellectual (or 'noetic') aspects of our existence. We do so much that is wrong because of the shameful desires of our hearts. As Jeremiah once mourned aloud to God when he observed the constant straying of the sheep of God's flock, 'the heart is deceitful above all things and beyond cure. Who can understand it?' (*Jer.* 17:9).

While Jeremiah certainly does not overstate the problem, he almost seems to overstate the mystery of it. For do we not all know that our minds willingly work overtime to find reasons to justify the desires of our hearts? Why have we 'turned away'? What makes us so 'worthless'? Why are our 'throats' the openings of graves which allow spiritually dead words to escape into the world? Why does Paul summarize so many verses that speak negatively of our tongues, lips, and feet and the way in which each is marked by 'ruin and misery' rather than 'peace'? In short, why is 'there no one who does good, not even one'? It is because, as Paul says at the beginning and ending of his paragraph, that we do not 'understand'; there is no proper 'fear of God before our eyes'. Our hearts and minds conspire together to seek after everything, it seems, except the God to whom we are accountable (*Rom.* 3:10-19).

What God said about mankind in Noah's day can be said of the average man in many ages: 'every inclination of the thoughts of his heart was only evil all of the time' (*Gen.* 6:5). The unattractive truth is that we are totally depraved, in the sense that we are defiled in 'all the faculties and parts of soul and body'. To put it another way, no part of who we are remains untouched by the plague of sin, not least our minds and consciences (*Titus* 1:15). It is true that we could be much worse. It is a great mercy that God has allowed no human being to be as bad as they could be. And yet we must not minimise the astonishing effects of the fall. God really does permit seasons, places, and persons of great evil. There are open advocates of evil and chiefs among sinners. The Apostle Paul looked back on his own life and considered himself to be one of the latter. But the most astonishing news of all is that Christ Jesus came into the world to save such sinners and to 'display his unlimited patience' in people like Paul, or perhaps in you or me, 'as an example for those who would believe on him and receive eternal life' (*1 Tim* 1:15, 16).

Historic Text	*Modern Version*
6.3 They being the root of all mankind, the guilt of this sin was imputed,[f] and the same death in sin and corrupted nature, conveyed to all their posterity descending from them by ordinary generation.[g]	**6.3** Since they were the root of all mankind, the guilt of this sin was imputed to—and the same death in sin and corrupted nature were conveyed to—all their posterity descending from them by ordinary generation.
6.4 From this original corruption, whereby we are utterly indisposed, disabled, and made opposite to all good,[h] and wholly inclined to all evil,[i] do proceed all actual transgressions.[k]	**6.4** From this original corruption, by which we are utterly disinclined, disabled, and antagonistic to all that is good and wholly inclined to all that is evil, all actual transgressions proceed.

Scripture Proofs

6.3 [f] Gen. 1:27,28, and Gen. 2:16,17, and Acts 17:26, with Rom. 5:12,15-19, and 1 Cor. 15:21,22,49. [g] Psa. 51:5; Gen. 5:3; Job 14:4; Job 15:14.

6.4 [h] Rom. 5:6; Rom. 8:7; Rom. 7:18; Col. 1:21. [i] Gen. 6:5; Gen. 8:21; Rom. 3:10-12. [k] James 1:14,15; Eph. 2:2,3; Matt. 15:19.

The root of all mankind

The first two paragraphs of chapter 6 summarize the Bible's teaching on the fall of Adam and Eve. The third and fourth paragraphs speak of our fall into sin.

That the human race did fall is amply evidenced all around us, and even inside us, as sin does its work. But the comprehensiveness of the human fall is also obvious from the fact that the 'root' of the great tree of humanity is found in the union of Adam and Eve. As a Jew from Tarsus explained to Greeks in Athens, God 'has made from one man every nation of mankind' (*Acts* 17:26). This is the natural history of human beings, according to the Bible. And so when the poison of disobedience was absorbed into the root of mankind, it could not help but spread that decay to the furthest branches of the human race.

Thus it was that when the man and the woman tasted death (*Gen.* 2:16, 17) and fell from God's favour, 'all their posterity' fell with them— or at least all of their posterity who descended 'by [and not because of] ordinary generation'. Here the confession mentions in passing a very important point: sin did not pass from person to person, or even from parent to child by physical generation (or ordinary procreation). The sexual union of Adam and Even could not communicate righteousness before the fall, and did not communicate sin after the fall. Fallenness is not communicated by acts of procreation—after all, it was God who told them to be fruitful and multiply (*Gen.* 1:27, 28). No, the confession is simply saying that fallenness is communicated to all who *become people* by procreation—which refers to all but three people of the human race.

And how we are fallen! As Paul told the Corinthians, 'death came through a man', and 'in Adam all died'. To use a garden-variety metaphor again, our bodies are now 'sown' in a 'perishable' state. They begin life in 'dishonour' and 'weakness', for that is the 'natural body' we now inherit at birth (*1 Cor.* 15:21-49). The Word of God speaks to the same effect in Romans 5: corruption is communicated. Adam and Eve were dead in sin and corrupt in their nature, and so, although the very act of procreation was good, they could still produce only their own kind in death and depravity. Adam produced children in 'his own likeness' (*Gen.* 5:3). To be made in the likeness of God entailed holiness. Now, to be made in the likeness of Adam entailed wickedness. Job was right to ask who could bring something pure out of something impure, and right again to conclude that no man or woman was righteous (*Job* 14:4; 15:14).

Adam and Eve's corrupt natures were passed on from generation to generation, from body to body.

However, we do not want to over-extend a corporate metaphor, and the confession is a little too egalitarian here, always including both Adam and Eve in its discussion of the fall. Paragraph 3 seems to suggest that guilt is imputed from the same two persons, and for the same reasons, that corruption is imparted. But guilt is different from corruption. Guilt itself is not a mental or biological condition, but a judicial declaration.

Yet it is true that we are born guilty, and elsewhere the writings of the Westminster assembly more clearly echo Scripture when in explaining the imputation of guilt it focuses on the responsibility and headship of Adam exclusively.[1] We are born united to the first Adam. He is our

[1] WLC 22 and 193, but especially WSC 16.

representative, and so his guilt is imputed or credited by God to all of his descendants. When he fell, we fell with him.[1]

And so, although God 'desires truth in the inner parts' and patiently teaches us 'wisdom in the inmost place', we must candidly confess with David that we are sinful at birth, indeed, sinful from the time our mothers conceived us. We are born into the family that has foolishly feuded with its Father in heaven. We are born in that city of man that raised its own walls, and then flew its own banner, proclaiming war on the city of God. There is no stage of innocence. No baby arrives in this world with a blank slate (*Psa.* 51:5, 6). This grim reality results from original sin. By that theologians do not mean Adam's first sin in the garden but the original sinful state into which we all are born.

Sin

Unhappily the story gets worse before it gets better. We have considered original sin. We must also consider actual sins, and the Westminster assembly offers us some guidance in chapter 6 paragraph 4. There we are told that 'original corruption' leaves us 'utterly indisposed, disabled, and made opposite to all good'.

This is a bleak assessment. And lest one should think this is too extreme a picture, the Westminster divines direct us to lines in the Apostle Paul's letters. There he declares that we are 'without strength'. What is more, our minds war against God; our intellects are not subject to God's

---

[1] The portrayal in WCF 6.3 of Adam and Eve as the dual source of human guilt reflects an older Christian tradition that emphasizes our participation in the effects of their sin by reason of our biological connection to the corrupt human nature of our first parents. Nonetheless, the description of both Adam and Eve as 'the root of all mankind' is comparatively unusual in English theology before and after 1646. George Walker offers the more common understanding of the phrase when he restricts this 'root' to Adam. See, *e.g.,* Walker, *History of Creation as It Was Written by Moses*, pp. 197, 207, and Walker, *The Key of Saving Knowledge* (London, 1641), p. 20, where he refers to Adam as the 'common stock and root of mankind', and Walker, *A Sermon Preached in London by a Faithful Minister of Christ* (London, 1642), p. 12, where he calls Adam the 'common father and root of all mankind'. In the years following the assembly the most prominent person to note the assembly's phrase in 6.3 was the Irish Bishop Jeremy Taylor, who catalogues it as a fault, and lists it within a larger condemnation of assembly doctrines. See Jeremy Taylor, *Deus justificatus* (London, 1656), pp. 29-30.

law—they cannot be. That is because nothing good lives in us and we cannot find the way forward to do what is right. We are alienated from God. We are his enemies (*Rom.* 5:6; 7:18; 8:7; *Col.* 1:21).

Again, the ringing indictments that God sounds before and after the flood are as true today as they were thousands of years ago (*Gen.* 6:5; 8:21). The only difference is that God has promised not to destroy the world again until the final day of judgment. As we read our histories and look around our world, we note the same phenomena that Paul described in his letter to the Romans and the biblical poets described in their own writings: no one is righteous, no, not one (*Rom.* 3:10-12; *Psa.* 14:1-3; 53:1-3; *Eccles.* 7:20). It is not the case that, in spite of their birth in sin, some people still naturally want to follow God. No; no one is seeking after God. If they have gone out of the way it is not to find good, but evil. We are unprofitable to God, even useless (*Rom.* 3:10-12).

An additional point is made here, however: from this *state* of sin erupts a *life* of sin. Paul states at one moment that no one *is* good. He declares at the next that no one *does* good, no, not one (*Rom.* 3:12). So it is from 'this original corruption' that 'all actual transgressions' 'do proceed'. Original sin can be distinguished from our actual sin from day to day. But the two can never be separated, for sins well up from inside us. As James says, 'every man is tempted, when he is drawn away of his own lust, and enticed'. And this begins a lethal spiral, for 'when lust has conceived, it brings forth sin: and sin, when it is finished, brings forth death' (*James* 1:14-15).

This spiralling of sinners into ever more sin has different forms, of course. As Paul points out to the Ephesians, we can be caught walking with the world, being deceived by the dictates of Satan, and then turn inward to seek fulfilment in the desires of our own flesh and the constructs of our own minds (*Eph.* 2:2, 3). The helix of sin can twist in different directions but its tendency is always downwards, unless stopped by the grace of God.

Some sinners suddenly wake to the horror that out of their own hearts are streaming 'evil thoughts' and then 'murders, adulteries, fornications, thefts, false witness' and even 'blasphemies' (*Matt.* 15:19). Some never wake from their sins at all. And some wake from this nightmare and repent of their sins. They continue to sin, of course, and the next paragraph in the confession will discuss this sad reality. But they rejoice to remember that there is *one* child of Adam who was not born by ordinary generation. Let us place all our hope on that one who was made opposite to all evil, and wholly inclined to all good.

Historic Text	**Modern Version**
6.5 This corruption of nature, during this life, does remain in those that are regenerated;[l] and, although it be, through Christ, pardoned, and mortified, yet both itself, and all the motions thereof are truly and properly sin.[m]	**6.5** During this life, this corruption of nature remains in those who are regenerated. Even though it is pardoned and put to death through Christ, yet both this corruption of nature and all its expressions are in fact really sin.
6.6 Every sin, both original and actual, being a transgression of the righteous law of God, and contrary thereunto,[n] does, in its own nature, bring guilt upon the sinner;[o] whereby he is bound over to the wrath of God,[p] and curse of the law,[q] and so made subject to death,[r] with all miseries spiritual,[s] temporal,[t] and eternal.[u]	**6.6** Every sin—both original and actual—is a transgression of the righteous law of God and contrary to it. Therefore, every sin in its own nature brings guilt upon the sinner, on account of which he is bound over to the holy wrath of God and the curse of the law. Consequently, he is subject to death, with all miseries—spiritual, temporal, and eternal.

Scripture Proofs

6.5   [l] 1 John 1:8,10; Rom. 7:14,17,18,23; James 3:2; Prov. 20:9; Eccles. 7:20. [m] Rom. 7:5,7,8,25; Gal. 5:17.

6.6   [n] 1 John 3:4. [o] Rom. 2:15; Rom. 3:9,19. [p] Eph. 2:3. [q] Gal. 3:10. [r] Rom. 6:23. [s] Eph. 4:18. [t] Rom. 8:20; Lam. 3:39. [u] Matt. 25:41; 2 Thess. 1:9.

Remaining corruption

We have heard that all of humanity is fallen in sin from birth. The heartrending reality is that most live in sin and die in sin, never turning in faith and repentance to God in Christ. But this is not true of all people. Some do find a new life in Christ. And so what can we say of them? Can someone be united to Christ and still be damaged by our history with

Adam? Can one be a Christian and still be a sinner? The confession looks at both of these questions in turn and answers, yes.

'This corruption of nature' that we inherited from Adam, at least 'during this life', does remain 'in those that are regenerated'. That is just the battle we see pictured in Romans 7. Every honest Christian can say there is something powerful 'in the members of my body, waging war against the law of my mind and making me a prisoner of the law of sin' (*Rom.* 7:23; see 14-23). Because of that, we 'all stumble in many ways' (*James* 3:2).

Amidst all the varied utterances of the preacher of Ecclesiastes we hear the ring of truth when he makes the all-embracing comment, 'there is not a righteous man on earth who does what is right and never sins' (*Eccles.* 7:20). The Apostle John is saying just this when he reminds us, 'If we say that we have no sin, we deceive ourselves, and the truth is not in us.' He powerfully underlines that this is God's own judgment about Christians. Thus, 'If we say that we have not sinned', then we are saying something about God—'we make him a liar, and his word is not in us' (*1 John* 1:8, 10).

Do we not know this ourselves? 'Who can say, "I have kept my heart pure; I am clean and without sin"' (*Prov.* 20:9)? The problem is that we are not pure; rather, we are living examples of the effects of corruption. We are not clean; rather, we are dirtied by sin. Thankfully John also tells us, 'If we confess our sins, he is faithful and just and will forgive us our sins and purify us from all unrighteousness' (*1 John* 1:9). But although we are 'through Christ pardoned and mortified', sin is still 'truly and properly' called sin, even its very first stirrings in our hearts. Those who have been born again by the Spirit are new creatures in Christ, but there is a battle of desires that continues even after Christ's Spirit begins to dwell in us. Paul describes that battle in Romans 7 (*Rom.* 7:5, 7, 8, 25); he summarises it in Galatians 5: 'the flesh lusteth against the Spirit, and the Spirit against the flesh: and these are contrary the one to the other: so that ye cannot do the things that ye would' (*Gal.* 5:17 KJV). Sin has had a shelf-life, and then a lingering potency that perhaps exceeds even the devil's expectations.

Original sin and actual sins

The confession ends the sixth chapter with a taxonomy of sin. This chapter has discussed original sin and actual sin, and now it reminds us that all these sins are contrary to God's law and, by nature, violations of it. As John says, 'sin is the transgression of the law' (*1 John* 3:4). In its very nature, law-breaking always brings guilt. So, in speaking of law-breaking, Paul can say that 'all the world' is 'guilty before God'. And since the law is written on our hearts, it brings knowledge of our guilt (*Rom.* 2:15).

Since we are guilty sinners, we also deserve God's wrath, the law's curse, and life's death. Naturally, we are 'in sin' and 'under the law' (*Rom.* 3:9, 19). When the confession states that we are 'bound over to the wrath of God', this is no more than what Paul says when he reminds us that we were born 'children of wrath' (*Eph.* 2:3). When the confession speaks of the 'curse of the law', it is merely paraphrasing a line in the letter to the Galatians (*Gal.* 3:10). And when we are threatened by news of death, we are only hearing the old warning cry of Romans 6:23, 'the wages of sin is death'.

In short, without Christ we must expect 'all miseries spiritual, temporal, and eternal'. Is it not misery to 'be alienated from the life of God' (*Eph.* 4:18)? Is it not misery to be 'subjected to frustration' through this life (*Rom.* 8:20) and to be punished for our sins (*Lam.* 3:39)? Is it not hopeless misery to hear the Saviour say, 'Depart from me, you who are cursed, into the eternal fire prepared for the devil and his angels' (*Matt.* 25:41)—and to be 'punished with everlasting destruction and shut out from the presence of the Lord and from the majesty of his power'? This world has done all that it can to palliate the effects of sin, but its curse is still at work in us.

In reminding us of the Scriptures' teaching that every sin deserves death, the Westminster divines are not denying that some sins are worse than others; neither are they denying that sins can be further aggravated by the person who commits them, by the place and time where they are committed, or by the one who is sinned against. It is worse for a minister of the gospel to sin than for a new convert. Stealing is bad, but it is especially bad to pick someone's pocket during a worship service. And while breaking the laws of the land is a serious crime, breaking any law of the King of kings is always a capital offence.[1]

There are distinctions between the gravity of sins, but in reminding us of the Scriptures' teaching that every sin deserves death, the Westminster divines are also arguing against one of the most famous distinctions in the history of sin. Sadly, the Roman Catholic Church teaches that some sins are mortal (or deadly), and others are only venial (or not so consequential). How flawed this understanding of sin is!

As this chapter explains, and as the Scriptures make all too clear, there are no venial sins. The truth is that every sin is a mortal sin. And yet at the same time, as later chapters will explain, every sin can be forgiven, for there is one who took our sin and guilt. Sin is misery, but we have a Saviour who paid sin's deadly price. And so it is that there will come a day, not 'during this life', but after, when our nature will know no more corruption, and we shall no longer sin.

---

[1] WLC 150-152.

CHAPTER 7:

OF GOD'S COVENANT WITH MAN

Historic Text

7.1 The distance between God and the creature is so great, that although reasonable creatures do owe obedience unto him as their Creator, yet they could never have any fruition of him as their blessedness and reward, but by some voluntary condescension on God's part, which he has been pleased to express by way of covenant.[a]

7.2 The first covenant made with man, was a covenant of works,[b] wherein life was promised to Adam, and in him to his posterity,[c] upon condition of perfect and personal obedience.[d]

Modern Version

7.1 The distance between God and the creature is so great that, even though rational creatures are responsible to obey him as their Creator, yet they could never experience any enjoyment of him as their blessing and reward except by way of some voluntary condescension on his part, which he has been pleased to express by way of covenant.

7.2 The first covenant made with man was a covenant of works in which life was promised to Adam and, in him, to his posterity, upon condition of perfect and personal obedience.

Scripture Proofs

 7.1 [a] Isa. 40:13-17; Job 9:32,33; 1 Sam. 2:25; Psa. 113:5,6; Psa. 100:2,3; Job 22:2,3; Job 35:7,8; Luke 17:10; Acts 17:24,25.

 7.2 [b] Gal. 3:12. [c] Rom. 10:5; Rom. 5:12-20. [d] Gen. 2:17; Gal. 3:10.

A distance so great

Following the order of topics in the Westminster Confession of Faith, we have looked first at God and then at man. Now we look at the two together. We should not expect it to be easy to keep both the Creator and the creature in our sights at once, for the distance between them is very great. Isaiah once wrote that, in comparison to God, all 'the nations are like a drop from a bucket' or 'dust on the scales' (see *Isa.* 40:13-17).

God is not a man, Job reminded his friends (*Job* 9:32, 33). We need to sense the amazement of the psalmist that 'the LORD, he is God!' (*Psa.* 100:2, 3). He is the one who is seated on high and looks down to us (*Psa.* 113:5-6).

Although we are made in God's image, there is a great difference between God and us, as these old covenant authors emphasize. To be clear, the confession has in view here not ethical differences, but differences in our very beings. It is not discussing our fallenness and God's holiness, but our smallness and God's greatness. But having said that, we can, in fact, also use the lens of sin to see the great distance between ourselves and God. Old Eli tried to tell his sons this very truth when they abused the Israelites who had come to worship the Lord: there was a big difference in sinning against another human being and sinning against God himself ('but they would not listen', *1 Sam.* 2:25).

As Eli and the psalmist both mention, all creatures which are able to reason owe to God their loyalty. The idea is not that we can somehow be profitable to God in our service; he is not like a rich landowner who needs working servants for personal gain (*Job* 22:2, 3). God is not in need of us, and that is just the point Paul makes when he talks to the pagans in Athens (*Acts* 17:24, 25). At a most basic level, we are not in a position to give, and God as our creator has no need to receive (*Job* 35:7, 8). It is more the case that we are to do all that we are commanded, and then, just like the servant in Jesus' parable, we are to admit that 'we have only done what was our duty' (*Luke* 17:10).

A covenant

God is immeasurably great and we owe him our obedience. But the fact is that we could hardly have even a working relationship with God if he had not voluntarily condescended to meet us where we are. God himself is the greatest blessing and highest reward that any person could have, but all human contact with God would have been fruitless if God had not freely decided to come to us and set terms where we could have fellowship with him, an arrangement which we call a covenant.

Most Reformed theologians are comfortable calling this first God-ordained relationship a 'covenant'. But notable theologians like John

Calvin were slow to call God's statement of terms to Adam a covenant, and John Murray actually argues against this common designation, since the word 'covenant' is not used in Genesis 1-2 (but see *Hos.* 6:7).[1] Nonetheless, we do not always need to see a term employed to know that the reality exists. If you spot four English ladies sipping tea, eating scones and savouring the local gossip at four o'clock in the afternoon, you do not need a label to know what is going on: there is a tea party. Yes, it is possible you have stumbled on an international spy-ring or the caucus of a drug cartel; but if you are familiar with tea parties you should be able to spot the difference. We could call this the 'tea party principle' and it easily applies to covenants. Any time one spots a sovereignly determined and administered arrangement between God and man, with penalties and promises, you have a covenant. Even if the members of the assembly did not call their principle of interpretation the 'tpp', it is clear that in Genesis 1-2 we have at least this: God sets the terms, man owes him obedience.

If a covenant ordinarily contains sanctions and promises, the sanction in the covenant with Adam is obvious: the threat of death (*Gen.* 2:17). It is likely that we can also see the idea that man's faithfulness to the covenant would have been blessed with life. That is part of the significance frequently drawn from God's requirement that Adam and Eve be kept from the tree of life after their fall into sin (*Gen.* 3:22-24). This promise requires us to connect the dots, but it is not difficult to do so and the emerging picture is covenantal in shape.

A covenant of works

Since the Bible does not supply a name for this covenant, as it does for some others, it could sensibly be called any number of things. Indeed, it could have just been numbered as the 'first covenant' made with man.

---

[1] Assembly members tend to be open but not committed to Hosea 6:7 as a reference to Adam in covenant. See, *e.g.,* Jeremiah Burroughs, who takes the opposing view in *An Exposition with Practical Observations Continued upon the Fourth, Fifth, Sixth and Seventh Chapters of Hosea* (London, 1650), pp. 621-22; or William Strong, *A Discourse of the Two Covenants* (London, 1678), p. 176. Their caution is reflected in the fact that they do not use Hosea 6:7 as a proof text at this point, nor in WLC 20 or WSC 12.

We could have called it the 'Adamic covenant', mentioning the person representing us in this divine arrangement. It could have been called a 'covenant of death', for Adam was to be punished with nothing less should he not abide by the simple terms of this covenant. But no one calls it that. The Shorter Catechism calls it the 'covenant of life', looking to the blessing implicitly promised to Adam, and in him to his posterity should they obey God.

In paragraph 2 of this chapter the covenant focus is on obedience, and the Westminster assembly calls it a 'covenant of works'. Here the assembly focuses on the works-principle of the covenant: the idea that the law of God requires perfect and personal obedience.[1] The one who does what is required in the law would live by it (*Rom.* 10:5; *Gal.* 3:12). *Doing* was the important verb. As it was, Adam did not keep the one simple, almost elegant law that was explicitly put before him. In spite of God's command to avoid the tree of the knowledge of good and evil, Adam ate its fruit. Disobeying God, he came under the law's curse and the penalty of death (*Gal.* 3:10; *Gen.* 2:17). This was an immense tragedy, for life was not only within sight, it was even within reach. Covenant-keeping really would have led to a more abundant life (*Rom.* 10:5; *Gal.* 3:12).[2]

---

[1] WCF 19.1 adds that this obedience must also be 'perpetual'.

[2] In considering the life that Adam could have lived, Romans 5 seems to provide an important pointer. There Paul talks of two Adams and tells us that those united to the second Adam have a new abundance of grace that the first Adam did not know (*Rom.* 5:12-20), but perhaps would have known if he had obeyed God in the garden. A second clue to the character of this promised life is found in 1 Corinthians 15:44-49, which speaks of the character of the resurrection body that we have through the second Adam. There we read of a body that is real, but is called a 'spiritual body'. It is this spiritual body that fallen Adam and his posterity lost title to in the garden, and now can regain only through Christ at the resurrection. It should be noted that even if the garden offered a probationary period, the obedience Adam was to offer needed to be a perpetual obedience (see WCF 19.1).

Historic Text	*Modern Version*
7.3 Man, by his fall having made himself incapable of life by that covenant, the Lord was pleased to make a second,[c] commonly called the covenant of grace; wherein he freely offers unto sinners life and salvation by Jesus Christ, requiring of them faith in him that they may be saved,[f] and promising to give unto all those that are ordained unto life, his Holy Spirit, to make them willing, and able to believe.[g]	**7.3** Since man, by his fall, made himself incapable of life by that covenant, the Lord was then pleased to make a second covenant, commonly called the covenant of grace. In it God freely offers life and salvation by Jesus Christ to sinners, requiring of them faith in him, that they may be saved, and promising to give his Holy Spirit to all those who are ordained to eternal life, to make them willing and able to believe.
7.4 This covenant of grace is frequently set forth in Scripture by the name of a testament, in reference to the death of Jesus Christ the testator, and to the everlasting inheritance, with all things belonging to it, therein bequeathed.[h]	**7.4** This covenant of grace is sometimes presented in the Scriptures by the name of a will or testament, with reference to the death of Jesus Christ (the testator) and to the everlasting inheritance—with all that belongs to it—bequeathed in it.

Scripture Proofs

7.3 [c] Gal. 3:21; Rom. 8:3; Rom. 3:20,21; Gen. 3:15; Isa. 42:6. [f] Mark 16:15,16; John 3:16; Rom. 10:6,9; Gal. 3:11. [g] Ezek. 36:26,27; John 6:44,45.

7.4 [h] Heb. 9:15-17; Heb. 7:22; Luke 22:20; 1 Cor. 11:25.

The covenant of grace

In the opening paragraphs of chapter 7, we heard that man had only one bond with God, forged by the Creator himself. Paragraph 3 opens by reminding us of that moment of supreme foolishness when man severed that life-giving bond and marked himself out for death. Humanity was no longer capable of attaining life by that first covenant.

The first covenant contained a fair and a just requirement, with the strong muscle of a threat behind it. But as we reflect on the covenant and the actions of our first parents we can see that the law did not give life. And once they had broken the law of that covenant, we must agree with the Apostle Paul that it could not give life (*Gal.* 3:21). By the 'works of the law' no one could 'be justified' in God's sight (*Rom.* 3:2).

Unexpectedly, from the perspective of human participants, and perhaps angelic observers, 'the Lord was pleased to make a second' covenant, which theologians commonly call 'the covenant of grace'. It is a covenant because it is another God-ordained bond, this time with sinners.[1] It is gracious because it contains a glorious promise, completely undeserved. The seed of that promise is found as early as Genesis 3:15, and it grows in the writings of the prophets (*e.g., Isa.* 42:6). Throughout the Law and the Prophets we hear whispers of its existence, stories of a 'righteousness of God' that is 'without' a law (*Rom.* 3:21). And when we begin reading the New Testament, we find that it is all true, and that the promise comes to full flower. There we read that what 'the law could not do' God did do 'by sending his own Son in the likeness of sinful flesh', 'condemning' the sin that had once condemned us (*Rom.* 8:3).

So we can have confidence in this covenant of grace, where God 'freely offers unto sinners life and salvation' to undo our death and sin. Where the first covenant is a deep expression of God's willingness to have fellowship with mere creatures, this second covenant is a staggering display of God's willingness to forgive and to have fellowship with those who are unworthy.

We can have confidence in this covenant because in this gracious offer God gives his own Son. It is in the New Testament that we clearly see that Christ himself is the new covenant; he is the promise; he is the covenant and bond of grace. There is nothing abstract or fictitious in this gospel. It is as real as the Lord Jesus Christ himself, Son of man and Son of God.

This is good news; and it gets even better, for we find that if there is any debt, Jesus has paid it all. There is nothing for us to do. We simply put all our faith in him, and 'whoever believes in him will not perish, but have everlasting life' (*John* 3:16).[2] In this gospel we find 'a righteousness' which is based on faith in Christ (*Rom.* 10:6), as we believe in our hearts that 'God has raised him from the dead'. It is by this we are saved (*Rom.* 10:9). We live by faith (*Gal.* 3:11), which is to confess that we actually live by the power and grace of Christ and not by ourselves.

[1] From the words 'requiring them' and 'promising . . . those' it appears that WCF 7.3 presents the covenant as made with sinners; it does not specify whether the covenant is made with sinners in Christ. In WCF 7.6 it is clear that the substance of the covenant of grace is Christ himself.

[2] Echoes of *John* 3:16 are found in *Mark* 16:15, 16, a passage with a weak manuscript testimony.

What gospel could be more free? And what could be more full, answering our every need, and even our doubts? For lest these promises should daunt us, the confession reminds us of a corresponding biblical promise. God gives us his Son and he also promises to give 'his Holy Spirit' to all those who are his people. When Ezekiel recorded God's promise of a 'new heart' for heartless sinners, he was also told to tell of 'a new Spirit' who would be 'within' us (*Ezek.* 36:26). It is by this Spirit that the Father would 'draw us' to the waters of salvation, and teach us to come to Christ (*John* 6:44, 45).

Does your faith ever waver? Remember the Holy Spirit, for he too is promised in this covenant that is all of grace. The Spirit will make us 'willing' to believe in a crucified Saviour and 'able to believe' in an empty tomb—it is he who begins our salvation. And remember too that this gift is for those who are 'ordained unto eternal life' and nothing less. For in this second covenant, the Father, the Son and the Holy Spirit have offered a relationship to us that will never end.

A testament?

Up to this point the confession has referred to a covenant, but it is worth observing, as a footnote, that one can also speak of a 'testament'. 'Covenant' is the usual term Scripture uses, but 'the covenant of grace is frequently set forth in the Scripture by the name of a testament'—or at least it is so in the Greek translation of the Old Testament.[1] It is probably for that reason that the word 'testament' is used sometimes in the King James Version of the Bible (*e.g., Heb.* 9:15-17; *Heb.* 7:22; *Luke* 22:20; *1 Cor.* 11:25).

The term 'testament' invokes biblical themes and biblical language. It reminds us that great gifts have been bequeathed to us. It evokes the idea of a 'testator', in Jesus Christ, and of an 'everlasting inheritance, with all things belonging to it'. On one level, in making this point, the members of the Westminster assembly are avoiding contention over words, for we all know that arguments about words have been more than a cottage industry in the Christian church. The gospel can be described in the dialect of covenantal theology, or in the language of a last will and testament.

[1] Anthony Burgess, *Vindiciae Legis* (London, 1647), p. 125.

Nonetheless this fourth paragraph is also reminding us that while there are dominant ways in which God's Word teaches Christian truth, we are wise to use the full range of biblical expressions. And the middle verses of Hebrews 9, at least, do appear to connect the reality of the covenant with the concept of a 'will' (ESV) or a 'testament' (KJV, ASV). In a few words, these verses teach us that the law of Moses was filled with blood and sacrifices in order to teach God's people something: that someone had to die before the great promise could 'take effect' (*Heb.* 9:15-17).

And what a powerful picture this is. The language of covenants has helped very many Christians understand the gospel. But, for others, the reality of God's gift may only come home with the language of 'wills' and of 'testaments'. For we all know who must die before a last will and testament can come into effect. It is the one who made it. And so it is that the Son of God bled out his life for us so that we would receive an everlasting inheritance.

Historic Text	*Modern Version*
7.5 This covenant was differently administered in the time of the law, and in the time of the gospel:[i] under the law, it was administered by promises, prophecies, sacrifices, circumcision, the paschal lamb, and other types and ordinances delivered to the people of the Jews, all fore-signifying Christ to come:[k] which were, for that time, sufficient and efficacious, through the operation of the Spirit, to instruct and build up the elect in faith in the promised Messiah,[l] by whom they had full remission of sins, and eternal salvation: and is called, the old testament.[m]	**7.5** In the time of the law, this covenant was administered differently than in the time of the gospel. Under the law, it was administered by promises, prophecies, sacrifices, circumcision, the passover lamb, and other types and ordinances given to the Jewish people, all of which foreshadowed Christ to come. These were, for that time, sufficient and efficacious, through the work of the Spirit, to instruct and build up the elect in their faith in the promised Messiah, by whom they received complete forgiveness of sins and eternal salvation. This covenant administration is called the old testament.
7.6 Under the gospel, when Christ, the substance,[n] was exhibited, the	**7.6** Under the gospel, Christ (the reality) having been revealed, the ordinances by

ordinances in which this covenant is dispensed, are the preaching of the Word, and the administration of the sacraments of baptism, and the Lord's supper:[o] which, though fewer in number, and administered with more simplicity, and less outward glory; yet, in them, it is held forth in more fullness, evidence, and spiritual efficacy,[p] to all nations, both Jews and Gentiles;[q] and, is called the new testament.[r] There are not therefore two covenants of grace, differing in substance, but one and the same, under various dispensations.[s]

which this covenant is dispensed are the preaching of the Word and the administration of the sacraments of baptism and the Lord's supper. Although these are fewer in number and are administered with more simplicity and less outward glory, yet in them the covenant is set forth in greater fullness, clarity, and spiritual efficacy to all nations, both Jews and Gentiles, and is called the new testament. Therefore, there are not two covenants of grace differing in substance, but only one, under various administrations.

Scripture Proofs

7.5 [i] 2 Cor. 3:6-9. [k] Heb., chapters 8-10; Rom. 4:11; Col. 2:11,12; 1 Cor. 5:7. [l] 1 Cor. 10:1-4; Heb. 11:13; John 8:56. [m] Gal. 3:7-9,14.

7.6 [n] Col. 2:17. [o] Matt. 28:19,20; 1 Cor. 11:23,24,25. [p] Heb. 12:22-28; Jer. 31:33,34. [q] Matt. 28:19; Eph. 2:15-19. [r] Luke 22:20. [s] Gal. 3:14,16; Rom. 3:21-23,30; Psa. 32:1, with Rom. 4:3,6,16,17,23,24; Heb. 13:8; Acts 15:11.

The Old Testament

So far, chapter 7 has outlined how the covenant of works and the covenant of grace are God's gifts to men, women and children. It then goes on, in paragraph 4, to explain the different language used in the Bible to describe the realities of the covenant of grace. In these two final paragraphs, we are reminded that the covenant of grace was 'administered' differently 'in the time of the law, and in the time of the gospel'. The one time is symbolized by the law engraved on stones, which was 'glorious;' the other is symbolized by the giving of the Spirit, in 'much more . . . glory' (*2 Cor.* 3:7, 9).

As paragraph 5 explains, the 'time of the law' was a time of 'promises, prophecies, sacrifices, circumcision, the paschal lamb, and other types and ordinances'. Not one of these things was complete in itself—each pointed to something that would be better and come later, as the letter to the Hebrews teaches us (*Heb.* 8-10). Furthermore, this time in the distant past was one of restrictions: the promises, prophecies and ceremonies, and the message they communicated, were limited to 'the people of the Jews', and those who would join these people.

The redeeming feature of this time of the law was that these types and ordinances all pointed directly to a coming Christ—God's anointed one, sent to take away the stench of our sin which had risen to heaven itself. Circumcision, for example, always had a spiritual meaning, as Paul explains in Romans and again in Colossians: it symbolized the removal of the body of sin and served as a seal of the righteousness of faith (*Col.* 2:11, 12; *Rom.* 4:11). It painfully pictured the forgiveness of sin and the gift of Christ's righteousness, so central to the gospel message. The passover meal, to choose another example, indirectly reminded believers to put away the old leaven of sin that ferments even in the church itself. But it most clearly preached to all who saw in it 'Christ our Passover is sacrificed for us' (*1 Cor.* 5:7).

Each of the promises embedded in these ceremonies and sacrifices were only 'fore-signifying Christ to come' but they were used by the Holy Spirit to communicate the great gospel of grace to God's people of old. They really 'were, for that time, sufficient and efficacious . . . to instruct and build up the elect'. Perhaps that is why Abraham could rejoice to see Jesus' day (*John* 8:56). That is why the faithful in the earliest eras of God's covenant community could see and 'welcome' the promises of God 'from a distance' (*Heb.* 11:13). Of course these gifts from God needed 'the operation of the Spirit'. They required 'faith in the promised Messiah'. Some people, in fact, did not have the gift of the Spirit or the grace of faith. For some it was simply remarkable that the Red Sea parted, and a good thing that they escaped the bondage of Egypt. For some it was convenient that meat flew from the sky and water flowed from rocks. But for others the rescue of God's people was a picture of God's deliverance through a coming Messiah, as Paul explains in the opening verses of 1 Corinthians 10. For the faithful, the feeding of many thousands in the wilderness was more than a regularly scheduled picnic. It was a foretaste of a spiritual food from God and a spiritual drink that reminded them of the Rock of Ages, the Rock that is Christ, as Paul explains in the following verses in 1 Corinthians 10.

Only those who had faith in this coming Saviour found the 'full remission' of all their sins; it is by the working of his Spirit that each and every believer discovered 'eternal salvation'. And all believers today are the spiritual 'children' of those believers from long ago; we share in their blessings (*Gal.* 3:7-9, 14). It is true that the administration of these blessings was 'called the Old Testament'. But let us never forget that it was always a good testament and full of glory.

The New Testament

Under the law everything was a promise or type either speaking of or visibly portraying what was to come. But 'under the gospel' we find Christ himself, the Word made flesh, exhibited before the world. Christ, of course, is the 'substance' of all the old prophecies and sacrifices and he is the substance of the covenant of grace. He himself is the gospel, the good news we proclaim. Paul sums this up memorably when he tells us that all the Old Testament ordinances were 'a shadow of the things to come, but the body', the reality that cast the shadow back into the Old Testament, was always Christ (*Col.* 2:17).

Therefore, in the era of the gospel, it is appropriate to focus solely on the living Christ who is with us. We do not celebrate the old rites that advertised that he would be coming soon. Although we preach about these Old Testament types and promises, it is Christ we see in 'the preaching of the Word'. Although we do have 'the sacraments of baptism and the Lord's supper', we baptize in the name of the one who, with his Father and Spirit, is with us 'always, even to the end of the world' (*Matt.* 28:19, 20). Although we partake of a spiritual meal of bread and wine, we do it all in remembrance of Christ (*1 Cor.* 11:23-25).

Admittedly, these simple New Testament ordinances are 'fewer in number' than those in the Old Testament. Admittedly, they are 'administered with more simplicity, and less outward glory'. After all, not even at major Christian conferences do preachers' faces shine in giving the gospel like Moses' face shone in giving the law. And yet, as the writer to the Hebrews explains in some of his closing words, what we have is so much better. Yes, it must have been glorious to see Mount Sinai at the giving of the law. Nonetheless, we have come 'to Mount Zion, to the heavenly Jerusalem, the city of the living God'. How marvellous it must have been to worship with throngs of God's people in the great Old Testament festivals. And yet we have come 'to thousands upon thousands of angels in joyful assembly'. Our names might not belong to ancient families that can trace their roots back to David or Abraham or Abel. But our 'names are written in heaven'. And what we have today in the gospel is not a future hope only. The Bible says that we '*have* come to God, the judge of all men, to the spirits of righteous men made perfect, to Jesus the mediator of a new covenant, and to the sprinkled blood that speaks a better word than the blood of Abel' (*Heb.* 12:22-24; *cf. Jer.* 31:33, 34).

So it is that we can truthfully confess that in the age of the gospel, and in its means of grace, we see God's goodness 'held forth in more fullness, evidence, and spiritual efficacy' than it ever was before. All restrictions are lifted as we teach 'all nations, both Jews and Gentiles', no longer discriminating in favour of those who are 'nigh' and against those who are 'afar off' (*Matt.* 18:19; *Eph.* 2:15-19).

It is for that reason that Christians hold such affection for what is called the New Testament or new covenant (*Luke* 22:20), while at the same time maintaining that there are not 'two covenants of grace differing in substance'. Rather, there is but 'one and the same' covenant 'under various dispensations' or ways and contexts of administering the covenant.[1] And the substance and reality of that one covenant of grace is the Lord Jesus Christ (*Gal.* 3:14, 16; *Acts* 15:11; *Rom.* 3:21-23, 30; *Heb.* 13:8; *Psa.* 32:1 compared with *Rom.* 4:3, 6, 16,17, 23, 24).

---

[1] The confession is not teaching the system of biblical interpretation which is later termed 'dispensationalism'.

CHAPTER 8:

OF CHRIST THE MEDIATOR

Historic Text

8.1 It pleased God, in his eternal purpose, to choose and ordain the Lord Jesus, his only begotten Son, to be the mediator between God and man;[a] the prophet,[b] priest,[c] and king,[d] the head, and saviour of his church,[e] the heir of all things,[f] and judge of the world:[g] unto whom he did from all eternity give a people, to be his seed,[h] and to be by him in time redeemed, called, justified, sanctified, and glorified.[i]

Modern Version

8.1 God was pleased, in his eternal purpose, to choose and ordain the Lord Jesus, his only begotten Son, to be the mediator between God and man. As the mediator, he is the prophet, priest, and king, the head and saviour of the church, the heir of all things, and the judge of the world. God gave to him, from all eternity, a people to be his seed and to be by him, in time, redeemed, called, justified, sanctified, and glorified.

Scripture Proofs

8.1 [a] Isa. 42:1; 1 Pet. 1:19,20; John 3:16; 1 Tim. 2:5. [b] Acts 3:22. [c] Heb. 5:5,6. [d] Psa. 2:6; Luke 1:33. [e] Eph. 5:23. [f] Heb. 1:2. [g] Acts 17:31. [h] John 17:6; Psa. 22:30; Isa. 53:10. [i] 1 Tim. 2:6; Isa. 55:4,5; 1 Cor. 1:30.

The mediator

So much of God and his plan is beyond us, and so many of our thoughts about God and his self-revelation remain loose and disjointed where we would like them to be tight and coherent. But as we come to chapter 8 of this confession we are reminded that there is one thing that every Christian knows with clarity: that 'God so loved the world, that he gave his one and only Son, that whosoever believes in him should not perish, but have everlasting life' (*John* 3:16). To put it a different way, we know that 'it pleased God, in his eternal purpose, to choose and ordain the

Lord Jesus, his only begotten Son, to be the mediator between God and man'.

What Christians know today, God's people have known in some form from the beginning. After all, this chosen one from God was once the subject of prophecy, a suffering servant beloved of God and filled with the Spirit (*e.g., Isa.* 42:1). But we have the clearest vision of him today, for he 'was revealed in these last times for' our sakes (*1 Pet.* 1:20). Now we can see how it is that a saviour could be 'chosen *before* the creation of the world'; now we can understand how one could be ordained as the 'mediator between God and man' (*1 Tim.* 2:5) at a time when only God existed—it was because the saviour was the Son of God himself.

Prophet, Priest and King

It is one of the great wonders of the incarnation and our salvation that the all-glorious and only begotten of the Father could humble himself and become a man. It is another wonder that at the same instant he took to himself new titles and works as our mediator which give us even more scope for praise than we ever had before. He was promoted as a prophet greater than Moses himself (*Acts* 3:22). He was declared an eternal high priest, who would offer up the one sacrifice to do away with all of our sin for all time (*Heb.* 5:5, 6). He was established as a king of Zion, and his kingdom shall never end (*Psa.* 2:6; *Luke* 1:33). As prophet, he is our teacher. As priest, he is our mediator and only hope. As king, he is our defender and ruler.

Obviously the Son of God is not only 'the saviour', as if that were a small thing. No, as our prophet, priest and king 'Christ is' also 'the head of the church' (*Eph.* 5:23). This threefold office of Christ as prophet, priest and king together with his headship over the church has vast implications for the way we consider his church. Plainly, it ought to shape how we think and speak of it, how we order it, how we serve in it, and how we worship in it—for it is his church, and we must seek his will diligently and constantly in all that we do.

Even this is, of course, only the beginning of our Saviour's perfections—and who can understand them all? This is God's Son, and, in him, God is well pleased. He 'appointed' him 'heir of all things'—heir of the worlds he once made, and still loves, as only God can (*Heb.* 1:2). This is our mediator.

With the Son of God as a mediator between God and man, what Christian has a right to be afraid of death and judgment? No, we have reason only for confidence, for not only can we be sure that God 'will judge the world in righteousness', we can also be sure that he has ordained Christ himself to serve as our judge (*Acts* 17:31). In John 3:16 Jesus speaks of himself as the Son who is given to all who believe. How clear it is that in Christ we have been given a gift like no other.

The gift

Strikingly, however, the end of this first paragraph reminds us of the other side of the story. The heir of all things has been given a gift too, a gift promised to him 'from all eternity'. We can only imagine what a gift the Son deserves. How surprising it is that Christians are that gift to the Son. The Son wanted 'a people' for himself. The eternal Son asked for a 'seed', children whom he could gaze upon with pleasure for all of his days (*Psa.* 22:30; *Isa.* 53:10). Who would have ever thought it? For we know what we are like. We are just like the complaining, arguing, fearful disciples of Jesus' own day. And yet, in a rare glimpse of trinitarian fellowship, we overhear the Son giving thanks—for what? That his Father kept his word, and gave him a people out of the world (*John* 17:6). On the eve of his crucifixion, this is what moved the Son to offer praise to the Father!

Although we feel so unfit for life with Christ, here is the wonder of it all: we could never enter his presence all spattered with sin; we could never escape the clutches of sin, Satan, and death; and so in time he came and redeemed us, giving himself as a ransom (*1 Tim.* 2:6). Although we were sheep once deaf to the Shepherd's voice, by his mighty power he called us to hear and come. In fact, in Christ Jesus we find our wisdom, our righteousness, our sanctification (*1 Cor.* 1:30). Stopping at nothing, he will also make us glorious, for he is remaking us in his image, for himself (*Isa.* 55:4, 5).

Historic Text	*Modern Version*
8.2 The Son of God, the second person in the Trinity, being very and eternal God, of one substance, and equal with the Father; did, when the fullness of time was come, take upon him man's nature,[k] with all the essential properties, and common infirmities thereof, yet, without sin:[l] being conceived by the power of the Holy Ghost, in the womb of the virgin Mary, of her substance.[m] So that, two whole, perfect, and distinct natures, the Godhead and the manhood, were inseparably joined together in one person, without conversion, composition, or confusion.[n] Which person, is very God, and very man, yet one Christ, the only mediator between God and man.[o]	**8.2** The Son of God, the second person of the Trinity, being truly and eternally God, of one substance and equal with the Father, did, when the fullness of time had come, take upon himself man's nature, with all its essential properties and common frailties, yet without sin. He was conceived by the power of the Holy Spirit in the womb of the virgin Mary and of her substance. In this way, two whole natures, the divine and the human, perfect and distinct, were inseparably joined together in one person without being changed, mixed, or confused. This person is truly God and truly man, yet one Christ, the only mediator between God and man.

Scripture Proofs

8.2 [k] John 1:1,14; 1 John 5:20; Phil. 2:6; Gal. 4:4. [l] Heb. 2:14,16,17; Heb. 4:15. [m] Luke 1:27,31,35; Gal. 4:4. [n] Luke 1:35; Col. 2:9; Rom. 9:5; 1 Pet. 3:18; 1 Tim. 3:16. [o] Rom. 1:3,4; 1 Tim. 2:5.

God and man

In the first paragraph of chapter 8 we were introduced to the one mediator between God and man. In this second paragraph we are informed that the mediator is himself both God and man. This is the clear teaching of the Word of God. It is this mediator we meet in the opening chapter of the Gospel of John: 'In the beginning was the Word, and the Word was with God, the Word was God' (*John* 1:1). There we see 'the Son of God, the second person in the Trinity' is 'very God'—for John says he 'was God'. There too we see that he is 'eternal God'—for John says this was true 'from the beginning'. Elsewhere John says that Jesus 'is the true God, and eternal life'; he is this life for us, because eternal life abides in him (*1 John* 5:20).

Much more could be said. For example, since the Son is God as much as the Father (or for that matter the Holy Spirit), it is almost an understatement to note that they are of 'one substance' or to say that they are 'equal', as Paul does in his letter to the Philippians (*Phil.* 2:6). But the main point is that we should never cease to marvel that 'in the fulness of time God sent forth his Son' (*Gal.* 4:4). How hard it is to grasp even the edges of this astonishing fact, that the same Word that was God 'was made flesh, and dwelt among us'. Who can fail to hear John's humbled amazement as he tells the world what he and his fellow disciples saw: 'we beheld his glory, the glory as of the only begotten of the Father' (*John* 1:14)!

The real humanity of this incarnated or enfleshed God is revealed in many places in the Bible, including the letter to the Hebrews. This mediator did not take on the form of angels. No, he was 'made like his brothers in every way'. To the extent that we 'are partakers of flesh and blood, he also himself likewise took part of the same' (*Heb.* 2:14, 16, 17). But he took a human nature, not a fallen human nature; he took our nature without the sin of our nature; sin assaulted but did not conquer his mind or body. As the writer to the Hebrews notes, our mediator is not one 'who is unable to sympathize with our weaknesses'. On the contrary, 'we have one who has been tempted in every way, just as we are—yet was without sin' (*Heb.* 4:15). Jesus would bear our sin, but it would always be our burden that he carried, and not his own. We must never forget that a chasm of difference exists between being tempted to sin and actually falling to temptation.

The sheer extent of our human wonder at the incarnation can make us forget sometimes that this event is part of human history. But history it is, and we can see it simply but eloquently narrated for us by a real historian in Luke 1. There, in the first chapter of his Gospel, Luke records how an angel revealed to Mary that she would conceive a child by the power of the Holy Spirit, while still a virgin. The child would be 'called the Son of God' (*Luke* 1:27, 31, 35; *cf. Gal.* 4:4). At the same time this child really would be hers.

Even so, as we wonder, we must continue to pay careful attention to biblical truth. This is not a case of man becoming God (which will never happen). This is God becoming man. We must also try to understand the *words* we use. Often the great creeds of the church had stressed that the Son of God was 'of the same substance' as the Father. By that, clear-headed theologians meant that Jesus is really divine. Here, the confession helpfully reminds us that he was also of Mary's substance. By that these theologians meant that Jesus is really human.

And yet how are we to understand the divinity and humanity of Christ? How do they relate in the one person that is Jesus Christ of Nazareth? I think we need to remember the words of the angel: the 'one to be born will be called the Son of God' (*Luke* 1:35). To put it differently, 'in Christ all the fullness of the Deity lives in bodily form' (*Col.* 2:9). Or, as Paul puts the mystery to the Roman Christians, we can trace a 'human ancestry of Christ', and at the same time we remember that he 'is God over all' (*Rom.* 9:5).

The Bible consistently refers to 'two whole, perfect and distinct natures' of Jesus Christ. There is the 'Godhead' or deity; and there is the 'manhood' or humanity. Jesus was truly human. Humans are able to die. 'Christ died for sins' (*1 Pet.* 3:18). Yet this really was God who was 'manifest in the flesh'. Again, a real man was 'justified in the Spirit' and 'seen of angels'. A real God was 'preached unto the Gentiles, believed on in the world, received up into glory' (*1 Tim.* 3:16). These two 'were inseparably joined together in one person'. There was no 'conversion'—the divinity was not lost in humanity, or humanity in divinity. There was no 'composition'—the incarnation did not result in some new creature that was neither God nor man. In fact, there was no 'confusion' between the human nature and divine nature at all.

What we must believe is that there is one 'person' who is 'very God, and very man'. He is our 'one Christ', and so we can say with Paul that God's 'Son Jesus Christ our Lord' truly 'was made of the seed of David according to the flesh', and truly was 'declared to be the Son of God with power' (*Rom.* 1:3, 4). He is our Messiah, and so we trust in his salvation and we pray in his name, confessing with all Christians through all ages that 'there is one God and one mediator between God and men, the man Christ Jesus' (*1 Tim.* 2:5).

Historic Text

8.3 The Lord Jesus, in his human nature thus united to the divine, was sanctified and anointed with the Holy Spirit, above measure,[p] having in him all the treasures of wisdom and knowledge;[q] in whom, it pleased the Father, that all fullness should dwell;[r] to the end, that being holy, harmless, undefiled, and full of grace and truth,[s] he might be thoroughly furnished to execute the office of a mediator, and surety.[t] Which office he took not unto himself, but was thereunto called by his Father,[u] who put all power and judgment into his hand, and gave him commandment to execute the same.[w]

Modern Version

8.3 In his human nature, united to the divine nature, the Lord Jesus was set apart and anointed with the Holy Spirit beyond measure, having in him all the treasures of wisdom and knowledge. In him the Father was pleased to have all fullness dwell, so that—being holy, blameless, and undefiled, full of grace and truth—he might be completely equipped to fulfill the office of a mediator and guarantor. He did not take this office to himself but was called to it by his Father, who put all power and judgment into his hand and commanded him to execute it.

Scripture Proofs

8.3 [p] Psa. 45:7; John 3:34. [q] Col. 2:3. [r] Col. 1:19. [s] Heb. 7:26; John 1:14. [t] Acts 10:38; Heb. 12:24; Heb. 7:22. [u] Heb. 5:4,5. [w] John 5:22,27; Matt. 28:18; Acts 2:36.

The Holy Spirit

The previous paragraph explained that the divine Son of God took to himself a human nature. He was fully man and fully God. As this paragraph explains, he was also full of the Holy Spirit. I think it is true for many of us that when we read the Gospels, or meditate on our salvation, we often marvel at the sheer extent of wise perception and profound understanding found in Christ. He is a man like no other man. He is the one who was 'sanctified' (or set apart) from all others.

When we seek to understand our Lord, it can be tempting to think that the answer to his uniqueness lies in one direction only: that the man Jesus was divine. But as we are reminded here, the reason for the uniqueness of our Saviour also lies with the Holy Spirit. Jesus Christ was completely 'sanctified and anointed with the Holy Spirit'. He alone could give the Spirit without measure because he, as John the Baptist once explained, had a measure of the Spirit that was without limit and beyond measuring (*John* 3:34).

This anointing of the Spirit is spoken about directly in the Bible. It can also be detected when we look at the results of the Spirit's work. Christ is and was the great treasure store 'of wisdom and knowledge', as Paul recalls in Colossians (*Col.* 2:3). The psalmist speaks of how he was anointed 'with the oil of gladness above' his fellows (*Psa.* 45:7). This was not the only fruit of the Spirit that we have seen in unique abundance in the life of Christ. Was he—and is he!—not also 'holy, blameless and pure', as the letter to the Hebrews says (7:26); and 'full of grace and truth', as the Gospel of John says (*John* 1:14)?

We hear the Scriptures tell us that Jesus was filled with the Spirit; we see the evidence of this in his life. And, of course, we also need to remember that Jesus Christ had to be full of the Holy Spirit because 'God was pleased to have all his fullness dwell in him' (*Col.* 1:19). The fact that the fullness of divinity dwelt in Christ did not remove the need for the Spirit—it only amplified it.

Surely all of this was and is for a purpose. The reason is that, as the Spirit-filled one, Christ might be thoroughly equipped to take up the highest office of all: to be the mediator and surety—the covenant head of the church. Christ was full of the Spirit so that he would be full of all other good things necessary for effective mediatory intercession, and for effective covenantal representation. This is the Jesus that was needed in his own day, as Peter explained to Cornelius and his household: 'God anointed Jesus of Nazareth with the Holy Spirit and power'. Why did he do this? So that he could go 'around doing good and healing all who were under the power of the devil'. He could do this 'because God was with him' (*Acts* 10:38). He was a mediator then, on earth, as he is now, in heaven.

Christ as 'surety'

The other side of the work of the mediator is that of a 'surety'. We distinguish between the two, but we cannot separate them. A surety is a 'person who undertakes some specific responsibility on behalf of' someone else. The surety is the guarantor, the person 'who makes himself liable for the default or miscarriage of another' (*OED*)—no matter what the cost.

Jesus was the guarantor of the covenant, the covenant discussed in the previous chapter. And he knew what the cost of serving as a guarantor would be, for he knew that we are perpetual covenant breakers. No matter how great the blessing, no matter how sweet the promise, men and women will not and cannot keep covenants, as Adam and Eve showed clearly when they broke the first covenant made in the garden of Eden. What a task this would be! One could not be a mediator unless there was some basis on which to mediate. Christ could be the 'mediator' of a 'new covenant' that speaks 'better things' as Hebrews 12 says, only if he also 'became the guarantor [or surety] of that better covenant' as Hebrews 7 says (*Heb.* 12:24; 7:22). Yet in his grace and mercy Jesus accepted that office. Incredibly, he considered it an honour to do so. No man takes this honour, this glory to himself—he awaits the call of God, as Hebrews 5 explains (*Heb.* 5:4, 5). And that call came. Our Lord was 'called by his Father' to be our mediator, and the Father gave him all that he needed for his task. Of course he gave him the Holy Spirit beyond all measure, for his work was appallingly arduous and his suffering would be great.

However, it would be a mistake to think of the mediator only in his weakness, and not in his strength. Our mediator is one who was given all power (*Matt.* 28:18), and to him is committed all judgment (*John* 5:22, 27). He died, but did not remain dead; he has risen and has ascended to the heavens. As Peter explained to a great guilty crowd almost two-thousand years ago, that 'same Jesus' who once was crucified has been made by God 'both Lord and Christ' (*Acts* 2:36). It is through this risen and ascended mediator that we worship our God.

Historic Text	**Modern Version**
8.4 This office, the Lord Jesus did most willingly undertake;[x] which that he might discharge, he was made under the law,[y] and did perfectly fulfill it,[z] endured most grievous torments immediately in his soul,[a] and most painful sufferings in	**8.4** This office the Lord Jesus most willingly undertook, and in order to discharge its obligations he was born under the law and perfectly fulfilled it. He endured most grievous torments in his soul and most painful sufferings in

his body;[b] was crucified, and died;[c] was buried, and remained under the power of death; yet saw no corruption.[d] On the third day he arose from the dead,[e] with the same body in which he suffered,[f] with which also he ascended into heaven, and there sits at the right hand of his Father,[g] making intercession,[h] and shall return to judge, men, and angels, at the end of the world.[i]

his body; he was crucified, died, and was buried; he remained under the power of death, yet his body did not undergo decay; and he arose from the dead on the third day with the same body in which he had suffered. In this body he ascended into heaven, where he sits at the right hand of his Father, making intercession, and he shall return to judge men and angels at the end of the age.

Scripture Proofs

8.4 [x] Psa. 40:7,8, with Heb. 10:5-11; John 10:18; Phil. 2:8. [y] Gal. 4:4. [z] Matt. 3:15; Matt. 5:17. [a] Matt. 26:37,38; Luke 22:44; Matt. 27:46. [b] Matt., chapters 26,27. [c] Phil. 2:8. [d] Acts 2:23,24,27; Acts 13:37; Rom. 6:9. [e] 1 Cor. 15:3,4. [f] John 20:25,27. [g] Mark 16:19. [h] Rom. 8:34; Heb. 9:24; Heb. 7:25. [i] Rom. 14:9,10; Acts 1:11; Acts 10:42; Matt. 13:40-42; Jude v. 6; 2 Pet. 2:4.

A willing mediator

The opening paragraphs of this chapter on Christ the mediator stress that the Son of God was called to be our high priest; he did not appoint himself to this office, but accepted his task and carried it out in the power of the Spirit. Although he was called to be our mediator, this was an office that our Lord Jesus Christ 'most willingly' undertook. As our Lord himself explained to his disciples, it was in his power to lay down his life, and in his power to take it up again. It was the Father's will—even his commandment—but the Son was also eager to help those who cannot help themselves (*John* 10:17, 18).

It was Christ's loving eagerness that the author of the letter to the Hebrews noted as he reflected on the meaning of Psalm 40. He points out that just after the psalmist dismissed the sufficiency of temple sacrifices and offerings in verse 6, a person suddenly appears in verses 8-9 who says that he is coming, that he would delight to do God's will and obey God's law. Who else could this be but Christ himself? He would serve as the true intermediary, and he would keep God's law (compare *Psa.* 40:6-9 with *Heb.* 10:5-12) and become obedient 'to the point of death, even death on a cross' (*Phil.* 2:8).

So it was that when God sent forth his Son, born of a woman, this Son was born 'under the law' (*Gal.* 4:4). The second person of the Trinity placed himself under all the obligations of the moral law, designed from eternity to reflect his own perfect character. The one who is wisdom itself accepted the tutelage of the ceremonial law. The one who was life itself submitted to the curse and the horror of the sacrificial law, seeing it in the temple, ending it on the cross. Our gracious Saviour perfectly fulfilled God's law, from the time that he stood in the Jordan, with water pouring over his head, to the moment when he fulfilled the Law and the Prophets, and could say for all to hear, 'It is finished!' (See *Matt.* 3:15; 5:17, *John* 19:30). And he did so as our mediator.

Torments of the soul, suffering of the body

As our mediator, Jesus Christ also endured most 'grievous torments', and the Westminster assembly insisted on mentioning that too. This suffering was not simply his anguish as he awaited and then experienced the brutal pain of scourging, humiliation and then crucifixion, as if that were some small thing. No, Jesus endured much more than that; for as he entered the garden of Gethsemane he began to groan under an invisible pressure greater than the fear of death. Christians have long recognized that before his tormentors could begin their dirty work, Jesus had already discovered in a garden the agonizing pangs of the penalty reserved for sinners (*Matt.* 26:37, 38; *Luke* 22:44). John Calvin called this Christ's 'descent into hell', borrowing a phrase in the Apostles' Creed to make his point. It was on the cross that Jesus finally cried out in anguish, 'My God, my God, why have you forsaken me?' (*Matt.* 27:46). But it was in the garden that the hell of eternity entered time, as God punished the sinless Saviour with the punishments that our sins deserved.

This agony in his soul must have been the worst that Jesus endured, but it was not the most obvious. The pain that all could see was the suffering in his body, at the hands of the priests and Jewish leaders; and then before Pilate; and then before Herod; and then before some soldiers. Finally he was crucified before the crowds, like a runaway slave; and hanging naked in shame and pain, he died (*e.g., Matt.* 26-27; *Phil.* 2:8).

So often we recall that Jesus was dying. We need to remember that Jesus was dead. That is why it is worth remembering that Jesus was actually buried, and that he remained under the dreadful dominion of death for a time (*Rom.* 6:9). Even though his body did not remain so long in the grave as to rot away, his living body had become a lifeless corpse (*Acts* 2:23-27; 13:37).

A risen Saviour

Thankfully, our mediator did not remain in the grave. As Paul reminds us in 1 Corinthians 15, it is not only a matter 'of first importance' that 'Christ died for our sins in accordance with the Scriptures', and 'that he was buried'; it is also a matter of first importance that 'he was raised on the third day in accordance with the Scriptures' (*1 Cor.* 15:3, 4). The Father was pleased with his Son's work; all that was necessary for our salvation was accomplished; and so he raised our Saviour from the dead and provided witnesses to testify to this astonishing event (*1 Cor.* 15:5). He also provided a doubting Thomas who wondered if Jesus had actually risen in his own physical body, a reality Jesus insisted on with all his disciples (*e.g., John* 20:25-27).

An ascended Saviour

It was in that 'same body' that Jesus ascended into heaven from a hilltop near Bethany (*Luke* 24:50-53; *1 Pet.* 3:22).[1] Even in heaven Christ remains our embodied mediator, for Jesus did not stop caring for his people on that hill near Bethany; he did not stop working on the day that he ascended. He cleared a pathway to heaven, and in a very real way he continues to prepare us for heaven, just as he prepared heaven for us. He has been busy gathering his church from around the world, giving her gifts and graces, defending her from enemies, and guiding her in truth and holiness. And, as we are reminded in the letter to the Romans, Christ 'makes intercession for us' (*Rom.* 8:34).

This is the promise of God's Word. In spite of our daily failings, in spite of the accusations of our enemies, he is there to quieten our

---

[1] The Westminster assembly cites Mark 16:19, a passage with a weak manuscript testimony.

consciences, to encourage our prayers, and to accept us and our services. He is our advocate and his very appearance in the presence of God (*Heb.* 9:24)—his scarred body in that perfect place—fully pleads our desperate case. He is able to silence our accuser, for in heaven it is a known fact that 'there is now no condemnation for those who are in Christ Jesus' (*Rom.* 8:1).

The return of the king

Christ ever lives to make intercession for us (*Heb.* 7:25), but one day he will 'return to judge men and angels'. That will be the most splendid of all days for God's people, and the most dire of days for all others. A whole chapter of the confession is devoted to this subject. For now, it is enough for us to remember the assuring words of the pair of angels that stood beside the dumbfounded disciples who had just witnessed the ascension: 'This Jesus, who was taken up from you into heaven will come in the same way as you saw him go into heaven' (*Acts* 1:11). This second coming will in turn be followed by a judgment of all human beings and all angels 'at the end of the world' (*Matt.* 13:40; *Acts* 10:42). The Bible tells us that many rebellious angels are already 'reserved in everlasting chains' waiting in darkness for the assessment of that great day (*2 Pet.* 2:4; *Jude* 6). The same is true for rebellious people too.

The main point is that 'we will all stand before the judgment seat of God' (*Rom.* 14:10). This should teach us not to busy ourselves judging one another. The Lord will do this for us. This should also teach us to prepare ourselves for that day—and the only way to do so is to consider Jesus Christ, the Son of God who became the Son of man, and willingly undertook the office of mediator.

Historic Text	**Modern Version**
8.5 The Lord Jesus, by his perfect obedience, and sacrifice of himself, which he, through the eternal Spirit, once offered up unto God, has fully satisfied the justice of his Father;^k and purchased, not	**8.5** The Lord Jesus, by his perfect obedience and sacrifice of himself—which he through the eternal Spirit once offered up to God—has fully satisfied the justice of his Father. He purchased not

only reconciliation, but an everlasting inheritance in the kingdom of heaven, for all those whom the Father has given unto him.[l]

only reconciliation but also an everlasting inheritance in the kingdom of heaven for all those whom the Father has given to him.

Scripture Proofs

8.5 [k] Rom. 5:19; Heb. 9:14,16; Heb. 10:14; Eph. 5:2; Rom. 3:25,26. [l] Dan. 9:24,26; Col. 1:19,20; Eph. 1:11,14; John 17:2; Heb. 9:12,15.

Fully satisfied justice

The only mediator between God and man is the Lord Jesus Christ. He is fully God and fully man, and full of the Holy Spirit. Knowing who he is, and what he has done, this paragraph explains what he purchased by his obedience and sacrifice.

Priests had long been required to give offerings to God on account of the sins of God's people, and to atone for their *own* imperfect obedience. But our mediator did not give an offering for that dual reason. He was a high priest like no other, for he offered 'perfect obedience' to God. He obeyed the whole of God's law for the whole of his life. Nothing that he should have done was left undone. And nothing that he should not have done was done. As the Son of man he obeyed every command that the law required of man. As the Son of God, he honoured his Father in coming to this world to save God's people. Surely it is the whole of this obedience—both Christ's general obedience to the whole law and Christ's special obedience in his role as mediator—that is in view in Paul's letter to the Romans. There he speaks of 'the obedience of one man', Jesus Christ, through which many are 'made righteous' (*Rom.* 5:19). The same may be in view here.

So, too, we must conclude that when our Lord Jesus Christ offered a sacrifice, he must have been doing it for others—for those who are sinners. That is in fact what the letter to the Hebrews says: Christ's conscience was clear, and so he made an offering to 'purge' our 'consciences from dead works' (*Heb.* 9:14). Yes, Christ was tempted like all other people—in fact above and beyond any allurement or provocation that we may ever face. But he did not fall to temptation, both because of who he was and because he had the Spirit above all measure. As Hebrews 9 explains, it was 'through the eternal Spirit' that Christ 'offered himself without spot to God'. And surely that is the most amazing fact of all: that the offering that Jesus Christ gave was his own self. That is an offering like no other—an offering of infinite merit and infinite worth. As Hebrews 9 tells us again, this was 'necessary' for our salvation (*Heb.* 9:14, 16).

What love! And what an irony! One man finally came into the world to obey the Father. Here was the first man who did not need to die, and yet the very spotlessness and perfection of our Lord was the thing that qualified him to die on our behalf. But this is a divine irony, according to the divine plan. No wonder that the Scriptures never tire of telling this old, old story. We find it in the Old Testament, in every sacrifice, in every feast, in every day of atonement. We find it in the New Testament, in each of the Gospels and throughout the epistles. This is what Paul told the Ephesians when he reminded them: 'Christ loved us and gave himself up *for us* as a fragrant offering and sacrifice to God' (*Eph.* 5:2). This is what the writer to Hebrews says: 'by one sacrifice he has made perfect forever those who are being made holy' (*Heb.* 10:14). The sacrifice of Jesus was perfect: it needed to be offered up only once, and it is in this sacrificed Jesus that we find our own perfection and righteousness.

Jesus gave himself as a sacrifice, but we need to remember that it is just as true to say that it was God who presented Jesus 'as a sacrifice of atonement'. Jesus was to propitiate the wrath of God—he was to appease the wrath of God by a sacrifice (*Rom.* 3:25); but God wanted to be appeased, so he gave his Son. And that is what he did. He alone *could* 'fully satisfy the justice of his Father', and he alone *did*; the penalty was paid. Christians rejoice in his penal substitution.

It will take an eternity to fully grasp the rich rewards of this one offering of obedience and sacrifice. But it takes only a moment to realize that through Christ's work we are the beneficiaries of every good gift (*James* 1:17). In paying the price of God's justice, Christ 'purchased, not only reconciliation, but an everlasting inheritance in the kingdom of heaven' (*cf. Eph.* 1:11-14).

We are those who have received a good gift. For the Scriptures repeatedly tell us that all of this was done for us. Daniel speaks of a Messiah that would come, and would be cut off, left with nothing (*Dan.* 9:26).

The letter to the Colossians says that through his blood he was reconciling us to God (*Col.* 1:19, 20), and the letter to the Hebrews says the same (*Heb.* 9:12-15). And so it is that we can sing,

> I belong to Jesus, he has died for me;
> I am his and he is mine, through eternity.

Christians praise God because the Scriptures repeatedly tell us that Christ gave himself for us. But we also praise him because the Father gave us to Christ. It is this fact that Jesus mentions in his prayer to the Father recorded in John's Gospel (17:1, 2). It is the gift from the Father, the gift of all his people, that Christ reckons as one part of his great glory.

And so we can also sing

> I belong to Jesus, I am not my own.
> All I have and all I am, shall be his alone.

Historic Text	*Modern Version*
8.6 Although the work of redemption was not actually wrought by Christ till after his incarnation, yet the virtue, efficacy, and benefits thereof were communicated unto the elect in all ages successively from the beginning of the world, in, and by those promises, types, and sacrifices, wherein he was revealed, and signified to be the seed of the woman which should bruise the serpent's head; and the Lamb slain from the beginning of the world: being yesterday, and today the same, and forever.ᵐ	**8.6** Although the work of redemption was not actually accomplished by Christ until after his incarnation, yet the power, efficacy, and benefits of it were applied to the elect in all ages successively from the beginning of the world, in and by those promises, types, and sacrifices by which Christ was revealed and signified to be the seed of the woman who would bruise the serpent's head, and to be the Lamb slain from the beginning of the world. He is the same yesterday, today, and forever.

Scripture Proofs

8.6 ᵐ Gal. 4:4,5; Gen. 3:15; Rev. 13:8; Heb. 13:8.

Redemption applied or 'communicated'

Thus far chapter 8 has offered a glimpse of the person of our mediator and his work as it applies to Christians living after the death and resurrection of Christ. But what are we to think about those who died before the saving actions of Christ were complete? After all, 'the work of redemption was not actually wrought by Christ till after his incarnation'. Was there salvation for those who died before Christ came? And if so, how did that salvation come to them?

In this section we are told that Old Testament believers did find salvation. Every spiritual mercy and blessing was available long before the incarnation. Nothing less than the spiritual 'virtue, efficacy, and benefits' of the rich treasures of redemption were 'communicated' or given to God's 'elect in all ages', right 'from the beginning of the world'. Sometimes we remind others that it is never too late to find salvation; this paragraph reminds us that there was also no time in history when it was too early.

Were Old Testament saints saved? The answer to this question is most clearly found in the New Testament. If there is 'only one mediator between God and man' (*1 Tim.* 2:5), then the answer in some way has to be obvious to every reader of the Bible: God's chosen people were saved. And their salvation was brought about by the Lord Jesus Christ. He is the one whom 'God sent forth' in 'the fullness of time' (*Gal.* 4:4, 5). At just the right moment, he was 'made of a woman', and 'made under the law'. He came to redeem all those who were under the condemnation of the law, through all time. It is not only we who can look back and see that this coming of Christ was revealed from the beginning. Old Testament saints could look ahead and see that it is Christ who was preached in all the promises of the Old Testament; he is the one pictured in its types; every one of those bloody offerings pointed to his bloody sacrifice for sin. Throughout the Old Testament it is clear that people could not save themselves. Romans 4 tells us that Abraham was righteous, but he was righteous by faith in someone else. It was not the marvel of Abraham's own amazing life that saved him. He put his faith in the truly righteous one to come. Did not Jesus say that Abraham rejoiced to see his day (*John* 8:56)?

Abraham, those before him, and those after him, needed a saviour and there is only one saviour who is revealed in Holy Scripture: the Lord Jesus Christ. He alone is signified or foreshadowed as the 'seed of the woman' promised in Genesis 3:15. He is the one who would 'bruise the serpent's head' and ultimately undo what sin had done. This salvation was so sure, and is so sure, that translators of Scripture were comfortable speaking as though our redemption was finished before it started, as though Christ had died at the very moment when God had chosen a people for his Son. Considering the permanent efficacy of Christ's redemptive work from the earliest times, they thought that one passage of Scripture spoke of a 'Lamb slain from the foundation of the world' (*Rev.* 13:8). The passage, however, is better rendered as a warning to 'everyone whose name has not been written before the foundation of the world in the book of life of the Lamb that was slain'.

This section in the confession is useful for helping us understand the salvation of Old Testament saints. At the same time, there is much here that we do not understand. How did the Holy Spirit apply a redemption that was not yet accomplished to these Old Testament sinners? How did they receive all the fruits of union with Christ before Jesus was even born? How is it, as Paul says, that 'this grace was given us in Christ before the beginning of time'? (*2 Tim.* 1:9). These things I do not understand, but I know they are true, for as one age succeeds another, and as saints come and go, there is one who never changes, one in whom people of all ages can always put their trust: 'Jesus Christ the same yesterday, and today, and for ever' (*Heb.* 13:8).

Historic Text	*Modern Version*
8.7 Christ, in the work of mediation, acts according to both natures, by each nature doing that which is proper to itself:ⁿ yet, by reason of the unity of the person, that which is proper to one nature, is sometimes in Scripture attributed to the person denominated by the other nature.°	**8.7** In the work of mediation, Christ acts according to both natures. Each nature does what is proper to itself; yet, by reason of the unity of his person, that which is proper to one nature is in Scripture sometimes attributed to the person designated by the other nature.

Scripture Proofs
  8.7 ⁿ Heb. 9:14; 1 Pet. 3:18. ° Acts 20:28; John 3:13; 1 John 3:16.

One person, two natures

This seventh paragraph of chapter 8 harkens back to an earlier section. You may recall that the second paragraph explained that God the Son took on a human nature, and by so doing became a person with two natures, the divine and the human. The third paragraph went on to tell us how Christ the mediator was enabled to fulfil his task because he was filled with the Spirit. Subsequent sections explained what the work of the mediator was. And then we come to this seventh paragraph which adds more depth to the discussion of the person and natures of Christ.

Here, in the first place, we are reminded again that it was Christ who acted 'in the work of mediation'—Christ who was both God and man. It is important to understand, and the confession states this here, that it is not the human nature of Christ that saves us. Nor is it the divine nature of Christ that saves us—no, it is Christ himself 'acting according to both natures' who is our Saviour and Deliverer.

It is a person who saves us

The confession aims to stress this point when it tells us that each nature of Christ was 'doing that which is proper to itself'. In one sense, this is inevitably an imprecise manner of speaking, for natures do not do anything apart from the person. As Hebrews 9:14 tells us, it was *Christ's* blood that purges us from a guilty conscience; or as 1 Peter 3:18 tells us, it was *Christ* who suffered. A great number of verses say the same, and they refer to the work of Christ who is, of course, a whole person.

And yet while we must always keep the person of Christ in view, the two natures of Christ must never be forgotten: Hebrews 9 also tells us that it was blood that was needed to save us, and 1 Peter 3 reminds us that suffering was required for our salvation. This blood and suffering were Christ's, but they were Christ's because the eternal Son of God became an embodied man with a human nature.[1]

---

[1] The assembly's own intention behind the Hebrews and 1 Peter citations was probably to argue that references to the Spirit in these two passages refer to Christ's divine

It is important to remember that Christ is for evermore one person with two natures and that he remains, as a whole person, our mediator. We need, in other words, to remember the 'unity of the person' of Christ. I say we need to remember this, but who can fully understand it? This is as great a mystery as the doctrine of the Trinity. There is no one like Christ, and no true analogy to the incarnation.

The communication of attributes

This will not be easy to understand, but one thing about which we need to be clear is how the two natures of Christ relate to his person. What is important to see is that what is true of either nature of Christ is also true of the person of Christ. This is usually called the communication of attributes (or the *communicatio idiomatum*). That is, what can be said of the humanity of Christ can be said of his person; what can be said of the divinity of Christ can be said of his person.

However, we must not think that what can be said of one nature is true of the other nature. For example, Christ's human nature did not exist from all eternity. And the divine nature of Christ could never die. The teaching of the communication of attributes of Christ's natures to his person is assumed when the divines say that what 'is proper to one nature' is 'attributed to the person'.

nature. Each passage sets up a dichotomy: Hebrews 9:14, the blood of Christ and eternal Spirit, and 1 Peter 3:18, body and Spirit. The tradition of interpreting these passages is varied and the differences can be illustrated with two authors. In his commentary on 1 Peter Calvin says both that 'the power of the Spirit' (meaning the Holy Spirit) and that 'divine power' (a less clear reference) is in view in 1 Peter 3:18. John Calvin, *The Epistle of Paul the Apostle to the Hebrews and the First and Second Epistles of St Peter*, trans. W. B. Johnston, eds. D. W. Torrance and T. F. Torrance (Grand Rapids, 1963), p. 292. In his commentary on Hebrews Calvin asserts that the Holy Spirit is in view in Hebrews 9:14 (*ibid.*, 121). Calvin's *Institutes* discusses only Christ's weakness in relation to 1 Peter 3:18. John Calvin, *Institutes of the Christian Religion* (Philadelphia, 1960), II.xiii.2. The three references to Hebrews 9:14 in his *Institutes* do consider Christology proper (II.xvi.6; III.xvi.2; and IV.xiv.21). Assembly member William Gouge, on the other hand, holds that 'eternal Spirit' in Hebrews 9:14 refers to Christ's divine nature. See Gouge, *Hebrewes*, Part 2, pp. 356-8. This same interpretation is found in *Annotations upon All the Books of the Old and New Testament* (London, 1651), *sub loc.* Contrary to Gouge and the assembly, these biblical texts more likely refer to the Holy Spirit and thus better support the contention of WCF 8.3 than the point of WCF 8.7.

Biblical language

Nonetheless the confession is saying more than this in the second half of this paragraph, for it states that 'that which is proper to one nature is sometimes in Scripture attributed to the person denominated by the other nature'. This too is hard to understand. Here the confession is actually interested in teaching us how to understand biblical language about Christ. It is attempting to keep us from oversimplifying biblical language.

Sometimes the humanity of Christ is expressed using divine categories and sometimes the divinity is expressed in human categories. There is an occasional cross-fertilization of language, even if there must not be confusion between the two natures of Christ. To state it differently, something may be true only of one nature; and yet in Scripture it may be attributed not only to the person of Christ (which we should expect), but it may also be attributed to Christ by reference to his other nature. Something that is only true of Christ's human nature (say, dying on the cross) may in Scripture be attributed to Christ by reference to his divine nature.

For example, in Acts 20:28, the Ephesian elders were warned to take care of 'the church of God, which he hath purchased with his own blood' (*cf. 1 John* 3:16).[1] We know that God does not have blood; it is the person of Jesus Christ in view, including his humanity. Scripture even refers to God dying, in 1 John 3:16.

The opposite example is found in John 3:13, where we are told of the Son of man who came down from heaven. Here the reference is really to the Son of God, who became the Son of man—the new vicegerent in the first Adam's place. We know that the humanity of Christ was not in heaven before the incarnation and ascension of our Lord. And yet here is a reference to the humanity of Christ, linked to a descent from heaven, that brings to mind his divinity.

Is this difficult to understand? Yes it is. Some things in Scripture are hard to fathom. On another level, we all know what this means: the second person of the Trinity came to save us. He came for his church, 'the church of God, which he hath purchased with his own blood'. This

---

[1] Some modern translations render this 'with the blood of his Own [Son]'.

is our Saviour. Let us worship him, the one who gave his life for us, while remembering his resurrection, ascension, and eternal kingship.

Historic Text

8.8 To all those for whom Christ has purchased redemption, he does certainly, and effectually apply, and communicate the same,[p] making intercession for them,[q] and revealing unto them, in, and by the Word, the mysteries of salvation,[r] effectually persuading them by his Spirit, to believe, and obey, and governing their hearts by his Word and Spirit,[s] overcoming all their enemies by his almighty power and wisdom, in such manner, and ways, as are most consonant to his wonderful and unsearchable dispensation.[t]

Modern Version

8.8 To all those for whom Christ purchased redemption, he certainly and effectually applies and communicates it. He makes intercession for them and reveals to them, in and by the Word, the mysteries of salvation. He effectually persuades them by his Spirit to believe and obey, and governs their hearts by his Word and Spirit. He overcomes all their enemies by his almighty power and wisdom in such a manner, and by such ways, as are most agreeable to his wonderful and unsearchable administration.

Scripture Proofs

8.8 [p] John 6:37,39. John 10:15,16. [q] 1 John 2:1,2; Rom. 8:34. [r] John 15:13,15; Eph. 1:7-9; John 17:6. [s] John 14:16; Heb. 12:2; 2 Cor. 4:13; Rom. 8:9,14; Rom. 15:18,19; John 17:17. [t] Psa. 110:1; 1 Cor. 15:25,26; Mal. 4:2,3; Col. 2:15.

A certain and effective application

This final paragraph, 'Of Christ the Mediator', serves as a bridge to take us from Christ's accomplishment of our redemption in past history to his application of that redemption in our present lives. For it was not for nothing that Christ died. No, he always had in view 'all those' who were his. Before he purchased redemption, he had already chosen each person that would receive the gift he would buy at the price of his own life.

Since this was Christ's purpose from the beginning, we can be sure of how it will end: he will certainly apply and communicate that redemption. This is all according to God's plan. He does not simply hope that what he has done will be applied to his people. No, he makes sure that his work is effectively communicated to each child of God. Nothing less than this could have been in view when our Lord spoke to that vast gathering on the edge of the Sea of Galilee. There Jesus had promised his hearers, 'whoever comes to me, I will never drive away' (*John* 6:37). These are some of the sweetest words sinners can hear. Whoever you are, if you turn to the Saviour you will find him already waiting to accept you.

But just as important to remember is the first half of the same verse, where Jesus confidently states the corresponding truth, 'All that the Father gives me *will* come to me' (*John* 6:37; *cf.* 6:39). He can say this because he certainly and effectually applies his salvation. These parallel truths taught to one crowd in John 6 are taught to another in John 10. There our Lord reminds us that he did not lay down his life for the good of the world in some abstract sense. No, he laid down his life for his sheep, and he knows that they will hear this good news and respond to the call of the Good Shepherd because he will ensure that 'they will listen' to his voice (*John* 10:15, 16). The work that Christ has begun he will surely complete.

Christ's interceding and revealing

Paul tells us in Romans 8 that sinners such as we can be sure to find salvation and not condemnation because Christ intercedes for us (*Rom.* 8:34). John tells us that Jesus Christ advocates our cause in heaven just as he propitiated for our sins on earth (*1 John* 2:1, 2). Here and elsewhere we see Christ revealing to us, 'in and by the Word, the mysteries of salvation'.

The very fact of revelation is a sign of Christ's love toward us, and we are told this often in Scripture. For example, Jesus told his disciples just that in John 15. On the one hand, we know that he is our friend because he laid down his life for us; on the other hand, we also know that he is our friend because he makes known to us what he has learned from the Father (*John* 15:13, 15).

Ephesians 2 commends the same truth to us in a different way. God lavished his love on us by showing us the riches of his grace. He also showed us his 'good pleasure' by making 'known to us the mystery of his will' in Christ (*Eph.* 1:7-9). And in his prayer to his Father, our Lord

Jesus rejoiced that he had revealed the Father 'to those whom you gave me out of the world'. 'They were yours,' Jesus said. 'You gave them to me and they have obeyed your word' (*John* 17:6). God is so good. He gave us his Son; in his Son he gives us all things. In so many ways we remain unworthy of his gifts and unable to see the wonder of them. What is his response? He continues to intercede for us, and reveal himself to us.

The effectual work of Christ's Spirit

As we seek to understand the work that Christ has authored, and is now perfecting (*Heb.* 12:2), we need to understand that Christ is working in us by his Holy Spirit. The Spirit that filled Christ is the same Spirit that fills us. Christ is effective in all that he does as he works in us by his Spirit. The work of the Spirit is all encompassing, for it is he who helps us in the Christian faith and life. He is the Spirit of our faith (*2 Cor.* 4:13) and he persuades us to 'believe'. He is the Spirit who controls and leads us (*Rom.* 8:9, 14), and he persuades us to 'obey'.

Christ uses the power of his Holy Spirit to govern our hearts (*Rom.* 15:18-19), and the Holy Spirit makes us holy by his Word, the Bible. It is in the Bible that the way of salvation and sanctification is laid out for us. This is Jesus' prayer to his Father for all of his people, that they would be 'sanctified by the truth'. And of course, 'God's word is truth' (*John* 17:17).

Given how indispensable the Spirit is to all that we are and all that we hope to be, how good it is that our Lord promised that this Spirit would abide with us forever (*John* 14:16), teach us all we need to know, and remind all Christ's disciples what he has taught them in one way or another (*John* 14:26).

Admittedly, we sometimes do not sense the abiding of the Spirit. More often than not it is because Christians want to 'feel' or 'know' the Spirit apart from his Word to us. Let us make it our ambition to be Spirit-filled Christians through a life immersed in the Scriptures.

Overcoming all

By this same Word and Spirit Christ not only overcomes all of our sins and keeps us in step with the Spirit, but he also overcomes our 'enemies by his almighty power and wisdom'. Although God's enemies fight and squirm, he can take one and all and use them as his footstool (*Psa.* 110:1). All his enemies, from first to last, will be put under his feet (*1 Cor.* 15:25, 26). One day, as the Bible tells us, God will even trample them underfoot (*Mal.* 4:2, 3).

In a very real way, this work was already begun while Christ was on earth; for 'having disarmed the powers and authorities, he made a public spectacle of them, triumphing over them by the cross' (*Col.* 2:15). We, of course, could never express such wrath or exercise such judgment in an appropriate way—at least not while we are in this world. That is why we leave judgment to God: because he does all things well. Our Lord Jesus Christ overcomes all his enemies, all our sin, and even death itself as he does all things—in a manner that is in perfect harmony with his wonderful arrangement of the world, and in a way that exposes the unsearchable greatness of our mediator.

SALVATION

CHAPTER 9:

OF FREE WILL

Historic Text

9.1 God has endued the will of man with that natural liberty, that it is neither forced, nor by any absolute necessity of nature determined to good or evil.[a]

Modern Version

9.1 God has endowed the will of man with such natural liberty that it is neither forced nor—by any absolute necessity of nature— determined to good or evil.

Scripture Proofs
9.1 [a] Matt. 17:12; James 1:14; Deut. 30:19.

A natural liberty, unforced

The previous chapter reflects on the person and work of Christ our mediator, and concludes that Christ's work will certainly and effectively be applied to believers. The absolute certainty of Christ's work as saviour and judge raises questions about the relative freedom of our wills. Chapter 9 addresses that subject.

The opening sentence frames the entire discussion of the will as it makes two points. In the first place, God has endowed or supplied 'the will of man with [a] natural liberty', a liberty that is not 'forced', but free. Since ancient times there have been philosophers and religions that have denied any true liberty of the will. Here we are told the contrary: we do have freedom to make decisions.

In telling us this, we are not being told anything new. For is this not what Jesus said long ago about those who persecuted John the Baptist? They did to him 'whatever they wished' and they would do so again when it was time for Jesus himself to undergo suffering (*Matt.* 17:12).

This corresponds also with our own experience. We are conscious that we have choices and make choices. I eat a ham and cheese sandwich, and avoid the tuna. It is a free choice. Negatively, we know there is such a thing as coercion, when decisions are made under duress—in which case I do eat the tuna.

A natural liberty, without natural determination

In the moral realm (from which we can provisionally exclude the eating of tuna sandwiches!) we know that we are responsible for our actions. All of Scripture teaches us that we will answer for what we do and say. And that brings us to the second point of this opening section: there is no 'absolute necessity of nature' that determines whether we shall choose 'good or evil'.

That is to say, there is no action or decision of ours that can be reduced to some natural law, some kind of inevitable system of causation, some force of the universe, some biological inheritance from our parents. Thus, to consider one sort of influence, if a boy always wills very bad things, it cannot all be blamed on the father; if a woman grows up to will the best things, her mother cannot claim all the credit. We are not determined by these factors.

At the same time, we need to be clear that the will does have powerful influences acting upon it, such as those just mentioned. Relevant are the desires of the heart, levels of spiritual and intellectual understanding and, in short, the whole state of the person before God. In listing these things we are not intending to minimize the wholeness of a human being by dividing that being into all different components, like parts of a machine. What we are trying to confess is that we are complex individuals, and that we cannot speak of the will without speaking in the same sense of other dimensions of who we are as people. Decisions are involved processes (as we are sometimes painfully aware) and are often shaped and prompted by our 'whole intellectual and emotional state at the time'.[1] Decisions are complex, but we must not forget that the will does still have the power of self-decision. God really has 'endued the will of man with that natural liberty, that it is neither forced, nor by any absolute necessity of nature determined to good or evil'.

[1] A. A. Hodge, *The Confession of Faith* (1869; London, 1961), p. 160.

Sometimes for convenience we talk about the will almost like it has a force or power of its own. Of course, the will is not a person. When we consider the human will, we are really considering the whole person acting: our decision-making, our choices, our ability to make decisions and choices. When we are speaking about the will we are speaking about an aspect of our existence, and not about an abstraction.

The will in any state

What is more, it is also important to recognize that this first paragraph of chapter 9 is not considering human beings only as they were created, or as they are fallen, or as they are redeemed, or as they will be one day in heaven or hell. It is saying something that is true of the will through every stage of history and at any point in our lives in time or eternity.

As we shall see in subsequent sections, it is true that our wills may be in bondage to sin and Satan. There is even a sense in which we may be enticed to sin because we are dragged away by our own evil desires, as James tells us (*James* 1:14). And yet we sin because these are our desires. We freely will to sin.

Furthermore, it is also true that God can change our wills irresistibly, by his grace, making us long for the salvation we once despised. And yet we turn to him because we have chosen to do so. Moses really could call the often-wandering Israelites to 'choose life'. He could 'set before' them 'life and death, blessing and cursing' (*Deut.* 30:19). We freely will to love God.

Far be it from me to minimize the effects of the fall or the power of God. But we need to see that neither a fall into the fullness of sin nor salvation by sovereign grace destroys the will or obliterates its liberty. And so it is that we will go on to see that sin takes away our ability to do good and our desire to do good. Only grace can set the will free to do good and to want good. And yet we know, and the Bible assumes, that we have a natural liberty, that our wills are free in a genuine sense, although not in an unqualified sense. That is what this confession of faith is stating in its opening declaration on the will.

A difficult doctrine

It has always been difficult to state this doctrine correctly. It is at once very simple and very demanding. When a committee of the Westminster assembly first tried to put this sentence into words, it had to be sent back to draft it again.[1] One member of the assembly, later writing on the subject, was surely not the first to ask his hearers to 'consider that the grace of God is necessary to guide us in this point'. He went on to say that Augustine of Hippo also acknowledged this difficulty: 'when grace is defended, we are thought to destroy free-will, and when a free-will is acknowledged (though in some sense only) we are thought to deny free-grace'.[2] This is why Christians need to pray for God's assistance, asking him to help us understand who we are, and to rejoice in the grace of Christ and the irresistible work of his Holy Spirit.

Historic Text	Modern Version
9.2 Man, in his state of innocency, had freedom, and power, to will, and to do that which was good, and well pleasing to God;[b] but yet, mutably, so that he might fall from it.[c]	**9.2** Man, in his state of innocence, had freedom and ability to will and to do what was good and well pleasing to God, and yet not unalterably, so that he might fall from it.
9.3 Man by his fall into a state of sin, has wholly lost all ability of will to any spiritual good accompanying salvation:[d] so as, a natural man, being altogether averse from that good,[e] and dead in sin,[f] is not able, by his own strength, to convert himself, or to prepare himself thereunto.[g]	**9.3** Man, by his fall into a state of sin, has completely lost all ability to choose any spiritual good that accompanies salvation. Therefore, an unregenerate man, because he is opposed to that good and is dead in sin, is unable by his own strength to convert himself or to prepare himself to be converted.

[1] Van Dixhoorn, ed., *The Minutes and Papers of the Westminster Assembly*, vol. 4, pp. 180-1, Session 666.

[2] Burgess, *A Treatise of Original Sin*, p. 311.

Scripture Proofs

    9.2 ^b Eccles. 7:29; Gen 1:26. ^c Gen. 2:16,17; Gen 3:6.

    9.3 ^d Rom. 5:6; Rom. 8:7; John 15:5. ^e Rom. 3:10,12. ^f Eph. 2:1,5; Col. 2:13.
^g John 6:44,65; Eph. 2:2-5; 1 Cor. 2:14; Titus 3:3-5.

Innocence

The opening paragraph of chapter 9 discussed the freedom of the will. There we are told that the will of human beings is naturally free, and that this freedom is not in any way compromised by the worst or by the best things, not even by the fall of man and sin, nor by sovereign and irresistible grace and salvation. This has always been true of humanity in some sense, and before sin entered the world it was true in the fullest sense. The following four paragraphs in this confession (9.2-9.5) look at the will of man through four different stages of redemptive history.

Paragraph 2 considers Adam and Eve as they were created. In the state of innocence, we are told, people had the 'freedom and power to will and to do that which was good and well-pleasing to God'.

It is important to see that this discussion of the human will is linked to human ability. Before sin entered the world, people were not only left with the freedom to choose good, but were also able to choose that good. The writer of Ecclesiastes was surely right when he noted, 'God made man upright' (*Eccles.* 7:29). Men and women needed to be upright so they could choose to exercise a wise and God-pleasing dominion over creation, the very task they were created to do (*Gen.* 1:26).

Free and able as Adam and Eve were to do good, they were nonetheless also free and able to do evil. The state that they were in was changeable; they were perfect, but they could fall from that perfection. God informed them of their mutability. He warned our first parents not to eat of the tree of the knowledge of good and evil, and he told them that to choose disobedience would be to choose death (*Gen.* 2:16, 17).

Everyone who has read the Bible knows what happened. Adam and Eve were given the freedom and ability to please God, but they filled their eyes with images of forbidden fruit and their ears with the counsel of the serpent. The time came when they chose to do evil. They willed what they should never have even thought (*Gen.* 3:6). They fell, and all the world groaned with them.

The fall

And yet even after the fall, at least in some sense, the wills of Adam and Eve remained free. They freely chose to run and hide from God. And when their Maker called them to stand before him, they freely blamed one another and willingly evaded responsibility for their sin. Without restraint they chose their own way, but look at the way they chose. Was it a path that led to repentance? Contrition? Pleas for mercy? Falling before God and begging his forgiveness? Nothing appears to have been further from their minds. After reading Genesis 3 and 4, and on through the whole of the Bible, what could be a more obvious conclusion than the one we find in the opening lines of paragraph 3 of this chapter: 'Man, by his fall into a state of sin', had 'wholly lost all ability of will to [do] any spiritual good accompanying salvation'.

It was not that they could only sin. After all, Adam and Eve argued with one another, but they did not go on to kill one another. And it was not that they could do no good—they did speak some truth when they answered God's questions. But all who read the Scriptures can see that they were no longer able to do anything good, sensible or wise for their salvation. They were free to do good, but they had lost the ability to help themselves spiritually. They were 'without strength'—the words Paul uses to describe all those who are ungodly (*Rom.* 5:6). They were embattled against their Creator, and their sinful minds were 'hostile to God'. They did 'not submit to God's law' nor could they do so (*Rom.* 8:7). Their wills might have been free, but as God looked upon the man and the woman he had made, nothing could be plainer than the fact that without him they were helpless (*John* 15:5).

Fallen man

How horrible this picture is, but it is nothing other than the teaching of Scripture. It used to be natural for Adam and his wife to please God. It would now be natural for all men and women to be altogether averse from doing good. Paul's words to that effect in Romans 3 ring this fact out slowly, solemnly, relentlessly: 'There is no one righteous'. 'No not one'. 'There is no one who seeks God'. 'They are all gone out of the way'. 'All have turned away'. 'They have together become worthless'. 'There is no one who does good'. 'Not even one' (*Rom.* 3:10-12). These awful lines, one after another, toll out distinctly like a church bell at a funeral.

Of course, it was a funeral, the funeral of the world. All mankind was now dead in sin, as Paul writes again and then again in his letters to the Ephesians and the Colossians (*Eph.* 2:1, 5; *Col.* 2:13). This includes us. Outside of Christ we are dead too. Who is able to convert or change himself into something worthy of salvation? Who is able to prepare herself to receive God's grace? Christ himself twice said, 'no one can come to me unless the Father has enabled him' (*John* 6:44, 65).

As Paul told the Corinthians, 'the man without the Spirit does not accept the things that come from the Spirit of God, for they are foolishness to him, and he cannot understand them, because they are spiritually discerned' (*1 Cor.* 2:14). And so it is that we are 'enslaved by all kinds of passions and pleasures', and we stand in desperate need of the 'kindness and love of God our Saviour'. Our only hope is 'his mercy'; we need his salvation; 'the washing of regeneration, and renewing of the Holy Ghost' (*Titus* 3:3-5).

How horrible it is that we use our freedom to do evil! How desperately sad it is to lack the ability to do what is necessary for our own salvation! How tragic it is, as we are reminded in Paul's letter to the Ephesians, that we tend to walk in the ways of the world and gratify our cravings! But thanks be to God, as Paul goes on to say, that 'because of his great love for us, God, who is rich in mercy, made us alive with Christ even when we were dead in transgressions—it is by grace you have been saved' (*Eph.* 2:2-5).

Historic Text	*Modern Version*
9.4 When God converts a sinner, and translates him into the state of grace, he frees him from his natural bondage under sin;[h] and, by his grace alone, enables him freely to will, and to do that which is spiritually good;[i] yet so, as that by reason of his remaining corruption,	**9.4** When God converts a sinner and brings him into the state of grace, he frees him from his natural bondage to sin, and by his grace alone he enables him freely to will and to do what is spiritually good. Yet, because of his remaining corruption, he does not perfectly

he does not, perfectly, nor only, will that which is good, but does also will that which is evil.[k]

nor only will what is good, but also wills what is evil.

9.5 The will of man is made, perfectly, and immutably free to good alone, in the state of glory only.[l]

9.5 The will of man is made perfectly and unchangeably free to do good alone, only in the state of glory.

Scripture Proofs

   9.4 [h] Col. 1:13; John 8:34,36. [i] Phil. 2:13; Rom. 6:18,22. [k] Gal. 5:17; Rom. 7:15,18,19,21,23.

   9.5 [l] Eph. 4:13; Heb. 12:23; 1 John 3:2; Jude v. 24.

Free to will what is good

Previous sections in chapter 9 discuss freedoms native to all people. Both before the fall and after the fall, we are not forced to act in ways that are fundamentally contrary to our character. But tragically, our characters are twisted by the fall and so we willingly walk in a way that leads to death. That is what we do and what we shall always keep on doing unless God 'converts a sinner, and translates him into the state of grace'. And thank the Lord, that is just what he does. He delivers us from the power and dominion of darkness, and transfers us into the kingdom of the Son that he loves (*Col.* 1:13). And as he rescues us from our natural slavery to sin we find that everything in our world changes. When the Son of God sets us free, we are free indeed (*John* 8:34, 36)!

   As God delivers us by his grace alone, he changes our characters. We learn that he is working in us to will and to work for his good pleasure, and we find ourselves increasingly happy to have this new will and to do this new work (*Phil.* 2:13). We are freed by God's grace alone, and then his Scriptures call us to 'become slaves of righteousness'. As Paul tells the Roman Christians of his day, 'you have been set free from sin and have become slaves of God' (*Rom.* 6:18, 22). As new creatures, we have new inclinations and abilities, and we can act according to them: we are able to freely will and do that which is spiritually good.

Free to will what is evil

But is that what always happens? Do we joyfully serve our Father all our days? Do we easily submit to his will and the hand of his providence? No. Caught between heaven and earth, God and the devil, Christians remain a conflicted people. As Galatians 5 and Romans 7 candidly discuss, the effects of corruption remain with us. 'The desires of the flesh are against the Spirit, and the desires of the Spirit are against the flesh, for these are opposed to each other, to keep you from doing the things you want to do' (*Gal.* 5:17). We do not perfectly or solely desire 'that which is good'. The devil still hisses; the world still calls; at times we feel like there is no strength left in us to escape or resist. Frankly, as Paul himself admits, we sometimes do not even understand our own actions. We do not follow through with the good we plan to do; we stumble into the evil that we intended to avoid. Sin remains in us; there is Christian warfare within and without (*Rom.* 7:15-23, esp. verses 15, 18, 19, 21, 23). As saved sinners we are free to do what is good, but we are also free to will what is evil.

Free to do good alone!

That is one more reason why we long for heaven. God's gracious alteration to our characters results in a change for good in what we desire and will. But because this change is incomplete in this life, we continue to choose what is wrong alongside what is right—but only until our Saviour takes us home.

Really, the only irrevocable solution to this conflict, and the only end to our wrong desires, is for our characters to be finally perfected in 'the state of glory'. That is when Christian men and women and children will forever find their wills made perfectly and unchangeably free to do 'good alone'. That is when we reach spiritual maturity; that is when we, by grace, measure up to Christ; when we too will be perfectly holy—we will all 'reach unity in the faith and in the knowledge of the Son of God'. We will even 'become mature, attaining to the whole measure of the fullness of Christ' (*Eph.* 4:13). That is when the righteous will be 'made perfect' (*Heb.* 12:23). One part of that perfection is the perfection of our will.

Naturally there is much that we do not understand about this—all that we shall be has not yet appeared to us. 'But we know' with the Apostle John 'that when he appears we will be like him, because we shall see him as he is' (*1 John* 3:2). Seeing Jesus is one part of that final change for good. For he is the one who is able not only 'to keep you from stumbling' in your desires and decisions, but also 'to present you blameless before the presence of his glory with great joy' (*Jude* 24).

CHAPTER 10:

OF EFFECTUAL CALLING

Historic Text

10.1 All those whom God has predestinated unto life, and those only, he is pleased in his appointed and accepted time, effectually to call,[a] by his Word and Spirit,[b] out of that state of sin and death, in which they are by nature, to grace and salvation by Jesus Christ;[c] enlightening their minds, spiritually, and savingly to understand the things of God;[d] taking away their heart of stone, and giving unto them an heart of flesh;[e] renewing their wills, and by his almighty power determining them to that which is good,[f] and effectually drawing them to Jesus Christ:[g] yet so, as they come most freely, being made willing by his grace.[h]

Modern Version

10.1 All those—and only those—whom God has predestined to life, he is pleased to call effectually in his appointed and accepted time, by his Word and Spirit. He calls them from the state of sin and death—in which they are by nature—to grace and salvation by Jesus Christ. In this calling, God enlightens their minds spiritually and savingly, so that they understand the things of God. He takes away their hearts of stone and gives them hearts of flesh, renews their wills, and by his almighty power turns them to what is good and effectually draws them to Jesus Christ. Yet he does this in such a way that they come most freely, being made willing by his grace.

Scripture Proofs

  10.1   [a] Rom. 8:30; Rom. 11:7; Eph. 1:10,11.   [b] 2 Thess. 2:13,14; 2 Cor. 3:3,6. [c] Rom. 8:2; Eph. 2:1-5; 2 Tim. 1:9,10.   [d] Acts 26:18; 1 Cor. 2:10,12; Eph. 1:17,18. [e] Ezek. 36:26.   [f] Ezek. 11:19; Phil. 2:13; Deut. 30:6; Ezek. 36:27.   [g] Eph. 1:19; John 6:44,45.   [h] Song of Sol. 1:4; Psa. 110:3; John 6:37; Rom. 6:16-18.

Predestination and the divine call

Chapter 10 paragraph 1 begins its discussion of effectual calling by reminding us that there is such a thing as predestination. From the beginning of the chapter the emphasis—reflecting the emphasis of the

Bible—is on the effectiveness of God's choice (*Rom.* 11:7, 8), on God's predestining and gathering a people for himself in Christ (*Eph.* 1:10, 11). However, chapter 10 of the confession also echoes clearly the language of Romans 8, where we are told that all whom God 'predestinated, he also *called*' (*Rom.* 8:30). All people hear some calls. Every human being hears the whole of creation calling us to praise our good God. Men and women cannot help but hear their consciences calling them to repentance when they live contrary to God's law. And whenever we gather to hear the Word of God we hear another call. It is the call of the preached Word knocking on the door of our heart with the gospel.

Each of these calls is significant in its own way, but this section talks about a call which, when heard, is louder and clearer than any other call. For as the external call of a preacher knocks at the human heart, it is the inner call of God which unlocks and opens it.

By Word and Spirit

As we consider this call of God, it seems that we always end up considering God himself. For why else is this call effective, except that it is God who chooses those whom he would call, and because it is God himself who does the calling? It is God who uses his 'Word and Spirit' to call us to himself. The effectual calling of God is always effective because by his Spirit, in the appointed and accepted time, God takes his Word, whether it is preached or read, and sends it straight to our hearts. That is why we are 'bound to give thanks' to God for what we see in one another, as Paul tells the Thessalonians. 'From the beginning God chose you to be saved' and he does so by his Spirit and through the truth (*2 Thess.* 2:13, 14).

It is important to remember, as the Westminster assembly seemed not to tire of saying, that in his effective call to his people, God does not use the Spirit alone: we are not saved unless the teaching of Scripture is brought to bear on our minds and hearts. Second Corinthians 3 tips us off, and helps us to see, that in his effective call to his people, God does not use the Word alone; for these truths are complementary. The Spirit uses the Word. And no amount of exposure to the Word of God, direct or indirect, will prove useful unless God writes this Word on our hearts by his good Spirit.

Out of sin and death, into grace and salvation

Of course, the teaching of Scripture can come to us indirectly through the witness and testimony of others, and often does. The assembly's proof text, cited here, makes this point clearly. The Apostle Paul even tells us that, as we are hearing God's call by his holy Word, we actually become a word from God for others to read. We discover, as Paul says, that each Christian is a kind of fresh 'epistle from Christ' addressed to the world; our lives are letters 'written not with ink but with the Spirit of the living God, not on tablets of stone but on tablets of human hearts' (*2 Cor.* 3:3; *cf.* 3:6). But when that word is passed on by a preacher, or by a friend, it is still the word which God uses.

We need this writing on our lives; we also need God to make us into something on to which he can write. We are like old parchments needing to be scraped off and cleaned up before we can be used to new purposes. We need God to erase our sin and the sentence of death; we also need him to write his graces into our lives.

Christians are grateful that the effectual call of God is like no other call, and his voice like no other voice. We are thankful to know what God's voice can do, to know that at creation he spoke, and it was done. Today we need him to speak to us with life-giving force, for him to do something supernatural: we need him to take us from our hopeless state of sin and death and bring us into the endless state of grace and salvation by Jesus Christ. We need a call that transforms. The members of the Westminster assembly were clear that without this calling our ears would remain forever blocked and our hearts would remain obstinately opposed to God. We need the 'Spirit of life' (*Rom.* 8:2) to deliver us from the spiritual death that Paul describes in Ephesians 2, especially verses 1-5. We need this 'holy calling' because we shall never be saved 'because of our works', but only 'because of his own purpose and grace . . . in Christ Jesus', for it is he 'who abolished death and brought life and immortality to light through the gospel' (*2 Tim.* 1:9, 10). Stated openly, no man, woman or child will ever live in heaven without the effectual calling of God on earth.

The mind, the heart, the will

You see, it is this effectual call of God that is used to enlighten our minds—to 'open our eyes' spiritually, to borrow a phrase that a preacher used with a king (*Acts* 26:18). Naturally we might wonder how a call from God can actually change us. How is it that the call of the Spirit helps us to understand the things of God and to search them out? How is this call made effective?

The answer is that God does not merely call us, but in calling us, comes to us. In Paul's words, we actually receive God's Spirit; we receive him, and he never leaves us. 'We have not received the spirit of the world but the Spirit who is from God, that we may understand what God has freely given us' (*1 Cor.* 2:10, 12).

Is this hard to understand? Probably. But then you too can pray 'that the God of our Lord Jesus Christ, the Father of glory, may give you the spirit of wisdom'. Then 'the eyes of your understanding will be enlightened' and you will 'know the hope to which he has called you' (*Eph.* 1:17, 18). Then, too, you will see that the call of God not only reaches the mind, but also the heart. We know what it is like to have a heart of stone. But what is this sad and heavy fact to God? He can lift our spirits, and what is more (as God more than once prophesied through Ezekiel), he will insert a new heart within us. He will remove our heart of stone and give us a heart of flesh (*Ezek.* 11:19; 36:26).

God gives understanding to our minds and love to our hearts, and all the while he renews our wills. 'By his almighty power' he sets us on a path toward all that is good. God gives us a 'new spirit', to use prophetic language (*Ezek.* 11:19); God 'works in' us so that we begin 'to will and to work for his good pleasure', to use apostolic language (*Phil.* 2:13). He will 'circumcise' our hearts, to use covenantal language (*Deut.* 30:6). God will dwell with us, he will be our God, and we will be his people, to use heavenly language (*Ezek.* 37:27).

He effectively draws us to Jesus Christ, the very personification of goodness. Christians give thanks for the 'immeasurable greatness of his power' and 'the working of his great might' (*Eph.* 1:19) because we believe what Jesus taught about the Father: that 'no one' can ever come to him 'unless the Father . . . draws him'; and the Father draws us by teaching us about Jesus, for 'everyone who has heard and learned from the Father comes to [his Son]' (*John* 6:44, 45).

And yet, as chapter 9 of the confession would lead us to expect, even as God himself draws us, we come 'most freely, being made willing by his grace'. Like people in love, when one pulls, the other comes running (*Song of Sol.* 1:4). Tasting God's power, we offer ourselves 'freely' (*Psa.* 110:3). All who are given to Jesus come to him of their own volition (*John* 6:37). We are slaves of God, but we are at the same time 'obedient from the heart' (*Rom.* 6:16-18).

Reflecting on these lines in the confession, Archibald Alexander Hodge once commented wisely that 'it cannot be inconsistent with a . . . free will to deliver it from bondage'.[1] The nineteenth-century theologian Robert Shaw states the case positively and reminds us that when God calls us our will is not destroyed; rather, 'its obstinacy is overcome, its perverseness taken away, and the whole soul powerfully, yet sweetly, attracted to the Saviour'.[2] To put it differently, the Holy Spirit makes us see how lovely the gospel is, and then we freely crave it. For many Christians, the scriptural teaching on God's effectual call is full of comfort. It is reassuring for preachers to know that every word preached will find its target and do its work because each is guided by the Spirit of God. It is a comfort for believers to know that when God intends to add to his church, nothing will stop him, because by his almighty power his grace is irresistible, and therefore always effectual. Let us continue to pray that he will call sinners to himself. Perhaps today he will call someone for whom you have been praying for many years.

---

[1] Hodge, *The Confession of Faith*, p. 173.
[2] R. Shaw, *Exposition of the Westminster Confession of Faith* (Edinburgh, 1845; Fearn, Ross-shire, 1992), p. 121.

Historic Text

10.2 This effectual call is of God's free, and special grace alone, not from anything at all foreseen in man,[i] who is altogether passive therein, until being quickened and renewed by the Holy Spirit,[k] he is thereby enabled to answer this call, and to embrace the grace offered, and conveyed in it.[l]

Modern Version

10.2 This effectual call is from God's free and special grace alone, and not from anything at all that God foresees in man, who is entirely passive in it, until—being made alive and renewed by the Holy Spirit—he is enabled to answer the call and embrace the grace offered and conveyed in it.

Scripture Proofs

10.2 [i] 2 Tim. 1:9; Titus 3:4,5; Eph. 2:4,5,8,9; Rom. 9:11. [k] 1 Cor. 2:14; Rom. 8:9; Eph. 2:5. [l] John 6:37; Ezek 36:27; John 5:25.

God's grace and our helplessness

The opening paragraph in chapter 10 provides a general description of God's sovereign and effective call to his people; the next two paragraphs shift emphasis slightly as they discuss the people that are summoned to salvation.

Paragraph 2 begins by reviewing one of the most basic facts about God and his effectual call: that its source is 'God's free and special grace alone'. It is God who saves us; he calls us to trust in Christ. This same sentence also specifies that this call is free—there is no obligation for God to love his enemies or to call out to those who turn away from him, as Romans 9 makes clear. This call is special—God speaks to each of his people directly and personally. This call is gracious, for it comes at no cost to ourselves, and at great cost to God.

It is the graciousness of this call that dominates the New Testament epistles. In them we see that one way in which God underlines his graciousness is to set it repeatedly beside our helplessness. We are told in one place that it was 'because of his great love for us' that God 'made us alive with Christ', and then we are reminded that this life came to us 'even when we were dead in transgressions'. We are also told that 'it is by grace you have been saved', and then we are reminded that 'this is not from yourselves' and 'not by works' (*Eph.* 2:4, 5, 8, 9). The message Paul gave to the Ephesians was the same one that Timothy and Titus were to pass on to others. We are saved 'not according to our works, but according to his own purpose and grace' (2 *Tim.* 1:9). It is 'not by works of righteousness which we have done, but according to his mercy he saved us, by the washing of regeneration, and renewing of the Holy Ghost' (*Titus* 3:4, 5).

Some have suggested that God sees something good in us that motivates him to come to us. But the Scriptures do not suggest such a thing, and so the confession states that this salvation is 'not from anything at all foreseen in man'. The baseline of Scripture is always about what God has done, and not what we might do, and so here we are told that God's invitation to salvation does not come to a sinner because God saw something unique or special in each person called. Of course, God foresees everything in every person's life, but he does not choose to save us because he peered into the future and noticed that certain people would have religious insight where others would not.

Made alive

Instead, what Scripture repeatedly sets before us is a picture of death in ourselves and life in Christ through the power of the Spirit. When it comes to salvation, we are 'altogether passive'; there is nothing that we can do until we are quickened or made alive, and we are helpless to help ourselves until we are 'renewed by the Holy Spirit'—and even then, we are utterly reliant on his grace.

Without the Spirit of Christ we can 'not accept the things that come from the Spirit of God', and so there was never a time when God could look into the future and find people that were in themselves spiritually discerning. No, all spiritual discernment comes from him alone. He must call us to our senses, because for those who are 'without the Spirit' all spiritual things 'are foolishness' (*1 Cor.* 2:14). That is why the confession's chapter on effectual calling discusses 'quickening', being made a new creature, coming to life again. Thanks be to God that 'even when we were dead in our trespasses' he 'made us alive together with Christ' (*Eph.* 2:5). Thanks be to God that we are 'not in the flesh but in the Spirit' and have the Spirit of God dwelling in us (*Rom.* 8:9).

Answering the call

New life comes when we are united to Christ and given his Spirit. No one can be joined to Jesus, the risen Saviour, and not experience new life. No one can be filled with the Spirit and not be renewed. And so it is that by the Spirit's power we are 'enabled to answer this call' from God. When Christ embraces us by his Spirit, we in turn find ourselves able 'to embrace the grace offered and conveyed in it'. Really, what good would God's offer of grace be if he did not convey or communicate that grace to us at the same time?

Again, we can be sure of this offer, for it is just one part of the faithfulness of our triune God to himself. We know that we will be able to come, and that we will not be driven away, because it is the Father who gave us as a gift to his Son (*John* 6:37). Furthermore, we know that the Spirit will come to all of God's people, because God has done it for his own honour and glory. He puts his Spirit in us so that we will be moved to follow his decrees and be careful to keep his laws (*Ezek.* 36:27).

Perhaps it is best to end this section by remembering some words of our Lord recorded in John's Gospel. There he promised, 'a time is coming and has now come when the dead will hear the voice of the Son of God and those who hear will live' (*John* 5:25). Surely these words point to the final day of the world and the resurrection that we all await. But they also signal that with the resurrection of Jesus Christ, the realities of the last day have a dramatic importance for every day. Even now, dead sinners hear his voice, and live.

Every Sunday churches are filled with those who were once dead— dead until they heard 'the voice of the Son of God'. And as they heard God's call, they experienced God's grace. It is because of this great call that we listen at all to those who call us to worship. We praise him for his call of grace. But when we worship God, our congregations also often contain those whose ears cannot, as of yet, hear God's call. There will be those who need the sovereign work of the Spirit in their lives. Let us rejoice over all who are called to worship the King. At the same time let us pray that all of us 'will hear the voice of the Son of God', and that we shall all learn the blessed truth that 'those who hear will live'.

Historic Text	*Modern Version*
10.3 Elect infants, dying in infancy, are regenerated, and saved by Christ, through the Spirit,[m] who works when, and where, and how he pleases:[n] So also, are all other elect persons who are incapable of being outwardly called by the ministry of the Word.[o]	**10.3** Elect infants who die in infancy are regenerated and saved by Christ through the Spirit, who works when, where, and how he pleases. So also are all other elect persons who are incapable of being outwardly called by the ministry of the Word.

Scripture proofs

10.3 [m] Luke 18:15,16, and Acts 2:38,39, and John 3:3,5 and 1 John 5:12, and Rom. 8:9, compared. [n] John 3:8. [o] 1 John 5:12; Acts 4:12.

Elect infants

The whole point of this chapter on effectual calling is to remind us that it is God who summons us to salvation. His call is all of grace; we do not deserve it, and without his help we cannot even hear it and respond to it. God's sovereignty in saving his people should always be good news as we pray for a sinner's salvation, but it is most obviously so when we think of how God helps those who cannot lift a finger to help themselves.

It is the most helpless of people of whom we are reminded in paragraph 3. There are infants, for example, who die in infancy. They certainly have no hope of coming to faith in Christ; there is no step that they can take towards eternal life. But this does not stop or even slow our God. All those whom he has elected to save, including infants dying in infancy, 'are regenerated, and saved by Christ, through the Spirit'.

We should not be surprised by this. Some Christian traditions give the impression that Christianity is really for adults, and that the developed confession of an old man is more to be trusted than the fumbling testimony of a young child. We listen to some Christians explain the gospel, and suspect that they might have told Nicodemus to grow up, rather than to be born again.

Our Lord is of a different mind, for he tells us in the Gospels that the kingdom of heaven is well represented or characterized by children. In fact, there is something in a child's dependency that pleases the Lord, and even calls for our imitation. Perhaps, for that reason, Jesus was willing to give his blessing to the children of those parents who believed that he could do them good (*Luke* 18:15, 16). Perhaps, for that reason, Peter could assure the quietened crowd at Pentecost that the promise of salvation was for all whom God would call—not only for those who would repent and believe, but also for their children, even though Peter had no idea how old their children would be. The emphasis is on the power of God's 'call', not the age or abilities of God's people (*Acts* 2:38, 39).

Normally the Spirit unites us to Christ by faith. Usually God's people grow up to confess him, to repent of their sins, and to live their lives for the kingdom. But he is not tied to any one means, for he 'works when, and where, and how he pleases', as Jesus told Nicodemus one night long ago (*John* 3:8). The non-negotiable for salvation is not faith, but the Spirit, by whom we have Christ, by whom, in turn, we have the Father (*1 John* 5:12; *Rom.* 8:9).

Paragraph 3 ends by telling us that this is as relevant for uncomprehending infants as it is for those who grow up in their bodies, but never in their minds. All 'elect persons who are incapable of being outwardly called by the ministry of the Word' can still be saved through Jesus Christ (*Acts* 4:12). There are no limits to the effectiveness of God's call.

In considering these 'special cases', it is instructive to feel for a moment the full weight of the assertion made in paragraph 2. There we were told that the effectual call was of God's free and special grace alone, and not from anything foreseen in man. When we turn to the subject of paragraph 3, we can see one more reason why we should love this doctrine—one more reason why we are relieved to hear that we have nothing to do with our salvation. For if one were to be elect on the basis of foreseen faith or obedience, what parents could have hope for their dying baby, or for their aging, but mentally inhibited child?

Nonetheless, let us also be clear what is not being taught. First, it is important to see that this discussion begins with a focus on elect infants. The Westminster divines wisely restrict their comments to what they can know and say with certainty—which is that elect infants are heaven bound. Often there is a tendency to drop the qualifying word 'elect' from the word 'infants', with the suggestion that all babies go to heaven.[1]

---

[1] Hodge correctly argues that only 'elect infants' will be saved. Unfortunately, he then assumes that 'we have good reason to believe that *all* infants are elected'. *The Confession of Faith*, p. 175.

The Scriptures do not allow us to draw this conclusion. Apparent innocence does not rise to the height of an eternal entitlement.

Second, the confession is not saying that infants and the mentally handicapped are saved or elected because they are infants, or because they are handicapped. Rather, they are saved because they are elect, chosen, just like any other person who is elect. The reason why they are effectually called does not change. Only the manner of their being called has changed.

Most of all, we need to remember that the foundation for our salvation never changes. Even if they cannot receive Christ by faith, salvation for infants and adults still rests in receiving Christ's righteousness and in Christ's receiving their sin. Salvation still depends on Christ bearing wrath and punishment for our trespasses. The ordinary means (or application) of salvation and grace are replaced by the extraordinary—but the basis of salvation remains the same. As chapter 8 of the confession properly insisted, upon the firm foundation of Scripture, there is only one mediator between God and man, the man Christ Jesus. There is no salvation outside of him.

Before we close, one more note is necessary. This section discusses what *God* can do. But *we* do not know who are chosen by God. So let Christian parents remember not only God's power, but also his mercy. Let us remember that our children were his before they were ours, and let us by his grace live in faith in the power of the gospel, and not fear in the depravity of man.

Historic Text	*Modern Version*
10.4 Others, not elected, although they may be called by the ministry of the Word,[p] and may have some common operations of the Spirit,[q] yet they never truly come unto Christ, and therefore cannot be saved:[r] much less can men, not professing the Christian religion,	**10.4** Although other persons who are not elected may be called by the ministry of the Word and may experience some common operations of the Spirit, yet they never really come to Christ and therefore cannot be saved. Much less can men not professing to be Christians

be saved in any other way whatsoever, be they never so diligent to frame their lives according to the light of nature, and the law of that religion they do profess.[s] And, to assert and maintain, that they may, is very pernicious, and to be detested.[t]

be saved in any other way, no matter how carefully they may order their lives by the light of nature and by the laws of whatever religion they profess. To assert and maintain that they may be saved in some other way is very pernicious and is to be detested.

Scripture Proofs

10.4 [p] Matt. 22:14. [q] Matt. 7:22; Matt. 13:20,21; Heb. 6:4,5. [r] John 6:64-66; John 8:24. [s] Acts 4:12; John 14:6; Eph. 2:12; John 4:22; John 17:3. [t] 2 John v. 9-11; 1 Cor. 16:22; Gal. 1:6-8.

The non-elect

Paragraph 3 explained that all 'elect persons who are incapable of being outwardly called by the ministry of the Word' can still be saved through Jesus Christ (*Acts* 4:12). There are no limits to the effectiveness of God's call. The point clearly made in the third paragraph of this chapter is presented from another angle in the fourth.

Here we are reminded that there are some who are able to hear the ministry of God's Word but not the true call of God. Our Lord sums this up by saying, 'many are called, but few are chosen' (*Matt.* 22:14). They may joyfully hear preaching and decide to change their lives (*Matt.* 13:20, 21). Incredibly, they might be permitted to prophesy, cast out demons, do wonderful works, and even have a taste of the work of the Spirit (*Matt.* 7:22; *Heb.* 6:4, 5). And yet they might not genuinely love Christ at all.[1]

Our Lord spoke very plainly about this problem in his own day. He rebuked some of his momentary admirers, for he knew 'from the beginning which of them did not believe and who would betray him' (*John* 6:64; *cf.* 6:65, 66; 8:24). Christians today do not have that kind of knowledge about apparent believers; we cannot pretend to point fingers,

[1] In 1648 assembly member Thomas Hill explained that the idea of 'common operations of the Spirit' did not entail any understanding of a hypothetically universal extent to the redemption purchased by Christ. His reason is that when we 'speak of any thing as to Salvation, there is a commensuration betwixt the three persons in the Trinity, and their workings'. Thomas Hill, *The Spring of Strengthening Grace in the Rock of Ages, Jesus Christ* (London, 1648), p. 5.

nor do we wish to do so. But that does not mean that we need to be naïve about the fact that not all hearers of, and even responders to, the gospel really hear God. There are some who appear to come to Christ, but while their feet carry them down an aisle, or the confession of their mouths brings them into the visible church, their hearts have never been moved by the gospel. They did not really come to Christ at all.

The church is not to be swept off her feet by every person professing love to Jesus. She must be especially careful to resist the calls of men who look good but do not profess 'the Christian religion'. It does not ultimately matter how 'diligent' they may be to 'frame their lives according to the light of nature', heeding their conscience and trying to love those around them. It does not matter if they are faithful to all 'the laws of that religion they do profess'. It will do nothing for their salvation.

Now this can be hard news to hear. Timothy had to hear this message from the Apostle Paul, even though Timothy's own father was a pagan. But Timothy was engaging in cross-cultural evangelism and he needed to be absolutely clear that 'salvation is found in no one' other than Jesus Christ. 'There is no other name under heaven given to men by which we must be saved' (*Acts* 4:12). 'I am the way and the truth and the life', Jesus insisted. 'No one comes to the Father except through me' (*John* 14:6; *cf. John* 4:22; 17:3). This is the clear testimony of Scripture, and we cannot redecorate or renovate the truth to make it more palatable to our contemporaries. 'To assert and maintain' anything to the contrary of a salvation found in Jesus alone is nothing short of 'pernicious'. It is a different gospel altogether from the one revealed to us in God's holy Word, and the Apostle Paul even uses his authority to curse those who preach such a thing (*1 Cor.* 16:22; *Gal.* 1:6-8).

Thus, if someone insists on a contrary position, in spite of clear instruction, it is not too strong to say that such teaching is 'to be detested'.[1] To claim that there is another way of salvation besides the one that Jesus Christ proclaimed and purchased, is to call our Lord a liar and his whole life a great mistake. We ought never to welcome those who would like to teach that all roads lead to heaven, whether that message

---

[1] It is on this point of doctrine that the Thirty-nine Articles, the English forerunner to the Westminster Confession of Faith, issue their only anathema (Article 18).

comes to us from the grandest cathedrals or from the most humble house church (*2 John* 9-11).

To be 'without Christ', Paul once wrote, is to be 'without hope, and without God in the world' (*Eph.* 2:12). Let us never forget this. Let us come to Christ. Let us cling to his cross, rejoice in his resurrection, and worship him alone. As we come to worship our great God, let us remember the good news of the gospel. To have Christ, as Paul never tired of saying, is to have 'the gift of God' and 'eternal life' (*Rom.* 6:23).

CHAPTER 11:

OF JUSTIFICATION

Historic Text

11.1 Those whom God effectually calls, he also freely justifies:[a] not, by infusing righteousness into them, but by pardoning their sins, and by accounting and accepting their persons as righteous; not, for anything wrought in them, or done by them, but for Christ's sake alone; nor, by imputing faith itself, the act of believing, or any other evangelical obedience, to them, as their righteousness, but, by imputing the obedience and satisfaction of Christ unto them,[b] they receiving, and resting on him and his righteousness by faith; which faith, they have, not of themselves, it is the gift of God.[c]

Modern Version

11.1 Those whom God effectually calls he also freely justifies, not by infusing righteousness into them, but by pardoning their sins and by accounting and accepting them as righteous. It is not for anything wrought in them, or done by them, but for Christ's sake alone that they are justified. It is not by imputing faith itself, the act of believing, or any other act of Christian obedience to them, as their righteousness, but by imputing the obedience and satisfaction of Christ to them who receive and rest on him and his righteousness by faith. Men do not have this faith of themselves; it is the gift of God.

Scripture Proofs

11.1 [a] Rom. 8:30; Rom. 3:24. [b] Rom. 4:5-8; 2 Cor. 5:19,21; Rom. 3:22,24,25,27,28; Titus 3:5,7; Eph. 1:7; Jer. 23:6; 1 Cor. 1:30,31; Rom. 5:17-19. [c] Acts 10:44; Gal. 2:16; Phil. 3:9; Acts 13:38,39; Eph. 2:7,8.

A free justification

In assuring us that God will finish what he starts, Paul told the Romans that all those whom God predestines he also calls, and those he calls he also justifies. The Westminster assembly connected chapters 10 and 11 of the confession with this quotation from Romans 8:30. But the assembly felt free to explain that Paul is promising the blessing of justification for all those whom God *effectually* calls. The apostle is promising that if you have been predestined to eternal life, you will be called to Christ and you will be justified.

As Paul says elsewhere in Romans, when Christ justifies us, he justifies us freely (*Rom.* 3:24). It is because this free justification is such a valued gift that this section takes the time and space to state the matter both negatively and positively. First it gives us the definition, clarifying what justification is and what it is not. Second, we are given the grounds of justification, identifying clearly the bases on which we are not justified, and the basis on which we are. Third, we are told what this righteousness is and what it is not. Finally, we are told in the simplest terms possible how we receive this great blessing.

Justification: what it is not and what it is

It is God who justifies, and he does so 'freely', needing nothing from ourselves. But we have questions. How does God freely justify? And while a free justification is convenient, what if we feel that we have something to contribute? After all, Roman Catholic teachers have argued that God infuses righteousness into us, and then declares us righteous because he actually makes us righteous. Is it not possible for God to justify us on the basis of the grace and righteousness that he works in us?

A proper response to Roman Catholic teaching will embrace the idea that God does indeed make us increasingly righteous and holy; the Bible usually calls this sanctification. But this sanctifying process is always incomplete in this life, and sometimes radically incomplete, so it is both a mark of wisdom and honesty to push aside the rickety platform of our own righteousness and stand on something better. The fact is that in this life even saints remain sinners, which is why Paul could tell the earliest Roman church that God actually justifies the ungodly (*Rom.* 4:5).

The way in which God justifies this ungodly world, or at least one part of it, is to forgive their sins. The forgiveness of sins is the happiness of Christians. We are blessed if our iniquities are forgiven and our sins are covered. 'Blessed is the man to whom the Lord will not impute sin' (*Rom.* 4:6-8; *2 Cor.* 5:19). This is a joy almost beyond compare: to count up all our sins, and then to know that God will not count them against us. But how is this possible? Because there was one who knew no sin in his own life and yet was made sin for us (*2 Cor.* 5:19-21). He carried the awful weight of our sin and was then crushed for our iniquities.

> Because the sinless Saviour died,
> My sinful soul is counted free.[1]

Nonetheless, to be justified is not to be left just as if we had never sinned, and no more. Rather, justification also involves being accounted and accepted as righteous. The good news is that not only did Jesus Christ once don our filthy sins, but he also forever clothes us in his spotless righteousness. We 'are justified freely by his grace through the redemption that came by Christ Jesus'. In other words, the righteousness of God comes to us in Christ alone (*Rom.* 3:22-28).

The grounds of justification: not because of us, but because of Christ

So why are we justified? Is there something that God sees in us? Is there something we can do to become better candidates for salvation? What must we do to be saved? God's Word gives us the only answer. We find our salvation 'not on the basis of deeds which we have done in righteousness, but according to his mercy'. We are justified by his grace (*Titus* 3:5, 7). It is not for anything worked in us or done by us. It is 'in him' that 'we have redemption'—that is, in Christ. We are justified 'through his blood'. It is because of him that we find 'the forgiveness of our trespasses, according to the riches of his grace' (*Eph.* 1:7). That is why in a prophecy of Jeremiah we are told that the Saviour will be called 'The LORD our Righteousness' (*Jer.* 23:6). We are accepted through Christ alone. Our righteousness is not some part of us. Our righteousness is Jesus.

Saving righteousness: not our faith or obedience, but Christ's

When our hearts and minds are properly calibrated to the Word of God, this comes to us as very good news. But Christians have often been out of line, and so the Westminster assembly had the good sense to state

---

[1] Charitie Lees Smith, 'Before the throne of God above.'

once more what saving righteousness really is. Traditional Arminianism affirmed that our faith stands as our righteousness in place of our works. Traditional Reformed thinking rejected this construction. God does not graciously accept our act of believing in place of the other righteous acts that we should have performed but did not. Nor is our repentance, the sincerity of our prayer, or any other evangelical obedience substituted as our righteousness. Again, we are not saved 'by works of righteousness that we have done' (*Titus* 3:5).

God established Jesus Christ as the only one that we need. He is our wisdom, our holiness and our redemption. And he is certainly our righteousness (*1 Cor.* 1:30, 31). God justifies us by imputing the obedience and satisfaction of Christ to us. The essence of the gospel is that 'one act of righteousness leads to justification and life for all men'. There are none who come to God another way. It is only through 'the one man's obedience' that 'the many will be made righteous' (*Rom.* 5:17-19), and that man is Jesus.

Justified by faith

And so it is that we rest on Jesus Christ and his righteousness by faith. We hear the Word (*Acts* 10:44) and we respond. Paul writes this clearly in Galatians 2:16: we are justified through faith in Jesus Christ, he says. We believe in Christ Jesus, in order to be justified by faith, and not by works.

Is not that the way we want it in the end? I want to 'be found in him, not having a righteousness of my own that comes from the law, but that which comes through faith in Christ, the righteousness from God that depends on faith' (*Phil.* 3:9). My freedom from sin is found through Jesus Christ (*Acts* 13:38, 39).

We are saved by faith in another. But salvation is so much a gift, and we are so greedy for praise, that Scripture comforts and humbles us by announcing that it was 'by grace you have been saved through faith', and that even faith is not something that originates with ourselves. That too, is a gift of God (*Eph.* 2:7, 8). So, 'what is justification? Justification is an act of God's free grace, wherein he pardons all our sins, and accepts us as righteous in his sight, only for the righteousness of Christ imputed to us, and received by faith alone' (WSC 33). Praise the Lord for this benefit that we receive through the Lord Jesus Christ.

Historic Text

11.2 Faith, thus receiving and resting on Christ and his righteousness, is the alone instrument of justification;[d] yet is it not alone in the person justified, but is ever accompanied with all other saving graces, and is no dead faith, but works by love.[e]

11.3 Christ by his obedience, and death, did fully discharge the debt of all those that are thus justified, and did make a proper, real, and full satisfaction to his Father's justice in their behalf.[f] Yet, in as much as he was given by the Father, for them;[g] and, his obedience and satisfaction accepted in their stead;[h] and, both, freely, not for anything in them; their justification is only of free grace;[i] that, both the exact justice, and rich grace of God, might be glorified in the justification of sinners.[k]

Modern Version

11.2 Faith—receiving and resting on Christ and his righteousness—is the only instrument of justification; yet it is not the only grace in the person justified, but is always accompanied by all other saving graces. Justifying faith is not dead, but works by love.

11.3 Christ, by his obedience and death, fully discharged the debt of all those who are justified. He made a proper, real, and full satisfaction to his Father's justice in their behalf. Yet, because he was freely given by the Father for them, and because his obedience and satisfaction were freely accepted in their stead, and not for anything in them, their justification is only of free grace. It was God's purpose in the justification of sinners to glorify both his exact justice and his rich grace.

Scripture Proofs

11.2 [d] John 1:12; Rom 3:28; Rom. 5:1. [e] James 2:17,22,26; Gal. 5:6.

11.3 [f] Rom. 5:8-10,19; 1 Tim. 2:5,6; Heb. 10:10,14; Dan. 9:24,26; Isa. 53:4-6,10-12. [g] Rom. 8:32. [h] 2 Cor. 5:21; Matt. 3:17; Eph. 5:2. [i] Rom. 3:24; Eph. 1:7. [k] Rom. 3:26; Eph. 2:7.

Faith alone

The second paragraph of this chapter expands on the concluding note in the first: the idea of 'receiving and resting on Christ and his righteousness'—the doctrine of justification by 'faith'.

What is faith? Faith is just resting on what Jesus has done. Faith is the abandoning of any attempt to please God on our own with our goodness, and trusting in Christ and his righteousness. Faith is simply believing that Jesus Christ has paid any debt that we owe, and endured any punishment that we deserved. Faith is decidedly *not* some kind of virtue in us, either some little thing or some important work that we do. It is giving up on ourselves and trusting God in Jesus Christ. Justifying faith is, as the confession states here, receiving and resting on Christ alone.

John reminds us in the opening of his gospel that the thing which characterises children of God is that they 'believe on his name' (*John* 1:12). Little wonder that Paul writes once and again in his letter to the Romans that we are 'justified by faith' (*Rom.* 3:28; 5:1). Faith is the only instrument that justifies us, so to speak, because it is the only good way of describing trust placed in Christ and not in ourselves.

Faith never alone

We are justified by faith alone. Yet at the same time we should remember that faith is never alone in the person justified. Faith is a gift of grace and it is the sole gift by which we receive justification. Nonetheless, for those who are justified, faith is given plenty of company. This one saving grace is accompanied by all other saving graces. Other graces like patience and hope and love are no mere optional puddings or desserts that we can select from among the buffet of Christian virtues. They are part of the main course, the essential food groups for a well-nourished Christian. In fact, without these Christian graces there is no Christian life at all.

Our understanding of salvation must always seek to be as robust as the Holy Scripture's teaching of salvation. James makes it abundantly clear that faith must be living and never dead (*James* 2:17, 22, 26). No, even as we look in faith to Christ, we begin to love not only our Saviour, but also his people and, in important ways, his world. As Paul once explained to the Galatians, 'in Jesus Christ' the only thing that avails anything 'is faith working by love' (*Gal.* 5:6).

Christ's obedience and death

Even while it discusses justification, the confession is keen to see that we do not lose sight of Jesus, and so the work of Christ is recapped for us in paragraph 3, by emphasizing that the justification we have is in Christ and is both just and gracious. All those who are justified are debtors. We owe a debt of obedience to God that we, like Adam, have failed to pay. Nor is there any hope of payment. We cannot be cast into a debtors' prison such as the kind we find in Jesus' parables or Dickens' novels and ever expect to emerge alive. Really, in this case, prison is not even an option, for rebellion against the King of kings deserves the death penalty.

What a cheerless case to be in for men, women and children! As we see the effects of sin in our lives and in the lives of those around us, who can forget that 'by one man's disobedience many were made sinners' (*Rom.* 5:15)? We are sinners, and our case would be hopeless; but as Paul delights to explain, there was one who was not disobedient, and 'by the obedience of the one shall many be made righteous'. Although Christ was treated as a ringleader of a rebellion (*Luke* 22:47-53), the truth was that Christ was a leader of righteousness. He obeyed his Father where we did not and, as our representative, he obeyed on our behalf.

The astonishing thing is that, when we were lost, God loved us, and he 'demonstrated his own love for us in this: while we were still sinners, Christ died for us'. We are 'justified by his blood'. We are 'saved from wrath through him'. We 'are reconciled to God by the death of his Son', because that death was a proper, real and full satisfaction of the Father's justice (*Rom.* 5:8-10).

This is the news that is broadcast all across the Bible. Whose is the righteousness that Daniel sees in the future (*Dan.* 9:24, 26)? What is the salvation that Isaiah pictures (*Isa.* 53:4-6, 10-12)? Who pays the ransom that Paul mentions to Timothy (*1 Tim.* 2:5, 6)? Who is in view in the letter to the Hebrews when it speaks of a body that was offered on behalf of sinners (*Heb.* 10:10, 14)?

Every Christian knows that each of these questions has only one answer: it is the Lord Jesus Christ, in whom our faith must find its resting place. He is the one who was given to us by the Father, delivered up for us all, so that he could freely give us all things (*Rom.* 8:32). It is his obedience and satisfaction on the cross that is accepted in our stead, for 'God made him who had no sin to be sin for us, so that in him we might become the righteousness of God' (*2 Cor.* 5:21). There was only one in whom the Father was well pleased, and he 'loved us and gave himself up for us as a fragrant offering and sacrifice to God' (*Matt.* 3:17; *Eph.* 5:2).

The wonder of it all sometimes leads Christians to weep with joy or laugh with astonishment—a variety of the astonished laughter that sometimes comes when something seems too good to be true, and yet it is true. I know who I am. I know this gift cannot come because of anything in me, and yet this justification comes freely to me and to you from God—it is grace as free as grace can be (*Rom.* 3:24; *Eph.* 1:7).

Ultimately, Jesus Christ has purchased for us the proof of both the exact justice and the rich grace of God, because God wished to be glorified in the justification of sinners. He wanted to show us that he is just 'and the one who justifies those who have faith in Jesus', as Paul explains. And he did this 'in order that in the coming ages he might show the incomparable riches of his grace, expressed in his kindness to us in Christ Jesus' (*Rom.* 3:26; *Eph.* 2:7).

Historic Text

11.4 God did, from all eternity, decree to justify all the elect,[l] and Christ did, in the fullness of time, die for their sins, and rise again for their justification:[m] nevertheless, they are not justified, until the Holy Spirit does, in due time, actually apply Christ unto them.[n]

11.5 God does continue to forgive the sins of those that are justified:[o] and, although they can never fall from the state of justification;[p] yet, they may by their sins, fall under God's fatherly displeasure, and not have the light of his countenance restored unto them, until they humble themselves, confess their sins, beg pardon, and renew their faith and repentance.[q]

11.6 The justification of believers under the old testament, was, in all these respects, one and the same with the justification of believers under the new testament.[r]

Modern Version

11.4 God, from all eternity, decreed to justify all the elect. In the fullness of time, Christ died for their sins and rose again for their justification. Nevertheless, they are not justified until, in due time, the Holy Spirit actually applies Christ to them.

11.5 God continues to forgive the sins of those who are justified. Although they can never fall from the state of justification, yet they may by their sins fall under God's fatherly displeasure and not have the light of his countenance restored to them until they humble themselves, confess their sin, plead for pardon, and renew their faith and repentance.

11.6 The justification of believers under the old testament was, in all these respects, one and the same with the justification of believers under the new testament.

Scripture Proofs

11.4 ¹ Gal. 3:8; 1 Pet. 1:2,19,20; Rom. 8:30. ᵐ Gal. 4:4; 1 Tim. 2:6; Rom. 4:25. ⁿ Col. 1:21,22; Gal. 2:16; Titus 3:4-7.

11.5 ° Matt. 6:12; 1 John 1:7,9; 1 John 2:1,2. ᵖ Luke 22:32; John 10:28; Heb. 10:14. ۹ Psa. 89:31-33; Psa. 51:7-12; Psa. 32:5; Matt. 26:75; 1 Cor. 11:30,32; Luke 1:20.

11.6 ʳ Gal. 3:9,13,14; Rom. 4:22-24; Heb. 13:8.

Justification in eternity?

The second half of this chapter on justification discusses the timing of justification, the experience of justification, and the way in which people were and are justified before and after the death, resurrection and ascension of the Son of God.

Paragraph 4 begins by telling us that God decreed 'from all eternity' that he would justify his elect people. There is an eternal dimension to justification. We get a glimpse of this when we are told that Old Testament believers had a confident expectation that God would be justifying people in the future (*Gal.* 3:8). It may be the eternal plan of justification that Peter has in view when he explains that according to God's foreknowledge we were chosen to benefit from Christ's obedience and the sprinkling or washing of his blood—blessings which come to us in the form of justification (*1 Pet.* 1:2; *cf.* 1:19, 20). Paul too connects justification with election when he tells us that all those whom God 'predestined', he also, amongst other things, 'justified' (*Rom.* 8:30).

Justification in history

Justification is determined in eternity, but it is vitally important to see that the doctrine assumes an event in history. For forgiveness and righteousness to be realities, someone had to come 'in the fullness of time' (*Gal.* 4:4). Jesus Christ had to come as our 'ransom' at the 'proper time' (*1 Tim.* 2:6). He needed to be 'delivered over to death for our sins' and 'raised to life for our justification' (*Rom.* 4:25). For Christians, for those united with Christ, there is a very real sense in which we can say that we are justified with Jesus, 2,000 years ago.

Unfortunately, over the centuries some Christians have so focused on God's eternal decree to justify, and others on the justification by Christ's death and resurrection, that they have lost sight of the fact that justification actually occurs at a point in time in the life of the person justified. To deny the reality of justification as an occurrence in the life of a person is most unhelpful and does not account for the emphasis of Holy Scripture itself.

Does not Scripture tell us again and again that we are justified by faith? Is there not a reason why Christians are identified as believers? A person is not a Christian until he believes in Jesus Christ as his Saviour. But if we are actually justified in eternity, or at Christ's cross, or at his empty tomb, we cannot really be 'justified by faith'. Faith must at most be a recognition of some existing justification, accomplished long ago.

Problems with a purely eternal or historical justification prove that these doctrines are unsustainable. Does not the Bible teach that there was once a time when we were alienated from God and accused before him—and then reconciled to him through Christ (*Col.* 1:21, 22)? In fact, do not some of us actually remember the weight of that accusation, and perhaps even recall the very moment that our sins were washed away? But how can this experience be genuine if we were already justified in eternity, or two millennia ago in history? At least since the time that this confession was written, there have always been people so eager to affirm God's verdict that we are *not* justified by works of the law, that they forget his statement that we *are* justified by faith (*Gal.* 2:16).[1] They also forget the work of the Holy Spirit in our salvation, for if we were justified long before we were born, the Spirit's work in uniting us to Christ cannot really be relevant to our salvation (*Titus* 3:4-7). And yet, properly speaking, Christians are not justified until the Holy Spirit, in due time, actually applies Christ to us.

---

[1] Like the mainstream Reformed orthodox, seventeenth-century antinomians opposed the classic Arminian understanding of faith that made it a new 'work' in the covenant of grace, in place of the works which we ought to, but cannot, perform. A subset of antinomians combatted Arminianism by positing a justification in eternity. They thus reduced faith to a mere evidence of justification, or they taught people to look in faith to their justification, rather than teaching them to look in faith to Jesus Christ. See C. Van Dixhoorn, 'The Strange Silence of Prolocutor Twisse', *The Sixteenth Century Journal*, 11:2 (Summer 2009), pp. 404-7.

Saved sinners

Justification is a declaration that is made about individual people by God during their lifetime. It is made on the basis of Christ's righteousness and it has eternal implications. Nonetheless, as paragraph 5 goes on to explain, and as every Christian believer knows, justified people still sin. There is a reason why our Lord taught us to pray, 'forgive us our debts' (*Matt.* 6:12).

There is also a reason, however, why the Apostle John assures us that we shall be forgiven. 'The blood of Jesus Christ his Son' really does 'cleanse us from all sin' and 'if we confess our sins' he 'is faithful and just to forgive us our sins, and to cleanse us from all unrighteousness' (*1 John* 1:7, 9). We need to hear, 'if any man sins, we have an advocate with the Father, Jesus Christ the righteous'. When we look at the vast world of our own sins, we need to be reminded that Jesus Christ 'is the propitiation for our sins: and not for ours only, but also for the sins of the whole world' (*1 John* 2:1, 2).

Christians are in a state of justification and we cannot fall out of it. As Jesus once prayed that Peter would not fall, so Christ continues to pray the same for us (*Luke* 22:32). The words our Lord spoke to Jewish people in the porch of the Jerusalem temple are just as true for us today, wherever we might be: when Jesus gives 'eternal life', those who receive that life 'will never perish'. Our Lord himself has promised: 'no one can snatch them out of my hand' (*John* 10:28). The effect of his sacrifice endures forever (*Heb.* 10:14).

A Father's discipline

Christians cannot fall under God's judicial sentence. But we must not forget that we can in our sin fall under God's 'fatherly displeasure'. In recognizing that this is God's fatherly disapproval, not his judicial condemnation, Christians are in no way to see this as a minimization of that disapproval. While we have a loving and a merciful Father, his displeasure is genuine, and like the just anger of an earthly father, the anger of a heavenly Father is not something with which we want to live.

The experience of God's disfavour is very trying to bear, as David confessed on more than one occasion (*Psa.* 51:7-12; *Psa.* 32:5; compare God's statement in *Psa.* 89:31-33, and believers' experiences in *Matt.* 26:75; *I Cor.* 11:30, 32; *Luke* 1:20). But remember that God shows us his displeasure so that he may restore the light of his countenance to us. He wants us to humble ourselves, confess our sins, beg his pardon—he wants us to renew our flagging faith and our often random repentance.

The old and new Testaments

Lastly, we are told in paragraph 6 that 'the justification of believers under the old testament was, in all these respects, one and the same with the justification of believers under the new testament'. In saying this the authors of the confession are being consistent with what they wrote about the covenant in general in chapter 7, and what they wrote about Christ the mediator in chapter 8: God's salvation is one and the same through all time unto eternity. Men have always, like Abraham, been justified by grace, through faith in the Messiah (*Gal.* 3:9, 13-14; *Rom.* 4:22-24). It has always been a gift of God.

In the Old Testament saints looked forward in faith to be justified. In the New Testament saints look backward to be saved. But it is the work of the one who is 'the same yesterday, today, and forever' that saves us all (*Heb.* 13:8). Could our zeal no respite know, could our tears forever flow, could Adam's, Abraham's, Peter's or Priscilla's tears forever flow, all for sin could not atone. Christ must save, and Christ alone.[1]

---

[1] See the hymn 'Rock of Ages' by Augustus M. Toplady (1740–78).

CHAPTER 12:

OF ADOPTION

Historic Text

12.1 All those that are justified, God vouchsafes, in, and for his only Son Jesus Christ, to make partakers of the grace of adoption:[a] by which they are taken into the number, and enjoy the liberties and privileges of the children of God,[b] have his name put upon them,[c] receive the spirit of adoption,[d] have access to the throne of grace with boldness,[e] are enabled to cry, Abba, Father,[f] are pitied,[g] protected,[h] provided for,[i] and chastened, by him, as by a Father;[k] yet, never cast off,[l] but sealed to the day of redemption,[m] and inherit the promises,[n] as heirs of everlasting salvation.[o]

Modern Version

12.1 All those who are justified God graciously guarantees to make partakers of the grace of adoption in and for his only Son, Jesus Christ. By this act they are taken into the number of God's children and enjoy the liberties and privileges of that relationship; they are given his name; they receive the Spirit of adoption; they have access to the throne of grace with boldness; and they are enabled to cry, 'Abba, Father.' Like a father, God has compassion on, protects, provides for, and chastens them; yet, they will never be cast off, but are sealed to the day of redemption, and will inherit the promises as heirs of everlasting salvation.

Scripture Proofs

12.1 [a] Eph. 1:5. [b] Gal. 4:4,5; Rom. 8:17; John 1:12. [c] Jer. 14:9; 2 Cor. 6:18; Rev. 3:12. [d] Rom. 8:15. [e] Eph. 3:12; Rom. 5:2. [f] Gal. 4:6. [g] Psa. 103:13. [h] Prov. 14:26. [i] Matt. 6:30,32; 1 Pet. 5:7. [k] Heb. 12:6. [l] Lam. 3:31. [m] Eph. 4:30. [n] Heb. 6:12. [o] 1 Pet. 1:3,4; Heb. 1:14.

Blessings as a package

The most noteworthy fact about this chapter on adoption is that there is a chapter at all. Biblical sonship is the Cinderella of Christian theology and has only recently been recognized as the royal topic that it really is.

It was not treated as an independent topic at the Reformation, and has often been lost from view since the time that this chapter was written.

Nonetheless, the second most striking aspect of the chapter is its brevity. This twelfth chapter is the confession's shortest for at least three reasons. First, there was a limited pool of theological reflection on this subject from which the assembly could draw. Second, and related, the assembly could offer a crisp statement on the doctrine of adoption because it could state the truth without correction of error. In contrast to the chapter on justification, for example, there was no rubble to be cleared away when the Westminster divines came to compose chapter 12. They tackled no dissent and treated no heterodoxy, for orthodoxy on this subject had no serious competitors. Third, there is considerable thematic overlap between the doctrine of adoption and the doctrine of assurance of faith and salvation, and some aspects of the experience of God's children are related in chapter 18 on assurance. This allows the confession to state a large doctrine in a little space.

This chapter begins by reminding us that the saving blessings and graces that come from Jesus Christ always come as a package. Just as we were justified in Christ, so too God graciously grants that we will be adopted in Christ. Adoption has always been part of God's plan. In fact, 'God sent forth his Son', as Paul explains in Galatians 4, so that those who 'were under the law . . . might receive the adoption of sons' (*Gal.* 4:4, 5). This grace comes to us only in Christ and for Christ, since it was 'the good pleasure' of God's eternal will (*Eph.* 1:5) that our Saviour should bring many sons to glory.

The uniqueness of adoption

Every gift from God is a wonder of grace, but many Christians experience this gift of adoption into God's family most keenly, and treasure it most deeply. Admittedly, there are few greater joys than knowing that one is justified before God, to hear the verdict that we are forgiven and as righteous in the sight of our judge as any man could ever be. Likewise, it is a great thing to be sanctified—to know that the great physician is at work, to know that our wounds are healing, the disease is leaving, the mortal illness of sin is mortal no longer. But neither of these pieces of news is fully realized and enjoyed outside the context of adoption.

The happiness we find in a family is different from that found in a courtroom or a doctor's surgery. Those who have been blessed with good parents can imagine the qualitative difference between leaving the judge in the courtroom without fear, and going home to a father with great joy. There is nothing like being a child of God and enjoying all the liberties and privileges of God's own family. What a freedom it is to be able to address God as our Father even though he is in heaven and we on earth! What a privilege it is to have brothers and sisters in every corner of the globe! What an honour it is to even have the power to be joint heirs with God's own Son (*Rom.* 8:17, *John* 1:12)!

Called by the Father's name

Consider what it means to be called by God's name—to have the Lord God Almighty give us his family name (*Jer.* 14:9; *2 Cor.* 6:18; *Rev.* 3:12). Just think of what it means for us to receive the Holy Spirit, who is the Spirit of adoption (*Rom.* 8:15), the one who through faith (*Rom.* 5:2) gives us 'access to the throne of grace with boldness' and 'confidence', as Paul reminded the Ephesians (3:12). Indeed, even sinners as wayward and weak as the Galatians were reminded that they too were enabled by the Spirit to cry out in simple trust, 'Abba', or in our language, 'Father' (*Gal.* 4:6).

The focus so far has been on what we receive, but the story can be told just as clearly from the perspective of what God gives. The psalmist reminds us that when we are pathetic, the Father pities the children who fear him (*Psa.* 103:13). The writer of Proverbs tells us that when we need refuge, God's children are protected (*Prov.* 14:26). The Lord Jesus tells us that we have no need to worry about our food or drink or clothes, for the Father knows how to provide for us (*Matt.* 6:30-32). In short, we can cast all our cares on him, because he cares for us (*1 Pet.* 5:7).

Chastisement

It is just because the Father cares for us that he also sometimes must discipline us. After all, as the writer to the Hebrews clearly says, it is precisely those whom the Lord loves that he disciplines, and it is those who are accepted as sons and daughters that the Father wisely punishes (12:6). Yet it is worth emphasizing that the Father is never vengeful or vindictive. He does not respond in wrath. Rather, we are chastened by him as by a loving Father. Sometimes we may need a severe mercy to bring us back to that straight and narrow road our Father has prepared for us. But God's discipline is always a mercy—by no means does it indicate that he has deserted us. It is worth remembering that it is right in the middle of Jeremiah's book of Lamentations that we are given the sweet promise that men and women 'are not cast off by the Lord forever' (*Lam.* 3:31).

On the contrary, one reason why we are given the Spirit of adoption is that the Spirit is God's seal 'to the day of redemption' (*Eph.* 4:30). God has a plan for his people, and all that he does for us, to us, and with us, is designed to prepare us for that great day. He is teaching his family members how to hold heavenly treasures in earthen vessels. It is his will that we, 'through faith and patience' (*Heb.* 6:12), will inherit all that he has promised. God has planned that we will be 'heirs of everlasting salvation', and that we will receive 'an inheritance that can never perish, spoil or fade—kept in heaven' for us (*1 Pet.* 1:4).

Father and children

When we have fellowship with other believers, we are with those who have been adopted by the living God as his own children. As we think of God the Father we must also think of God's family.

Our most basic alignment in this world is toward our Father who is in heaven. He is the one we adore and worship; it is in him that we trust, and we owe him the loyalty of our hearts. Our second most important relationship is with his children. We are God's family, one family, with one elder brother and one Spirit of adoption. For that reason Christian brothers and sisters ought to do all that they can to foster love and unity in this family, seeking its good and holding back from harming their fellow members of God's household.

As we think about our place in God's family, the last line in the first chapter of the letter to the Hebrews proves to be particularly significant. There we are told that 'all angels' are actually 'ministering spirits'. And incredibly, one of their main tasks is to give themselves to help God's family on earth. They are 'sent' by our Father 'to serve those who will inherit salvation' (*Heb.* 1:14). If this is the case, if the angels of God who stand before his throne are sent as servants of people here on earth, how much more ought we to serve the same family ourselves! Surely such service is appropriate thanks for the great salvation that we will inherit. Certainly it is an approved way to praise our Father and live to his glory, when we do all that we can to help our brothers and sisters on their way to the heavenly home we will share together.

CHAPTER 13:

OF SANCTIFICATION

Historic Text

13.1 They who are effectually called, and regenerated, having a new heart, and a new spirit created in them; are further sanctified, really, and personally, through the virtue of Christ's death and resurrection,[a] by his Word, and Spirit dwelling in them:[b] the dominion of the whole body of sin is destroyed,[c] and the several lusts thereof are more and more weakened and mortified;[d] and they, more and more quickened and strengthened in all saving graces,[e] to the practice of true holiness, without which no man shall see the Lord.[f]

Modern Version

13.1 Those who are effectually called and regenerated, having a new heart and a new spirit created in them, are further sanctified—truly and personally—through the power of Christ's death and resurrection, by his Word and Spirit dwelling in them. The dominion of the whole body of sin is destroyed, its various lusts are more and more weakened and put to death, and those called and regenerated are more and more enlivened and strengthened in all saving graces, leading to the practice of true holiness, without which no man shall see the Lord.

Scripture Proofs

13.1 [a] 1 Cor. 6:11; Acts 20:32; Phil. 3:10; Rom. 6:5,6. [b] John 17:17; Eph. 5:26; 2 Thess. 2:13. [c] Rom. 6:6,14. [d] Gal. 5:24; Rom. 8:13. [e] Col. 1:11; Eph. 3:16-19. [f] 2 Cor. 7:1; Heb. 12:14.

Regeneration and sanctification

When God begins a work, he is faithful in completing it. One of the miraculous works that God does is to effectually call and revitalize those who are spiritually dead. He gives them a new heart, a new spirit—in fact, it is not too much to say that he gives them new life. Paul termed it 'regeneration' in his letter to Titus (*Titus* 3:5). Jesus called it being 'born again' in his late-night conversation with Nicodemus (*John* 3:1-8).

God furthers his faithful plan by taking, washing and feeding his newborns; he takes those he regenerates and sanctifies them (*1 Cor.* 6:11). Christians are really and personally set apart and made holy. Paul calls this being 'built up'; every Christian needs this, because the inheritance God has set aside for us is only for those who are sanctified, as Paul explained to the Ephesians (*Acts* 20:32).

It is important to remember that sanctification is God's work because Christians sometimes summarize salvation as if one part of its progress is to be credited to God and one part to us. Doubtless this is said with good intent, and with the hope of making us serious about the Christian life. Nonetheless, we must insist that the only way to play a part in cleansing oneself is by clinging to the one who is white as snow. Those who want to walk the path of self-sanctification must be reminded of Romans 6: there we are told that sanctification only happens in Christ; there we are told that the only way to be dead to sin is to see 'our old self . . . crucified with [Christ] in order that the body of sin might be brought to nothing, so that we would no longer be enslaved to sin' (*Rom.* 6:5, 6). Like every Christian blessing and benefit, sanctification is found in union with Christ. Only by a willingness to identify with a Saviour who suffered will we find ourselves dead to sin, and only by looking with faith at Christ's empty tomb do we find the resurrection power for which Paul prayed (*Phil.* 3:10).

Word and Spirit

This sanctifying work is preeminently the work of the Spirit of the resurrected Christ. Paul told the Thessalonians, 'God chose you as the first fruits to be saved, through sanctification by the Spirit and belief in the truth' (*2 Thess.* 2:13). He said this because it is the Spirit of God who unites us to Christ and because the Spirit is our teacher. We learn in his school and his assigned textbook is the Word of God. It was Jesus' prayer to his Father, just after he promised the Holy Spirit to his disciples, that his Father would sanctify his people by his truth; by 'his truth' he meant the Scriptures (*John* 17:17).

It is the Spirit of God the Father and God the Son who sanctifies us, and the principal means he uses for our growth in grace is Scripture.

This is the tool the Spirit uses to shape us. Even when Scripture alludes to our being sanctified and cleansed with water, it is not water without the Word, but with the Word (*Eph.* 5:26). Even the sacraments of baptism and the Lord's supper are Word-dependent: our understanding of the sacraments and their usefulness are guided by the Word of God, and no water, bread or wine is truly a special sign without the spoken word.

The main point, which the Reformers and their heirs understood so well, and which the Westminster assembly mentions here for the third time, is that we are sanctified by 'Word and Spirit', because the Spirit uses the Word to teach us truth. Truth is transforming. With the truth of God's Word the Holy Spirit will make us grow spiritually and will sanctify us by his truth. Without it we will stagnate. Christians who do not know their Bibles remain immature and childish. Churches that do not teach the truth of God's Word will never rise above the nursery, even if they do separate the adults from the children in their services of worship.

Milk is fed to the young, but they will soon outgrow 'baby food' and will need to be moved on to 'solids' and ultimately to strong meat. No church should offer only one or the other of these necessities to God's people. We sometimes wonder why we do not grow, why we are so mediocre. It is not a mystery. It is not the fault of the Spirit, for he has told us about the important function the Bible has to our growth in grace. *Tolle lege!* Pick it up and read!

Destroying the dominion of sin

This is a serious business for all Christians. We want to have the Word of God dwelling richly in us because we want to see sin's dominion destroyed. Sin wants to enslave us; it is a cruel master that intends no good but does not want to run away. The only way for most slaves to escape their masters was through death. This has always been true, and Paul uses this as a striking illustration when he says that 'our old self was crucified with him', that is Jesus, 'in order that the body of sin might be brought to nothing, so that we would no longer be enslaved to sin', and that 'sin will have no more dominion' (*Rom.* 6:6, 14).

Elsewhere Paul sheds light on our mortal combat with sin as he explains that Christians crucify their sinful flesh with its passions and desires (*Gal.* 5:24). We do all we can to weaken the power of sin because it is a life and death battle: 'For if you live according to the flesh you will die, but if by the Spirit you put to death the deeds of the body, you will live' (*Rom.* 8:13).

Being strengthened in saving graces

This is the other half of the story. The full idea of sanctification is not summed up sufficiently by 'the mortification of the flesh', to use an old phrase; we must also be 'quickened', to use another. The flesh must be dealt a fatal wound but we must also live a new life. We not only need to subdue sin but also to become more and more alive to God's righteous demands. We need to see sin weakened. We also need to be 'strengthened in all saving graces'. What Paul wished for the Colossians we should all wish for one another: 'May you be strengthened with all power, according to his glorious might, for all endurance and patience with joy' (*Col.* 1:11). That is what it is like to live united to a resurrected Saviour.

Perhaps one of the most powerful summaries of a sanctified life is the one the Lord has reserved for us in Ephesians 3. There we overhear another apostolic prayer, which bears careful consideration:

> I pray that out of his glorious riches he may strengthen you with power through his Spirit in your inner being, so that Christ may dwell in your hearts through faith. And I pray that you, being rooted and established in love, may have power, together with all the saints, to grasp how wide and long and high and deep is the love of Christ, and to know this love that surpasses knowledge—that you may be filled to the measure of all the fullness of God (*Eph.* 3:16-19).

These prayer requests exemplify what sanctification truly is. It is about the practice of true holiness and it is about seeing Jesus. The two are intimately related. We will never be perfect; but without some practice in holiness we will not see the Lord, neither in this life nor in the next. God promises to change his people. So, 'since we have these promises, beloved', let us heed the Holy Scriptures that call us to 'cleanse ourselves from every defilement of body and spirit, bringing holiness to completion in the fear of God' (*2 Cor.* 7:1). As the letter to the

Hebrews urges, let us 'pursue peace with all men', and let us also pursue sanctification, 'without which no one will see the Lord' (*Heb.* 12:14).

How are we to do that? By trusting in the virtue of Christ's death and resurrection; by diligent study, trust, and application of the Word of God; and by humbly asking the Spirit of God to help us fight sin and love what is good, by his grace and through his power.

Historic Text	*Modern Version*
13.2 This sanctification is throughout, in the whole man;[g] yet imperfect in this life, there abiding still some remnants of corruption in every part:[h] whence arises a continual, and irreconcilable war; the flesh lusting against the Spirit, and the Spirit against the flesh.[i]	**13.2** This sanctification, although imperfect in this life, is effected in every part of man's nature. Some remnants of corruption still persist in every part, and so there arises a continual and irreconcilable war—the flesh warring against the Spirit, and the Spirit against the flesh.
13.3 In which war, although the remaining corruption, for a time, may much prevail;[k] yet, through the continual supply of strength from the sanctifying Spirit of Christ, the regenerate part does overcome:[l] and so, the saints grow in grace,[m] perfecting holiness in the fear of God.[n]	**13.3** Although in this war the remaining corruption may strongly prevail for a time, yet, through the continual supply of strength from the sanctifying Spirit of Christ, the regenerate nature overcomes, and so the saints grow in grace, perfecting holiness in the fear of God.

Scripture Proofs

  13.2 [g] 1 Thess. 5:23. [h] 1 John 1:10; Rom. 7:18,23; Phil. 3:12. [i] Gal. 5:17; 1 Pet. 2:11.

  13.3 [k] Rom. 7:23. [l] Rom. 6:14; 1 John 5:4; Eph. 4:15,16. [m] 2 Pet. 3:18; 2 Cor. 3:18. [n] 2 Cor. 7:1.

Sanctification throughout

The Westminster assembly's opening statement on sanctification provided us with some direction as we define this Christian grace. These following sections remind us of its existential dimensions. They tell us about the *experience* of sanctification.

The first thing we are told is that sanctification penetrates our whole being. Because sanctification is for the whole man, Scripture teaches us to pray that 'the God of peace' will 'himself sanctify you completely', both 'soul and body' (*1 Thess.* 5:23). Since every part of us is marred by sin, every part of us needs to be affected and changed by the grace of God. Certainly sanctification is a matter of the heart, but it is also intellectual: God's grace changes the way we think. It is physical: the Spirit changes the way in which we use our bodies, and the things we do. It is verbal: sanctified speech is controlled and purposeful, and it avoids dirty words and jokes.

However, the very fact that we need to pray for sanctification shows how different it is from justification and adoption. Christians do not pray that God would justify them—our sins are already forgiven; Christ's righteousness is already ours. Christians do not ask the Lord to adopt them—we already belong to his family. But Christians do earnestly ask that we would be sanctified by Word and Spirit. We ask that our 'whole spirit and soul and body' would 'be kept blameless at the coming of our Lord Jesus Christ' (*1 Thess.* 5:23), because God's sanctifying work is 'imperfect in this life'. It is not defective, but it is incomplete.

Remaining corruption

The truth is that, in all of us, corruption still exists. If we could X-ray our minds and hearts, a theological radiologist would see 'remnants of corruption in every part' of us. The Apostle John, an intern trained by the Great Physician himself, said that if we deny the presence of sin in our lives we make God a liar. To live in denial of sin does not prove that there is no sin in us. It proves that God's 'word is not in us' (*1 John* 1:10).

Surely, if we are half as honest as we ought to be, we will admit the problem of lingering sin to be painfully true. We 'have the desire to do what is right, but not the ability to carry it out'. The Apostle Paul speaks for all of us when he admits that sin remains a powerful force in life. He wishes it were a case of mind over matter; he wishes he could just announce that all is at peace; instead, he finds himself warring against sin, because sin longs to hold each of us as its prisoner (*Rom.* 7:18-23, especially verses 18 and 23). Paul did not obtain the heights that he wanted to reach. He freely told the Philippians that he was not perfect (*Phil.* 3:12). This must be true of lesser men also.

A necessary war

It is just because the enemy has not left us that we press on. We engage in battle. The Christian is conscripted to 'a continual, and irreconcilable war' precisely because 'the desires of the flesh are against the Spirit, and the desires of the Spirit are against the flesh' (*Gal.* 5:17). We would be fools not to fight, because whether we resist temptation or not, our sinful desires will 'wage war' against our souls (*1 Pet.* 2:11). Every Christian should try and live at peace with other sinners, but no Christian should try to live in harmony with a little sin. Sin and sanctification, the desires of the flesh and the desires of the Spirit, 'are opposed to each other' (*Gal.* 5:17).

Growing in grace

Our struggle emerges as all the more necessary because the remaining corruption in Christians may sometimes even get the upper hand—it 'may much prevail', at least 'for a time', as the pastors of the Westminster assembly remind us in the final paragraph of this chapter on sanctification. Our Lord claims us as his own; he plants his flag and announces his sovereignty over the whole of his church and over all that we are. But guerilla warfare continues and we still find Christians who are 'captive to the law of sin' (*Rom.* 7:23).

The good news is that Christians are regenerate people. We truly have been born again and are new creatures who have been given the Holy Spirit. 'Through the continual supply of strength from the sanctifying Spirit of Christ' we gradually overcome our enemy. As we engage in the spiritual exercise of running to Jesus and running from sin, and as we soak ourselves in the Word of God, we grow in our fitness to combat sin.

It is not easy to describe this bifurcated existence of the Christian. A seasoned apostle managed to express this difficulty eloquently, but even the Westminster assembly was grasping for words when it wrote about corruption in every part of us, while in the same breath telling us about what is true of our entire being.

No doubt they were reflecting normal human speech, for we some-times say that part of us wants to do what is right, and part of us wants to do what is wrong. In any case, we surely know what this third paragraph means when it says that 'the regenerate part' of us ultimately overcomes. This kind of phrasing is not denying that sanctification is throughout, in the whole man, when affirming that sin will no longer have dominion over us. The point is that we are not under law, but under grace (*Rom.* 6:14). We are being assured that 'everyone who has been born of God overcomes the world' (*1 John* 5:4). These theologians from long ago are reminding their readers of the eternal truth that Christians will eventu-ally 'grow up in every way into him who is the head, into Christ, from whom the whole body, joined and held together by every joint with which it is equipped, when each part is working properly, makes the body grow so that it builds itself up in love' (*Eph.* 4:15, 16).

To put it in more familiar words, sinners are also 'saints', and saints 'grow in grace'. Scripture calls all Christians to desire this growth—growth 'in the grace and knowledge of our Lord and Saviour Jesus Christ' (*2 Pet.* 3:18). All who are united to the living Lord will grow; it is not too much to say that we are being 'transformed . . . from one degree of glory to another'. It may not always feel like that, but growth is what 'comes from the Lord who is the Spirit' (*2 Cor.* 3:18). That is why Paul calls us to 'cleanse ourselves from all filthiness of the body and spirit, perfecting holiness in the fear of God' *(2 Cor.* 7:1).

Christian brothers and sisters need to encourage one another to walk in the fear of God. And as we do so, let us be earnest in our dependence on the Word and the Spirit, for it is through humble dependence on God's power that the strongholds of sin are brought down, and holiness is brought to completion.

CHAPTER 14:

OF SAVING FAITH

Historic Text

14.1 The grace of faith, whereby the elect are enabled to believe to the saving of their souls,[a] is the work of the Spirit of Christ in their hearts;[b] and is ordinarily wrought by the ministry of the Word:[c] by which also, and by the administration of the sacraments, and prayer, it is increased and strengthened.[d]

Modern Version

14.1 The grace of faith, by which the elect are enabled to believe to the saving of their souls, is the work of the Spirit of Christ in their hearts, and is ordinarily produced through the ministry of the Word. This faith is increased and strengthened by the same means, and also by the administration of the sacraments and prayer.

Scripture Proofs

14.1　[a] Heb. 10:39.　[b] 2 Cor. 4:13; Eph. 1:17-19; Eph. 2:8.　[c] Rom. 10:14,17.
[d] 1 Pet. 2:2; Acts 20:32; Rom. 4:11; Luke 17:5; Rom. 1:16,17.

Faith

By this point in the confession, readers have encountered the word 'faith' over a dozen times. It is time to properly define this Christian grace.

Sometimes, as is well known, the Bible refers to faith as something objective. In that sense 'the faith' refers to a set of orthodox doctrines as laid out in Scripture itself. Here the confession is interested in the more common use of the word 'faith' as it is found in the Scriptures, that is, the grace that enables the elect to believe 'to the saving of their souls' (*Heb.* 10:39). As the chapter title indicates, the Westminster assembly wanted its readers to reflect on 'saving faith' in particular.

The work of the Spirit

One of the first things that needs to be said about saving faith is what we find stated early on in this paragraph: saving faith is God's gift. Although the Bible says that we are 'saved through faith' (*Eph.* 2:8), and that faith is our own, every Christian also knows that faith comes to us only by God's grace. In fact, we can say more than that, for we can also deduce that faith is worked in us by God the Holy Spirit.

Consider, for example, the opening chapter of Paul's letter to the Ephesians. Notice that it is the Spirit who conveys wisdom and the other Christian graces that come from God (*Eph.* 1:17). Note also that our saving belief in Christ is ascribed to God's mighty power (*Eph.* 1:19). If the Spirit works grace and if faith is worked by God's mighty power, we can probably deduce that it is the Holy Spirit in particular who works faith in us. It is certainly striking, then, to see that in Paul's second letter to the Corinthians he refers to the 'Spirit of faith' (*2 Cor.* 4:13). The Westminster divines are not the first to conclude that when Paul refers to the 'Spirit of faith' he does not mean our *attitude* of faith. No, this should be understood as an uppercase 'S'—Paul is referring to a divine Spirit of faith, a Spirit who brings faith to a people who tend not to believe what they ought to believe.

There is so much we do not understand about the nature of faith and the Spirit's work. But surely the confession is clear enough when it talks about God's chosen people and says that saving faith 'is the work of the Spirit of Christ in their hearts'.

The ordinary means

Surprisingly, this section goes on to say that the Spirit 'ordinarily' works this saving faith in our hearts 'by the ministry of the Word'—that is, by preaching. One of the members of the Westminster assembly, Anthony Burgess, states that the faithful ministry of the Word is 'the sure and ordinary way for conversion of men from their evil wayes'.[1] He states this even more strongly in an exposition of 1 Corinthians 3: 'The Ministry is the only ordinary way that God hath appointed, either for the beginnings

---

[1] Anthony Burgess, *Spiritual Refining* (London, 1658), p. 500; see also p. 494.

or encrease of grace'. After all, 'faith is said to come by hearing',[1] and Paul's own text informs the Corinthians that Paul and Apollos were the 'ministers by whom ye believed'.[2] In 1649, William Greenhill, another member of the assembly, agreed. In his judgment, 'where the Word of God is not expounded, preached, and applyed' the people 'perish'.[3]

This focus on preaching was often unpopular in the 1640s for many of the same reasons that it is unpopular today. After all, are there not other means that can be used to build up the church? If the Bible is as good as chapter 1 of the Westminster Confession of Faith says it is, and if a sermon must always be judged by the Bible anyway, why not simply read the Bible? Or perhaps the Bible and Christian literature?

The response of another assembly member, Jeremiah Burroughs, is typical: 'You will say, "Cannot we sit at home and read a sermon?"' Today we might ask if we could stay at home and get something edifying off a website. No. 'The great ordinance is the preaching of the Word, faith comes by hearing (the Scripture saith) and never by reading'.[4] Burroughs softens this somewhat when he admits that his readers 'may think that this or the other means may do the deed as well', but expects that 'because God hath appointed this to be his ordinance, therefore in obedience to him [they] wil[l] attend upon this means rather than upon other means', just like Naaman did when he could not see the point of God's command for him.[5] Thomas Goodwin suggests that good books and conversations are helpful, particularly in times of spiritual drought, but a steady use of these in the absence of preaching is akin to a reliance on 'watering-pots' in the place of rain.[6]

There are a variety of responses that have been, and can be, given to those who doubt that the ministry of the Word is useful. And naturally in those responses we should make allowances for those who are unable

---

[1] Romans 10:17.

[2] 1 Corinthians 3:5; Anthony Burgess, *Scripture Directory* (London, 1659), p. 69.

[3] William Greenhill, 'To All Lovers of Divine Truths', The epistle dedicatory of *An Exposition Continued upon the Sixt, Seventh, Eighth, Ninth, Tenth, Eleventh, Twelfth, and Thirteenth Chapters of the Prophet Ezekiel* (London, 1649; Edinburgh, 1994), p. v.

[4] Jeremiah Burroughs, *Gospel Worship* (London, 1648), p. 167 (Morgan, PA, 1996), pp. 201-202.

[5] *Ibid.*

[6] Thomas Goodwin, *Works* (1861-66; Eureka, CA, 1996), vol. 11, p. 360.

to be where the Word is preached. Nonetheless, in normal situations, Romans 10 should always weigh heavily in the discussion. There we are not only told that faith comes by hearing, but also that hearing comes from preaching (*Rom.* 10:14, 17). If the Apostle Paul announces that 'faith comes by hearing, and hearing by the word of God', then we need to think twice about elevating any other means of communication above preaching—the means that Paul explicitly singles out for attention.

The ministry of the Word is used by the Spirit to work saving faith in us. It should be added that the Word of God can increase and strengthen our faith.

What new Christian and what seasoned saint will not confess that his or her faith is often weak? All the honest ones will. For that reason Christian elders impress upon every believer the importance of attending as often as possible to the preaching of the Word. We want to see trust in Christ grow and be strengthened as the weeks and years go by. The Apostle Peter once urged believers to desire what he called 'the pure milk of the word' precisely so that they would 'grow up into salvation' (*1 Pet.* 2:2). Paul said much the same to the leaders of the Ephesian church when he commended his listeners to the 'word of his grace, which can build you up' (*Acts* 20:32). This is biblical advice; the soundest sort of wisdom.

The sacraments and prayer

Preaching helps to strengthen faith. So too do the sacraments. We see this even in the Old Testament, for its old covenant sacrament of circumcision was linked to faith (*Rom.* 4:11). We know this in our own day too, for many people have had their faith strengthened from witnessing a baptism, or by partaking in the Lord's supper.

As we think of the Spirit's work of bringing faith and increasing faith, we should never forget the privilege of prayer, and we should be often in prayer for our faith and for that of others. After all, we have the strongest encouragements to pray. The apostles themselves set us an example, when in a moment of doubt they collectively cried out to Christ, 'Lord, increase our faith' (*Luke* 17:5). This is a prayer that Christ is pleased to answer by his Spirit. And this too, is the testimony of many Christians.

Perhaps it is best to sum up our reflections on saving faith by recalling the words of the Apostle Paul. Under the inspiration of the Holy Spirit Paul testified that he was 'not ashamed of the gospel, for it is the power of God for salvation to everyone who believes'. It does not matter if you are a Jew or a Gentile, Paul explained. If you want to know the power of God for salvation, you need saving faith. This is the non-negotiable that this chapter in the confession puts before us. After all, as Paul went on to say, the righteous will only 'live by faith' (*Rom.* 1:16, 17).

Historic Text	*Modern Version*
14.2 By this faith, a Christian believes to be true, whatsoever is revealed in the Word, for the authority of God himself speaking therein;ᵉ and, acts differently upon that which each particular passage thereof contains; yielding obedience to the commands,ᶠ trembling at the threatenings,ᵍ and embracing the promises of God for this life, and that which is to come.ʰ But the principal acts of saving faith, are, accepting, receiving, and resting upon Christ alone for justification, sanctification, and eternal life, by virtue of the covenant of grace.ⁱ	**14.2** By this faith, a Christian believes to be true whatever is revealed in the Word, because of the authority of God himself speaking in it. He also responds differently to what each particular passage contains—obeying the commands, trembling at the threatenings, and embracing the promises of God for this life and that which is to come. But the principal acts of saving faith are accepting, receiving, and resting upon Christ alone for justification, sanctification, and eternal life, by virtue of the covenant of grace.
14.3 This faith is different in degrees, weak, or strong;ᵏ may be often and many ways assailed, and weakened, but gets the victory;ˡ growing up in many to the attainment of a full assurance through Christ,ᵐ who is both the author and finisher of our faith.ⁿ	**14.3** This faith varies in degrees. It may be weak or strong. It may often, and in many ways, be assailed and weakened, but it gains the victory. It matures in many to the attainment of a full assurance through Christ, who is both the author and the perfecter of our faith.

Scripture Proofs

14.2 ᵉ John 4:42; 1 Thess. 2:13; 1 John 5:10; Acts 24:14. ᶠ Rom. 16:26. ᵍ Isa. 66:2. ʰ Heb. 11:13; 1 Tim. 4:8. ⁱ John 1:12; Acts 16:31; Gal. 2:20; Acts 15:11.

14.3 ᵏ Heb. 5:13,14; Rom. 4:19,20; Matt. 6:30; Matt. 8:10. ˡ Luke 22:31,32; Eph. 6:16; 1 John 5:4,5. ᵐ Heb. 6:11,12; Heb. 10:22; Col. 2:2. ⁿ Heb. 12:2.

Faith in the Word of God

The first paragraph in this chapter told us who works saving faith and how. This second asks what faith does, and in whom it is placed.

The first port of call for faith is the Scriptures: 'A Christian believes to be true whatsoever is revealed in the Word'. At a minimum, Christians need to be like the Samaritan villagers who heard Jesus speak and trusted him completely because they came to know that he was the Christ (*John* 4:42). But we need to believe more than the words that Jesus spoke on earth. Saving faith trusts the whole of the Bible, and does so because of the full 'authority of God' speaking in it. Actually, the Samaritans ought to have believed in Christ without actually having met him, for they could have believed the Old Testament record that God gave about his Son (*1 John* 5:10).

That was what characterized Paul—he not only worshipped 'the God of his fathers', but he did so 'believing all things which [were] written in the law and in the prophets' (*Acts* 24:14). It is this faith that Paul also wanted to see in others, and thus he commends the Thessalonians for their willingness to 'receive the word of God' (*1 Thess.* 2:13).

Obeying, fearing and embracing the Word

This section in the confession explains that a trust in the Word of God ought to be a defining mark of a Christian believer. It also points out that different passages in God's Word have different emphases. We need to heed the meaning of each passage of Scripture and act accordingly. This is important for a right interpretation of the Bible. The assembly members assume, quite rightly, that we cannot draw whatever point we please from any passage, like travellers who come to a well and expect it to yield their beverage of choice. We need to pay attention to what the Bible actually says. Nor can we (or should we) make the same point out of all passages. A preacher should not be expecting to find his hobby-horse saddled and ready to ride as he approaches every biblical text. We need to see, for example, if a passage is commanding, threatening, or promising, and adjust our teaching accordingly.

Moreover, we should recognize that if passages have different emphases, they may require different responses. The Apostle Paul explained to Christians in Rome that obedience needed to accompany their faith (*Rom.* 16:26). The prophet Isaiah emphasized that God wanted people to tremble at his message (*Isa.* 66:2). And prior to Paul and Isaiah, patriarchs such as Abel and Enoch, Noah and Abraham were taught to embrace God's promises in faith (*Heb.* 11:13).

Faith in Christ

So saving faith accepts the whole of God's Word, and seeks to act as God requires and to trust what God promises, both 'for this life and that which is to come' (*1 Tim.* 4:8). But saving faith does have a special focus. The principal thing that saving faith does is to 'receive' Christ, as John puts it (*John* 1:12); to 'believe' Christ, as Peter puts it (*Acts* 15:7); or to 'accept' Christ or 'rest on' Christ, as this confession puts it. No matter how it is said, the point is that faith does not simply look to promises. Nor does faith look to the blessings that Christ brings to Christians, such as the forgiveness of sin or the gift of righteousness. No, faith looks to Jesus Christ himself.

It is only through Christ that justification, sanctification and eternal life are given to sinners. We make no attempt to isolate Jesus from all the benefits that come to us when we believe in him. After all, it is by virtue of his gospel, his covenant of grace, that we are saved. Thus when we are spreading the good news, it should always be clear that the good news is Jesus himself—it is through our Saviour that all blessings flow. Is that not just what John was saying when he explained that those who received Christ became sons of God (*John* 1:12)? Is this not what Paul meant when he told the Philippian jailor to believe on the Lord Jesus Christ to be saved (*Acts* 16:31)? In both cases, the answer must be yes. Our hope of eternal life is placed in Christ, for 'we believe it is through the grace of our Lord Jesus that we are saved, just as they are' (*Acts* 15:11). This is certainly what Paul was teaching when he told the Galatians to look to Christ, for we live 'by faith in the Son of God'. For Paul, this was the only hope because, as he explained, it is Jesus 'who loved me, and gave himself for me' (*Gal.* 2:20).

Faith that grows

This confidence in Christ, indeed a firm faith in the whole of God's Word, ought to characterize every Christian. But it does not, and so paragraph 3 of chapter 14 makes one additional point.

It is well known that there are some Christians whom the Scripture describes as babes needing milk, while it speaks of others as adults needing meat (*Heb.* 5:13, 14). The Bible refers to those who are 'weak in faith', and 'strong in faith', and our Lord comforted those of 'little faith' and delighted in those of 'great faith' (*Rom.* 4:19, 20; *Matt.* 6:30; 8:10). Nonetheless, Christians with even a small degree of self-awareness know that faith not only varies in strength from person to person, but also in strength in our own individual experience. The reality is that our faith is often 'assailed' by sin, suffering, and the devil. It is, at times, 'weakened'. A robust confidence of our salvation in Christ is not the constant companion of every Christian. After all, our Lord himself prayed that Peter's faith would not fail (*Luke* 22:32), and Paul urged the Ephesians to take up the shield of faith to protect themselves from the same enemy who attacked Peter (*Eph.* 6:16).

Because of the weakness that accompanies us wherever we go, we need to remember that there is a 'victory' for Christians. Indeed, the Apostle John tells us that the very existence of our faith *is* in some way the victory that overcomes the world (*1 John* 5:4). Although we are often tempted, the experience of many Christians is to have an authentic assurance of faith in our salvation and in our final victory, even in the midst of our greatest trials. The letter to the Hebrews speaks of a 'full assurance of hope' that comes from faith and patience; elsewhere it urges us to draw near to God in 'full assurance of faith' (*Heb.* 6:11, 12; 10:22). This is not a blind trust but one that Paul refers to as a 'full assurance of understanding' (*Col.* 2:2).

Need we add that the one in whom we are to hope and trust and understand is Jesus. This is really the most important thing to understand about faith; we should always be found 'fixing our eyes on Jesus, the author and perfecter of faith, who for the joy set before him endured the cross, despising the shame, and has sat down at the right hand of the throne of God' (*Heb.* 12:2), and where he continues to intercede for us.

CHAPTER 15:

OF REPENTANCE UNTO LIFE

Historic Text

15.1 Repentance unto life, is an evangelical grace,[a] the doctrine whereof is to be preached by every minister of the gospel, as well as that of faith in Christ.[b]

15.2 By it, a sinner, out of the sight and sense not only of the danger, but also of the filthiness and odiousness of his sins, as contrary to the holy nature, and righteous law of God; and, upon the apprehension of his mercy in Christ to such as are penitent, so grieves for, and hates his sins, as to turn from them all unto God,[c] purposing and endeavouring to walk with him in all the ways of his commandments.[d]

Modern Version

15.1 Repentance unto life is a gospel grace, the doctrine of which is to be preached by every minister of the gospel, just as is the doctrine of faith in Christ.

15.2 By it a sinner—seeing and sensing not only the danger but also the filthiness and hatefulness of his sins, because they are contrary to God's holy nature and his righteous law—turns from all his sins to God in the realization that God promises mercy in Christ to those who repent, and so grieves for and hates his sins that he determines and endeavours to walk with God in all the ways that he commands.

Scripture Proofs

15.1 [a] Zech. 12:10; Acts 11:18; [b] Luke 24:47; Mark 1:15; Acts 20:21.

15.2 [c] Ezek. 18:30,31; Ezek. 36:31; Isa. 30:22; Psa. 51:4; Jer. 31:18,19; Joel 2:12,13; Amos 5:15; Psa. 119:128; 2 Cor. 7:11. [d] Psa. 119:6,59,106; Luke 1:6; 2 Kings 23:25.

Repentance that leads to life

The previous chapter in this confession stressed the importance of faith in Christ for all of life and for the life that is to come. But when the Scriptures speak of life, they also speak of the repentance that leads to life, or 'repentance unto life' (*Acts* 11:18), and thus the Westminster assembly offered a discussion of this 'evangelical grace'.

Repentance is a gospel or an evangelical grace because repentance involves believing something about ourselves and something about Christ. The authors of the confession may be making this point when they direct readers to an ancient prophecy. Every Christian knows that true repentance involves a serious consideration of our own sin. The prophet Zechariah declared that when the Holy Spirit would be poured out in a special measure, God's people would especially consider the cost of their sin—they will look 'on him whom they have pierced'. We mourn what sin required of the Son of God—indeed, Zechariah says, we 'mourn for him as one mourns for an only child, and grieve bitterly for him as one grieves for a firstborn son' (*Zech.* 12:10). As we look on Christ, the one who was pierced for our transgressions, we begin to see the full measure of our sin.

Repentance is important for our salvation, and this fact 'is to be preached by every minister of the gospel, as well as' the need for 'faith in Christ'. We see the importance of preaching repentance in the Bible. At the beginning of his ministry John the Baptist preached that the time had come for sinners to 'repent and believe the gospel' (*Mark* 1:15). At the end of his earthly ministry, our Lord himself sounded a similar note. He told his disciples that not only 'the forgiveness of sins' but also 'repentance' would 'be preached in his name to all nations, beginning at Jerusalem' (*Luke* 24:47). The Apostle Paul, too, testified 'both to the Jews and also to the Greeks' that they had need for 'repentance toward God, and faith toward our Lord Jesus Christ' (*Acts* 20:21).

Turning from sin and turning to God

So repentance contemplates our sin and the *cost* of our sin to the Saviour. Paragraph 2 goes on to remind us that people being led to repentance should see and sense the *danger* of their sin too. The Lord God himself urges his people to see their peril. Through the prophet Ezekiel he calls them to 'Repent!'. 'Turn away from all your offences; then sin will not be your downfall. Rid yourselves of all the offences you have committed, and get a new heart and a new spirit. Why will you die?' (*Ezek.* 18:30, 31)

Here is a call that Christians wish every sinner would not only hear but heed. But sinners must not only see the danger, but also the *filthiness and repulsiveness* of their sins. That too was preached by Ezekiel. Sinners were to 'remember [their] evil ways and wicked deeds' and 'loathe [themselves] for [their] sins and detestable practices' (*Ezek.* 36:31). These are strong words, but sin is a strong poison. Indeed, Isaiah compares the disposal of cherished idols to the disposal of a menstrual cloth (*Isa.* 30:22). We must never forget that sin is a dirty affair because it is absolutely 'contrary to the holy nature' of God.

Sin is also a *personal* affair, for sin is set against God himself, the one to whom we ought to have been faithful. Is that not why King David was so stricken with grief when he was confronted by Nathan the prophet? 'Against you, you only, have I sinned and done what is evil in your sight', he cried to the Lord. It was to God that he spoke when he confessed that his Maker was 'proved right' when he spoke, and 'justified' when he judged (*Psa.* 51:4; *cf. Jer.* 31:18, 19). All sin is to be judged, for it breaks the 'righteous law of God'. It is because we consider God's precepts to be right, that we come to 'hate every wrong path' (*Psa.* 119:128).

Sinners may sink into great depths of sorrow for sin, but we need to understand that remorse is not the same thing as repentance. What Paul calls a 'godly sorrow' is distinguished from 'worldly sorrow' by a Godward change (*2 Cor.* 7:11). True repentance not only sorrows for sin but sees a Saviour. This is so important for us to grasp. As we consider what God thinks of sin, we must also consider his mercy to sinners. After all, he is the one who spoke through the prophet Joel, urging his people to 'Return to the Lord your God, for he is gracious and compassionate, slow to anger and abounding in love, and he relents from sending calamity' (*Joel* 2:12, 13). We can treasure the powerful understatement of Amos, who told his hearers to repent, for 'perhaps the Lord God Almighty will have mercy' (*Amos* 5:15). And as we consider God's mercy we will begin to so grieve for and hate our sins, as to turn from them all toward God.

Is this not the most basic need that each one of us has? We were made to be with God, to enjoy fellowship with him. We want to be in a situation where we are no longer 'put to shame' when we consider our Creator's commands. We want to consider our ways, and turn our steps to walk according to God's statutes. Indeed, we want simply to follow God's righteous laws (*Psa.* 119:6, 59, 106). That is our purpose, our endeavour: to be upright in God's sight (*Luke* 1:6), and to turn to the Lord with all our heart and with all our soul and with all our strength, in all the ways of his commandments (*2 Kings* 23:25). Let us pray that this would be the main purpose of our repentance. Let us not only cease our foolish wanderings, but by God's grace follow in the footsteps of our Saviour, until the day dawns when we shall see him in his glory and sin will be no more.

Historic Text	*Modern Version*
15.3 Although repentance be not to be rested in, as any satisfaction for sin, or any cause of the pardon thereof,[e] which is the act of God's free grace in Christ;[f] yet is it of such necessity to all sinners, that none may expect pardon without it.[g]	**15.3** Although repentance is not to be relied on as any payment of the penalty for sin, or any cause of the pardon of sin (which is God's act of free grace in Christ); yet repentance is so necessary for all sinners, that no one may expect pardon without it.
15.4 As there is no sin so small, but it deserves damnation;[h] so there is no sin so great, that it can bring damnation upon those who truly repent.[i]	**15.4** No sin is so small that it does not deserve damnation. Nor is any sin so great that it can bring damnation upon those who truly repent.

Scripture Proofs

    15.3 [e] Ezek. 36:31,32; Ezek. 16:61-63.   [f] Hos. 14:2,4; Rom. 3:24; Eph. 1:7.   [g] Luke 13:3,5; Acts 17:30,31.

    15.4 [h] Rom. 6:23; Rom. 5:12; Matt. 12:36. [i] Isa. 55:7; Rom. 8:1; Isa. 1:16,18.

Repentance as 'self-satisfaction' or the 'cause' of pardon?

The first two sections of chapter 15 tell us what repentance is. It is a work of God's grace that sees us pulled out of the swamp of our sin and despair and walking instead down the straight and narrow path that leads to God and eternal life. But how essential is our repentance to our salvation? Paragraphs 3 and 4 aim to answer this question.

In the first place, we should not exaggerate the importance of our repentance in salvation. God forgives us when we turn from our sin to him in Christ, but he does not forgive us because he considers our repentance a deed that deserves a reward. Nor does he forgive us because he thinks that in repenting of our sin we are atoning for our own wrong-doing. Our repentance does not earn God's pardon; that was the late medieval view of penance in its crassest form. Penance came to be understood as the sinner's self-satisfaction—the sinner paying the price for his own sin by pious deeds before God. This mind-set is something that we slip into effortlessly on our own without lessons in medieval church history!

Here the basic point is that we ought not to think that our change in attitude and action impresses the Lord—a message which the Lord passed on more than once through his prophet Ezekiel. The covenant Lord declared through the prophet that he was going to show mercy to his wayward people. He was going to give them a new heart, and cause them to walk in his statutes and keep his laws. These people were going to be transformed. But they needed to remember that God was not doing it for their sakes; that is, not for anything that they had done or were about to do. He was helping them in spite of themselves, and only because he is merciful. Their only appropriate stance was shame for sinful ways and gratitude for the Lord's mercy. Pride for their recent transformation was not to even register on their spiritual radar (*Ezek.* 36:31, 32; 16:61-63).

God's free grace in Christ

We do not rely on repentance as the ground of our pardon. No, we rely on 'God's free grace in Christ'. It is 'free grace' that God emphasized through the life and teaching of the prophet Hosea. 'I will heal their waywardness', God promised, speaking of those who had come to rely on human helpers and false religion. I will 'love them freely', he went on to say, 'for my anger has turned away from them' (*Hos.* 14:4; *cf.* 14:2, 3).

God justifies penitent people 'freely by his grace' and he does so in Christ, or, as Paul says in Romans 3, 'through the redemption that came by Christ Jesus' (*Rom.* 3:24). We find this teaching in more than one place in Paul's letters. It is not our new walk of life that saves us; rather, our redemption comes only through Jesus' blood. To put it differently, 'the forgiveness of sins' is not in accordance with the quality of our repentance, but 'in accordance with the riches of God's grace' (*Eph.* 1:7).

The necessity of repentance

Though repentance is not the cause of God's pardon, we must also be clear that there is no pardon without repentance. Ponder the parallel, even if it is not a perfect one: God requires faith in Christ, but faith does not save us. In a similar way, God requires repentance, but repentance does not save us. However, that does not mean that either faith or repentance remain unimportant to God. On the contrary, both are 'of such necessity to all sinners, that none may expect pardon without' them.

Jesus said this on more than one occasion, and once he said it twice in a row: 'unless you repent', he told a crowd, 'you too will all perish' (*Luke* 13:3-5). This is as true for people on the streets of Jerusalem as it is for the philosophers on the Acropolis: as Paul declared, God 'commands all people everywhere to repent' (*Acts* 17: 30-31).

Comfort for sinners

Everyone is commanded to repent because 'all have sinned' (*Rom.* 5:12). Everyone is commanded to repent, even the people who commit small sins, because 'there is no sin so small but it deserves damnation'. Paul did not suggest that the wages of really major sin is death. He said, 'the wages of sin is death', without any qualification (*Rom.* 6:23). Who will leave the bar of heaven breathing a sigh of relief that God did not care about the little sins? Who can sincerely say that the Word of God is not including us and our sins in its sweeping declarations about humanity and human sin?

Remember the words of our Lord Jesus Christ. It was he who said, 'men will have to give account on the day of judgment for every careless [or idle] word they have spoken' (*Matt.* 12:36). When we recall this, some of us will find great comfort in this divine truth expressed in human words: 'There is no sin so great, that it can bring damnation upon those who truly repent.' Is that not near the very heart of God's message in Isaiah? 'Let the wicked forsake his way', he says, 'and the evil man his thoughts. Let him turn to the LORD, and he will have mercy on him, and to our God, for he will freely pardon' (*Isa.* 55:7). Or as Paul put it to the church in Rome, 'there is now no condemnation for those who are in Christ Jesus' (*Rom.* 8:1).

That is good news for sinners. Perhaps that is why this comfort is placed prominently in the opening paragraphs of Isaiah's long prophecy: 'take your evil deeds out of my sight!' the Lord commands; 'Stop doing wrong.' And what does the Lord promise to those who heed this call? He promises, 'though your sins are like scarlet, they shall be as white as snow; though they are red as crimson, they shall be like wool' (*Isa.* 1:16, 18). Have you wounded others with your careless words? Are you stained with sin that you cannot wash away? Then look to the grace of God in Christ, and repent of your sins. If you do, you will surely find a gracious redemption that is full and free.

Historic Text	*Modern Version*
15.5 Men ought not to content themselves with a general repentance, but it is every man's duty to endeavour to repent of his particular sins, particularly.[k]	**15.5** No one should be satisfied with a general repentance; rather, it is everyone's duty to endeavour to repent of each particular sin, particularly.
15.6 As everyman is bound to make private confession of his sins to God, praying for the pardon thereof;[l] upon which, and the forsaking of them, he shall find mercy:[m] so, he that scandalizes his brother, or the church of Christ, ought to be willing by a private or public confession, and sorrow for his sin, to declare his repentance to those that are offended,[n] who are thereupon to be reconciled to him, and in love to receive him.[o]	**15.6** It is the duty of each one to make private confession of his sins to God, praying for pardon (and whoever confesses his sins, prays for forgiveness, and forsakes those sins shall find mercy). Similarly, anyone who has scandalized a brother, or the church of Christ, ought to be willing by private or public confession, and sorrow for his sin, to declare his repentance to those that are offended, who are then to be reconciled to him and receive him in love.

Scripture Proofs

15.5 [k] Psa. 19:13; Luke 19:8; 1 Tim. 1:13,15.

15.6 [l] Psa. 51:4,5,7,9,14; Psa. 32:5,6. [m] Prov. 28:13; 1 John 1:9. [n] James 5:16; Luke 17:3,4; Josh. 7:19; Psa. 51:1-19. [o] 2 Cor. 2:8.

General and particular repentance

So far we have reflected on what repentance is and why it is important. These final sections discuss the details of how repentance ought to look. Indeed, the need for details is the first thing mentioned in paragraph 5: we ought not to be content with a general confession of sin.

Almost everyone will acknowledge that they are not perfect, and all Christians will confess that they are sinners. But sweeping admissions of sin should never satisfy us. Many Christians will have met people who have made general confessions of sin a science, or one of the fine arts. Listen to them pray and they can confess sin in general eloquently, seemingly without end.

The problem is not with their 'general repentance'. The problem is that their repentance is *always* general. They will never be heard confessing a particular sin. They will not admit that they are wrong, either to their family, their friends, their co-workers, or their elders; nor are they much more particular on their knees. That is why the confession goes on to remind us that 'it is every man's duty to endeavour to repent of his particular sins, particularly'. We should consider this instruction in our own prayers, in the prayers of our children, and in the prayers of our leaders, such as parents and elders and deacons. Those who piously content themselves with general confessions of their sinfulness often prove to be the most stubborn sinners.

The first step to repenting of particular sins is to realize that we commit individual sins. David prayed that the Lord would keep him from 'wilful sins'; assumed in this prayer request is the admission that as a sinner, David could consciously commit acts of sin (*Psa.* 19:13).

The second aspect of particular repentance is actually naming sin. Even while stating that ignorance and unbelief contributed to his sin, the Apostle Paul was willing to confess that he had been a blasphemer, a persecutor, a violent man. A particular confession did not require him to repeat his blasphemies, to recall the details of his persecutions or to retell violent stories. No one needed to hear all of that. But it would not have been enough if Paul had merely asserted that he was the chief of sinners (*1 Tim.* 1:13, 15).

Finally, particular repentance is evidenced in turning away from particular sin. That is one of the evils of contenting oneself with a general repentance—no particular sin is ever identified, so no particular sin is left behind and no Christian grace is embraced. How different this is from the case of Zacchaeus the tax collector. He did not simply announce that he was a sinner. He said, 'I give half of my possessions to the poor, and if I have cheated anybody out of anything, I will pay back four times the amount' (*Luke* 19:8). There was nothing vague about that!

Public and private repentance

Having explained the difference between general and particular repentance, the confession goes on to remind us of the Bible's teaching about private and public repentance. We must always confess our sin to God, privately (at least) and perhaps sometimes publicly. We see confession of sin again and again in Psalm 51. David could not help but cry out to God, for it was against God first that he had sinned. It was his cry to his Lord that he would be cleansed and that the sins that haunted him would be hidden away (*Psa.* 51:4-5, 7, 9, 14). We see the same in Psalm 32, where the king acknowledged his sin to God, covering nothing. He confessed his 'transgressions to the LORD' and urged 'everyone who is godly' to pray to God while he may be found (*Psa.* 32:5, 6).

The good news is that when we forsake our sin we will 'find mercy'. It is a sound proverb that 'he who conceals his sins does not prosper, but whoever confesses and renounces them finds mercy' (*Prov.* 28:13). As the Apostle John once wrote, and as Christians have often recalled, 'if we confess our sins, he is faithful and just to forgive us our sins, and to cleanse us from all unrighteousness' (*1 John* 1:9).

A private confession to God is a necessity. In his presence believers will always find mercy. But there are some cases, particularly when we have scandalized or hurt a brother or sister, when we ought to be willing to confess the sin to other people. A truly repentant person will not shrink from a true repentance before the one that has been wounded. A husband must be ready to confess his sin to his wife, a mother to her daughter. There is no need to publish our sins, especially some sins, for all to hear. But there is good reason to repent of our particular sins before those whom we have personally wounded—in fact God's Word calls us to it: 'confess your sins to each other and pray for each other' (*James* 5:16). The principle of meeting with people to discuss our sin is raised in the Gospel of Luke as well (*Luke* 17:3, 4). So this is instruction we cannot afford to ignore.

Nonetheless, what if we have sinned publicly? Perhaps during dinner, with friends witnessing our rude comments? In front of the family when we lose self control? What if our behaviour has tarnished the name of Christ in the whole community, or in his church? In such a case we are in Achan's situation. As everyone already knows what we have done, we ought to confess the act ourselves, as sin—no matter what the consequences. In Achan's case, the confession did not help him to escape his penalty. But he was assured that in his public death-row confession he was giving glory to God (*Josh.* 7:9). Maybe it is that sort of public confession we see in one of David's psalms, where the very title of his psalm publicly announces that he had committed adultery with his neighbour's wife (*Psa.* 51).

However, we cannot end here. Just as we were reminded that God will forgive those who repent of their sins to him, we are told that we need to forgive those who repent of their sins against us—whether privately or publicly. When a brother, sister or neighbour repents of their sin, we must be reconciled. More than that, we must receive them in love. We need to be ready to forgive and comfort, as Paul urged the Corinthians to do, lest anyone be 'overwhelmed by excessive sorrow'. We need to reaffirm our love to those who repent (*2 Cor.* 2:7, 8). And in doing so, we will be showing the same mercy to others that our Father in heaven has shown to us in Christ.

CHAPTER 16:

OF GOOD WORKS

Historic Text

16.1 Good works are only such as God has commanded in his Holy Word,ᵃ and not such as, without the warrant thereof, are devised by men, out of blind zeal, or upon any pretence of good intention.ᵇ

16.2 These good works, done in obedience to God's commandments, are the fruits and evidences of a true and lively faith:ᶜ and, by them, believers manifest their thankfulness,ᵈ strengthen their assurance,ᵉ edify their brethren,ᶠ adorn the profession of the gospel,ᵍ stop the mouths of the adversaries,ʰ and glorify God,ⁱ whose workmanship they are, created in Christ Jesus thereunto;ᵏ that, having their fruit unto holiness, they may have the end, eternal life.ˡ

Modern Version

16.1 Good works are only such as God has commanded in his holy Word, and not such as, without the warrant of Scripture, are devised by men out of blind zeal or any pretence of good intention.

16.2 These good works, done in obedience to God's commandments, are the fruits and evidences of a true and living faith. By them believers show their thankfulness, strengthen their assurance, build up their fellow believers, adorn the profession of the gospel, shut the mouths of the adversaries, and glorify God. They are his workmanship, created in Christ Jesus for good works, so that, bearing fruit unto holiness, they may attain the outcome, which is eternal life.

Scripture Proofs

16.1 ᵃ Mic. 6:8; Rom. 12:2; Heb. 13:21. ᵇ Matt. 15:9; Isa. 29:13; 1 Pet. 1:18; Rom. 10:2; John 16:2; 1 Sam. 15:21-23.

16.2 ᶜ James 2:18,22. ᵈ Psa. 116:12,13; 1 Pet. 2:9. ᵉ 1 John 2:3,5; 2 Pet. 1:5-10. ᶠ 2 Cor. 9:2; Matt. 5:16. ᵍ Titus 2:5,9-12; 1 Tim. 6:1. ʰ 1 Pet. 2:15; ⁱ 1 Pet. 2:12; Phil. 1:11; John 15:8. ᵏ Eph. 2:10. ˡ Rom. 6:22.

Good works that God commands

This confession has focused for many chapters on God's good work in our salvation. The chapter before us considers our good works, and it begins with a definition: good works are works that 'God has commanded' in his Word.

The Lord explains what is good whenever he spells out his requirements—such as acting justly, loving mercy, or walking humbly in his ways (*Mic.* 6:8). If we want to know or test what is pleasing, what is good or even perfect, then we must study God's will revealed in the Bible (*Rom.* 12:2). He alone is the one who can show 'us what is pleasing to him', and he is, as the writer to the Hebrews explains, the only one who can equip us 'with everything good for doing his will . . . through Jesus Christ' (*Heb.* 13:21).

Good works devised by men

Christians need to heed what God has to say about good works, and they need to avoid the so-called good works that are invented by men. This is true especially in the most important things that we do. It is true for our worship, to choose an example found in the assembly's proof texts.

In practice, we follow some rules or directions every time a congregation worships together, whether we make them up anew each week, or whether we follow the tradition of centuries. Given that we do have rules, we need to evaluate them wisely, for as the prophet Isaiah tried to teach his hearers, God is not simply displeased when people honour him with their mouths and not with their hearts. He will also punish them when 'their worship' is 'made up only of rules taught by men' (*Isa.* 29:13). This phrase is repeated by our Lord, who explains that man-styled worship is empty, hopeless and ultimately vain (*Matt.* 15:9).

But there is a larger point in view here. Sometimes these purportedly 'good' works are done out of zeal; but if God has not required them, then we are working blindly. There is a zeal for God, as Paul once explained, that 'is not based on knowledge' (*Rom.* 10:2). This lack of knowledge is not only useless for anyone who imposes his or her works on others. It is often dangerous for others. It is a sad fact of history, predicted by our Saviour, that people have even thought that in killing Christ's disciples they were somehow 'offering a service to God' (*John* 16:2).

Sometimes these so-called good works can claim the authority of a 'good intention', and sometimes they are an empty pretence.[1] King Saul once tried to justify breaking God's Word by a show of worship, but as the prophet Samuel put it memorably to Saul, 'obedience is better than sacrifice' (*1 Sam.* 15:21-23). Actually, both are needed, and it took Christ's obedience and sacrifice to redeem God's people from the bondage of the empty traditions that were handed down to them from their forefathers. We have a liberty from works imposed on us by others—a freedom that was not purchased 'with perishable things such as silver or gold' (*1 Pet.* 1:18). Let us take that freedom seriously.

The value of good works

One way of keeping from the snare of a man-made piety is to focus on the value of keeping God's own commandments. After all, obedience is a fruit and evidence of a 'true and lively faith'. As James puts it, our works both show and complete our faith in Christ (*James* 2:18, 22).

Through good works believers confirm their 'thankfulness' to God. The psalmists are hardly alone in wanting to render thanks to God for all of his goodness to us (*Psa.* 116:12, 13). After all, through Christ we are a 'chosen people, a royal priesthood, a holy nation, a people belonging to God'. What else should we do but 'declare the praises of him who called us out of darkness into his wonderful light' (*1 Pet.* 2:9)? Expressing thankfulness is only the beginning of those good works we can do by God's grace. They can strengthen our assurance, edify our brethren, and properly gild our 'profession of the gospel'.

This is the straightforward teaching of the New Testament. John tells us that if we want to 'be sure' that we know Christ, we need to keep his commandments (*1 John* 2:3, 5). Peter says the same when he links a chain of Christian graces and tells us that these will help us 'make our calling and election sure' (*2 Pet.* 1:5-10).

The Bible is equally clear about edification. Paul tells us that if we want to bless one another and stir up more zeal, then we need to engage in practical works such as giving to the needy (*2 Cor.* 9:2). In the words of our Lord, 'let your light shine before others, so that they may see your good works and give glory to your Father who is in heaven' (*Matt.* 5:16).

---

[1] 'Pretence' can have morally neutral or negative overtones. See *OED*, s.v.

And with respect to making our profession of faith more attractive, Paul tells Titus that we need to 'renounce ungodliness and worldly passions, and to live self-controlled, upright, and godly lives in the present age' if the 'doctrine of God our Saviour' is to be 'adorned' (*Titus* 2:5, 9-12). He tells Timothy that good works are necessary if the gospel is not to be 'reviled' (*1 Tim.* 6:1).

Christian obedience does suggest that our actions will sometimes speak louder to the world than words, so that, as Peter once explained, 'by doing good you should put to silence the ignorance of foolish people' (*1 Pet.* 2:15). Peter says this in the context of another exhortation: 'Live such good lives among the pagans', he urges, so that 'though they accuse you of doing wrong, they may see your good deeds and glorify God on the day he visits us' (*1 Pet.* 2:12).

We cannot ignore the world in all that we do, but the chief purpose of all of our labours is to 'glorify God'. We want to be 'filled with the fruit of righteousness that comes through Jesus Christ', Paul told the Philippians, because our concern is 'the glory and praise of God' (*Phil.* 1:11). Here he is echoing the words of his Master, who told his disciples that it is to the 'Father's glory, that you bear much fruit' (*John* 15:8). This emphasis on the importance of good works should hardly be surprising. Paul tells us that we were actually 'created in Christ Jesus to do good works, which God prepared in advance for us to do' (*Eph.* 2:10).

Bearing good fruit will show that we are Christ's disciples (*John* 15:8). For you see, 'now that you have been set free from sin and have become slaves of God, the fruit you get leads to sanctification and its end, eternal life' (*Rom.* 6:22). So let us take Christian obedience seriously.

Historic Text	*Modern Version*
16.3 Their ability to do good works, is not at all of themselves, but wholly from the Spirit of Christ.ᵐ And that they may be enabled thereunto, besides the graces they have already received, there is required an actual influence of the same	**16.3** Their ability to do good works is not at all from themselves, but entirely from the Spirit of Christ. And—in order that they may be enabled to do these things—besides the graces believers have already received, there must

Holy Spirit, to work in them to will and to do, of his good pleasure:[n] yet are they not hereupon to grow negligent, as if they were not bound to perform any duty, unless, upon a special motion of the Spirit; but, they ought to be diligent in stirring up the grace of God that is in them.[o]

also be an actual influence of the same Holy Spirit working in them both to will and to do God's good pleasure. This truth, however, should not cause believers to become negligent, as though they were not bound to perform any duty without a special moving of the Spirit; rather, they ought to be diligent in stirring up the grace of God that is in them.

16.4 They, who in their obedience, attain to the greatest height, which is possible in this life, are so far from being able to supererogate, and to do more than God requires, as that they fall short of much which in duty they are bound to do.[p]

16.4 Those who attain the greatest heights of obedience possible in this life are so far from being able to go beyond duty and to do more than God requires, that they fall short of much that is their duty to do.

Scripture Proofs

16.3 [m] John 15:4,5; Ezek. 36:26,27. [n] Phil. 2:13; Phil. 4:13; 2 Cor. 3:5. [o] Phil. 2:12; Heb. 6:11,12; 2 Pet. 1:3,5,10,11; Isa. 64:7; 2 Tim. 1:6; Acts 26:6,7; Jude v. 20,21.

16.4 [p] Luke 17:10; Neh. 13:22; Job 9.2,3; Gal. 5:17.

Depending on the Spirit

The opening paragraphs of chapter 16 tell us what good works are and why they are important. Paragraphs 3 and 4 discuss our ability to do good works and the extent to which we can expect to keep God's commands.

Firstly, we are told that the 'ability to do good works' does not come from ourselves, but 'wholly from the Spirit of Christ'. Apart from Christ, we cannot bear good fruit. As Jesus once explained to his disciples, if we are not united to him by his Spirit, we are like branches trying to grow grapes while detached from the vine (*John* 15:4, 5). To change the metaphor, if we want to keep the Lord's 'statutes and be careful to obey' his rules, we need the Spirit: we need God to remove our hearts of stone and give us each a heart of flesh (*Ezek.* 36:26, 27).

The importance of the work of the Spirit must not be underestimated. There is nothing in us that can generate good works. We can do many things as Christians, but we need to say with Paul that we 'do all things through him who strengthens me' (*Phil.* 4:13). If we pretend otherwise, a line from 2 Corinthians 3 will always stop us in our tracks: it is 'not that we are sufficient in ourselves to claim anything as coming from us'. The reality is that 'our sufficiency is from God' (*2 Cor.* 3:5). Nor is it the case that the graces we receive from Christ are themselves able to generate good works. It is not the case that God sets the ball rolling and the rest is up to us. Rather, to paraphrase Philippians 2:13, we need God himself to continue working in us, making us *willing* to do, and then actually *to do* what is God's good pleasure.

Stirring up God's grace

Our work relies on the Spirit's work but that does not give us room to grow negligent in keeping God's commandments. It is not as though we can ignore all of our duties unless we feel the Spirit personally prompting us into action. God's graces given to us in Christ must not, and in God's people cannot, be left gathering dust. We need to stir up, to rouse what is sluggish (*Isa.* 64:7; *Heb.* 6:11, 12). Elders, deacons and ministers, as well as ordinary church members, need to 'fan into flame the gift of God' that has been given them (*2 Tim.* 1:6).

There is a sense in which we should hope to 'attain' eternal life, to use a biblical verb (*Acts* 26:6, 7). Hence Paul urges us to 'work out' our 'own salvation with fear and trembling' (*Phil.* 2:12). And Jude directs his readers by saying, 'build yourselves up in your most holy faith; pray in the Holy Spirit; keep yourselves in the love of God' (*Jude* 20, 21).

Perhaps it is Peter who most unmistakably sets these key truths beside one another: the Spirit's working and our working. It is clear in Peter's Second Epistle that God's 'divine power has granted to us all things that pertain to life and godliness'. For 'this very reason' the apostle tells us to 'make every effort to supplement' our faith with virtue, knowledge, self-control, steadfastness, godliness, brotherly affection and love. Peter says still more by way of command, and more with strong words of warning. But his basic point is that although God is working in us, we are to be 'diligent to make [our] calling and election sure'. For, as the apostle explains, 'if you do these things, you will never fall, and you will receive a rich welcome into the eternal kingdom of our Lord and Saviour Jesus Christ' (*2 Pet.* 1:3, 5, 10, 11).

The limits of good works

We are to spare no effort to do good works by God's grace, but we need to remember what the Word of God says about our limitations. There are those who attain to great heights of obedience in this life. Take, for example, the Old Testament leader, Nehemiah. He was a faithful man, used by God to transform a nation for God's glory. He is a man who can shamelessly catalogue a number of his achievements (*Neh.* 13:22). But the striking thing is that after listing his good works, Nehemiah approaches the end of his book with the prayer that the Lord would 'spare [him] according to the greatness of [God's] steadfast love' (*Neh.* 13:22). Even Nehemiah could not assume that he could actually satisfy God's righteous standard by all that he had accomplished and he definitely did not assume that he could do more than God required. No one can reach a standard where we may seriously argue our goodness before God. This is something we can learn from almost any place in the Bible, whether from Nehemiah, or from Job, or, in a very different way, from Jesus (*Job* 9:2, 3; *Luke* 17:10).

At the end of every day, and at the end of our lives, God's people confess how far we have fallen short of the glory of God. We may entertain a high view of what God is doing in others. But we should not be so naïve as to expect that we or others are capable of works of supererogation, of doing 'more than God requires'. The reality is that Christ's righteousness super-abounds, but ours does not.

Of course, there are reasons for our deficiencies. Paul takes the time to explain one of them to the Galatians, and in doing so, speaks for all Christians. Even with the best of God's people, 'the desires of the flesh are against the Spirit, and the desires of the Spirit are against the flesh, for these are opposed to each other, to keep you from doing the things you want to do' (*Gal.* 5:17). The Spirit is working in us, but there is a battle going on. Christians are saved by God's grace, but they remain saved sinners.

The good news is that we can be led by the Spirit to a great extent, and that we can live by the Spirit through Jesus Christ our Lord. And the best news is that Jesus reached the highest heights, the very pinnacle of good works. He obeyed his Father and laid down his life for those who fail in their duties but have faith in the Saviour.

Historic Text	*Modern Version*
16.5 We cannot, by our best works, merit pardon of sin, or eternal life at the hand of God, by reason of the great disproportion that is between them and the glory to come; and, the infinite distance that is between us and God, whom, by them, we can neither profit, nor satisfy for the debt of our former sins,^q but, when we have done all we can, we have done but our duty, and are unprofitable servants;^r and, because, as they are good, they proceed from his Spirit;^s and, as they are wrought by us, they are defiled, and mixed with so much weakness and imperfection, that they cannot endure the severity of God's judgment.^t	**16.5** We cannot, by our best works, merit forgiveness for sin or eternal life at the hand of God. This is true because of the great disproportion between our best works and the glory to come, and because of the infinite distance between us and God. We cannot benefit God by our best works nor render satisfaction for the debt of our former sins, for when we have done all we can, we have done merely our duty and are unprofitable servants. This is because, insofar as they are good, these deeds proceed from the Spirit; and, insofar as they are done by us, they are defiled and mixed with so much weakness and imperfection that they cannot endure the severity of God's judgment.

Scripture Proofs

16.5 ^q Rom. 3:20; Rom. 4:2,4,6; Eph. 2:8,9; Titus 3:5-7; Rom. 8:18; Psa. 16:2; Job 22:2,3; Job 35:7,8. ^r Luke 17:10. ^s Gal. 5:22,23. ^t Isa. 64:6; Gal. 5:17; Rom. 7:15,18; Psa. 143:2; Psa. 130:3.

Our best works and God's best: why we cannot merit eternal life

Good works are works that God commands, 'the fruits and evidences of a lively faith' in Christ. Our works are the fruit of the Holy Spirit's work in us, but the Spirit's work in us is not perfected until we are raised from the dead. Indeed, we fall short of what God requires.

Paragraph 5 of chapter 16 provides more detail of the Christian account of good works, moving from a discussion of the limitations of the best people, to the limitations of the best works. The most obvious limitation to our best works is that they do not 'merit pardon of sin, or eternal life'. When in Romans 3 Paul specifies that we cannot be saved by 'the works of the law', he seems to have in view religious activities in particular. But even if he has in view Jewish works in particular, he is merely providing us with a prominent example of a general principle: good works, things we do, religious or otherwise, are not enough to please God (*Rom.* 3:20).

Now, there is a sense in which good works could give us a little scope for boasting before one another, or so it seems if we listen to ourselves from week to week. But we could never boast before God about our works. We could never claim that salvation is not God's gift but our due. Our blessedness is that God imputes righteousness apart from our works as Paul declares in Romans 4 (*Rom.* 4:2, 4, 6). The same point is developed elsewhere in his other epistles. As Paul explained to the Ephesians, 'it is by grace you have been saved, through faith—and this not from yourselves, it is the gift of God'. Apparently some did think that salvation might be gracious, but that a little bit of it might come from themselves. Paul rules this out. Salvation is 'not by works, so that no one can boast' (*Eph.* 2:8, 9).

There has never been a time when this truth has not been doubted in one or another corner of the church. The actual insufficiency of our best works needs to be reaffirmed as clearly today as it was in the seventeenth century or the sixteenth, or the fifth or the first. The fact is that there is a huge disproportion between the best of our works and the least of God's glories.

How can we seriously set our shining acts of piety, even our most serious sacrifices for Christ, beside the splendour of 'the glory to come'? The truth is 'that our present sufferings are not worth comparing with the glory that will be revealed in us' (*Rom.* 8:18). How can we think that what we do in this life could ever earn us eternal life? The truth is that God 'saved us, not because of works done by us in righteousness, but according to his own mercy, by the washing of regeneration and renewal of the Holy Spirit' (*Titus* 3:5). How can we 'become heirs according to the hope of eternal life'? Only because the Spirit is 'poured out on us richly'; only 'through Jesus Christ our Saviour'; only because we are 'justified by his grace' (*Titus* 3:6, 7). Only because God has dealt with 'our former sins', and not because of anything that we can do.

At root, the reason why there is such a distance between our good works and God's, and between our piety and our reward, is because there is a chasm of difference between God and us. This fact is an all-important reference point. In God all goodness dwells. But the same is not true of us. Apart from him we have no good thing (*Psa.* 16:2). All God's goodness profits us, but what can we add to God? This is a question that is raised more than once in the book of Job, and the answer is obvious (*Job* 22:2-3; 35:7-8). When we have 'done all' that we 'were commanded', we are to say, 'We are unworthy servants; we have only done what was our duty' (*Luke* 17:10). These are the words of Jesus, and he knows the mind of God.

A debt to the Spirit

Our best works cannot merit God's pleasure because they will never be good enough for God and because what is good in our works is really owing to the Holy Spirit. Again and again the Scriptures associate most closely the gracious work of the Spirit with our own efforts. Is there any 'love, joy, peace', or 'patience' in your life? Are you seeing 'kindness, goodness', and 'faithfulness' in your roommate or your spouse? Have you noticed any 'gentleness and self-control' in your Christian friends or children? If so, we instinctively know who is at work. This is 'the fruit of the Spirit', and he must be assigned the credit (*Gal.* 5:22, 23).

That is the true assessment of our behaviour. The good in us proceeds from the Holy Spirit. That which comes from us alone can be 'good' only in the most pedestrian sense of the word. It is useful to accept this general sense of goodness—it would be difficult to thank, praise and encourage each other without it. And yet we must remember, especially when considering ourselves, that our best works are still defiled, because they are 'mixed with so much weakness and imperfection' and confused intentions (*cf. Gal.* 5:17; *Rom.* 7:15, 18; *Isa.* 64:6). Our works can pass the muster of a kind friend, or, if we are already Christians, a benevolent Father in heaven, as we will see elsewhere. But they could never 'endure the severity of God's judgment', let alone win us salvation. If the Lord 'should mark iniquities . . . who could stand?' (*Psa.* 130:3) We must confess, with the psalmist's masterly economy of words, that 'no one living is righteous before' God (*Psa.* 143:2)—no one, except the One.

Historic Text	*Modern Version*
16.6 Yet notwithstanding, the persons of believers being accepted through Christ, their good works also are accepted in him,ᵘ not as though they were in this life wholly unblameable and unreproveable in God's sight;ʷ but that, he looking upon them in his Son, is pleased to accept, and reward that which is sincere, although accompanied with many weaknesses and inperfections.ˣ	**16.6** Nevertheless, because believers are accepted through Christ, their good works are also accepted in him. They are accepted not because believers are in this life unblamable and unreprovable in God's sight, but because he, looking upon them in his Son, is pleased to accept and reward that which is sincere, even though it is accompanied by many weaknesses and imperfections.
16.7 Works done by unregenerate men, although, for the matter of them, they may be things which God commands, and of good use both to themselves, and others:ʸ yet, because they proceed not from an heart purified by faith;ᶻ nor are done in a right manner, according to the Word;ᵃ nor, to a right end, the glory of God;ᵇ they are therefore sinful, and cannot please God, or make a man meet to receive grace from God.ᶜ And yet, their neglect of them is more sinful, and displeasing unto God.ᵈ	**16.7** Although the works done by unregenerate men may in themselves be things which God commands and things which are useful to themselves and others, yet—because they do not come from a heart purified by faith, are not done in a right manner according to the Word, and are not done for the right purpose, which is to glorify God—they are therefore sinful, and cannot please God or make one suitable to receive his grace. Yet, neglecting them is even more sinful and displeasing to God.

Scripture Proofs

   16.6 ᵘ Eph. 1:6; 1 Pet. 2:5; Exod. 28:38; Gen. 4:4, with Heb. 11:4. ʷ Job 9:20; Psa. 143:2; ˣ Heb. 13:20,21; 2 Cor. 8:12; Heb. 6:10; Matt. 25:21,23.

   16.7 ʸ 2 Kings 10:30,31; 1 Kings 21:27,29; Phil. 1:15,16,18. ᶻ Gen. 4:5, with Heb. 11:4; Heb. 11:6. ᵃ 1 Cor. 13:3; Isa. 1:12. ᵇ Matt. 6:2,5,16. ᶜ Hag. 2:14; Titus 1:15; Amos 5:21,22; Hos. 1:4; Rom. 9:16; Titus 3:5. ᵈ Psa. 14:4; Psa. 36:3; Job 21:14,15; Matt. 25:41-43,45; Matt. 23:23.

The good works of believers: accepted in Christ

How can obedience ever be acceptable when our good works are so bad? That is one question which this chapter raises and which these two final paragraphs seek to answer with respect to the believer and to the unregenerate person.

   For the Christian, and we say this with mingled joy and wonder, the answer is that our good works are accepted through our mediator. We often recall that God accepts *us* 'in the beloved', as Paul says in Ephesians 1:6. But he also accepts *the good that we seek to do*, the 'spiritual sacrifices' that become 'acceptable to God through Jesus Christ', as the Apostle Peter affirms (*1 Pet.* 2:5).

The Father receives our work because we have a high priest who intercedes for us. This is pictured clearly already in the Old Testament. In that time before Christ, when an Israelite came to God with a gift in hand, it was never perfect. So obvious was this that the high priest had to symbolically 'bear the guilt involved in the sacred gifts the Israelites consecrate, whatever their gifts may be' (*Exod.* 28:38; *cf. Gen.* 4:4 with *Heb.* 11:4).

Again we can see that it is 'not as though [these works are] in this life wholly unblamable and unreprovable in God's sight'. We do not have such confidence. For example, it would be hard to point to a man more admirable than Job, and yet in one of his most striking lines, this philosopher and philanthropist states, 'if I justify myself, mine own mouth shall condemn me: if I say, I am perfect, it shall also prove me perverse' (*Job* 9:20). If that is true of Job, then the psalmist is certainly right to say that 'no one living is righteous before' God (*Psa.* 143:2).

Nonetheless, the point is that in spite of the many dark blotches on all of our best works, God looks 'upon them in his Son'. We need to be clear regarding every point in this discussion about good works, but here is an overriding concern that we may stress with unequal emphasis. God can and actually does work 'in us that which is pleasing in his sight, through Jesus Christ' (*Heb.* 13:20, 21). Our Father understands us, he knows our limitations as humans and as sinners, and at the very least, he judges our gifts based on what we *can* do and not on what we *cannot* do (*2 Cor.* 8:12). Is this not how a Father receives the gifts of a child, even his disobedient children? Because of Jesus he 'is pleased to accept and reward that which is sincere' even though it is 'accompanied with many weaknesses and imperfections'. Our works have no merit that earns mercy, nor are they given any meritorious worth by God. But in accepting us in Christ, our Father accepts all that we are and do.

As the writer to the Hebrews explains, 'God is not unjust; he will not forget your work and the love you have shown him as you have helped his people and continue to help them' (*Heb.* 6:10). It is true that we will one day say that we have been unworthy servants, doing only our duty at the best of times. But it is a wonderful truth that our Master will say, 'Well done, good and faithful servant! You have been faithful with a few things; I will put you in charge of many things. Come and share your master's happiness' (*Matt.* 25:21, 23).

The good works of unbelievers: useful, but unacceptable, and necessary

Unfortunately we cannot end on that point, for we also need to remember that there are those who are outside of Christ who will not repent of their sins and trust the Saviour. These people may do things which God commands. Furthermore, what they do is in some sense good—or at least it has a 'good use both [for] themselves and others'. God told the idol-worshipping Jehu that he had 'done well', in part because Jehu was less evil than the kings before him (*2 Kings* 10:30, 31). And God even acknowledged that there was humility to be found in King Ahab, and so promised him relief from suffering in his lifetime (*1 Kings* 21:27, 29). We need to be comfortable saying that unbelievers can do well, because God says as much in his holy Word. We ought to have Paul's perspective about the works of others. He once stated that whenever Christ is preached, he rejoiced. This was a good work and he would acknowledge it as such. He was not naïve about the true character of this work. He knew that some people did good 'out of goodwill' while others did it 'out of envy and rivalry' (*Phil.* 1:15, 16, 18). But he still rejoiced, and was determined to 'continue to rejoice' about such things.

So we can rejoice and give God praise for the good that unregenerate people do. We can thank others for their kindness. Yet we must also be clear that God knows that these things 'proceed not from an heart purified by faith' in Christ. As we survey the landscape of good works, Cain and Abel's sacrifices look alike. Yet to God it made all the difference that Abel was a faithful man (*Gen.* 4:5 with *Heb.* 11:4, 6). Works that come from an impure heart are not performed 'according to the Word' of God. You see, I can 'give all I possess to the poor and surrender my body to the flames'. It will look most impressive. Stories will be told about it. Nonetheless, the Word of God says that if I am lacking in another compartment, such as 'love, I gain nothing' (*1 Cor.* 13:3). The Lord will ask why we do what we do, and we will not survive his cross-examination unless Christ is our advocate (*Isa.* 1:12).

In short, there is one thing that the unbeliever refuses to take into account: 'the glory of God'. Those who do not work for the glory of God ultimately work for their own selves, their own goals, their own glory. As Jesus explained to his audience, 'they have their reward' (*Matt.* 6:2, 5, 16). But it is a fleeting reward offered by this world, and not the eternal reward from the Lord. Truly, these works are in God's sight 'sinful', and it is God's sight that matters. They simply 'cannot please God'. They most assuredly will not induce God to reward them with grace. The Bible declares this repeatedly, but perhaps nowhere as clearly as in Paul's letter to Titus: 'to the pure, all things are pure, but to the defiled and unbelieving, nothing is pure' (*Titus* 1:15). That is a problem which an unbeliever cannot overcome.

God hates the most solemn worship service that is empty (*Amos* 5:21, 22). He declares unclean the work of unbelieving hands (*Hag.* 2:14). He will punish the Jehus of this world, impressive as they might seem (*Hos.* 1:4).[1] It can be our prayer that our neighbours will come to see that God's approval 'depends not on human will or exertion, but on God, who has mercy' (*Rom.* 9:16, *Titus* 3:5). Perhaps they will turn to Christ, and find life in him.

At the same time, let us pray for our own good and for theirs, that they would not neglect what good they do, for wherever we turn in Scripture we can see that the abandonment of good is even 'more sinful and displeasing unto God' (*e.g., Psa.* 14:4; 36:3; *Job* 21:14, 15; *Matt.* 23:23; 25:41-43, 45). Let us pray that evildoers who never seem to learn, will 'call on the Lord', trusting Christ, and not their good works which, in God's reckoning, are woefully inadequate.

---

[1] See also Titus 3:5; Psalm 36:3; Job 21:14-15; Matthew 25:41-43, 45; 23:23.

CHAPTER 17:

OF THE PERSEVERANCE OF THE SAINTS

———

Historic Text

17.1 They, whom God has accepted in his Beloved, effectually called, and sanctified by his Spirit, can neither totally, nor finally, fall away from the state of grace: but shall certainly persevere therein to the end, and be eternally saved.[a]

Modern Version

17.1 Those whom God has accepted in his Beloved, effectually called, and sanctified by his Spirit, can neither totally nor finally fall away from the state of grace, but shall certainly persevere in it to the end and be eternally saved.

Scripture Proofs

17.1   [a] Phil. 1:6; 2 Pet. 1:10; John 10:28,29; 1 John 3:9; 1 Pet. 1:5,9.

What God has done

One way of thinking about our own perseverance in our Christian pilgrimage is to remember who we are. We are people 'accepted' in Christ, God's beloved Son. We are people who have been 'effectually called and sanctified' by God's Holy Spirit—and so much more besides. In short, we are people for whom the triune God has already done great things. And if God has done so much for us, if he has given us his own Son and Spirit, will he not give us all that we need to run our race, to finish our journey, to win the crown? This is the sort of logic that Paul uses when he assures the Philippians 'that he who began a good work in you will bring it to completion at the day of Jesus Christ' (*Phil.* 1:6). This is the clear teaching of the Scriptures. When God calls us to life in Christ, he calls us forever. When he begins a good work, he finishes it.

Strikingly, one of the clearest statements about our eternal security in Christ was made at a time when the enemies of our Lord were circling around him, doing all that they could to catch him and ultimately kill him. It was at that unlikely moment that the Great Shepherd chose to explain that he would never lose a single sheep in his fold. 'I give them eternal life', he declared, 'and they will never perish, and no one will snatch them out of my hand'. The reason for this confidence was at once so simple and so grand: 'My Father, who has given them to me, is greater than all'. For that reason 'no one is able to snatch them out of the Father's hand' (*John* 10:28, 29). We are the object of a divine gift exchange, and no one will steal a gift from the Father to the Son.

What God will do

This confession determines that we 'can neither totally nor finally fall away from the state of grace'. Yet every Christian knows that we sometimes stumble, and some have discovered by bitter experience that if we neglect to light our path with the lamp of God's Word, we will lose our way. It matters very much how we walk before our God. He never once encourages us to take his promises as excuses for carelessness. Churches in the Reformation tradition have never taught a bare doctrine of preservation. They affirm a biblical doctrine of perseverance.

Surely it is both wise and weighty that we are not only reminded in this paragraph that we are preserved by God's grace, but also that we are to 'persevere' to the end. Is this not exactly what Peter teaches? 'Be all the more diligent to make your calling and election sure'. Only then, he says, 'if you do these things', can he promise that 'you will never fall' (*2 Pet.* 1:10). Perseverance in sanctification is essential for those who would be eternally saved.

We should offer no encouragement to the idea that those people are Christians who confess Christ as their Saviour at one moment and then live a life of disobedience at every other. We may save a soul by reminding them that we have no reason to trust their testimony without evidence of change. Recall the words of the Apostle John who tells us that 'no one born of God makes a practice of sinning, for God's seed abides in him, and he cannot keep on sinning because he has been born of God' (*1 John* 3:9). People who are born again will feed on the milk of God's Word. They will learn to walk in his ways. They will mature to live in humble dependence on the Spirit of Christ.

We must be clear about this. After all, while the Bible does not teach us that there is such a thing as a 'carnal Christian', it does warn us that a person may confess Christ falsely, and eventually fall away. We need to call today's worldly Christians to trust in Christ and repent of their sins.

Let us follow Jesus down the hard path of obedience, and avoid the 'easy' road of sin. Let us turn to Christ when we falter, reminding the Lord in our prayers that by his power he can keep us from totally or finally falling away from sin. After all, it is by 'God's power' that we 'are being guarded through faith for a salvation ready to be revealed in the last time'. It is through trusting in Christ, the Scripture assures us, that you will obtain 'the outcome of your faith, the salvation of your souls' (*1 Pet.* 1:5, 9).

Historic Text	*Modern Version*
17.2 This perseverance of the saints, depends not upon their own free will, but upon the immutability of the decree of election flowing from the free and unchangeable love of God the Father;[b] upon the efficacy of the merit, and intercession of Jesus Christ;[c] the abiding of the Spirit, and of the seed of God within them;[d] and the nature of the covenant of grace:[e] from all which, arises also the certainty, and infallibility thereof.[f]	**17.2** The perseverance of the saints does not depend upon their own free will, but on the unchangeableness of the decree of election, flowing from the free and unchangeable love of God the Father; on the efficacy of the merit and intercession of Jesus Christ; on the continuing presence of the Spirit and the seed of God within them; and on the nature of the covenant of grace. These are grounds of the certainty and infallibility of their perseverance.
17.3 Nevertheless, they may, through the temptations of Satan and of the world, the prevalency of corruption remaining in them, and the neglect of the means of their preservation, fall into grievous sins;[g] and, for a time, continue therein:[h] whereby they incur God's displeasure,[i] and grieve his Holy Spirit,[k] come to be deprived of some measure of their graces and comforts,[l] have their hearts hardened,[m] and their consciences	**17.3** Nevertheless, they may—through the temptations of Satan and of the world, the pervasiveness of the corruption remaining in them, and the neglect of the means by which they are to be preserved—fall into grievous sins and for a time continue in them. In so doing they incur God's displeasure and grieve his Holy Spirit; some measure of God's graces and comforts is taken from them; they have their hearts hardened and

wounded,[n] hurt, and scandalize others,[o] and bring temporal judgments upon themselves.[p]

their consciences wounded; they harm others and give them occasion to sin, and bring temporal judgments upon themselves.

Scripture Proofs

17.2 [b] 2 Tim. 2:18,19; Jer. 31:3. [c] Heb. 10:10,14; Heb. 13:20,21; Heb. 9:12-15; Rom. 8:33-39; John. 17:11,24; Luke 22:32; Heb. 7:25. [d] John 14:16,17; 1 John 2:27; 1 John 3:9. [e] Jer. 32:40. [f] John 10:28; 2 Thess. 3:3; 1 John 2:19.

17.3 [g] Matt. 26:70,72,74. [h] Psa. 51, title, and v. 14. [i] Isa. 64:5,7,9; 2 Sam. 11:27. [k] Eph. 4:30. [l] Psa. 51:8,10,12; Rev. 2:4; Song of Sol. 5:2-4,6. [m] Isa. 63:17; Mark 6:52; Mark 16:14. [n] Psa. 32:3,4; Psa. 51:8. [o] 2 Sam. 12:14. [p] Psa. 89:31,32; 1 Cor. 11:32.

How Christians persevere

Christians are to remain steadfast in their pursuit of God, even in the face of troubling obstacles. Nonetheless, this constancy on our part does not simply depend on a decision of our own wills. It depends on God's will. We persevere because God has immutably decreed that we are his. He has unchangeably chosen us. It is his decision. 'The Lord knows those who are his' (*2 Tim.* 2:18, 19).

Our loyalty is secured because of God's gracious election, and the confession rightly observes that this election flows from the Father's free and boundless love. It is he who says, 'I have loved you with an everlasting love; I have drawn you with loving-kindness' (*Jer.* 31:3).

God's love is eternal. His love reminds us that he is triune. Our hope depends on the love of the Father, as well as on 'the efficacy of the merit and intercession of Jesus Christ'. In other words, our continuance in the Christian faith rests in Christ's single, 'once for all' offering of himself for our sin and in his continual pleading for our good. It is through 'the blood of the eternal covenant' that God will 'equip you with everything good for doing his will'. It is 'through Jesus Christ' that he will 'work in us what is pleasing to him' (*Heb.* 13:20, 21). All that he did, he did so that we 'may receive the promised eternal inheritance' (*Heb.* 9:12-15).

It is because of our Lord's death and, what is more, his resurrection and ascension, that Paul tells us that nothing 'will separate us from the love of Christ', that 'we are more than conquerors', that neither death, demons, 'nor anything else in all creation, will be able to separate us from the love of God that is in Christ Jesus our Lord' (*Rom.* 8:33-39). We have been given to the Son by the Father (*John* 17:11, 24) and the Son will always pray for us, and 'always lives to intercede' for us (*Luke* 22:32; *Heb.* 7:25).

We take courage from the Father and the Son, and also from the Spirit. When Jesus promised that the Father would give a 'helper', 'comforter' or 'counsellor', the cardinal point is that the Holy Spirit would be with us forever, and for our good (*John* 14:16, 17). He anoints God's people, setting them apart and teaching us what we need to know (*1 John* 2:27). Ultimately, the Spirit helps us persevere to the end because he keeps us from making 'a practice of sinning'; the Spirit dwells in us, and with this seed of God planted in us, we cannot be lost (*1 John* 3:9).

So much more could be said about how God keeps and preserves us. For now it may be enough to say that God has graciously covenanted to save us. That is what he promised long ago through Jeremiah: nothing short of 'an everlasting covenant', one where God would 'not turn away from doing good' to us, where a fear of God would reside in our hearts, where God will never let us depart from him (*Jer.* 32:40).

All of this gives rise to a certainty, even an infallibility of knowledge, that God's people will not fall away. It is in the context of this eternal decree, this salvation from a triune God, this everlasting covenant, that we are to read the great promises of the Bible. That is how we are to understand John 10:28, where Jesus says, 'I give them eternal life, and they will never perish, and no one will snatch them out of my hand'. That is how we are to hear 2 Thessalonians 3:3, where we are told that 'the Lord is faithful. He will establish you and guard you against the evil one'. That is also how we are to read solemn passages such as 1 John 2:19, where John reminds us what it really means when someone leaves the church of Christ: 'They went out from us, but they were not of us; for if they had been of us, they would have continued with us. But they went out, that it might become plain that they all are not of us.'

Temptation, hard hearts, and scandals

Some suddenly defect from the ranks of the church militant because they never had a heart for God. But it should also be acknowledged that there is a wide spectrum of experience among Christians who continue under Christ's banner. That is the point of paragraph 3. There really are 'temptations of Satan', the 'world', and our own sinful hearts. Perhaps we see all three at work in Peter's worst moments. Jesus warned him of the approaching tempter, but Peter still fell under the spell of an unbelieving mob in a palace, and his heart gave way under the fear of persecution (*Matt.* 26:70-74).

Peter fell into grievous sin in the midst of an intense spiritual battle, but it is also the case that he had neglected an important means for his own preservation. More than once he had been told to watch and pray, but he first denied the danger and then slept until it was upon him. He considered essential instruction from Jesus to be merely supplementary. We ought to be aware that we have an enemy, that there is no neutral territory in this world, and that we are weak soldiers at the best of times. And we ought to be quick to use every gracious support that the Lord has provided for us.

Yet there is something else we can learn from Peter's story. Though he fell he was raised back up on to his feet. He sinned, but was restored. A similar case is that of King David, as Psalm 51 eloquently testifies. David too fell into sin; he embraced his sin more fully, more deliberately, and for a longer period of time than did Peter, and the consequences of David's sin were more severe. That is a point we must recognize too. There are consequences to sin. There are times when God is angry with his people. It is not the anger of an enemy bent on the destruction of a foe. It is the anger of a father towards his disobedient children (*Isa.* 64:5, 7, 9). But it is a real anger nonetheless, and it comes with real punishments, as David also experienced (*2 Sam.* 11:27).

One consequence for a Christian is that we grieve the Spirit of God (*Eph.* 4:30). Grieving the Spirit—there is a mystery that we can only begin to understand, and surely never want to understand by experience. Yet another cost of unrepented sin is a loss of comfort and a sense of diminished usefulness and attractiveness as a Christian. If we live with sin we are deprived of the power of Christian 'graces and comforts'. As the psalmist writes, our bones feel broken, our hearts dirty, our joy decreased (*Psa.* 51:8-12). Our relationship with God can no more remain unaffected when we forsake him, our 'first love', than the relationship between two lovers can remain indifferent to uncertainties in affection (*Rev.* 2:4; *cf. Song of Sol.* 5:2-4, 6).

What is true of 'unrepentance' is also true of acts and thoughts that stem from unbelief. It leads to 'hardened hearts' (*Isa.* 63:17; *Mark* 6:52),[1] then sin which wounds our own consciences, leaving us to groan at our own foolishness and sin (*Psa.* 32:3, 4; 51:8). Even worse, our slipping and backsliding often 'hurt' or 'scandalize others'. David came to see that his adultery had consequences for others, but only after the fact (*e.g.,* 2 *Sam.* 12:14). Pray in advance that we will repent of our sins when they are still thoughts, and before they develop into words and actions. But if we do not, we can be sure that it will 'bring temporal judgments upon' ourselves, for we will be judged and disciplined by our own Lord 'so that we will not be condemned with the world' (*1 Cor.* 11:32; *cf. Psa.* 89:31, 32). And how is it that our sin can bring only temporal judgments on ourselves? How is it that we can receive the Lord's discipline, designed for our restoration and preservation? Because in love the Father chose to bring our eternal judgements upon his Son.

---

[1] Hardness of heart is also mentioned in Mark 16:14, a text with weak manuscript testimony.

CHAPTER 18:

OF THE ASSURANCE OF GRACE AND SALVATION

Historic Text

18.1 Although hypocrites and other unregenerate men may vainly deceive themselves with false hopes, and carnal presumptions of being in the favour of God, and estate of salvation;[a] which hope of theirs shall perish:[b] yet, such as truly believe in the Lord Jesus, and love him in sincerity, endeavouring to walk in all good conscience before him, may, in this life, be certainly assured that they are in the state of grace,[c] and may rejoice in the hope of the glory of God, which hope shall never make them ashamed.[d]

18.2 This certainty is not a bare conjectural and probable persuasion, grounded upon a fallible hope;[e] but, an infallible assurance of faith, founded, upon the divine truth of the promises of salvation,[f] the inward evidence of those graces unto which these promises are made,[g] the testimony of the Spirit of adoption witnessing with our spirits that we are the children of God:[h] which Spirit is the earnest of our inheritance, whereby we are sealed to the day of redemption.[i]

Modern Version

18.1 Although hypocrites and other unregenerate men may vainly deceive themselves with false hopes and fleshly presumptions that they are in God's favour and in a state of salvation, this hope of theirs will perish. Nevertheless, those who truly believe on the Lord Jesus, love him sincerely, and strive to live in all good conscience before him, may in this life be certainly assured that they are in the state of grace and may rejoice in the hope of the glory of God, a hope that shall never make them ashamed.

18.2 This certainty is not merely a conjectural and probable persuasion grounded on a fallible hope, but an infallible assurance of faith, founded on the divine truth of the promises of salvation, on the evidence in our hearts that the promised graces are present, and on the fact that the Spirit of adoption witnesses with our spirits that we are God's children. The Holy Spirit, by whom we are sealed for the day of redemption, is the pledge of our inheritance.

Scripture Proofs

18.1 ^a Job 8:13,14; Mic. 3:11; Deut. 29:19; John 8:41. ^b Matt. 7:22,23. ^c 1 John 2:3; 1 John 3:14,18,19,21,24; 1 John 5:13. ^d Rom. 5:2,5.

18.2 ^e Heb. 6:11,19. ^f Heb. 6:17,18. ^g 2 Pet. 1:4,5,10,11; 1 John 2:3; 1 John 3:14; 2 Cor. 1:12. ^h Rom. 8:15,16. ⁱ Eph. 1:13,14; Eph. 4:30; 2 Cor. 1:21,22.

Hypocrisy

Chapters 17 and 18 of the Westminster Confession of Faith are closely related. Chapter 17 discussed the perseverance of the saints and the certainty of our salvation. Chapter 18 treats a related topic when it asks what we ourselves can know about our own salvation.

However, the chapters are linked even more closely in their closing and opening lines. The last paragraph of chapter 17 reminded us of the Scripture's teaching about the perseverance of the saints, and it included a warning that some Christians may fall away for a time, causing much harm to themselves and others. Chapter 18 begins by addressing an even worse situation, that of 'hypocrites and other unregenerate' people.

Tragically, there are people who 'vainly deceive themselves' and they often begin their journey along a well-trodden track. You can recognize the path, for it is the one where true faith is forgotten after the first bend. One bad turn after another leads hypocrites away from the sad truth about themselves until finally, one day, far from where they started out, their 'false hopes' begin to diminish. Eventually their misplaced confidence is lost, and the emptiness of their religion is exposed. Worse still, it is hard to find the way back. Those who simply presumed or pretended that all was well discover that they were never tethered to the Word of God in the first place. The book of Job speaks of such as grasping a spider's web of self-deception (*Job* 8:13, 14).

Sometimes the way of the hypocrite is very subtle. At other times their pretences are obvious. As the prophet Micah explained, people can actually get to the point where they bribe judges, teach God's Word to get rich, or even produce prophecies for money, and still think that the Lord is among them and that no disaster will threaten them (*Mic.* 3:11). The reality is that such people are not blessed of God. They are trying to bless themselves (*Deut.* 29:19) while doing the devil's work (*John* 8:41). It is an understatement to declare that they are not in God's favour and not in a state of salvation. So, our Lord warns every hypocrite that there will come a day when many will say, '"Lord, Lord, did we not prophesy in your name, and in your name drive out demons and perform many miracles?" Then I will tell them plainly, "I never knew you. Away from me, you evildoers!"' (*Matt.* 7:22, 23).

The certainty of God's grace

This reminder about self-deception is doubtless a solemn beginning to a chapter on the assurance of God's grace and salvation, but it is by no means the end. There is much that can be said about faith, self-awareness and salvation, and some of that is said here.

First of all, Christians can really know they are Christians. There are people who 'truly believe in the Lord Jesus', who 'love him in sincerity', and who may not succeed, but do at least endeavour 'to walk in all good conscience before' their Lord. These people ought to know that they are Christians. Perhaps that is a description of you. If it is, then you may be certain and assured that you are no longer in a state of sin and judgment, but in a 'state of grace'.

There exists a clear association in Scripture between faith and obedience on the one hand and a certainty of God's grace toward us in Christ on the other. Would you like to know if you 'have come to know him', that you have 'passed out of death into life'? Do your leaders want to discern whether 'we are of the truth' and can legitimately 'reassure our heart[s] before' God? For Christians it is normal to want to know if Christ 'abides in us' by his Spirit, and that has been the norm since the days of the Apostle John. That is probably why in his First General Epistle he first puts down some frequently asked questions and then provides clear answers. If you want to know if you have 'eternal life', then 'believe in the name of the Son of God', 'obey' the Lord's 'commands', 'love the brothers'—and make sure that you are not loving 'in word or talk but in deed and in truth' (*1 John* 2:3; 3:14, 18, 19, 21, 24; 5:13). Then all that will remain for you is to 'rejoice in the hope of the glory of God' and, as Paul told the Romans, that hope will never 'put us to shame' (*Rom.* 5:2, 5).

What kind of assurance?

We are not speaking loosely when we talk about the certainty of our salvation. This certainty is not the same thing as an 'educated guess' or a 'likely bet'. This is no bare conjectural or probable persuasion. The author of the letter to Hebrews chose his words wisely, when in the sixth chapter he writes about a 'full assurance of hope until the end' and a 'sure and steadfast anchor of the soul' (*Heb.* 6:11, 19). It is not too much to say that this assurance is 'infallible', without error. Indeed our assurance is founded on God's truth, his promises about salvation. The same chapter of Hebrews tells us that God wanted to demonstrate his promises 'more convincingly'. He wanted his heirs to see 'the unchangeable character of his purpose'; the God who does not lie added an oath to his promise in order to give us 'strong encouragement to hold fast to the hope set before us' (*Heb.* 6:17, 18).

This hope is further confirmed by 'the inward evidence of those graces unto which these promises are made'. One only has to think again of John's statements on the subject (*1 John* 2:3; 3:14), statements similar to those made by Peter on one occasion (*2 Pet.* 1:4, 5, 10, 11), and by Paul on another (*2 Cor.* 1:12). Westminster assembly member Thomas Goodwin sums up the Bible's teaching about the relationship between personal sanctification and assurance of salvation when he comments that the Spirit writes 'first all graces in us, and then teacheth our consciences to read his handwriting'.[1]

And yet as the confession notes in this second paragraph, the Spirit does more than this. He also witnesses 'with our spirits that we are the children of God'. In the face of our sin or our suffering, as Paul explains in Romans 8, the Spirit of the Father and the Son reminds us that we belong to the divine family. He assures us that we really are God's children, and in doing so, he assures us of our salvation (*Rom.* 8:15, 16).

The Spirit, in his work and in his witness, is a foretaste or instalment or pledge (or to use an older word, an 'earnest') 'of our inheritance'. To paraphrase the Apostle Paul in Ephesians, it is the Spirit who seals our salvation, giving us a divine security until the day of our redemption, the day when Christ returns (*Eph.* 1:13, 14; 4:30). To quote the Apostle

[1] Goodwin, *Works*, vol. 6, p. 27.

Paul in 2 Corinthians, 'it is God who makes both us and you to stand firm in Christ. He anointed us, set his seal of ownership on us, and put his Spirit in our hearts as a deposit, guaranteeing what is to come' (*2 Cor.* 1:21, 22). The triune God assures us that we are his children, bought with the blood of his Son, and sealed by his Spirit. When this good news infuses our minds and hearts we will come more readily to God in prayer and worship, and be more eager to meet him with all his other children on the last day.

Historic Text	*Modern Version*
18.3 This infallible assurance does not so belong to the essence of faith, but that a true believer may wait long, and conflict with many difficulties before he be partaker of it:[k] yet, being enabled by the Spirit to know the things which are freely given him of God, he may, without extraordinary revelation, in the right use of ordinary means, attain thereunto.[l] And therefore it is the duty of everyone, to give all diligence to make his calling and election sure;[m] that thereby his heart may be enlarged in peace and joy in the Holy Ghost, in love and thankfulness to God, and in strength and cheerfulness in the duties of obedience, the proper fruits of this assurance:[n] so far is it, from inclining men to looseness.[o]	**18.3** This infallible assurance does not so belong to the essence of faith but that a true believer may wait long and contend with many difficulties before he partakes of it. Yet, because he is enabled by the Spirit to know the things which are freely given to him by God, he may—without any extraordinary revelation—attain this assurance by a proper use of the ordinary means. It is therefore the duty of everyone to be very diligent in making certain that God has called and chosen him. By such diligence his heart may grow in peace and joy in the Holy Spirit, in love and thankfulness to God, and in strength and cheerfulness in the duties which obedience to God requires—the proper fruits of this assurance. Thus it is far from inclining men to carelessness.

Scripture Proofs

18.3 [k] 1 John 5:13; Isa. 50:10; Mark 9:24; Psa. 88:1-18; Psa. 77:1-12. [l] 1 Cor. 2:12; 1 John 4:13; Heb. 6:11,12; Eph. 3:17-19. [m] 2 Pet. 1:10. [n] Rom. 5:1,2,5; Rom. 14:17; Rom. 15:13; Eph. 1:3,4; Psa. 4.6,7; Psa. 119:32. [o] 1 John 2:1,2; Rom. 6:1,2; Titus 2:11,12,14; 2 Cor. 7:1; Rom. 8:1,12; 1 John 3:2,3; Psa. 130:4; 1 John 1:6,7.

An unsure faith

Christians have every good reason to be confident about their salvation—but what if they are not? What are we to think of a faith in Christ that wavers, and wonders whether the Saviour has really died and risen 'for me'? Is weak faith still true faith? This is the question that the third paragraph of chapter 18 addresses.

The answer found here is that a full assurance of salvation does not belong to the very 'essence of faith'. It might be normal to be sure that one is a Christian, but one can be a Christian without being sure. In fact 'a true believer may wait long, and conflict with many difficulties, before' he or she is assured of God's grace and favour. This seems to be the issue that the Apostle John is addressing in his First Epistle, where he is writing to those 'who believe' in order that they may 'know' that they 'have eternal life' (*1 John* 5:13). The prophet Isaiah discusses those who fear the Lord and obey his servants, and yet walk in darkness. They need to be told to 'trust in the name of the LORD and rely' on God (*Isa.* 50:10). And we can hear this kind of distress first hand in Asaph's cries in Psalm 77, from the Sons of Korah in Psalm 88, or from the father in the Gospel of Mark who cried out to Jesus 'with tears' saying, 'Lord, I believe; help me in my unbelief' (*Mark* 9:24).

Finding light in darkness

Christians can find themselves struggling through dark days, but the Lord does offer us light. The spirit of this world may confuse us, but 'the Spirit who is from God' will enable us to know that the great gift of salvation is truly and freely given to us by God (*1 Cor.* 2:12). Indeed, by the gift of the Spirit 'we know that we abide in him and he in us' (*1 John* 4:13).

We must remind people that this assurance can be had without some 'extraordinary revelation'. We are only to rely on the Spirit, and show diligence in the pursuit of an assurance of salvation by a 'right use of ordinary means'—means which God himself has established for the strengthening of our faith (*Heb.* 6:11, 12).

If you are a professing Christian now lacking assurance of your salvation, pay attention to the preaching of the Word and turn to the Lord in prayer. Remain in the church and make full use of the sacraments 'so that Christ may dwell in your heart through faith'. Only then will you find yourself 'being rooted and established in love'. Only then will you find the 'power, together with all the saints, to grasp how wide and long and high and deep is the love of Christ, and to know this love that surpasses knowledge'. Only then, as Scripture promises, will you 'be filled to the measure of all the fullness of God' (*Eph.* 3:17-19).

It is by the Spirit, and through the resources of grace which God has given us that we 'make our calling and election sure' (*2 Pet.* 1:10). It is through these means that our hearts will be enlarged with 'peace and joy in the Holy Spirit', as Paul tells the believers in Rome (*Rom.* 14:17; *cf. Rom.* 15:13; 5:1, 2, 5 and *Psa.* 4:6, 7), with 'love and thankfulness', as he informs the Ephesians (*Eph.* 1:3, 4), and with 'strength and cheerfulness in the duties of obedience', of which the psalmist also speaks (*Psa.* 119:32).

Carefree but not careless

Some people and some traditions worry that if we are sure about our salvation, we will live carelessly—that we will 'continue in sin so that grace may abound'. By no means is this possible for true disciples of Christ (*Rom.* 6:1, 2). The truth is that children of God are stronger and more cheerful in their obedience when they delight in the love of their Father. The proper or natural fruit of a full assurance of our adoption into God's family and of the effective advocacy of Jesus Christ is that we stop sinning (*1 John* 2:1, 2). When the grace of God appears, it trains us 'to renounce ungodliness and worldly passions, and to live self-controlled, upright, and godly lives in the present age'. It makes us 'zealous for good works' (*Titus* 2:11, 12, 14). The knowledge that such promises from God belong to us, makes us want to clean up our act (*2 Cor.* 7:1).

When the psalmist finds that there is forgiveness with the Lord, he fears God with a solemn, new-found respect (*Psa.* 130:4). When Paul realizes that 'there is no condemnation' awaiting him, he understands that he is a debtor to a new master (*Rom.* 8:1, 12). When John realizes that he has hope in Christ, he seeks to purify himself because Christ is pure (*1 John* 3:2, 3).

Though a full assurance of grace and salvation is not necessary for our salvation, this should not prevent us from pursuing it and praying for it with heart and soul and mind. As the old Puritan Thomas Brooks once said, 'the being in a state of grace will yield a man heaven hereafter, but the seeing of himself in this state will yield him both a heaven here and a heaven hereafter'.[1] Or as Thomas Watson explained, 'it puts a man in heaven before his time'.[2] What these two friends of assembly members had to say was probably learned by considering what the Apostle John wanted his readers to see: if we have fellowship with Christ, then we find ourselves walking 'in the light, as he is in the light'; we discover that 'we have fellowship with one another'; and we rejoice for evermore that 'the blood of Jesus, his Son, purifies us from every sin' (*1 John* 1:6, 7).

Historic Text

18.4 True believers may have the assurance of their salvation divers ways shaken, diminished, and intermitted; as, by negligence in preserving of it, by falling into some special sin, which wounds the conscience, and grieves the Spirit; by, some sudden, or vehement temptation, by God's withdrawing the light of his countenance, and suffering even such as fear him to walk in darkness and to have no light:[p] yet are they never utterly destitute of that seed of God, and life of faith, that love of Christ and the brethren, that sincerity of heart, and conscience of duty, out of which, by the operation of the Spirit, this assurance may, in due time, be revived;[q] and by the which, in the mean time, they are supported from utter despair.[r]

Modern Text

18.4 True believers may have the assurance of their salvation shaken, diminished, or temporarily lost in various ways: as by negligence in preserving it, by falling into some special sin which wounds the conscience and grieves the Spirit, by some sudden or violent temptation, or by God's withdrawing the light of his countenance and allowing even those who reverence him to walk in darkness and have no light. Yet, true believers are never completely deprived of that seed of God and life of faith, that love for Christ and fellow believers, that sincerity of heart and conscience concerning duty, out of which—by the operation of the Spirit—this assurance may in due time be revived; and by which, in the meantime, they are supported from utter despair.

[1] Thomas Brooks, *Works*, (Edinburgh, 1861-67; Edinburgh, 1980), vol. 2, p. 14.
[2] Thomas Watson, *A Body of Divinity* (London, 1692; Edinburgh, 1992), p. 253.

Scripture Proofs

18.4 [p] Song of Sol. 5:2,3,6; Psa. 51:8,12,14; Eph. 4:30,31; Psa. 77:1-10; Matt. 26:69-72; Psa. 31:22; Psa. 88:1-18; Isa. 50:10. [q] 1 John 3:9; Luke 22:32; Job 13:15; Psa. 73:15; Psa. 51:8,12; Isa. 50:10. [r] Mic. 7:7-9; Jer. 32:40; Isa. 54:7-10; Psa. 22:1; Psa. 88:1-18.

Our sin and God's sovereignty

The major task of a chapter on assurance of grace and salvation is to talk about how ideal and normal this assurance is for Christians, and why it is helpful. The second task is to comfort those whose faith is weak and whose assurance might be lacking. Having touched on both of these themes, the final paragraph of chapter 18 takes this discussion deeper, and suggests reasons why Christians may struggle with doubt about their salvation.

In the experience of the authors of this confession, and according to their study of the Scriptures, it appears that assurance of salvation can be 'shaken, diminished, and intermitted' in a variety of ways. For instance, true believers can be negligent in preserving their faith, careless about using God's means of grace. Sometimes we are thoughtless about Bible reading and prayer, or pay little attention to preaching and the administration of the sacraments. We can become like the drowsy lover of the Song of Solomon who is slow, far too slow, in responding to her beloved when he knocks on her door, a lover who eventually goes away by the time she wants him (*Song of Sol.* 5:2, 3, 6).

Sometimes we struggle spiritually because we were too slow in doing what is good. Sometimes we struggle spiritually because we have succumbed to the very bad. It is then that we find our consciences wounded, or at any rate, deeply troubled. Perhaps you know what that is like. You know you ought to 'get rid of all bitterness, rage and anger, brawling and slander, along with every form of malice', or whatever your habitual sin might be. Instead you behave in such a way that you 'grieve the Holy Spirit of God, by whom you were sealed for the day of redemption' (*Eph.* 4:30, 31).

Even then, not all sin is habitual. Sometimes we walk into sin that is new or unusual for us. We may crumble under a 'sudden or vehement temptation'. Perhaps King David did this when he fell into adultery

(*Psa.* 51:8, 12, 14); and the Apostle Peter when he denied his friend and Lord (*Matt.* 26:69-72).

Furthermore, we must be clear that not everyone found in spiritual darkness has been negligent or has committed some particular sin. In our Sovereign's perfect plan, he sometimes sees fit to withdraw 'the light of his countenance', 'suffering even such as fear him to walk in darkness and to have no light', as we see in the case of Job, or the author of Psalm 73. We find ourselves stumbling through the dark (*Isa.* 50:10), or lying in the dark, unable to sleep (*Psa.* 77). Sometimes we lose almost all hope and perspective. Feeling cut off from God's sight (*Psa.* 31:22), we can even conclude that darkness is our closest friend (*Psa.* 88:18).

Light in the darkness

Things can be grim for God's people because we have failed or because God has seen fit to give us a season in life with diminished comforts and confidence. However, the Word of God speaks eloquently to the fact that even if we feel deserted, or even if God may choose to distance himself from us for reasons known only to him, yet we are never left utterly destitute and hopeless.

We are never left without the Spirit, the seed of God that is planted in us.[1] Therefore we are never so dead that there is no life of faith, no love for Christ and the brethren, no sincerity of heart or conscience about our duty. These things may be reduced or suppressed drastically. But the Spirit is still at work in us. Job was a troubled man in the midst of his deep suffering, and yet at moments he could still speak with great wisdom, and at other points with great faith, even vowing that if God were intent on ending his life, he would still hope in him (*Job* 13:15). Glimmers of godliness can also be seen amidst the spiritual depression that permeates Psalm 73 (*e.g.,* 73:15) or Psalm 51, and the prophet Isaiah could call even the most despondent to their duties (*e.g.,* 50:10).

This is the confession of many downcast Christians, who can say in truth that in his good time the Holy Spirit revived them, gave them confidence of their salvation, and enabled them to strengthen their brothers (*Luke* 22:32). But whether or not this is their conscious experience

---

[1] Perhaps this is the meaning of 1 John 3:9.

during moments of personal doubt, the reality is that 'in the mean time' the Holy Spirit uses all means at his disposal to support us and keep us above the line of 'utter despair'. This has been a dear doctrine of God's people from ancient times. This is the promise made to Isaiah and Jeremiah (*Isa.* 54:7-10; *Jer.* 32:40). It is the confession made by the psalmists, sometimes with confusion (*Psa.* 22:1; *Psa.* 88), and of Micah, with clarity (*Mic.* 7:7-9).

In whatever state we may be, let it always be an article of our creed that even in our deepest darkness, God will never leave us. Hope is the life-breath of Christianity. God is the one who gave us the Light of the world. Let us trust even in our gloomiest days that he will shine the light of his gospel into our lives, in answer to our prayers, and the prayers of all his dear children.

LAW AND LIBERTY

CHAPTER 19:

OF THE LAW OF GOD

Historic Text

19.1 God gave to Adam a law, as a covenant of works, by which he bound him, and all his posterity to personal, entire, exact, and perpetual obedience; promised life upon the fulfilling, and threatened death upon the breach of it: and endued him with power and ability to keep it.[a]

19.2 This law, after his fall, continued to be a perfect rule of righteousness, and, as such, was delivered by God upon Mount Sinai, in ten commandments, and written in two tables:[b] the four first commandments containing our duty towards God; and the other six, our duty to man.[c]

Modern Version

19.1 God gave Adam a law, in the form of a covenant of works, by which he bound him and all his descendants to personal, entire, exact, and perpetual obedience. He promised life if Adam kept the law and threatened death if he broke it. Moreover, he endowed Adam with power and ability to keep that law.

19.2 This law, after Adam fell, continued to be a perfect rule of righteousness and, as such, was given by God upon Mount Sinai in ten commandments written on two stone tablets. The first four commandments contain our duty to God, the other six our duty to man.

Scripture Proofs

19.1 [a] Gen. 1:26,27, with Gen. 2:17; Rom. 2:14,15; Rom. 10:5; Rom. 5:12,19; Gal. 3:10,12; Eccles. 7:29; Job 28:28.

19.2 [b] James 1:25; James 2:8,10-12; Rom. 13;8,9; Deut. 5:32; Deut. 10:4; Exod. 34:1. [c] Matt. 22:37-40.

God's gift to Adam

In chapter 19 we turn our attention to an important biblical subject: the law of God. Adam was the first to know that his creator was also life's regulator. Adam was told to exercise dominion over the world, in imitation of God (*Gen.* 1:26, 27). He was also told not to eat fruit from a particular tree (*Gen.* 2:17).

Not all of God's commands were necessarily delivered to Adam in an external or in a codified form. God spoke through the conscience: there was a 'law written in their hearts', as Paul explains in Romans (*Rom.* 2:14, 15). This law was given during a time of peace and perfection; it was to guide Adam for all of his life; it was God's gift to mankind. And this law took the form of a 'covenant'.

Law and covenant

Law and covenant have some things in common. Both involve rules or prescriptions. God required of Adam and all his children nothing less than a 'personal, entire, exact, and perpetual obedience'. Both law and covenant also include penalties for non-compliance. God 'threatened death' if his commands were ever broken (*Gen.* 2:17; *Rom.* 5:12; *Gal.* 3:10).

But there is also a difference between law and covenant, for a covenant contains more than law. It also contains a promise—made by the covenant-maker, God, to the potential covenant-keeper. In this case God promised an enduring life if his commands were kept—and indeed, God in his goodness made Adam upright (*Eccles.* 7:29), thus giving him the 'power and ability to keep' his covenant, to fear him, to turn away from evil.[1]

At least two housekeeping tasks must be performed before discussion of the covenant can be fruitful. First, terms must be explained. Theologians often refer to the covenant made with Adam as a 'covenant of works', because they are focusing on the law—what Adam was to do. But sometimes theologians refer to the covenant made with Adam as a covenant of life, because they are focusing on the promise—what God said he would do. We see both of these terms used by the Westminster assembly in the confession and catechisms (WLC 20; WSC 12).

Second, a word must be said about biblical usage. 'Covenant' is a broader term than 'law'; as explained above, it includes law but is not

---

[1] Some interpreters understood the 'man' in Job. 28:28 to refer to Adam. See *Annotations upon All the Books of the Old and New Testament, sub loc.*

subsumed under law. Yet law is such an important part of God's covenant that sometimes the two terms are used interchangeably in Scripture, or at the very least, the part (law) sometimes stands for the whole (covenant). That may very well be what we see in Romans 10:5, where we are told about 'the righteousness which is of the law, "That the man which doeth those things shall live by them"'. Here Paul refers to the law, and yet speaks of its reward, even though reward, strictly speaking, is an aspect of covenant.[2]

The perfect rule, pre- and post-fall

Unhappily, as we know and as paragraph 2 two reminds us, Adam broke God's law and this introduced no end of change in the world. Nonetheless, God did not change, nor did his law. To borrow a uniquely New Testament phrase and apply it to the Old Testament, it was always a 'perfect law' (*James* 1:25). After Adam's fall, the law that was always perfect, the law that the Lord had ordained, 'continued to be a perfect rule of righteousness'.[3] It is not safe to assume that the law is anything less than an infallible guide, or to think that one can turn aside from it toward the right or the left (*Deut.* 5:32). To paraphrase George Hendry, God's norm for good behaviour was not annulled by sin any more than normative statements about good health are annulled by sickness.[4]

If anything, the law was more clearly revealed than ever before. As human consciences corrupted, God openly codified his law. As their hearts hardened, God took what was written on their hearts, and had it inscribed on two tablets of stone (*Exod.* 34:1; *Deut.* 10:4). It was, essentially, the law of Adam that was revealed to Moses and summarized 'in ten commandments'. Naturally, Adam and those who followed after him may have related to and come to understand the law in a different way. Early humans may have understood the law more as, or only as, an interconnected unity, as Paul or James sometimes speak of it, rather than a list of instructions (see *Rom.* 13:8, 9; *James* 2:8, 10-12). Yet the content

---

[2] See also Romans 5:19 which would, I think, have been true of the first Adam if he had obeyed God; note too Galatians 3:12.

[3] The words 'as such' refer either to the 'rule of righteousness', or to 'this law' defined as 'a covenant of works' and a 'rule of righteousness'.

[4] G. S. Hendry, *The Westminster Confession for Today* (Richmond, 1962), p. 176.

remained the same. Cain knew that he ought to have worshipped God properly; he also knew that he ought not to have murdered his brother Abel.

It is often assumed that one tablet may have contained the first four commandments, the other tablet the other six. These two tablets of the law given on Mount Sinai were more likely two separate copies of the law, for this was the ancient pattern in covenant-making ceremonies. Either way, 'the four first commandments' evidently contain 'our duty towards God; and the other six, our duty to man'.[5] That, in fact, is just how Moses summed up the law, and how our Lord Jesus repeated this summary in Matthew 22: 'Love the Lord your God with all your heart and with all your soul and with all your mind', he urged. 'This is the first and greatest commandment. And the second is like it: "Love your neighbour as yourself." All the Law and the Prophets hang on these two commandments' (*Matt.* 22:37-40). May the Spirit of holiness help us to heed the precepts of God's law, whether in its totality, as it is summed up in these two commandments, or in its individuality, in each of the ten that the Lord gave Moses long ago.

Historic Text	*Modern Version*
19.3 Beside this law, commonly called moral, God was pleased to give to the people of Israel, as a church under age, ceremonial laws containing several typical ordinances, partly of worship, prefiguring Christ, his graces, actions, sufferings, and benefits;[d] and partly, holding forth divers instructions of moral duties.[e] All which ceremonial laws are now abrogated, under the new testament.[f]	**19.3** In addition to this law, commonly called the moral law, God was pleased to give the people of Israel—as the church under age—ceremonial laws, which contained several typological ordinances. These ordinances consisted partly of worship, prefiguring Christ, his graces, actions, sufferings, and benefits, and partly of various instructions of moral duties. All these ceremonial laws are now abrogated under the new testament.

[5] Here the Westminster assembly is also setting out the Reformed taxonomy of the Decalogue against the Lutheran and Roman Catholic divisions of the law.

19.4 To them also, as a body politic, he gave sundry judicial laws, which expired together with the state of that people; not obliging any other now, further than the general equity thereof may require.^{g}	**19.4** To the people of Israel, as a civil entity, he also gave various judicial laws which expired at the time their state expired. Therefore, these judicial laws place no obligation upon anyone now, except as they embody general principles of justice.

Scripture Proofs

19.3 ^{d} Heb., chapter 9.; Heb. 10:1; Gal. 4:1-3; Col. 2:17. ^{e} 1 Cor. 5:7; 2 Cor. 6:17; Jude v. 23. ^{f} Col. 2:14,16,17; Dan. 9:27; Eph. 2:15,16.

19.4 ^{g} Exod. 21:1-36; Exod. 22:1-29; Gen. 49:10, with 1 Pet. 2:13,14; Matt. 5:17, with vs. 38,39; 1 Cor. 9:8-10.

The ceremonial law

The Old Testament law of God has traditionally been divided into three categories: the moral law, the ceremonial law, and the judicial or civil law. Paragraphs 3 and 4 of chapter 19 discuss these forms of the law and explain how each relates to the Christian today.

Besides the moral law outlined above, God gave 'ceremonial laws'. We see these concentrated in Exodus, Leviticus and Numbers, and reviewed in Deuteronomy. As Paul explained to the Galatians, these laws were given to God's people because of their spiritual youthfulness. They needed these things to serve as tutors, guardians, or trustees to guide them along the way to maturity (*Gal.* 4:1-3).

God knew that they were not ready to learn without these laws. They needed such daily reminders and pictures of who he was. Of course God always speaks even to the wisest Christian as a father speaks to his little ones. But here we are reminded that what God still does to some extent for all his children, was done to a radical extent for all of his children before the time of Christ: he spoke to them through a variety of ordinances that were divinely designed to teach them something about himself, his covenant, and the Messiah.

Laws of worship and morality

All of these ordinances—religious ceremonies or rituals—were symbolic or, as the confession says here, they were 'typical'. Although all were symbolic or typical, these symbols and types were of two kinds.

Some of these ceremonies had to do with 'worship'. By their use in worship they pointed to Christ, his wonderful 'graces', or his 'actions', the things he would do. Sacrifices picture his 'sufferings'. Washing and cleansing rituals pictured the 'benefits' we receive from Christ, such as the washing away of our sins. We see a number of these rituals explained in Hebrews 9. It is there we learn that 'without the shedding of blood there is no forgiveness'. But it is not the blood of bulls and goats that washes away sin; it is the blood of Christ. As the opening verse of Hebrews 10 explains, the 'law is only a shadow of the good things that are coming—not the realities themselves. For this reason it can never, by the same sacrifices repeated endlessly year after year, make perfect those who draw near to worship' (*Heb.* 10:1; *cf. Col.* 2:17).

Other old covenant ceremonies had to do with 'moral duties'. These rituals portrayed the damaging effects of the sin we should seek to avoid. During the celebration of the Passover, for example, the Israelites were to avoid yeast or leaven in their bread. Paul explains that this was to remind them that just as leaven spreads through a loaf of bread, so sin spreads and swells through the whole person (*1 Cor.* 5:7). Ceremonies about unclean things and foods were to teach God's people that they were not to live in the same way as the rest of the world (*2 Cor.* 6:17). And Jude lets us see that even dirty clothes were to remind people of the filth of sin (*Jude* 23).

The end of the ceremonial law

The Christian church can be deeply enriched by the Old Testament and its ceremonial laws about worship and morality. Indeed, New Testament writers often echo the imagery and sometimes use the very words of these Old Testament laws to illustrate the gospel or to show believers what God thinks of sin.

Nevertheless, while the historical record of these laws is useful for a variety of purposes, we must be clear that these 'ceremonial laws' themselves 'are now abrogated under the new testament'. As the Apostle Paul once told the Christians in Colosse, God has 'cancelled the written code, with its regulations, that was against us and that stood opposed to us; he took it away, nailing it to the cross'. And the following verses make it very clear that it is the end of the ceremonial law that Paul has in view

(*Col.* 2:14, 16, 17; *cf. Eph.* 2:15, 16). It is even possible that the end of the ceremonial law is what Daniel predicted when he mentioned that someone would 'put an end to sacrifice and offering' (*Dan.* 9:27), a prophecy that found fulfilment temporarily before the time of Christ, and permanently at the destruction of Jerusalem.

Judicial laws

In addition to ceremonial laws God gave the people of Israel, as a political body, a set of 'judicial laws'. These laws can be found in many places, but one of the most concentrated collections is found in Exodus 21 to 23. Like the ceremonial laws, these judicial laws are no longer in force for God's people today, nor for any of God's people since the time of Christ and the destruction of the ancient Jewish nation in the days of the apostles. Perhaps this end of the judicial law of Israel was alluded to in Jacob's dying words to his children, even before the family became a nation (*Gen.* 49:10).

What is in force are the laws of men, as Peter clearly teaches (*1 Pet.* 2:13, 14). Whether our overlord be a king or a governor, we submit ourselves to their civil ordinances for the Lord's sake. We are not to try and enforce submission to the Lord's Old Testament ordinances for their sakes.

Once again, we need to remember that Jesus Christ came to fulfil the law. Of course he did not destroy it, as he says himself. But he came to that old body of legal and civil instructions and he showed the spirit of the law that had somehow been lost over time. That is why he would repeat time and again what others had heard about the law, but then as the new law-giver, the one greater than Moses, he would turn to the crowds, and announce with authority: 'But I say unto you . . .' (*Matt.* 5:17, 38, 39).

For the most part, these laws remain only to teach us general principles of equity and fairness.[1] To choose an example of the Apostle Paul,

---

[1] William Ames sees 'general equity' applying to the ceremonial law also. For example, the existence of Old Testament holy days shows that certain days can be set apart for worship in the new covenant era. William Ames, *The Marrow of Sacred Divinity* (London, 1642), p. 328. William Gouge uses the same example in his, *The Saints Sacrifice* (London, 1632), p. 243. Edward Reynolds thinks that Old Testament

if 'it is written in the Law of Moses: "Do not muzzle an ox while it is treading out the grain"', we should learn that we ought not to starve a preacher if he is working for the good of Christ's church (*1 Cor.* 9:8-10).

There is much to learn from these ceremonial and judicial laws. But to continue the judicial laws and their penalties would be to forget that the new Israel is the church, and not some political nation on earth. To continue the ceremonial laws would be to forget that Jesus Christ is our true high priest and our only sacrifice. Thus, we would be left with no gospel at all.

Historic Text	*Modern Text*
19.5 The moral law does for ever bind all, as well justified persons as others, to the obedience thereof;[h] and that, not only in regard of the matter contained in it, but also in respect of the authority of God the Creator, who gave it:[i] Neither does Christ, in the gospel, any way dissolve, but much strengthen this obligation.[k]	**19.5** The moral law binds all people at all times to obedience, both those who are justified and those who are not. The obligation to obey the moral law is not only because of its content, but also because of the authority of God the Creator, who gave it. In the gospel, Christ in no way dissolves this obligation, but greatly strengthens it.

Scripture Proofs
   19.5   [h] Rom. 13:8-10; Eph. 6:2; 1 John 2:3,4,7,8.   [i] James 2:10,11.   [k] Matt. 5:17-19; James 2:8; Rom. 3:31.

The moral law

With paragraph 5 we return to the subject of 'the moral law'. The previous sections explained that the ceremonial and judicial laws of the Old Testament expired along with the theocratic nation-state of Israel. This paragraph tells us that the moral law does not expire. In fact it always binds us to obedience, whether we are Christians justified by the blood of Jesus Christ, or whether we are not.

history shows that it is 'not universally against equity for one to suffer the punishment of anothers sinne' in *An Explication of the Hundred and Tenth Psalme* (London, 1632), pp. 445-446. Daniel Cawdrey, in a discussion of general equity equates it with a 'spirituall meaning'. Cawdrey, *Sabbitum Redivivum* (London, 1645), p. 38.

It is true, of course, that the Bible sometimes says that the law is fulfilled. But whatever is meant in these contexts, it cannot mean that the moral law is of no effect. Remember how, when Jesus said that the law was fulfilled, he went on to discuss the moral law and our obligations to keep it (*cf. Matt.* 5-7 with 5:17-19). When Paul wrote that 'love is the fulfilment of the law', he quoted from the Ten Commandments and explained how love binds and empowers us to greater obedience (*Rom.* 13:8-10).

In fact the New Testament is peppered with quotations from, and references to, the moral law (*e.g., Eph.* 6:2). John went so far as to say, 'by this we know that we have come to know him' that 'we keep God's commandments'. As far as the apostle was concerned, 'whoever says "I know him" but does not keep his commandments is a liar, and the truth is not in him'. Of course, the New Testament presents this law in new ways and in a new light. But while it can look like a 'new commandment', it is really the 'old commandment that you had from the beginning' (*1 John* 2:3, 4, 7, 8).

The matter or content of the moral law still binds each one of us, no matter who we are. But perhaps the most significant thing to keep in mind is the most basic relationship of all people to the one God who does not change. He forever remains the God of all power and authority; we remain his subjects. He is 'the Creator who is also the law-giver. We are his creatures, obliged to keep that law. This reality is not altered by the coming of Christ and the inauguration of the final age.

Again, Scripture teaches us that God's perfect law reflects not only his holiness but also the holistic-ness of his character. James once wrote that the God 'who said, "Do not commit adultery", also said, "Do not murder"'. There is nothing surprising about either statement. The interesting thing is that each part of the law relates to the other. As James explains, if someone 'keeps the whole law but fails in one point', God the Creator declares that he 'has become accountable for all of it' (*James* 2:10, 11).

Why are that idea and that passage so important to this discussion about our continued obligation to the moral law? Because if God's moral law is such a cohesive unity, as taught in the letter of James, it is all the more unlikely that any one part of the law could change over time without affecting the whole. It can develop; we see the development of the moral law within the Pentateuch. But expansion and clarification differ from erosion. It is also unlikely that any aspects of the law could be ignored without also affecting our view of God himself.

In spite of this, some Christians are left uneasy with this stress on the unity between the two Testaments and on the continuity of the law of God. They look at the teachings of Christ, or the contrasts between the law and the gospel, and suspect that the moral law has somehow changed. Some say that the moral law is actually dissolved or reconstituted in the New Testament. Arguably, people come to this conclusion usually because they do not understand the primacy of grace in the Old Testament, or because they do not distinguish between different types of law, or because they do not understand the relationship between law and faith in the New Testament.

Whatever the reason for thinking that the moral law of God has changed in the new covenant era, we have reason to think the Westminster Confession of Faith is correct in judging that Christ and his gospel actually *strengthen* our obligation to keep the law of God. After all, it was Jesus himself who said that he did not come 'to abolish the Law or the Prophets'. Perhaps his strongest statement about the muscle of the moral law was this: 'until heaven and earth pass away, not an iota, not a dot, will pass from the Law until all is accomplished' (*Matt.* 5:17, 18).

Now it is obvious that not everything that has been promised has been accomplished—to pick one notable example, our Lord needs to return before the heavens and the earth pass away. It is also obvious that it was the moral law that Jesus was reviewing as we can see from the context of Matthew 5 and thereafter. Jesus did not go on to consider ceremonial washings, animal sacrifices and regulations about cities of refuge, but love and murder as well as marriage and divorce. Thus there is no reason to think that Jesus intended to overthrow the moral law before his second coming. Indeed, he has eternity in view when he warns, 'whoever relaxes one of the least of these commandments and teaches others to do the same will be called least in the kingdom of heaven, but whoever does them and teaches them will be called great in the kingdom of heaven' (*Matt.* 5:19).

Nor did Jesus wipe away the Ten Commandments when he said they could be summarized as two. In a way, Jesus actually fortified the moral law when he simplified it. In telling us that the whole of the law hangs on two commandments—a whole-hearted love for our God and a warm-hearted love for our neighbour—Jesus presented a regal summary that James calls the royal law. James also understood this ongoing force of the law and he told the church that it would do well to keep it (*James* 2:8).

In the end, neither Jesus nor his gospel overthrow the statutes of God. Whatever Paul means when he pits the law against faith, he does not intend to disparage or diminish the claims of God's commandments.[1] That is an assumption embedded in Paul's Epistle to the Romans. After telling us that no one is righteous, that no one successfully observes the law of God, and that we are actually justified by trusting in Christ rather than in ourselves, Paul finally asks the almost inevitable question: do we somehow 'overthrow the law by this faith?' His answer is unequivocal: 'By no means! On the contrary, we uphold the law' (*Rom.* 3:31). Just how does Christian faith uphold the law? That is the question the following section of chapter 19 discusses.

Historic Text	Modern Version
19.6 Although true believers be not under the law, as a covenant of works, to be thereby justified, or condemned;[l] yet, is it of great use to them, as well as to others; in that, as a rule of life informing them of the will of God, and their duty, it directs, and binds them to walk accordingly;[m] discovering also the sinful pollutions of their nature, hearts, and lives;[n] so as, examining themselves	**19.6** Although true believers are not under the law as a covenant of works by which they are justified or condemned, nevertheless the law is of great use to them as well as to others. By informing them—as a rule of life—both of the will of God and of their duty, it directs and binds them to walk accordingly. It also reveals to them the sinful pollutions of their nature, hearts, and

---

[1] Paul pits law and faith or law and grace against each other when speaking of the basis for our justification.

thereby, they may come to further conviction of, humiliation for, and hatred against sin;[o] together with a clearer sight of the need they have of Christ, and the perfection of his obedience.[p] It is likewise of use to the regenerate, to restrain their corruptions, in that it forbids sin:[q] and, the threatenings of it serve to show, what, even their sins, deserve; and, what afflictions, in this life, they may expect for them, although freed from the curse thereof threatened in the law.[r] The promises of it, in like manner, show them God's approbation of obedience, and what blessings they may expect upon the performance thereof;[s] although, not as due to them by the law, as a covenant of works.[t] So as, a man's doing good, and refraining from evil, because the law encourages to the one, and deters from the other, is no evidence of his being under the law; and, not under grace.[u]

lives. Therefore, when they examine themselves in the light of the law, they may come to further conviction of, humiliation for, and hatred of their sin, together with a clearer view of their need of Christ and the perfection of his obedience. The law is also useful to the regenerate because, by forbidding sin, it restrains their corruptions. By its threats it shows them what their sins deserve, and, although they are free from the curse threatened in the law, it shows the afflictions that they may expect because of them in this life. The promises of the law likewise show to the regenerate God's approval of obedience and the blessings they may expect as they obey the law, although these blessings are not due to them by the law as a covenant of works. Therefore, the fact that a man does good rather than evil because the law encourages good and discourages evil is no evidence that the man is under the law rather than under grace.

Scripture proofs

19.6 [l] Rom. 6:14; Gal. 2:16; Gal. 3:13; Gal. 4:4,5; Acts 13:39; Rom. 8:1. [m] Rom. 7:12,22,25; Psa. 119:4-6; 1 Cor. 7:19; Gal. 5:14,16,18-23. [n] Rom. 7:7; Rom. 3:20. [o] James 1:23-25; Rom. 7:9,14,24. [p] Gal. 3:24; Rom. 7:24,25; Rom. 8:3,4. [q] James 2:11; Psa. 119:101,104,128. [r] Ezra 9:13,14; Psa. 89:30-34. [s] Lev. 26:1-14, with 2 Cor. 6:16; Eph. 6:2,3; Psa. 37:11, with Matt. 5:5; Psa. 19:11. [t] Gal. 2:16; Luke 17:10. [u] Rom. 6:12,14; 1 Pet. 3:8-12, with Psa. 34:12-16; Heb. 12:28,29.

Not under the law

Having treated different distinctions within the law, paragraph 6 turns to three great uses which apply to the moral law only. But first, by way of preface, readers are told that true believers do not relate to the law as an instrument that can either justify them or condemn them.

That Christians cannot be justified by the law has been stated clearly from the beginning of church history. The fact is, as Paul told the Galatians, 'a person is not justified by works of the law but through faith in

Jesus Christ'. Sometimes we are proud, and in our pride even boastful, about our small accomplishments in life. However, Paul tells us that we 'have believed in Christ Jesus, in order to be justified by faith in Christ and not by works of the law, because by works of the law no one will be justified' (*Gal.* 2:16).

The Scriptures are equally clear, on the other hand, that the law can no longer condemn us if we belong to Jesus. Sometimes the size of our sins blocks our vision, and we no longer see this truth clearly. At such times we need to stop and listen, because the truth of Scripture peals out the good news again and again: 'Christ redeemed us from the curse of the law by becoming a curse for us'; 'God sent forth his Son, born of woman, born under the law, to redeem those who were under the law' (*Gal.* 3:13; 4:4, 5); 'There is now no condemnation for those who are in Christ Jesus' (*Rom.* 8:1).

In every way that obedience to the law could not free us, faith in Christ has freed us (*Acts* 13:39). That is why we are not 'under the law' as Paul puts it (*Rom.* 6:14), certainly 'not under the law as a covenant of works', as the confession puts it.

The first use of the law: a rule of life

We do not have God's law in our lives as a covenant of works, but that does not mean it is of no use or relevance, either to us or to others. Three uses of the law are mentioned here in this section. As presented by the assembly, the first is that the law remains essential 'as a rule of life' for all people.[1] The law is a rule of life because it informs us of God's will. The psalmist longed to keep God's precepts 'diligently', steadfastly, and with a fixed focus because he longed to please God himself (*Psa.* 119:4). While ceremonies such as circumcision no longer count at all, keeping God's commandments counts a great deal (*1 Cor.* 7:19). Paul tells us that

---

[1] The assembly's ordering of the uses of the law has not proved as popular as that offered by John Calvin. The Genevan Reformer presented the law in a different order as (1) a sign-post directing us to our need for Christ and his grace, what has come to be called the 'paedagogical use' of the law (see Calvin, *Institutes*, II.vii.1-3, 5-9); (2) as a rule of life for everyone, or the 'civil use' of the law (*Institutes*, II.vii.8, 10-11); and (3) as a tool to restrain sin and encourage godliness among the regenerate, or the 'normative use' of the law (*Institutes*, II.vii.12).

God's commands are 'holy and righteous and good' and that we 'delight in the law' and 'serve the law' (*Rom.* 7:12, 22, 25). The 'whole law is fulfilled' in love, and can be summarized as walking by the Spirit, following his desires, bearing his fruit. 'Against such things there is no law' (*Gal.* 5:14-23). Far from it. In these precepts we see our duty and find ourselves directed. This, for the assembly, is the first use of the law, and with the help of the Holy Spirit, it leads to the second.

The second use of the law: a sign-post to Christ

As we seek to walk according to God's law, we eventually (and often quickly!) discover the 'sinful pollutions' of our 'nature, hearts, and lives'. The effects of this discovery can be so pronounced, that we find ourselves sharing Paul's surprise at the law's potency: 'if it had not been for the law, I would not have known sin' (*Rom.* 7:7). It is 'through the law' that the 'knowledge of sin' comes (*Rom.* 3:20).

Serious attempts at law-keeping help us to examine ourselves. When God tells us what to do, we instinctively take stock of what we have done and of what remains for us to do. For that reason, looking at the law is like looking in the mirror and finding ourselves unhappy with what we see (*James* 1:23-25). The law exposes us. We are alive and well 'apart from the law'—and then a commandment comes, sin comes alive, and we see that we are dead (*Rom.* 7:9). The hoped-for result is that we will remember what we see and learn—learn what it costs to be 'sold under sin', feel the bondage and long for deliverance. In other words, the law usefully convicts our consciences for our many failings, helps us to mourn our wretchedness, and fosters a longing for deliverance from our damning faults (*Rom.* 7:14, 24).

'Humiliation for' sin and 'hatred for sin' are common effects of this conviction. They should not be considered as ends in themselves but as means to a greater end. The humbling that comes from the law is intended by God to give us a 'clearer sight of the need' we have for 'Christ, and the perfection of his obedience'. Historically, each part of the old covenant law, including the moral law, was employed by God as a tutor, as an educational guardian that pointed to Christ until he himself came (*Gal.* 3:24). Existentially the moral law continues to function as a trainer or coach, pointing us to Christ, even though he has now come.

Therefore, it is the law that causes us to say with Paul, 'wretched man that I am!' But the law also prepares us to rejoice with the apostle and say, 'Thanks be to God through Jesus Christ our Lord!' (*Rom.* 7:24, 25). For through Jesus, God has done 'what the law . . . could not do'. He sent his Son 'in the likeness of sinful flesh', and through his Son he saves his people from their sin. Through the work Jesus accomplished 'the righteous requirement of the law' is 'fulfilled in us' (*Rom.* 8:3, 4).

The third use of the law: a restraint for sin

A third function of the moral law is that of a barricade to keep us from destructive rebellion, a preventative from sin. Even those who are 'regenerate' need the help of God's law to 'restrain their corruptions' and the law does this in at least four ways.

The straightforward way in which the law forbids sin can to some degree hold people back from sin. It matters a great deal to Christians that Scripture commands us not to commit adultery and murder; we come to realize that if we commit such acts we become transgressors of the law (*James* 2:11). The restraining force of the law is a repeated theme in Scripture's longest psalm, a function of the law for which the psalmist is very grateful (*e.g., Psa.* 119:101, 104, 128).

The corruption of sin is restrained in us by the bare fact that it is forbidden. Redeemed saints do not want to offend their God and Saviour. But the law also serves to restrain the corruption remaining within believers when it reminds them what 'their sins deserve' and the punishment they should suffer were it not for the mercy of God. Knowing the punishment we deserve, but have escaped by God's amazing grace, is a very powerful motivating force to avoid anything that would offend our Father in heaven. In a remarkable payer of confession offered on behalf of the nation of Israel, Ezra acknowledged that God punishes his own people 'less than our iniquities deserve'; yet that truth made him all the more eager to avoid any further sin (*Ezra* 9:13).

The third way in which the law restrains sin in believers is to remind them of the continuing consequences of law-breaking—even for Christians. Although we as Christians are 'freed from the curse . . . threatened in the law', our sins still earn 'afflictions in this life', and if we do not turn from those sins, we should expect to meet our Father's disfavour.

This is eloquently expressed in Psalm 89 with reference to David's off-spring. On the one hand, God warns, 'if his children forsake my law and do not walk according to my rules, if they violate my statutes and do not keep my commandments, then I will punish their transgression with the rod and their iniquity with stripes' (*Psa.* 89:30-32). On the other hand, God also issues an enduring promise for the very sinners who sometimes have to take their stripes, 'but I will not remove . . . my steadfast love or be false to my faithfulness. I will not violate my covenant or alter the word that went forth from my lips' (*Psa.* 89:33, 34).

The final way in which the law restrains our sin is by urging us on with promises of God's approval of obedience and the blessings which we can expect when the law is kept. In that regard it is significant that the promise attached to the fifth commandment under the old cove-nant is annexed to the same commandment under the new covenant (*cf. Exod.* 20:12 with *Eph.* 6:2-3). It is enlightening that the blessing extended to the meek in Psalm 37 becomes a beatitude taught by Jesus in Matthew 5 (*cf. Psa.* 37:11 with *Matt.* 5:5). It is instructive that some of the rich blessings promised to the nation of Israel are extended to the church in Corinth. God promises to make his dwelling with his obedient people, to walk with them, to be their God, and to own them as his people. These promises are cited in a different context. They take on a different hue; the promises become more personal, perhaps, and more eschatological, certainly. But they are considered real and abiding promises nonetheless (*cf. Lev.* 26:1-14 with *2 Cor.* 6:16). Psalm 19 captures the perspective of both Testaments towards the commandments of God when it states that 'by them is your servant warned; in keeping them there is great reward' (*Psa.* 19:11).

The rewards of the law

In speaking about warnings and blessings, we must be clear that just as God will not curse Christians who violate his law, so too he is not bound to bless those who keep his law. To be owed any blessing by God for the work we do would require us to be righteous before God, or justified by God according to a goodness which is our own.

Here the triple denial of such a possibility, issued by the Apostle Paul in Galatians 2:16, must be factored into our thinking: 'we know that a person is not justified by the works of the law'; we are 'justified by faith in Christ and not by works of the law'; 'by the works of the law no one will be justified'. Jesus tells us that even in the best of circumstances—an ideal scenario where we have done all that we are commanded—we shall at most say, 'We are unworthy servants; we have only done what was our duty' (*Luke* 17:10). No wonder that the Westminster divines concluded that neither cursing nor blessing is due to us as it would be in a covenant of works.

Promises and threats as motivations for Christians

The fact is that we *are* sometimes motivated to do good or refrain from evil because of the encouragements or deterrents of the law. Nonetheless, *ought* we to be so motivated? Is such motivation an evidence that a Christian is, to reverse a biblical phrase, 'under the law, and not under grace'?

To answer this question we must once more assemble the facts that we have already considered. First, as Paul explicitly says in Romans 6, those who are 'not under law but under grace' care a great deal about sin: they refuse its reign and dominion. We can conclude from this that truly liberated Christians evidently prefer to obey the law rather than submit to the 'passions' of sin (*Rom.* 6:12, 14). Second, we must consider the fact that God calls us to obedience in order that we 'may obtain a blessing'. This is not merely an old covenant way of thinking, for Psalm 34, promising rich benedictions for the obedient, is quoted extensively in 1 Peter 3 (*cf. 1 Pet.* 3:8-12 with *Psa.* 34:12-16). But the new covenant does inform and even transform our understanding of blessings by clarifying that any good thing comes to us as a gift from Christ; none is earned by right. Third, while we are grateful for God's gifts, while we are 'grateful' to be 'receiving a kingdom' from God 'that cannot be shaken', and while as members of the new covenant we no longer fear damnation, we at the same time recall God's warnings, and thus come before him with 'reverence and awe', remembering that 'our God is a consuming fire' (*Heb.* 12:28, 29).

The Bible presents three main categories of motivation for obedience, and we do well to consider all of them. First, we are to consider our guilt, God's grace, and then respond in gratitude. Second, we are called to be what we are—since we are new creatures, we need to live as new creatures. Third, as the Westminster assembly argues here, we are to pursue what is most worthwhile—the approval of our Father in heaven and the inheritance he offers, instead of the two-pound (or dollar) pleasures of sin which continue to fascinate us much more than they should.

Historic Text	*Modern Version*
19.7 Neither are the forementioned uses of the law contrary to the grace of the gospel, but do sweetly comply with it;ʷ the Spirit of Christ subduing, and enabling the will of man, to do that, freely and cheerfully, which the will of God, revealed in the law, requires to be done.ˣ	**19.7** These uses of the law do not conflict with the grace of the gospel, but are in complete harmony with it; for it is the Spirit of Christ who subdues and enables the will of man to do freely and cheerfully those things which the will of God, revealed in the law, requires.

Scripture Proofs
  19.7 ʷ Gal. 3:21. ˣ Ezek. 36:27; Heb. 8:10, with Jer. 31:33.

The law and the gospel

Chapter 19 has described the different ways in which the Bible speaks about the law of God. It described moral, ceremonial and civil laws, and explained how only the moral law continues in force today. Paragraph 6 then spelled out three uses of the law: how the law is useful to guide our lives, how it shows us our need for the Saviour, and how it restrains God's people from sin. The threats of the law teach us to fear disobedience, and its promises help to lead us in ways that God favours.

The final paragraph tells us explicitly that the law and its different uses are in no way contrary to a life of grace. Some people are of the opinion that Christians should not think about the law. They argue that we should never be motivated to obey God because of a hope of blessing for obedience or punishment for disobedience.

If the law were our only motivation in life, there would be a problem, not least because in so many ways we fall short of God's perfect standards every day. Our lives as Christians should be fundamentally fuelled by the grace and love of the gospel. But we should never think that God's law and God's gospel are at war with each other, and cannot coexist in the life and thought of believers. We need to raise this cautionary flag because of all that we have said about the law and gospel so far, and we can say this because Scripture itself addresses this very point.

Paul once asked, 'Is the law then against the promises of God?' The answer for him was obvious and emphatic. Definitely not. In fact, if there could have been a law which would have given life, this was it (*Gal.* 3:21). We need a Saviour not because of a problem with law, but because we are not the kind of people who can keep the law.

Spirit-enabled obedience

The fact is that 'the Spirit of Christ' both subdues and enables Christians to 'freely and cheerfully' heed the will of God which he has revealed in his law.

It is this Spirit whom God promised through Ezekiel, when he said, 'I will put my Spirit within you, and cause you to walk in my statutes and be careful to obey my rules' (*Ezek.* 36:27). What is more, God was speaking through the prophet Ezekiel about the new covenant, which is one more indication that the law is not contrary to the gospel.

In fact Jeremiah could see from afar that new-covenant believers would come to love the law. He spoke of a 'covenant that' God would 'make with the house of Israel', and one of its distinguishing features had to do with the law. Strikingly, we are not informed that these enlightened New Testament believers would distance themselves from the moral law of the Old Testament. On the contrary, they would be enlightened because the Lord would put his 'law within them', and would 'write it on their hearts'. It was in that way, among others, that God would prove his great declaration, 'I will be their God, and they shall be my people' (*Jer.* 31:33).

This is a note that we need to sound today, for evangelical Christians are increasingly unclear about their relationship with the law. Sometimes people are praying for guidance and discernment from God when they really need to pray for compliance and obedience to God. At other times, people have clear opinions about the law, but they are clearly wrong, as they fail to see that the moral law which was first given in the Old Testament has an abiding relevance in the New.

In fact we know that this is what New Testament believers needed to hear, because this is the passage which the writer of the letter to the Hebrews quotes at some length in the very place in which he describes the new covenant (*Heb.* 8:10). Of course he will go on to explain all the ways in which the new covenant is truly new. Under the new covenant we no longer worship in an earthly tabernacle or temple. Under the new covenant a high priest no longer continues to offer sacrifices day after day. Jesus Christ is our priest and he gave himself as a sacrifice once for all. Under the new covenant there is no longer a multitude of ceremonies that we need to keep—we are left with only two, baptism and the Lord's supper.

If he had thought it necessary to mention, or if it had spoken more directly to his argument, the writer of the letter to the Hebrews could have added that the judicial and civil laws of the Old Testament have been fulfilled. We can see the points of discontinuity between the two covenants. Nonetheless, there are connections between the two covenants, including this very important one: that 'the Spirit of Christ' grants new-covenant believers a love and respect for the moral law that was delivered under the old covenant. Let us express that respect ourselves, both in the way in which we think and speak about the law, and in the way in which—by the power of the Holy Spirit and the grace of God—we try to keep it from day to day.

CHAPTER 20:

OF CHRISTIAN LIBERTY,
AND LIBERTY OF CONSCIENCE

Historic Text

20.1 The liberty which Christ has purchased for believers, under the gospel, consists, in their freedom from the guilt of sin, the condemning wrath of God, the curse of the moral law;[a] and, in their being delivered from this present evil world, bondage to Satan, and dominion of sin;[b] from the evil of afflictions, the sting of death, the victory of the grave, and everlasting damnation;[c] as also, in their free access to God,[d] and their yielding obedience unto him, not out of slavish fear, but a childlike love and willing mind.[e] All which, were common also to believers under the law.[f] But, under the new testament, the liberty of Christians is further enlarged, in their freedom from the yoke of the ceremonial law, to which the Jewish church was subjected;[g] and in greater boldness of access to the throne of grace,[h] and in fuller communications of the free Spirit of God, than believers, under the law, did ordinarily partake of.[i]

Modern Version

20.1 The liberty which Christ purchased for believers under the gospel consists in their freedom from the guilt of sin, from the condemning wrath of God, and from the curse of the moral law. Furthermore, it consists in their being delivered from this present evil age, from bondage to Satan and the dominion of sin, from the evil of afflictions, from the sting of death, from the victory of the grave, and from everlasting damnation. It consists also in their free access to God and in yielding obedience to him, not out of slavish fear, but out of a childlike love and willing mind. All of these things were common to believers also under the law. Under the new testament, however, the liberty of Christians is further enlarged: they are free from the yoke of the ceremonial law to which the Jewish church was subjected; they have greater boldness of access to the throne of grace; and they experience in greater measure the gifts of God's free Spirit than believers under the law ordinarily partook of.

Scripture Proofs

    20.1   [a] Titus 2:14; 1 Thess. 1:10; Gal. 3:13.   [b] Gal.1:4; Col. 1:13; Acts 26:18; Rom. 6:14.   [c] Rom. 8:28; Psa. 119:71; 1 Cor. 15:54-57; Rom. 8:1.   [d] Rom. 5:1,2.

ᵉ Rom. 8:14,15; 1 John 4:18. ᶠ Gal. 3:9,14. ᵍ Gal. 4:1-3,6,7; Gal. 5:1; Acts 15:10,11.
ʰ Heb. 4:14,16; Heb. 10:19-22. ⁱ John 7:38,39; 2 Cor. 3:13,17,18.

What Christ has purchased

We turn in this chapter from the law to liberty. Christians are alive
when they believe the gospel and obey the law. They blossom when they
understand their liberty.

The first thing that needs to be said about Christian liberty is that
it is something which Christ has bought for us. Our liberties are not
frivolous freedoms. They come to us because Jesus Christ suffered and
died. We can see this immediately if we consider our foundational freedoms: freedom from guilt, from 'the condemning wrath of God', from
the dreaded 'curse of the moral law'. We have these freedoms because
Christ gave himself for us, to redeem us from all our sins (*Titus* 2:14);
because a Son from heaven, now raised from the dead, 'delivered us from
the wrath to come' (*1 Thess.* 1:10); because Christ himself 'redeemed us
from the curse of the law, being made a curse for us' (*Gal.* 3:3). Whatever
our liberties are, they are liberties owed to Christ and thus enjoyed only
under his lordship.

Christ has brought us into his Father's family, a place to stay where
the list of complementary gifts is staggering to conceive. In his presence
we are 'delivered from' the worst that 'this present evil world' has to offer.
We are set free from 'bondage to Satan'. And in Christ, we break loose
from the 'dominion of sin'. These are not benefits that we are left to infer
for ourselves. On the contrary, these are explicit announcements made
by the Apostle Paul in his letters. It was the will of the Father that Jesus
would deliver us from present evil (*Gal.* 1:4), from the power of darkness,
and from sin (*Col.* 1:13; *Rom.* 6:14); as Paul explained, the proclamation
of these freedoms was at the very core of his own mission (*Acts* 26:18).

In Christ we are granted immunity from the full effects of sin. The
'evil of afflictions' works for the good of those who love God (*Rom.*
8:28)—an astounding idea first heard in the Old Testament, where the
psalmist goes so far as to say that it was 'good' to be afflicted, and that
the experience helped him learn (*Psa.* 119:71). The 'sting of death', too,
loses its venom as a result of the victory of our Lord Jesus Christ over the

grave (*1 Cor.* 15:54-57). Beyond a mere victory over the grave, through Jesus Christ we are granted an everlasting exemption from 'eternal damnation'. As the old Geneva translation of the Bible put it, 'There is no condemnation to them that are in Christ Jesus' (*Rom.* 8:1).

Glorious as these realities are, we are not only emancipated from evil—we become fully franchised in the good. 'Since we have been justified by faith, we have peace with God through our Lord Jesus Christ'—a peace that is lived out in a free access to God by faith (*Rom.* 5:1, 2). Our whole mode of service is changed too. We no longer offer the cringing obedience of a terrified slave. We find a new kind of love that 'casts out fear'. As a completely new experience to us, we offer service in love, as children serving a Father they love, and doing so with a willing mind (*Rom.* 8:14, 15; *1 John* 4:18).

As we have already seen in passing, these liberties are common to believers under the law, by which we mean the Old Testament, and believers under the gospel, by which we mean the New Testament. As Paul explained to the Galatian believers, we are 'blessed along with faithful Abraham', for 'in Christ Jesus the blessing of Abraham' comes to Gentiles (*Gal.* 3:9, 14). At the same time the New Testament church enjoys freedoms which the 'Jewish church' of the Old Testament could hardly have imagined.

In the age of the gospel our freedom has been immeasurably enlarged and the burdens of life lightened as the heavy yoke of the ceremonial law is lifted from our shoulders. There was a childish and slavish aspect to the tutelage of the law. So radical was the end of this old order, and so unfamiliar this freedom, that some first-century (and some twenty-first-century) Jewish converts to Christianity could not (and cannot) imagine life without these old ceremonies. Many conflicts in the New Testament were caused by men and women who were like freed prisoners who had only known life in jail and who could imagine no other.

The apostles understood them. But they insisted on their rehabilitation and reorientation to the kingdom of God. With the coming of Christ the Father's appointed time had come. Slaves to ceremonies were set free and clearly declared to be sons with new responsibilities (*Gal.* 4:1-3, 6, 7). It is for this freedom that Christ has set us free; and we are warned to stand firm in this freedom, and never again submit to the yoke of slavery (*Gal.* 5:1). We were set free to own these freedoms and to defend them. It would be worthy of our final breath to die in the defence of these things. To think less of these liberties is to test God and to place a burden on the backs of Christians that our fathers in the faith were never able to bear themselves (*Acts* 15:10, 11).

Of course, these ceremonies and sacrifices are gone for a reason: we have now interceding for us a permanent priest who has finished his work on earth and has passed through the heavens to continue his work at his Father's side. That also means that we can draw near to the throne of grace with a new confidence (*Heb.* 4:14, 16). We now enter the holy presence of God in greater boldness by the blood of Jesus. There is a new way: *Jesus.* There is a living way: *Jesus.* We have a great high priest: *Jesus.* We can draw near with a true heart in full assurance of faith (*Heb.* 10:19-22).

And as we draw near to the Father, by the Son, we do so through the Holy Spirit. It is one of our greatest liberties that we live in the freest communication with the Spirit of God possible on this side of heaven, a freedom much fuller than was possible on the other side of the cross. The Holy Spirit flows from Christ to his people like a river of living water. The glorification of Jesus is celebrated by the abundant giving of the Spirit (*John* 7:38, 39). We can gaze at God's glory to a new extent—a veil is taken away. For, as Paul told the Corinthians, Jesus is present with us by his Spirit, 'and where the Spirit of the Lord is, there is freedom' (*2 Cor.* 3:13, 17, 18).

Historic Text	*Modern Version*
20.2 God alone is Lord of the conscience,[k] and has left it free from the doctrines and commandments of men, which are, in anything contrary to his Word; or beside it, if matters of faith, or worship.[l] So that, to believe such doctrines, or to obey such commands, out of conscience, is to betray true liberty	**20.2** God alone is Lord of the conscience and has left it free from the doctrines and commandments of men which are—in anything—contrary to his Word, or which—in matters of faith or worship—are in addition to it. Therefore, anyone who believes such doctrines or obeys such commands out

of conscience:[m] and the requiring of an implicit faith, and an absolute and blind obedience, is, to destroy liberty of conscience, and reason also.[n]

of conscience betrays true liberty of conscience. The requiring of an implicit faith, and an absolute and blind obedience, destroys both liberty of conscience and reason.

Scripture Proofs

20.2 [k] James 4:12; Rom. 14:4. [l] Acts 4:19; Acts 5:29; 1 Cor. 7:23; Matt. 23:8-10; 2 Cor. 1:24; Matt. 15:9. [m] Col. 2:20,22,23; Gal. 1:10; Gal. 2:4,5; Gal. 5:1. [n] Rom. 10:17; Rom. 14:23; Isa. 8:20; Acts 17:11; John 4:22; Hos. 5:11; Rev. 13:12,16,17; Jer. 8:9.

Liberation under lordship

Having tallied in the first paragraph some of the tremendous freedoms purchased for us by Jesus Christ, the authors of the confession here look at the liberating effects of Christ's lordship.

The first thing that we are told is that there is only one true Lord over our consciences: the God who is Lord over all. It is he alone who made us in his image. 'There is only one lawgiver and judge' (*James* 4:12) and he is the one who implanted in every human being a sense of what is right and good and true. It is before him that every person 'stands or falls' (*Rom.* 14:4).

Sometimes people can see immediately how this lordship liberates the Christian conscience. With God as our Lord, our lives are freed 'from the doctrines and commandments of men'—at the very least freed from those commands and teachings which are against God's Word. We are even more free in our Christian faith and worship. Not only should no one command us to believe anything in our doctrine or do anything in our worship which is against God's Word—but no one should even ask us in the name of God to believe or do anything that is 'beside' or in addition to the Word of God.

That should make sense to Christians. In no part of our life should we ever feel obliged to listen to and obey men instead of God. That is the point that Peter and John made to the Sanhedrin in Acts 4, and sharpened even more on another occasion in Acts 5, when 'Peter and the apostles answered, "We must obey God rather than men"' (*Acts* 5:29).

Nonetheless, this is a message of freedom that Christians too often forget. Paul had to tell the Corinthian church, 'you were bought with a price; do not become slaves of men' (*1 Cor.* 7:23). For some reason we find it hard to accept that God is our spiritual father and Christ our teacher (*Matt.* 23:8-10). Instead we have the tendency to rank the advice of men in the same league as the Word of God. It is knowledge of this sinful human tendency that makes the best shepherds wary of manipulating their sheep or lording their position over their people (*2 Cor.* 1:24; *1 Pet.* 5).

In no part of life are we to obey men instead of God. But we are to be especially careful in our approach to the two related subjects of doctrine and worship. In doctrine and worship we must be watchful to pay close heed to God's Word, for in listening to his Word we most clearly hear his voice. In worship and in doctrine we must not only avoid that which is contrary to the Word of God. We must also avoid all that is offered to supplement the Word of God. Jesus once quoted the following words from Isaiah's prophecy: 'in vain do they worship me, teaching as doctrines the commandments of men' (*Matt.* 15:9; *cf. Isa.* 29:13). Christians today must be careful lest that which was said of the contemporaries of Isaiah, and later of Jesus, also be said of us.

Indeed, we need to be on guard against believing the teachings of men that are not rooted in God's Word, or letting the commands of others rule our consciences, or to be persuaded that we should follow their dictates 'out of conscience'. To allow others to dictate in the realm in which God has already given us directions 'is to betray true liberty of conscience'. We cannot submit at the same time to the world's regulations for religion and to God's. Nor can we submit to man-made religious supplements—rules that say 'do not handle, do not taste, do not touch'. As Paul told the Colossians, such things not only displease God—they are also useless. They have 'an appearance of wisdom in promoting self-made religion and asceticism and severity to the body, but they are of no value in stopping the indulgence of the flesh' (*Col.* 2:20, 22, 23). We must choose one master, and only one will set his servants free.

It is impossible to secure both 'the approval of man' and 'of God' (*Gal.* 1:10). So we need to be on guard against those who will try to gather obedient followers around them. Really, they are bringing others into slavery after Christ purchased our liberty. To that spirit we must say with Paul that we will not 'yield in submission even for a moment, so that the truth of the gospel may be preserved' (*Gal.* 2:4, 5). This is a theme that runs through the Scriptures, not least in Paul's letters. We must never forget that it is not simply for forgiveness, but 'for freedom that Christ has set us free'. For that reason, we must not let ourselves 'be burdened again by a yoke of slavery' (*Gal.* 5:1).

This sort of conscience coercion can happen almost accidentally by well-meaning people who are over-prescriptive in giving advice. It can also happen deliberately by power-hungry people who want to control and manipulate crowds in the church. At its worst this suppression of Christian liberty of conscience has been institutionalized. Sadly the Roman Catholic Church has long required its members to believe and obey certain doctrines on the basis of what it calls 'an implicit faith' in the church. But when faith is placed in teaching that goes beyond the Word of God, it violates a key rule of the Word of God; for the Bible tells us that 'faith comes from hearing, and hearing through the word of Christ' (*Rom.* 10:17). To ask for an 'absolute' obedience in areas where the Bible is silent is to ask for a 'blind obedience' that quickly destroys 'liberty of conscience'. It destroys our 'reason' too. And such extra-biblical requirements confuse us, leading people to doubt, to act out of guilt, and sometimes to act against what they believe (*Rom.* 14:23).

Isaiah once spoke into a context where God's people were bombarded with teachers of everything but the truth. His instructions for God's people were clear. Where do we go in a situation like this? 'To the law and to the testimony!' If teachers 'do not speak according to this word, they have no light of dawn' (*Isa.* 8:20).[1] It was the hard task of another prophet to ask the Israelites what they planned to do now that they had rejected the word of the Lord—where did they expect to learn wisdom? (*Jer.* 8:9).

Our liberty rests in having the light of the gospel in our lives, in

---

[1] It may be that Hosea refers to a similar problem with the Ephraimites, facing judgment because they are going after filth, or, in another possible translation, 'following human precepts' (*Hos.* 5:11). See Jeremiah Burroughs, *An Exposition with Practical Observations Continued upon the Fourth, Fifth, Sixth and Seventh Chapters of Hosea*, p. 464.

being able to look to God's Word, and in knowing that we can measure all other words by it. It is for turning to the Bible that we remember the Bereans, those early Christians who used the Scriptures to evaluate the teaching of the Apostle Paul (*Acts* 17:11). Negatively, it is one sign of the beast in the book of Revelation that he forces false worship (*Rev.* 13:12, 16-17). Positively, it is a sign of the work of God in the church when worship is free and true. When we have the Word of God we can worship God with liberty, for we know what he wants (*John* 4:22). When we live under Christ's lordship and have God's Word as our guide, the truth will set us free.

Historic Text	**Modern Version**
20.3 They, who upon pretence of Christian liberty, do practice any sin, or cherish any lust, do thereby destroy the end of Christian liberty, which is, that being delivered out of the hands of our enemies, we might serve the Lord, without fear, in holiness and righteousness before him, all the days of our life.°	**20.3** Those who, on the pretext of Christian liberty, practice any sin or cherish any evil desire destroy the purpose of Christian liberty. This purpose is that, having been delivered out of the hand of our enemies, we may serve the Lord without fear, in holiness and righteousness before him all the days of our life.

Scripture Proofs

   20.3   ° Gal. 5:13; 1 Pet. 2:16; 2 Pet. 2:19; John 8:34; Luke 1:74,75.

Freedom within biblical bounds

This chapter underlines the many real freedoms that we have through Christ. It also considers how to avoid submitting ourselves to any rule and regulation which subverts the freedoms which Christ purchased for us with his own life blood. The previous section stressed that in no aspect of the Christian life are we to obey men instead of God. Especially in worship and doctrine we must not only avoid that which is contrary to the Word of God, but even that which is additional to its instruction. However, it is perhaps possible to make this point (or to take this point) in a way that could lead someone to wonder if there are any limits to Christian liberty. The Bible answers this question: there are limits, and this paragraph tells us what they are.

If someone, under the cloak of a free conscience, practises some sin, or comes to love some wrong, they are actually subverting the Scripture's teaching. The idea of Christian liberty is not that we are free to do or say or think whatever we can persuade our weak consciences to accept. On the contrary, one purpose of Christian liberty is to be freed from the power of sin itself; for, as our Lord explained to his hearers, 'everyone who commits sin is a slave to sin' (*John* 8:34).

Another purpose of Christian freedom is to be freed from those who would oppress us with their commands, for we are to live under the lordship of Jesus Christ. We are instructed not to obey enemies who want to dominate us for their own purposes. We are set free so that we can serve the one who is Master of all. In the words of Zechariah's song, we are 'being delivered from the hand of our enemies' by the Lord so that we 'might serve him without fear, in holiness and righteousness before him all our days' (*Luke* 1:74, 75).

Finding freedom from sin by serving the Lord and his people is the vision that God presents to us in his Word. We can hear part of this message in Paul's letter to the Galatians. He reminded them that they were 'called to freedom', but that they should not use their 'freedom as an opportunity for the flesh', rather, 'through love' they were to 'serve one another' (*Gal.* 5:13).

In the New Testament the Apostle Peter makes this point in a couple of different ways. The first is a straight-forward exhortation when he says, 'live as people who are free, not using your freedom as a cover-up for evil, but living as servants of God' (*1 Pet.* 2:16). In the second way he approaches the subject by warning about false freedoms. There are people who come to Christians and 'promise them freedom, but they themselves are slaves of corruption'. These people want to 'set us free' to go where no Christian has gone before; they are finding new freedoms from God's law that others never noticed. Perhaps it is something exciting, like a sexual revolution or a new definition of marriage. Perhaps it is something private, like a new spin on copyright laws that conveniently permits us to reproduce things that we have not purchased. But while we suppose ourselves to be blazing new frontiers in morality and ethics, we are overcome by sin and are enslaved ourselves (*2 Pet.* 2:19).

So here is a danger that we must all try to avoid. There is a vitally important difference between liberty and licence and we must pray that we will be given the willingness and the wisdom to see it. And we must use our freedom in a certain way: we are free to run from that which enslaves us; we are free to serve a Master whose yoke is easy and whose burden is light; we are free to help those around us, guided by God and blessed by his Spirit.

Historic Text	*RCF (1788) Text*	*Modern Version*
20.4 And because the powers which God has ordained, and the liberty which Christ has purchased, are not intended by God, to destroy, but mutually to uphold and preserve one another; they, who upon pretense of Christian liberty, shall oppose any lawful power, or the lawful exercise of it, whether it be civil or ecclesiastical, resist the ordinance of God.[P] And, for their publishing of such opinions, or maintaining of such practices, as are contrary to the light of nature, or to the known principles of Christianity, whether concerning faith, worship, or conversation; or, to the power of godliness; or, such erroneous opinions or practices, as either in their own nature, or in the manner of publishing	**20.4** And because the powers which God has ordained, and the liberty which Christ has purchased, are not intended by God to destroy, but mutually to uphold and preserve one another; they who, upon pretence of Christian liberty, shall oppose any lawful power, or the lawful exercise of it, whether it be civil or ecclesiastical, resist the ordinance of God.[I] And for their publishing of such opinions, or maintaining of such practices, as are contrary to the light of nature, or to the known principles of Christianity, whether concerning faith, worship or conversation; or to the power of godliness; or such erroneous opinions or practices, as either, in their own nature, or in the manner of publishing	**20.4** Because the powers which God has ordained and the liberty which Christ has purchased are not intended by God to destroy each other, but mutually to uphold and preserve one another, those who, in the name of Christian liberty, oppose any lawful power or any lawful exercise of it, whether civil or ecclesiastical, resist the ordinance of God. Those who declare opinions or maintain practices contrary to the light of nature, or to the known principles of Christianity (whether concerning faith, worship, or manner of life), or the power of godliness; or who are guilty of such erroneous opinions or practices, as either in their own nature, or in the manner of publishing or maintaining them,

or maintaining them, are destructive to the external peace and order which Christ has established in the church, they may lawfully be called to account, and proceeded against by the censures of the church,[q] and by the power of the civil magistrate.[r]	or maintaining them, are destructive to the external peace and order which Christ has established in the church; they may lawfully be called to account,[2] and proceeded against by the censures of the church.[3]	are destructive of the external peace and order which Christ has established in the church, may lawfully be called to account, and proceeded against, by the censures of the church.

Scripture Proofs (WCF)

20.4 [p] Matt. 12:25; 1 Pet. 2:13,14,16; Rom. 13:1-8; Heb. 13:17. [q] Rom. 1:32, with 1 Cor. 5:1,5,11,13; 2 John 10,11, and 2 Thess. 3:14, and 1 Tim. 6:3-5; Titus 1:10,11,13, and Titus 3:10, with Matt. 18:15-17; 1 Tim. 1:19,20; Rev. 2:2,14,15,20; Rev. 3:9.
[r] Deut. 13:6-12; Rom. 13:3,4, with 2 John 10,11; Ezra 7:23,25-28; Rev. 17:12,16,17; Neh. 13:15,17,21,22,25,30; 2 Kings 23:5,6,9,20,21; 2 Chron. 34:33; 2 Chron. 15:12,13,16; Dan. 3:29; 1 Tim. 2:2; Isa. 49:23; Zech. 13:2,3.

Scripture Proofs (RCF)

20.4 [1] Matt. 12:25; 1 Pet. 2:13-14,16; Rom. 13:1-8; Heb. 13:17; [2] Rom. 1:32 with 1 Cor. 5:1,5,11,13; 2 John 10-11 and 2 Thess. 3:14 and 1 Tim. 6:3-5 and Titus 1:10-11,13 and Titus 3:10 with Matt. 18:15-17; 1 Tim. 1:19-20; Rev. 2:2,14,15,20; Rev. 3:9; [3] Deut. 13:6-12; Rom. 13:3-4 with 2 John 10-11; Ezra 7:23,25-28; Rev. 17:12,16-17; Neh. 13:15,17,21-22,25 30; 2 Kings 23:5-6,9,20-21; 2 Chron. 34:33; 2 Chron. 15:12-13,16; Dan. 3:29; 1 Tim. 2:2; Isa. 49:23; Zech. 13:2-3.

Law and liberty

Jesus Christ has purchased for us every liberty we have as Christians and therefore he claims lordship over our consciences. It remains to be said, and is said here in this fourth paragraph, that there is no tension between the powers that God ordains in society and the freedom we find in Christ. Good government and Christian liberty are mutually complementary. They are designed by God to 'uphold and preserve' each other. God's kingdom is not 'divided against itself' (*Matt.* 12:25).

For that reason, to argue that we, in the name of the church or of Christian freedom, have a right to oppose civil powers or the legal exercise of power, is to destroy what God intends. If we resist lawful civil government by mayors, or members of congress, or prime ministers; if we resist church government (in local congregational or regional elder-ships or presbyteries), we are ultimately resisting God himself.

Indeed, Peter called early Christians under hostile governments to 'be subject for the Lord's sake to every human institution, whether it be to the emperor as supreme, or to governors as sent by him to punish those who do evil and to praise those who do good'. Of course, the same applies to us, as does Peter's additional exhortation that we 'live as people who are free, not using your freedom as a cover-up for evil, but living as servants of God' (*1 Pet.* 2:13, 14, 16). We can obey evil governments, unless they command us to do evil.

One of the fullest biblical treatments on the duties of Christians to their civil governments is found in the opening eight verses of Romans 13, where we are actually told to obey authorities not only because God appoints them, but also 'for conscience sake' (*Rom.* 13:1-8). In a similar way we are called to honour leaders in the church (*Heb.* 13:17).

No freedom for lawlessness

It is because we do not have the freedom to ignore God's Word or God's governments that we are to be held accountable for what we say and do. If we preach and print opinions, or maintain practices that are against the light of nature—such as the problem of incest that we see in the Corinthian church—then the church is to deal with such things (*cf. Rom.* 1:32 with *1 Cor.* 5:1, 5, 11, 13).

If we ignore key Christian doctrines about faith, worship or life; if we undermine the power or importance of godliness; if we hold to 'erroneous opinions or practices'; if we cling to things that are bad in themselves; or if we act in any way that destroys the structures of peace and order in society or in the church, we need to be 'called to account' through the regular means that God has appointed, such as the ones we see in Matthew 18:15-17.

Sometimes that discipline will take the shape of avoiding unnecessary contact with a troublemaker, as we see in 2 John 10, 11 or 2 Thessalonians 3:14. Sometimes we deal with the problem by just calling it what it is, as Paul does in 1 Timothy 6:3-5. Sometimes a sharp rebuke is in order, as Paul states in Titus 1:10, or some combination of the above, as Paul recommends in Titus 3:10.

This might not look like much to those who are outside the church. But the Bible has serious words for this discipline. It reserves its strongest language for those who foment trouble in the church, saying that they belong to the synagogue of Satan (*Rev.* 3:9). They are compared to King Balak the Moabite or Queen Jezebel the wicked wife of King Ahab (*Rev.* 2:2, 14, 15, 20)—and when people refuse to repent of their sins, the Bible tells us that there is a sense in which they are being handed over to Satan (*1 Tim.* 1:19, 20).

Church censures and civil magistrates

In short, any persistent sin that God's people refuse to leave behind can be 'proceeded against, by the censures of the church'. A subset of those things are so serious that they ought to be dealt with by 'the power of the civil magistrate'. Nonetheless the civil government should not be called to punish spiritual sins.

The denial that the civil government has any role in spiritual matters puts most Christian teachers today at odds with Christian teachers of the past. Of course, there are all sorts of Old Testament texts which refer to civil involvement in spiritual matters. There is the punishment of doctrinal sins in the nation of Israel, such as the death penalty for encouraging others to engage in idolatry (*Deut.* 13:6-12; *Zech.* 13:2, 3). Godly political leaders encourage or require obedience to the God of Israel (*Ezra* 7:23, 25-28; *Neh.* 13:15, 17, 21, 22, 25, 30; *2 Kings* 23:5, 6, 9, 20, 21; *2 Chron.* 15:12, 13, 16; 34:33). As if that were not enough a pagan king encourages all people to obey God in the book of Daniel (3:29), and in Isaiah 49 the Lord promises to make kings 'foster fathers' and queens 'nursing mothers', presumably with non-Israelite monarchs in view (verse 23).

Nevertheless, we need to remember that the New Testament analogy for Israel is not a modern nation. Israel is the church, and she is to be scattered among the nations. These Old Testament passages, provided by the Westminster assembly, teach us that sins deserve punishment—that we as sinners deserve death. But the church's task is not to execute or incarcerate; our discipline is to hand people over to a spiritual death unless they repent; we warn them of the imprisonment of the soul.

Of course some sins require the attention of the church *and* the civil government. And Christians have sometimes enjoyed the administration of governors who have encouraged Christianity through their own personal profession and public testimony, which is entirely commendable and in keeping with the prophecy of Isaiah 49. Nonetheless, Christian monarchs should not meddle with the affairs of the church (as they sometimes have done), and normally Christians should not refer their churchly quarrels and intra-personal problems to civil courts—in fact Paul warns against this. Certainly we need to employ other ways of bringing home the danger of sin (*cf. Rom.* 13:3, 4 with *2 John* 10, 11). Unless they have committed a civil felony, church members are not to be handed over to civil magistrates by church leaders. Prior to the American Revolution, Presbyterian leaders in the colonies recognized this, and rightly took issue with the final clause in the original form of paragraph 4 of chapter 20. American Presbyterians meeting in Philadelphia in 1788 actually deleted this final phrase, and revised other statements in the Westminster Confession of Faith dealing with the civil magistrate and religion.

So, what are the proper spheres of the church and the state in matters of discipline? The state is to prosecute all those who break its public laws. The church is to turn over to the courts all its sex-offenders, wife-beaters and tax-cheats—all those who break such laws of the state. The church is to pray that the state will perform its task well. We take seriously Paul's command to pray 'for kings and all those in authority', both for the good of our leaders themselves, for all society, and so 'that we may live peaceful and quiet lives in all godliness and holiness' (*1 Tim.* 2:2). This is God's command for our good and his glory. Let us thank him for freeing us and guiding us to serve him better.

WORSHIP

CHAPTER 21:

OF RELIGIOUS WORSHIP, AND THE SABBATH DAY

Historic Text

21.1 The light of nature shows that there is a God, who has lordship and sovereignty over all, is good, and does good unto all, and is therefore to be feared, loved, praised, called upon, trusted in, and served, with all the heart, and with all the soul, and with all the might.[a] But, the acceptable way of worshipping the true God, is instituted by himself, and so limited by his own revealed will, that he may not be worshipped according to the imaginations and devices of men, or the suggestions of Satan, under any visible representation, or any other way not prescribed in the Holy Scripture.[b]

Modern Version

21.1 The light of nature shows that there is a God who has lordship and sovereignty over all, that he is good and does good to all, and that he ought therefore to be feared, loved, praised, prayed to, trusted in, and served with all the heart, and with all the soul, and with all the might. But the acceptable way of worshipping the true God has been instituted by himself, and so limited by his own revealed will, that he may not be worshiped according to the imaginations or devisings of men, or the suggestions of Satan, or under any visible representation, or any other way not commanded in Holy Scripture.

Scripture Proofs

21.1 [a] Rom. 1:20; Acts 17:24; Psa. 119:68; Jer. 10:7; Psa. 31:23; Psa. 18:3; Rom. 10:12; Psa. 62:8; Josh. 24:14; Mark 12:33. [b] Deut. 12:32; Matt. 15:9; Acts 17:25; Matt. 4:9,10; Deut. 4:15-20; Exod. 20:4-6; Col. 2:23.

Worship by the light of nature

When we look at the package we call humankind, we find stamped on each one of us a divine imprint. We can 'clearly see' that we are made by God. The light of nature shows us this much and more. It is because we know something of the real God and his 'eternal power' that we know that he is 'Lord of heaven and earth' and reigns over us and all things, as Paul wrote to the Roman Christians and preached to the Athenian philosophers (*Rom.* 1:20; *Acts* 17:24).

When the New Testament tells us in its own words that we know that God is good, and that God is powerful as Lord and Sovereign of all, it is only building on the clear proclamations of the Old Testament. A psalmist tells us that God 'is good and does good' (*Psa.* 119:68). A prophet announces that God is the king of the nations (*Jer.* 10:7). His goodness and his kingship are realities that all creatures know, even if many choose to suppress this knowledge.

It is because God is who he is, and does what he does, that we are urged by commandment and by promise to fear God (*Jer.* 10:7), love God, praise God (*Psa.* 31:23), call on God (*Rom.* 10:12), trust God (*Psa.* 62:8), and serve God (*Josh.* 24:14). We know this is the right response to God because we are creatures, and our creator has left his mark of ownership on us. And since we have an inkling of God's majesty and greatness, we also know that we are to approach him wholeheartedly, with all our understanding, and with the undivided devotion of our souls (*Mark* 12:33).

The acceptable way of worshipping

Under the spotlight of our conscience, there is no hiding the truth about the existence of the invisible God. And we know in our conscience that we must worship him. However it is Scripture that teaches us that the only acceptable way of worshipping God is *his way*. It was after a discussion about worship, and before a discussion about false teachers, that the Lord told his old covenant people to do everything they were told, nothing more, and nothing less (*Deut.* 12:32). In other words, God institutes the practices of worship. We do not.

Embedded in the Lord's instructions throughout Scripture is the idea that what we do in worship is actually limited. God has identified areas where we must go and some where we must not (see below). Thankfully we do not need to guess these limits. Because he is not a capricious God, our Lord has revealed his will to us. We have such great imaginations, and we can generate so many devices for pleasing God (or pleasing ourselves) in worship, that God graciously gave his Word to be our guide and our boundary.

It was because God had already given his Word that Jesus was so critical of leaders whose worship was empty—who elevated the commandments of men as doctrines for the people (*Matt.* 15:9). God does not need us or our clever ideas (*Acts* 17:25), and neither does he need the worship we may devise in the hope of pleasing him.

When considering worship we also need to consider our temptation to false worship; for there is a tempter, one who is known to redirect worship away from God, and we are warned that he will continue this evil work of his until he is finally chained. When Jesus gave the command 'worship the Lord your God and him only shall you serve', he was not speaking to his mother, or to his disciples, or to religious leaders (*Matt.* 4:9-10), but to Satan.

One of the ways we are not to worship God is through the use of creative visual imagery (*Exod.* 20:4-6). On this score the Israelites were told to watch themselves very carefully. One of the reasons why they were told not to make images of God to assist them in their worship was that when God revealed himself at Sinai, he did not do so in a *visible* form. God did not offer himself to the artists. The Israelites were not supposed to make an educated guess about his appearance. They were especially warned not to take something in creation—whether the fish of the sea or the stars of the sky—and use it as a model for the creator (*Deut.* 4:15-20). There were many problems with idols. Ultimately, people fashioned idols in order to help them access and control the god they wanted to worship. This is offensive to God, but idol worship was also offensive because it involved a worship of God that was not ordered by his Word. The only religion that is healthy for us and acceptable to God is religion according to *his* prescription.

The call to do in worship what is *prescribed* in the Bible, rather than merely to avoid what is *proscribed* in the Bible, is an important regulating principle for worship. Members and friends of the Westminster assembly understood the sufficiency of Scripture for worship in a way that the Roman Church, Lutheran churches, and the hierarchy of the Church of England did not. As a principle, this attention to biblical prescription usefully keeps us from promoting in our churches any activity that sounds practical, appears beautiful, smells wonderful, feels comfortable or tastes vaguely theological, but that is not prescribed in the Bible.

Admittedly, this is hard for us, because, as the Apostle Paul pointed out, there are many practices, including worship practices, that have the 'appearance of wisdom'. But it turns out that self-made practices are useless. They have 'no value'. What has true value is worship that God endorses—no, worship that God commands—offered through Jesus our only mediator, by the power of the Holy Spirit.

Historic Text	*Modern Version*
21.2 Religious worship is to be given to God, the Father, Son, and Holy Ghost; and to him alone;[c] not, to angels, saints, or any other creature:[d] and, since the Fall, not without a mediator; nor in the mediation of any other, but of Christ alone.[e]	**21.2** Religious worship is to be given to God alone—Father, Son, and Holy Spirit. It is not to be given to angels, saints, or any other creature. And since the Fall, worship is not to be given except through a mediator, nor is it to be given through any mediator other than Christ.
21.3 Prayer, with thanksgiving being one special part of religious worship,[f] is, by God, required of all men:[g] and, that it may be accepted, it is to be made in the name of the Son,[h] by the help of his Spirit,[i] according to his will,[k] with understanding, reverence, humility, fervency, faith, love, and perseverance;[l] and, if vocal, in a known tongue.[m]	**21.3** Prayer with thanksgiving is a special part of religious worship and is required by God of all men. In order that prayer may be accepted, it is to be made in the name of the Son, by the help of his Spirit, and according to his will. Prayer is to be offered with understanding, reverence, humility, fervency, faith, love, and perseverance. If vocal, it must be offered in a language that is understood.
21.4 Prayer is to be made for things lawful,[n] and for all sorts of men living, or that shall live hereafter:[o] but, not for the dead,[p] nor for those of whom it may be known, that they have sinned the sin unto death.[q]	**21.4** Prayer is to be made for things that are lawful and for all kinds of men now alive or who will live at a later time. But it is wrong to pray for the dead or for those known to have committed the sin unto death.

Scripture Proofs

21.2 [c] Matt. 4:10, with John 5:23, and 2 Cor. 13:14. [d] Col. 2:18; Rev. 19:10; Rom. 1:25. [e] John 14:6; 1 Tim. 2:5; Eph. 2:18; Col. 3:17.

21.3 [f] Phil. 4:6. [g] Psa. 65:2; [h] John 14:13,14; 1 Pet. 2:5. [i] Rom. 8:26. [k] 1 John 5:14. [l] Psa. 47:7; Eccles. 5:1,2; Heb. 12:28; Gen. 18:27; James 5:16; James 1:6,7; Mark

11:24; Matt. 6:12,14,15; Col. 4:2; Eph. 6:18. [m] 1 Cor. 14:14.

21.4 [n] 1 John 5:14. [o] 1 Tim. 2:1,2; John 17:20; 2 Sam. 7:29; Ruth 4:12. [p] 2 Sam. 12:21-23, with Luke 16:25,26; Rev. 14:13. [q] 1 John 5:16.

Trinitarian worship

We were made to worship. Every one of us knows that there is one who is to be 'feared, loved and praised', and the Scriptures tell us whom we are to call upon, to trust in and to serve with all our hearts, and the assembly summarizes this teaching here: 'God, the Father, Son, and Holy Spirit'. Our worship is to be trinitarian, for the only God who has ever lived is one and three, and we are to worship him only.

As the Lord Jesus explained, it is not possible to worship the Father unless we also worship the Son (*John* 5:23), and we might add, the Spirit. We are reminded of this every time that we hear the apostolic blessing. The 'grace of the Lord Jesus Christ and the love of God and the fellowship of the Holy Spirit' must infuse our worship as they effect our salvation (*2 Cor.* 13:14). But in praising and in praying to the Three, we never cease to adore the One. We worship the Lord our God and him only shall we serve (*Matt.* 4:10).

God alone, but not alone

If we are to worship God only, it hardly needs saying that we are not to worship anyone else. We are not to worship angels (*Col.* 2:18), we are not to worship the greatest and most holy of all Christians, those popularly called 'saints' (*Rev.* 19:10). Indeed, it is one of the marks of a world in decline when it worships and serves 'the creature rather than the Creator, who is blessed forever!' (*Rom.* 1:25).

We are to worship God alone, but there is a sense in which we are not to worship him alone, that is, we are not to worship him by ourselves only. Since humanity's fall into sin we must never come near to God 'without a mediator', and we must never pretend that there is any other mediator than the Lord Jesus Christ. He is 'the way, and the truth, and the life' and no one comes to the Father except through him (*John* 14:6). It is only 'through him' that 'we . . . have access in one Spirit to the Father' as Paul told the Ephesians (*Eph.* 2:18). It was when Paul was instructing Timothy about worship that he told him 'there is one God, and there is one mediator between God and men, the man Christ Jesus' (*1 Tim.* 2:5).

We should also see that we need a mediator for worship because we need one for all of life—in 'whatever' we do, in 'word or deed', we are to 'do everything in the name of the Lord Jesus'. When we give thanks to God the Father, we do it 'through him' (*Col.* 3:17).

Prayer through Christ by the power of the Spirit

In paragraph 3 of chapter 21 we move from a discussion of worship in general to a discussion of the main parts of worship, such as prayer. Prayer—which Paul says is always to be accompanied 'with thanksgiving'—is properly seen as a 'special part' of worship (*Phil.* 4:6). Since we are made to enjoy fellowship with God, God calls all people to prayer (*Psa.* 65:2).

Of course, like the rest of worship, our prayers are accepted only in the name of Jesus, which is what our Lord taught his disciples (*John* 14:13, 14); whether our prayers are petitions or 'spiritual sacrifices' of praise, they must be offered to God in his name.

It is a wonderful blessing to know that our prayers are 'acceptable to God through Jesus Christ' (*1 Pet.* 2:5). But that is not all. God also assures us that we can have the Holy Spirit's help in our prayers, especially when we least know what to say (*Rom.* 8:26). This gives us tremendous confidence. It helps us to see 'that if we ask anything according to his will he will hear us' (*1 John* 5:14).

How we pray

It is important to seek God's will in our prayers. The basic orientation of our prayers is significant. But the manner in which we pray is also a matter of concern to the Lord. It is critical to pray with understanding, not being 'rash with our mouths' (*Eccles.* 5:1, 2); to pray with reverence, for we are coming before 'the King of all the earth' (*Psa.* 47:7; *cf. Heb.* 12:28); to pray with humility, because like Abraham we are only 'dust and ashes' (*Gen.* 18:27). We are to be fervent in prayer, recalling that 'the prayer of a righteous man is powerful and effective' (*James* 5:16). We are to come in faith (*James* 1:6, 7), believing that we will receive what we ask if it is good for us (*Mark* 11:24). And until the Lord answers according to his good timing and not our own, we must persevere, as Paul tells the Colossians and the Ephesians (*Col.* 4:2; *Eph.* 6:18).

Need I mention that we should come in love, forgiving others their sins before we ask the Lord to forgive ours (*Matt.* 6:12, 14, 15)? Certainly it is worth mentioning in the charismatic climate of modern Christianity that if our prayers are vocal, then they must be spoken in a tongue that is known to those who are joining with us in our prayers (*1 Cor.* 14:14).

For what are we to pray?

Two questions remain: for what we are to pray? And for whom? Obviously we should not pretend to know God's secret will; there are many chapters in our lives and the lives of others that God has written and we have not read. We need not worry about that. We can pray, however, for anything that is 'lawful', that is, anything in accordance with what God has revealed about himself and his will for Christians (*1 John* 5:14).

Obviously we are not to pray merely for ourselves. We are to pray for all sorts of people. The Apostle Paul does not merely suggest, he actually *urges* Christians 'that supplications, prayers, intercessions, and thanksgivings be made for all people, for kings and all who are in high positions, that we may lead a peaceful and quiet life, godly and dignified in every way' (*1 Tim.* 2:1, 2). I think our Lord also hints in his high-priestly prayer that we ought to pray for those who are yet to come to Christ, even as he prays for all who will one day believe in him (*John* 17:20). We find clearer evidence that we can pray for those who are yet to be born when we see the elders of Bethlehem praying for the children that were expected from Ruth and Boaz (*Ruth* 4:12). We see this again when Ruth's great-grandson David prayed for a blessing on his future family (*2 Sam.* 7:29).

Clearly we must pray for those who are living and we should probably pray for those who might yet live. We should not pray, however, for those who have already died. This too, David understood, for he ceased to pray for his child the moment he died (*2 Sam.* 12:21-23). David's Lord taught the same, for when he gave instruction about the afterlife he explained that nothing could or would be done to relieve the punishment of those who were suffering the torments of hell (*Luke* 16:25, 26). Those who die in the Lord are blessed. Those who do not are not (*Rev.* 14:13). The time to repent of our sins and believe in the gospel, the time for all of us to pray for ourselves and for others is now.

Is it possible to end on a more solemn note? Actually, yes. The Westminster divines mention that there are also those who have hardened themselves. There is one sin that leads to death, and that is the sin of unrepentant opposition to God. If that sin continues for all of life, then it will prove to be a 'sin that leads to death', as the Apostle John calls it (*1 John* 5:16). How do we know when a sinner has reached the point of spiritual death prior to their physical death? Can we know this? Perhaps this knowledge was obtained only by the prophets and apostles, who sometimes spoke and acted with confidence about the spiritual state of some of their contemporaries (perhaps *Jer.* 11:14; *Acts* 5:1-11; *Rev.* 2:20-23). We ourselves should be careful in judging the spiritual state of others, and normally, we would continue to pray for the salvation of the lost no matter what the circumstances.

Here the Westminster assembly cautiously repeats the command of the Apostle John, choosing not to close down the possibility that we may obtain knowledge of someone's spiritual death. And if we did have this knowledge, we would not pray for them because, to say it once again, God's judgment is final. But there is one place where we can confidently say we have already seen the finality and severity of God's judgment: at the cross, where Jesus Christ gave himself for sinners. Certainly that judgment on our Saviour provides us with abundant scope for worship, and for prayer with thanksgiving.

Historic Text	*Modern Version*
21.5 The reading of the Scriptures with godly fear;^r the sound preaching^s and conscionable hearing of the Word, in obedience unto God, with understanding, faith, and reverence;^t singing of psalms with grace in the heart;^u as also, the due administration, and worthy receiving of the sacraments instituted by Christ; are all, parts of the ordinary religious worship of God:^w beside religious oaths,^x vows,^y solemn fastings,^z and thanksgivings, upon special occasions,^a which are, in their several times and seasons, to be used, in an holy and religious manner.^b	**21.5** The various elements of the ordinary religious worship of God are the reading of the Scriptures with reverence; the sound preaching and conscientious hearing of the Word in obedience to God, with understanding, faith, and reverence; the singing of psalms with grace in the heart; and the proper administration and worthy receiving of the sacraments instituted by Christ. Also, on special occasions and at appropriate times, there are other elements of worship, namely, religious oaths, vows, solemn fasts, and thanksgivings. These are to be used in a holy and devout manner.

Scripture Proofs

21.5 ^r Acts 15:21; Rev. 1:3. ^s 2 Tim. 4:2. ^t James 1:22; Acts 10:33; Matt. 13:19; Heb. 4:2; Isa. 66:2. ^u Col. 3:16; Eph. 5:19; James 5:13. ^w Matt. 28:19; 1 Cor. 11:23-29; Acts 2:42. ^x Deut. 6:13, with Neh. 10:29. ^y Isa. 19:21; Eccles. 5:4,5. ^z Joel 2:12; Esth. 4:16; Matt. 9:15; 1 Cor. 7:5. ^a Psa. 107:1-43; Esth. 9:22. ^b Heb. 12:28.

Public worship—Reading

Having discussed worship in general and prayer in particular, the Westminster Confession goes on to treat other elements of public worship as well as some acts of worship that can be either public or private.

Among the ordinary requirements of worship is the reading of Scripture with godly fear. To read a portion of Scripture every Sabbath was the practice of God's people 'from ancient times' (*Acts* 15:21). God's people have always known that they need to hear God's Word. What else can lead and guide them? Indeed, the Bible itself actually stresses the benefit and blessing that God will send when his Word is read aloud, heard and kept (*Rev.* 1:3). And so reading God's Word with godly fear is a central feature of our worship.

Public worship—Preaching

Another normal part of worship is the careful, 'sound preaching' of the Word. Assembly member Anthony Burgess once commented that preachers 'must dresse every sermon at the glasse [mirror] of the Word; they must preach as they read in Scripture'.[1] That is why the Scriptures tell ministers to 'preach the word' faithfully (2 Tim. 4:2).

Public worship—Hearing

But it is also important how we listen to preaching. We must listen in a 'conscionable' way—that is, in a careful, conscientious manner. We want the expectant spirit of Cornelius who with his household waited patiently for Peter to preach (Acts 10:33). We need to listen obediently, not being hearers only, but 'doers of the word' (James 1:22). As we know from the parable of the sower, we need to listen 'with understanding' or the things we have heard will be easily snatched away from us again (Matt. 13.19). And as we know from the solemn warning given in Hebrews, our hearing will only benefit us if it is united with faith (Heb. 4:2).

Naturally, none of this can be achieved if the Word is not heard with 'reverence'. In November 1643 a member of the Westminster assembly, Jeremiah Burroughs, made use of a fragmentary quote from Isaiah 66:2, 'and that trembleth at my word', to cultivate a little reverence among his hearers. His sermon does not tell his hearers to fear God; instead, he paints a verbal picture of a God-fearer and allows his auditors to determine whether they fit that picture. A God-fearing man or woman, he says, does not come 'to hear the Word in an ordinary way, meerly to spend so much time, or to hear what a man could say'. Rather, the Word, 'either read or preached', is attended to 'with all reverence'. Such a one examines the preaching, but 'dares not cavil against it'. Burroughs holds up Moab's King Eglon as an example to be followed by the saints not, of course, in his 'heathenish' ways, nor in his untimely and disgusting death, but as one who rose to receive Ehud as an ambassador with 'a message from God' (Judg. 3:20). Burroughs then pushes the knife in a little deeper, questioning whether their 'hearts . . . swell against' preaching, asking them what they really think about preaching, and pointing

[1] Burgess, *Scripture Directory*, p. 141.

out the irony of those who think they have escaped the world but still show the worst pride in rebelling against the Word—the very opposite of hearing in a conscionable (or acceptable) way.[1]

Public worship—Singing

Needless to say, we are not only to use our ears in hearing but also our tongues in singing. We are to sing 'psalms with grace in the heart'. Essential in all our singing is that we are to make our melodies with our whole heart. Half-hearted singing does not please the Lord.

The seventeenth-century use of the term 'psalms' includes, of course, the one hundred and fifty psalms of the Psalter, and the Westminster assembly was agreed on their regular use in worship. The assembly's commitment to the Psalter in worship is amply evidenced in the enormous amount of time that its members invested in revising and proof-reading a new edition of the Psalter. The assembly's Psalter included no hymns, and its Directory for Public Worship commended psalm singing. The assembly clearly did not believe in exclusive hymnody. Nonetheless the commendation of the Psalms in the confession and the directory needs to take into account that early-modern use of the term 'psalm' is not limited to the Book of Psalms only. The common use of psalm almost always included hymns, and in its scriptural proof texts the assembly deliberately directs readers of the confession to passages like Colossians 3:16, Ephesians 5:19, and James 5:13, which call Christians to 'sing praise', or to sing 'psalms and hymns and spiritual songs'.

Public worship—Sacraments

The final aspect of 'ordinary religious worship' that ought to be mentioned here is 'the due administration' of the sacraments on the minister's part, and the 'worthy receiving of the sacraments' on the members' part. We are to administer those two sacraments that are 'instituted by Christ', baptism and the Lord's supper. That is what our Lord commanded his disciples to do in Matthew 28. That is what Paul reminds us to do in 1 Corinthians 11. That is what we see God's people doing in the book of Acts (*Acts* 2:42).

---

[1] Jeremiah Burroughs, *Gospel-Fear* (London, 1674), pp. 6-7, 9.

Private worship

All of these aspects of worship we offer through Jesus Christ our Lord. But Scripture also shows us, and later chapters in the confession will discuss, that there is also a dimension of worship to our oaths, wherein we call God as a witness (*Deut.* 6:13 with *Neh.* 10:29), or to our vows, wherein we make a promise to God (*Isa.* 19:21 with *Eccles.* 5:4-5).

Prayerful fasts (as opposed to crash diets) should also be a part of our private or public worship, as we can see from examples in Joel and Esther, Matthew and 1 Corinthians (*Joel* 2:12; *Esther* 4:16; *Matt.* 9:15; *1 Cor.* 7:5). So too should 'thanksgivings upon special occasions' as we see in the book of Esther (*Esther* 9:22), or hear of in the book of Psalms (*e.g., Psa.* 107).

Oaths, vows, fastings, and thanksgivings, just like prayer and singing, can be public or private. Each of these aspects of worship has its own time and season. But in all situations, 'since we are receiving a kingdom that cannot be shaken, let us be thankful, and so worship God acceptably with reverence and awe' (*Heb.* 12:28).

Historic Text	*Modern Version*
21.6 Neither prayer, nor any other part of religious worship, is now under the gospel, either tied unto, or made more acceptable by any place in which it is performed, or towards which it is directed:^c but God is to be worshipped everywhere,^d in spirit and truth;^e as in private families^f daily,^g and in secret, each one by himself;^h so, more solemnly, in the public assemblies, which are not carelessly, or wilfully to be neglected, or forsaken, when God, by his Word or providence, calls thereunto.ⁱ	**21.6** Under the gospel, neither prayer nor any other part of religious worship is now limited to—or made more acceptable by—any particular place where it is performed or toward which it is directed. On the contrary, God is to be worshiped everywhere in spirit and truth. He should be worshiped daily in families, and privately by individuals, and with greater solemnity in public worship services. Such worship services are not to be carelessly or wilfully neglected or forsaken when God by his Word or his providence calls people to them.

Scripture Proofs

21.6 ᶜ John 4:21. ᵈ Mal. 1:11; 1 Tim. 2:8. ᵉ John 4:23,24. ᶠ Jer. 10:25; Deut. 6:6,7; Job 1:5; 2 Sam. 6:18,20; 1 Pet. 3:7; Acts 10:2. ᵍ Matt. 6:11. ʰ Matt. 6:6; Eph. 6:18. ⁱ Isa. 56:6,7; Heb. 10:25; Prov. 1:20,21,24; Prov. 8:34; Acts 13:42; Luke 4:16; Acts 2:42.

No place for prayer?

At the dedication of the temple King Solomon prayed that the Lord would be merciful to his people, especially when they looked to the temple in their prayer. Presumably, looking at the temple was a symbol of their faith in the God they worshipped (*2 Chron.* 6:21), a symbol of which God approved. In many parts of the Christian world this tradition of looking in a particular direction while praying or worshipping continues. Paragraph 6 of this chapter teaches that such traditions are not helpful in the New Testament era. There is no special place that can enhance our prayers, or make our worship more acceptable. 'Neither prayer, nor any other part of religious worship, is now under the gospel, either tied unto, or made more acceptable by any place in which it is performed, or towards which it is directed.' We can say this with confidence because our Lord said as much to a Samaritan woman, explaining that neither Jerusalem nor her nation's holy place were to be considered special places for worship (*John* 4:21).

Prayer in every place, and on all occasions

In these last days all people are to pray (*1 Tim.* 2:8), and we are to worship God everywhere, 'from the rising of the sun to its setting' (*Mal.* 1:11). God requires only that we worship him in the power of the Spirit and in the One who is truth (*John* 4:24). But it is a requirement nonetheless, and he threatens judgment on all who will not call on his name (*Jer.* 10:25).

We are also to give worship to God in all different contexts and relationships. We praise him in families. There we pray for each other (*1 Pet.* 3:7), there parents instruct their children formally and informally (*Deut.* 6:6, 7), and there we read God's Word together. We see this in the Old Testament and in the New: in the lives of Job the business tycoon, David the king, and Cornelius the soldier—Scripture commends families and family leaders who pray (*Job* 1:5; *2 Sam.* 6:18, 20; *Acts* 10:2). Indeed, it is hard to escape the idea that the Lord's Prayer is particularly designed for families. Certainly the petitions of this prayer assume that we need the Lord every hour, and one of them makes it clear that we need him every day, in its request that the Lord 'give us this day our daily bread' (*Matt.* 6:11).

Personal and public worship

God is worshipped in 'families daily'; he is also to be worshipped by individuals secretly. Jesus assumes this when he discusses prayer in Matthew 6: 'when you pray', he says, 'go into your room and shut the door and pray to your Father who is in secret. And your Father who sees in secret will reward you' (*Matt.* 6:6). And if we are to take seriously Paul's command to be 'praying at all times in the Spirit, with all prayer and supplication' (*Eph.* 6:18), then that is one more reason why we need to worship God not only in families, but also to breathe up our prayers to God as part of our private lives before him.

Furthermore, if we are not to omit worship in families and in private, how much more we ought to praise God in the assembly of his people, since these meetings are solemn and important times of worship and foretastes of heaven. God by his Word regularly calls us to worship. In many churches such calls and encouragements to worship are heard at the start of each public service of worship. God also sometimes calls us to come back to him in worship by acts of his providence, by events that drive us to our knees, by conversations that draw us back to God's people. However he chooses to call us, the worship of God's name is not to be 'carelessly, or wilfully . . . neglected, or forsaken'.

We see that public prayer and worship are an essential part of the life of God's people. Isaiah reminds us that when we gather corporately we are to remember the breadth of God's plan of salvation: God's house is a 'house of prayer for all peoples' (*Isa.* 56:6, 7). And of course it is not only a house of prayer. It is also a house of Scripture, for God's Word was read and expounded in the synagogues, and on some occasions it was heard very eagerly (*Luke* 4:16; *Acts* 13:42, 43). Sometimes God's people are also spotted together in other public places—in the streets, markets, and city gates (*Prov.* 1:20, 21, 26).[1]

---

[1] The warning for rejecting wisdom in Proverbs 1:24 has led some scholars to

In the early church Christians 'devoted themselves to the apostles' teaching and fellowship, to the breaking of bread and the prayers' (*Acts* 2:42), and hungered for the Word (*Acts* 13:42). We are to hope for this same spiritual appetite for ourselves and our fellow Christians. It is because of the centrality of corporate worship that the writer of the letter to the Hebrews urges his readers not to 'give up meeting together, as some are in the habit of doing'. Much better to 'encourage one another—and all the more as you see the Day approaching' (*Heb.* 10:25).

Historic Text	***Modern Version***
21.7 As it is of the law of nature, that, in general, a due proportion of time be set apart, for the worship of God; so, in his Word, by a positive, moral, and perpetual commandment, binding all men, in all ages, he has particularly appointed one day in seven, for a Sabbath, to be kept holy unto him:^k which, from the beginning of the world to the resurrection of Christ, was the last day of the week; and, from the resurrection of Christ, was changed into the first day of the week,^l which, in Scripture, is called the Lord's day,^m and is to be continued to the end of the world, as the Christian Sabbath.^n	**21.7** As it is the law of nature that, in general, a proper proportion of time ought to be set apart for the worship of God, so God in his Word—by a positive, moral, and perpetual commandment binding all men in all ages—has specifically appointed one day in seven for a Sabbath to be kept holy to him. From the beginning of the world to the resurrection of Christ, the appointed Sabbath was the last day of the week. Beginning with the resurrection of Christ, the Sabbath was changed to the first day of the week, which in Scripture is called the Lord's day, a day to be continued until the end of the age as the Christian Sabbath.

Scripture Proofs

21.7 ^k Exod. 20:8,10,11; Isa. 56:2,4,6,7. ^l Gen. 2:2,3; 1 Cor. 16:1,2; Acts 20:7. ^m Rev. 1:10. ^n Exod. 20:8,10, with Matt. 5:17,18.

think that the wisdom referred to must be the Word of God. That, in turn, has led them to think that the Word of God was presented and taught in a variety of public gatherings in the Old Covenant community (see *Prov.* 1:20, 21). See *Annotations upon All the Books of the Old and New Testament, sub loc.*

A law of nature, a perpetual commandment

If, as Paul says in Romans 1, the very creation tells us that there is a God and we owe him not only obedience but also thanks, then it is fitting that we set aside part of our time to worship him (*Rom.* 1:18-25). Indeed, the members of the Westminster assembly went further and concluded that it is in fact a 'law of nature', woven into the very fabric of the world God made, that time should be set aside for the worship of the Creator.[1]

This general sense gleaned from the created world and from conscience is also specified in God's Word. In the Decalogue, the fourth commandment calls us to 'remember' a period of rest—and the Lord explains what he means. We are to recall his own resting after the creation of the world. The actions of God are to shape the patterns of human life. God's activities at the beginning of time are a model for all whom he has created. But they are especially a model for all his covenant people (*Exod.* 20:8, 10, 11). However, it is not too much to say that God's Word offers 'a positive, moral, and perpetual commandment binding all men in all ages'.

Nonetheless it was not simply the idea, or the principle of rest, or 'Sabbath' that was enshrined from the beginning. No, from the start God 'has particularly', or specially, 'appointed one day in seven, for a Sabbath, to be kept holy unto him'. We are to 'remember the Sabbath day'. As Isaiah explained, we are blessed if we keep the day, and do not profane it; we please the Lord when we hold fast to this covenant day; and the Lord promises joy for those who celebrate his day, especially the joy of seeing him make his day and his house a kind of sanctuary for all people (*Isa.* 56:2, 4, 6, 7).

For clarification: Sabbaths and the Sabbath

In speaking of the Sabbath day, it is really only one kind of Sabbath that is in view in this confession, although Sabbaths came in two different sizes. The first type of Sabbath in Scripture was special, almost always beginning a special festive time and almost always on the first day of the week or the first day of a feast. These days were often referred to in the

---

[1] The argument that it is a law of nature that we are to worship is a more complicated proposition to sustain than the idea that it is a law of nature that we are to rest.

plural, as they are in Paul's letter to the Colossians (*Col.* 2:16): they are often collectively called 'Sabbaths'.

Leviticus 23 is one of the passages in Scripture which mentions the special 'first day Sabbaths' and the feasts which they inaugurated.[1] There you will find the Feast of Tabernacles celebrating the end of desert wandering and the beginning of life in the promised land; the Feast of the Firstfruits marking the beginning of the harvest; the Feast of Weeks celebrating the end of the harvest; the Feast of Unleavened Bread celebrating the departure from Egypt; and the Feast of Trumpets celebrating rest itself with the blowing of trumpets.

In each of these cases the feasts began on 'the day after the Sabbath', on 'the first day', or (with the help of some mathematical skill) on 'the eighth day', or 'the fifteenth day', or 'the fiftieth day'—the reader can do the arithmetic, but the idea of seven plus one runs throughout these cycles. The point is that except for the Passover and the Day of Atonement, these were special Sabbaths celebrated not on seventh days, but on first days. Each was rich in meaning.

These first-day Sabbaths were special, but the high point of all these Old Testament Sabbaths was a year, and not a day. God decreed that every seven years the land of Israel was to be given rest from farming. Each of these was a great year in the life of God's people, but the biggest celebration came after seven of these cycles of seven years. After forty-nine years had passed, the next year was declared the grand Sabbath, the year of Jubilee. This Sabbath above all Sabbaths pictured rest and redemption. Not only was the land of Israel to be given rest from farming, but the slaves of Israel were to be set free from their lives of bondage.

The second type of Sabbath was a last-day Sabbath, the weekly Sabbath familiar to most readers of the Bible. This day is usually referred to in the singular, and is called 'the Sabbath'. This was the day of rest that marked the completion of God's work of creation (*Gen.* 2:2, 3). It was a day the Lord chose to honour.

---

[1] Leviticus 23 mentions 'first day Sabbaths' frequently but not exclusively.

The last is now first

It was the weekly Sabbath which the assembly had in view when it wrote that 'from the beginning of the world to the resurrection of Christ' this Sabbath 'was the last day of the week'. This pattern defined not only the first week, but all weeks. However, Christians also believe that 'from the resurrection of Christ' this day 'was changed into the first day of the week'.

Christians have long realized that it was no accident that the one who 'tabernacled among us' (*John* 1:14), the one who was the firstfruits of a great harvest (*1 Cor.* 15:23), the one who called himself the bread of life (*John* 6:35), the one who will return to this world with the sound of the trumpets of heaven—that the one who was the fulfilment of every Old Testament celebration and Sabbath—was raised from the dead on the first day of the week. That is why Christians began to worship on 'the first day of the week'. In fact the Apostle Paul clearly expected Christians to meet regularly on the first day of the week, whether they be in the great city of Corinth, or in the town of Troas, as we see in 1 Corinthians 16:1, 2 or Acts 20:7. He knew when they would meet, and why.

Just as the Sabbath was a day over which Jesus exercised special lordship (*Mark* 2:28), so it was fitting that God's people, following the lead of the Apostle John, should call this new day 'the Lord's day' (*Rev.* 1:10). And this day of rest, being part of that moral law from which no change is permitted, 'is to be continued to the end of the world, as the Christian Sabbath' (*cf. Exod.* 20:8, 10 with *Matt.* 5:17, 18).

Historic Text	*Modern Version*
21.8 This Sabbath is then kept holy unto the Lord, when men, after a due preparing of their hearts, and ordering of their common affairs before hand, do not only observe an holy rest, all the day, from their own works, words, and thoughts about their worldly employments, and recreations,° but also are taken up the whole time, in the public	**21.8** This Sabbath is then kept holy to the Lord when men, after due preparation of their hearts and arranging of their common affairs beforehand, not only observe a holy rest, all the day, from their own works, words, and thoughts concerning their everyday occupations and recreations, but also devote the whole time to the public and

and private exercises of his worship, and in the duties of necessity, and mercy.ᴾ

private exercises of God's worship and to the duties of necessity and mercy.

Scripture Proofs

21.8 ᵒ Exod. 20:8; Exod. 16:23,25,26,29,30; Exod. 31:15-17; Isa. 58:13; Neh. 13:15-17; 18-22. ᴾ Isa. 58:13; Matt. 12:1-13.

Keeping a day holy

Paragraph 8 of chapter 21 discusses the very practical question of keeping the Sabbath day holy. This is something that Christians will want to do because they know it is the Lord's day. Of course every day is his, but he has specially marked out one day of the week to be set apart, requiring us to 'remember the Sabbath day' and to 'keep it holy' (*Exod.* 20:8).

The first thing we are told about keeping the Sabbath day holy is that it does not start on the Sabbath. We need to plan ahead. We know the importance of planning ahead because we do this regularly for the other days of the week. If we want a successful holiday outing with friends, we will often have to think about it in advance. If we want to be ready for a meeting with an important client, we will need to order some events ahead of time.

We often need to give thought to the next day if it is to run smoothly, and this is no less true for the day when, in a special way, we meet with each other and with the Lord. We need to prepare our hearts, reminding ourselves why we need and want to worship the Lord. Furthermore, we need to order our many tasks. For it is a known fact in the Christian community that if we do not carefully attend to our work on six days of the week, we will not easily find rest on the remaining day.

To put it negatively, if we neglect proper preparation, instead of finding rest in Christ, and refreshment in the fellowship of God's people, we will find ourselves taking our work to church. But if we have focused on our work, and if we have taken the time to take stock of our week, then we will find our minds much more free on Sunday morning, afternoon, or evening. We will be less likely to be reviewing our own words and thoughts in the middle of the worship service, and more likely to focus on God's Word, thinking his thoughts after him. Rest is principally defined as non-work in the Decalogue and elsewhere, but work and rest need to be tied together in our thinking, just as they are in the Scriptures (*Exod.* 20:8-11; 31:15-17).

The confession mentions work; the same is true of pleasure. We need to find a way during the week to get the recreation we need. If we do not, we will almost inevitably find ourselves and our children pining for a second Saturday instead of enjoying our Sunday.

We see examples of people planning ahead in the Old Testament; indeed, God's people were commanded to do so. We also see how the Sabbath requires not only planning, but faith that God will provide when we take a day of rest (*Exod.* 16:23, 25, 26, 29, 30). When everyone else is treating the day like any other, it is hard to believe that we are not falling behind in enjoying life. Or when every other family in the neighbourhood has someone working, when every other student is studying, it is hard to believe that we will not fall behind in the rat-race of success. But we are not rats, we are humans, and we were designed to differentiate between the days. Indeed, many Christians can testify that working and playing harder for six days and resting more thoroughly for one day has been a pattern that God has used to bless them.

It is true that we do not want to lose sight of the fact that the Sabbath is special for God's sake first, and for our sakes second. Nonetheless, God does promise to bless those who 'call the Sabbath a delight and the holy day of the Lord honourable' (*Isa.* 58:13). And we can see how the church, at least, can learn from the example of Nehemiah, the great Old Testament reformer, who thought carefully about the implications of ignoring the Sabbath. He also instructed God's people, creating structures for them that would help them see that the day of rest was not intended to be a shopping jamboree (*Neh.* 13:15-19, 21, 22).

The character of the day

It seems clear that if we are to find our joy in the Lord (*Isa.* 58:14) then we need to think beyond going our own way on his day or, as the prophet Isaiah added, seeking our own pleasures instead of his glory, or talking idly instead of building up the good names of our neighbours (*Isa.* 58:13).

Just how this God-focused day will look will vary somewhat from family to family and person to person. But all of God's people should find their day characterized by public and private worship—both individual and corporate worship are important. The day should also be characterized by 'duties of necessity' and acts of 'mercy', as our Lord had to teach the heartless Pharisees (*Matt.* 12:1-13). It is an act of mercy to help the sick and feed the poor, and these works are needed every day. It is also an act of mercy to provide housing and to offer food to Christian travellers and strangers.

It is probably worth saying that activities of necessity and mercy should preferably be those best suited to the day. Thus tornadoes, earthquakes, fires and floods may require Christians to rush to the aid of our neighbours on the Lord's day. However, in most circumstances we should discern when it is wisest to use our different gifts and skills. Building houses for the needy, except in unusual circumstances, is best suited as a weekday activity. Practising hospitality, while important in many circumstances, is perfectly suited for the Lord's day.

The main point is that between worship, hospitality—and, since it is a Sabbath, could we add fellowship and rest?—Christians can easily devote their whole day to the Lord. A day with morning and evening worship, and fellowship and hospitality in between, tends to answer most Sabbath practice questions. Indeed we would do well to avoid being over-prescriptive in defining the structures and activities of that day. And we should be aware that pious efforts to justify some sensible Sunday activities are often far too fancy, and ultimately undermine the uniqueness of Sabbath worship and acts of mercy. We do not need to call a walk in the park an act of worship or a deed of mercy to legitimize it. That would only have the effect of redefining biblical categories so broadly that they could lose their usefulness. Let us be aware of our own needs and strengths as well as those of others, and then remember the maxim that our Lord left with the Pharisees: 'it is lawful to do good on the Sabbath' (*Matt.* 12:12).

If we remember the Sabbath day, worshipping our Lord and aiming to do good—if this is the longing of our hearts, with God's help, we cannot go far wrong. And if we do err, we can turn to the Lord of the Sabbath, who rose one Sunday morning so that sinners would find life and look forward to an eternal rest with him and all his people.

CHAPTER 22:

OF LAWFUL OATHS AND VOWS

Historic Text

22.1 A lawful oath is a part of religious worship,[a] wherein upon just occasion, the person swearing, solemnly calls God to witness what he asserts, or promises; and to judge him according to the truth, or falsehood of what he swears.[b]

22.2 The name of God only, is that by which men ought to swear; and, therein it is to be used with all holy fear and reverence.[c] Therefore, to swear vainly, or rashly, by that glorious and dreadful name; or, to swear at all, by any other thing, is sinful, and to be abhorred.[d] Yet, as in matters of weight and moment, an oath is warranted by the Word of God, under the new testament, as well as under the old;[e] so, a lawful oath, being imposed by lawful authority, in such matters ought to be taken.[f]

Modern Version

22.1 A lawful oath is a part of religious worship, in which—on an appropriate occasion—the person taking the oath solemnly calls upon God to witness what he asserts or promises and to judge him according to the truth or falsehood of what he swears.

22.2 The name of God is the only name by which men should swear, and they should do so with all holy fear and reverence. Therefore, to swear vainly or rashly by that glorious and fearful name, or to swear at all by any other thing, is sinful and to be abhorred. Yet since, in matters of weight and great importance, an oath is warranted by the Word of God under the new testament as well as under the old, therefore, a lawful oath ought to be taken when imposed in such matters by lawful authority.

Scripture Proofs

    22.1 [a] Deut. 10:20. [b] Exod. 20:7; Lev. 19:12; 2 Cor. 1:23; 2 Chron. 6:22,23.
    22.2 [c] Deut. 6:13. [d] Exod. 20:7; Jer. 5:7; Matt. 5:34,37; James 5:12. [e] Heb. 6:16; 2 Cor. 1:23; Isa. 65:16. [f] 1 Kings 8:31; Neh. 13:25; Ezra 10:5.

The good kind of swearing

It looks strange to modern eyes to see a chapter on oaths and vows in a confession of faith. However, if one were reminded of an oath every Monday morning, as were the members of the assembly, or if one had a high view of the State and of a Christian's civic duties, a discussion of oaths or vows makes considerable sense. Life in this world often requires us to take oaths of office, oaths in court, and oaths in other contexts as well.

From one perspective a lawful oath is actually a dimension of religious worship, broadly conceived. After all, as Deuteronomy 10:20 reminds us, when we swear it is always to be by God's name. In warning us not to use God's name in vain, the Ten Commandments assume that we will in fact use God's name (*Exod.* 20:7). There is a time and place to call God to witness our statements or promises.

We are not to do so 'falsely, and so profane the name' of God (*Lev.* 19:12). Nonetheless we may ask God to judge us 'according to the truth or falsehood' of what we swear. When we swear, we are, like Solomon, asking God to vindicate us and our honesty (2 *Chron.* 6:22, 23). It was when the apostle's motives were called into question by cantankerous Corinthians that Paul resorted to 'swearing'. He called God to witness against him if it were not true that he had avoided contact with Corinth out of mercy, rather than out of neglect or animosity (2 *Cor.* 1:23).

In God's name

We are to swear in God's name. It hardly needs to be said that we are to swear in his name *only* (*Deut.* 6:13). He alone is Lord; he alone knows all that is true; he is the one who will judge all lies. Obviously calling on God's name is so solemn an act that we ought to give serious consideration to our motives and actions before making an oath. We need to approach the moment of swearing 'with all holy fear and reverence'.

Truthfully, we have not been very good at this. Perhaps the sin of people long ago was, or of people far away still is, to swear by the names of those who are not gods at all (*Jer.* 5:7). The fault of most people today is to use God's name lightly—perhaps more lightly than any other name. People routinely 'swear vainly, or rashly' by the 'glorious and dreadful', or awesome, name of the Lord with a 'Jesus!' 'Jesus Christ!' or an 'O my God'! This really ought not to be.

Our Lord also told his contemporaries, as did James, to stop swearing so quickly. We simply need to let our yes be yes, and our no, no (*Matt.* 5:37; *James* 5:12). Adding 'I swear' to the end of each sentence as we tell a story hardly increases our credibility. Often it suggests that there may be some untruth or evil afoot. The Bible has stern words for those who swear lightly or take the Lord's name in vain, and those warnings should be heard today.

While some Christians have focused on passages prohibiting careless oaths, the authors of the confession are quite right to point out that 'in matters of weight and moment, an oath is warranted by the Word of God, under the new testament, as well as under the old'. The author to the Hebrews assumes that oaths are normal and good (*Heb.* 6:16). Paul, as mentioned, calls on God's name as a witness (*2 Cor.* 1:23). And the Old Testament is replete with such references (*e.g., Isa.* 65:16). It is for that reason that Christians ought to take a 'lawful oath' if it is 'being imposed by lawful authority', both in legal and in other contexts (*e.g., 1 Kings* 8:31; *Neh.* 13:25; *Ezra* 10:5).

Historic Text	*RCF (1903) Text*	*Modern Version*
22.3 Whosoever takes an oath, ought duly to consider the weightiness of so solemn an act; and therein to avouch nothing, but what he is fully persuaded is the truth.[g] Neither may any man bind himself by oath to anything but what is good and just, and what he believes so to be, and what he is able, and resolved to perform.[h] Yet is it a sin, to refuse an	**22.3** Whosoever takes an oath, ought duly to consider the weightiness of so solemn an act, and therein to avouch nothing but what he is fully persuaded is the truth.[1] Neither may any man bind himself by oath to anything but what is good and just, and what he believes so to be, and what he is able and resolved to perform.[2]	**22.3** Whoever takes an oath ought to consider seriously the great importance of such a solemn act, and in doing so should affirm nothing but what he himself is fully convinced is the truth. A person may bind himself by oath only to what is good and just, what he believes to be such, and what he is able and resolved to perform.

oath touching anything
that is good and just,
being imposed by lawful
authority.[i]

22.4 An oath is to be taken in the plain and common sense of the words, without equivocation, or mental reservation.[k] It cannot oblige to sin: but, in anything not sinful, being taken, it binds to performance, although to a man's own hurt.[l] Nor is it to be violated, although made to heretics, or infidels.[m]

22.4 The oath is to be taken in the plain and usual sense of the words, without equivocation or mental reservation. It cannot oblige a person to sin, but when it is taken in matters which are not sinful, it obligates performance of the oath even though it may hurt. The oath is not to be violated even though it is made to heretics or unbelievers.

Scripture proofs (WCF)

22.3 [g] Exod. 20:7; Jer. 4:2. [h] Gen. 24:2,3,5,6,8,9. [i] Num. 5:19,21; Neh. 5:12; Exod. 22:7-11.

22.4 [k] Jer. 4:2; Psa. 24:4. [l] 1 Sam. 25:22,32-34; Psa. 15:4. [m] Ezek. 17:16,18,19; Josh. 9:18,19, with 2 Sam. 21:1.

Scripture proofs (RCF)

22.3 [1] Exod. 20:7; Lev. 19:12; Jer. 4:2; Hos. 10:4. [2] Gen. 24:2-9; Neh. 5:12,13; Eccles. 5:2,5.

Speaking the truth and swearing to do good

If the first two paragraphs of this chapter speak truth, then it will be all the more important to see that whoever takes an oath will have to ponder the weightiness of what they are doing (*Exod.* 20:7), and take into consideration the urgent call of the prophet Jeremiah, that God's people swear by his name only 'in truth, in justice, and in righteousness' (*Jer.* 4:2). We need to make sure that we are justified and 'fully persuaded' of any assertion wherein we call God as witness.

As well, we need to make sure that we bind ourselves to do only something that we should do, can do, and plan to do. Abraham's servant was willing to help him in a quest for Isaac's wife; he felt it was something that he should do. But he would not plan to do it, and certainly would not swear to do it, until Abraham acknowledged that he might not be able to do it (*Gen.* 24:2, 3, 5, 6, 8, 9). We can learn from the example of this wise servant.

The last line of the original version of paragraph 22.3 is debated among Reformed people. Do people have no option but to swear an oath regarding anything that is 'good and just' if it is 'imposed by lawful authority'? Or do we have freedom to refuse to take an oath, even if demanded to do so by a lawful authority (see *Num.* 5:19, 21; *Neh.* 5:12; *Exod.* 22:7-11 for Old Testament examples). The Westminster assembly asserted the obligation. American Presbyterians at the turn of the twentieth century demurred from this position and deleted the final line from paragraph 3.

No equivocation

It remains to be said that an oath is meant to clarify and add credibility, and not to help someone equivocate and deceive. As Jeremiah urged God's people to swear 'in truth' (*Jer.* 4:2), so the psalmist reminds us that there are people who do not have 'clean hands and a pure heart' and who sometimes swear deceitfully (*Psa.* 24:4). It is because human society is corrupt, and riddled with lies and broken promises, that we swear oaths at all. It is because we treat oaths lightly that we have armies of lawyers; in trying circumstances (or in any context that involves money) few people can be trusted or feel that they can trust others.

We are never to deceive with our oaths. Not even if we are speaking to or about 'heretics, or infidels'. The Bible contains vivid accounts of those whom God punished for lying to unbelievers and enemies (*Ezek.* 17:16, 18, 19; *Josh.* 9:18, 19; *2 Sam.* 21:1). Nonetheless, if we realize that we have sinned by swearing to do what is wrong, then we must not add to our sin by proceeding to do that wrong. We must abandon our foolish oath. David once made an oath, asking God to destroy him if he did not destroy Nabal. It was a foolish oath; he should not have made it, and he was later thankful that he was kept from honouring it (*1 Sam.* 25:22, 32-34). And yet, although we cannot oblige ourselves to sin with an oath, we must bring ourselves to honour a righteous oath, even if we later find that its fulfilment is painful to us. It was David again who praised the person 'who swears to his own hurt and does not change' (*Psa.* 15:4). In considering the value of our oaths, we do well to remember our God, who swore in his own name, and kept his promises. In considering our difficult oaths, even oaths made before dubious authorities, let us remember our Lord Jesus Christ, who gave an answer under oath to Pontius Pilate, knowing that it would bring him hurt, even death, on behalf of unworthy sinners.

Historic Text	*Modern Version*
22.5 A vow is of the like nature with a promissory oath, and ought to be made with the like religious care, and to be performed with the like faithfulness.[n]	**22.5** A vow is similar in nature to a promissory oath and ought to be made with the same religious care and be performed with the same faithfulness.
22.6 It is not to be made to any creature but to God alone:[o] and, that it may be accepted, it is to be made voluntarily, out of faith, and conscience of duty, in way of thankfulness for mercy received, or for the obtaining of what we want; whereby we more strictly bind our selves to necessary duties; or, to other things, so far, and so long, as they may fitly conduce thereunto.[p]	**22.6** A vow is to be made only to God and not to any created being. In order for it to be acceptable, it is to be made voluntarily, out of faith and conviction of duty, either from thankfulness for mercy or from the desire to obtain what we lack. By taking a vow we bind ourselves more strictly to necessary duties, or to other things to the extent that they contribute to the performance of these duties.
22.7 No man may vow, to do anything forbidden in the Word of God, or what would hinder any duty therein commanded; or which is not in his own power, and, for the performance whereof, he has no promise of ability from God.[q] In which respects, popish monastical vows, of perpetual single life, professed poverty, and regular obedience, are so far from being degrees of	**22.7** No one may vow to do anything forbidden in the Word of God or anything which would hinder the performance of any duty it commands. No one may vow to do anything for which he has no ability and for which he has no promise of ability from God. With respect to these things, Roman Catholic monastic vows of perpetual single life, professed poverty, and regular

higher perfection, that they are superstitious and sinful snares, in which, no Christian may entangle himself.[r]

obedience—far from being steps to higher perfection—are in fact superstitious and sinful snares, in which no Christian may entangle himself.

Scripture Proofs

22.5 [n] Isa. 19:21; Eccles. 5:4-6; Psa. 61:8; Psa. 66:13,14.

22.6 [o] Psa. 76:11; Jer. 44:25,26. [p] Deut. 23:21-23; Psa. 50:14; Gen. 28:20-22; 1 Sam. 1:11; Psa. 66:13,14; Psa. 132:2-5.

22.7 [q] Acts 23:12,14; Mark 6:26; Num. 30:5,8,12,13. [r] Matt. 19:11,12; 1 Cor. 7:2,9; Eph. 4:28; 1 Pet. 4:2; 1 Cor. 7:23.

Fulfil what you vow

The first part of chapter 22 looks at the place of oaths in the Christian's life; the second part looks at vows. The two are similar in many respects, not least in the fact that they need to be made with similar care and executed with similar faithfulness. The Bible has a lot to say about carrying out the vows that we make (*Isa.* 19:21; *Psa.* 61:8; 66:13, 14). The author of Ecclesiastes is surely right to say that 'it is better that you should not vow than that you should vow and not pay'. We need to be mindful that our mouths do not lead us into sin—as they can when we make too many promises to God. To quote Ecclesiastes again, 'When you make a vow to God, do not delay in fulfilling it. He has no pleasure in fools; fulfil your vow' (*Eccles.* 5:4-6).

Vows are to the Lord

Unsurprisingly, it is to God that we owe this obedience because vows are made to God only. Oaths are promises that we make in God's presence. Vows are promises made to God himself. If these categories are rigid, and not fluid, then 'marriage vows' should probably be called marriage oaths, and most so-called ordination or membership vows need rephrasing. In any event, in biblical discussions about vows, both those that are done well (*Psa.* 76:11) and those done badly (*Jer.* 44:25-26), it is assumed that God is or should be the one to whom we vow.

The Bible also suggests that vows are promises with certain characteristics. For example, they are to be made 'voluntarily', as Moses explains in Deuteronomy, to encourage us in our duties. To put it negatively, 'if you refrain from vowing, you will not be guilty of sin' (*Deut.* 23:21-23). And vows are to be made with a purpose, perhaps to give thanks for God's mercy, as we see in Psalm 50:14; or to more powerfully plead for something we desire, as we see Jacob doing in Genesis 28 (verses 20-22; *cf. I Sam.* 1:11; *Psa.* 66:13, 14).

The basic idea behind a vow is that we 'more strictly bind ourselves to necessary duties' or perhaps to something that is not necessary, but still fitting and proper. In saying this we also recognize the limitations of our human natures. The sad reality is that we need helps and devices such as vows to spur us on in our duties, or to help us carry through our good intentions (*e.g., Psa.* 132:2-5). On account of our humanity we should also mention that wise vows will often have limitations—perhaps containing phrases such as 'so far as . . .' and 'so long as . . .'—for we need to remember that we are restricted in our abilities to keep our vows.

Foolish vows

In reflecting on our limitations and our frequent foolishness we must also reiterate some points made in the final paragraph of the chapter. We should not 'vow to do anything forbidden in the Word of God'. This applies, of course, to oaths and vows, and we see examples of such sinful promises when Jephthah swore to offer up whatever first came out of his house in the event of a victory in battle (*Judg.* 11:29-40), when Herod killed John the Baptist on account of his oath (*Mark* 6:26), and when Jewish militants bound themselves by an oath to attempt the assassination of the Apostle Paul (*Acts* 23:12, 14).

Not only must we avoid the wrong, we must also, as with oaths, not vow to do anything that would indirectly keep us from obedience. And again, we must not vow to do what we do not have the strength to carry out; and we must not promise to do what God has not promised to help us do. Strikingly, the Old Testament provided occasional contexts where daughters and wives could have their vows revoked if they were made thoughtlessly, although no such mercy was permitted to men (*Num.* 30:5, 8, 12, 13), and no such exception clause exists in the New Testament.

It is probably worth mentioning some of the most common foolish vows, many of which are associated with the Roman Catholic Church.

For example, Roman clergy make vows to remain perpetually unmarried. This idea of putting fences around the law of God is not new. Even in the time of Jesus, there were people who tried to avoid sins of lust by sterilizing themselves (*Matt.* 19:11, 12). But as Paul explained to the Corinthians, God's way to avoid the sin of lust is very different, and often includes the blessing of marriage (*1 Cor.* 7:2, 9). Certain religious orders also vow to remain poor, some of them living by begging only. But again, this vow of poverty inhibits obedience to other commands, such as Paul's injunction to hard work so that Christians will be able to help those who are truly in need (*Eph.* 4:28). Usually the whole package of 'popish' promises, as they are called here, are commitments to a regular, often austere, pattern of obedience which cannot be kept by men and women and have only the appearance of wisdom. They are unqualified, open-ended promises which bring the Lord's displeasure when they are made, and again when they are broken.

We need to remember that these high-powered promises do not help people live the rest of their earthly lives free from evil human desires, and happily bound to the will of God (*1 Pet.* 4:2). However well-meaning these vows may be, they do not lead us to a higher Christian life. If you scratch the surface, you will usually find superstition. If you observe the fruit of many man-made promises, you will see that they ultimately prove to be sinful snares.

We must not entangle ourselves with unwise vows. They return us to bondage and make us forget the warning of the Apostle Paul: 'You were bought with a price; do not become slaves of men' (*1 Cor.* 7:23). Since we have been bought by a Lord whose yoke is easy and whose burden is light, let us not needlessly multiply our promises to him, but revel in the promises he has made to us.

CHAPTER 23:

OF THE CIVIL MAGISTRATE

Historic Text

23.1 God, the supreme Lord and King of all the world, has ordained civil magistrates, to be, under him, over the people, for his own glory, and the public good: and, to this end has armed them with the power of the sword, for the defence and encouragement of them that are good, and for the punishment of evil doers.[a]

23.2 It is lawful for Christians to accept and execute the office of a magistrate; when called thereunto:[b] in the managing whereof, as they ought especially to maintain piety, justice, and peace, according to the wholesome laws of each commonwealth;[c] so, for that end, they may lawfully now, under the new testament, wage war, upon just and necessary occasion.[d]

Modern Version

23.1 God, the supreme Lord and King of all the world, has ordained civil authorities to be, under him, over the people for his own glory and the public good. For this purpose he has armed them with the power of the sword for the defence and encouragement of those who are good, and for the punishment of those who do evil.

23.2 It is lawful for Christians to hold public office when called to it. In such office they ought especially to maintain piety, justice, and peace, according to the wholesome laws of each commonwealth. For that purpose they may now, under the new testament, lawfully wage war upon just and necessary occasion.

Scripture Proofs

23.1 [a] Rom. 13:1-4; 1 Pet. 2:13,14.

23.2 [b] Prov. 8:15,16; Rom. 13:1,2,4. [c] Psa. 2:10-12; 1 Tim. 2:2; Psa. 82:3,4; 2 Sam. 23:3; 1 Pet. 2:13. [d] Luke 3:14; Rom. 13:4; Matt. 8:9,10; Acts 10:1,2; Rev. 17:14,16.

The Lord of the lords, and King of the kings

The first phrase of chapter 23 is perhaps its most important. It announces that God owns this world; the earth is his manor, the universe his kingdom—he is the 'supreme Lord and King'. As the ruler of all, he calls and orders some people to execute human government in a world under his authority. When Christians consider God's government on earth they have traditionally called his agents 'civil magistrates'. And when we consider the respect that is due to them, we should seek a wide definition of the term, doubtless including the full range of people mentioned by the Apostle Peter in his discussion of the topic. In his first general letter we are told to respect not only kings and governors, but also those who promote and enforce their laws (*1 Pet.* 2:13, 14).

Since God is ruler over all, civil magistrates are under him, and we, in turn, are under them. But we are also reminded in this opening paragraph that these men and women are under God and over us *for a reason:* they are there to promote God's glory and 'the public good', not to boost their own prestige, privilege or financial enrichment.

The sword

We all know that many people refuse to obey even the best civil governments; they refuse to submit 'to every ordinance of man for the Lord's sake' (*1 Pet.* 2:13). And so, because God is intent on his glory and the public good, and because some of us are not, God has permitted magistrates to bear and issue arms.

They are given 'the power of the sword' as ministers of God (*Rom.* 13:4). The sword can be used to defend, and in defending, to encourage those who are good. It can also be used to punish evildoers. Determining the scale and conditions of legitimate defence and punishment requires much wisdom. But the *idea* that both are to be administered by civil magistrates on God's behalf should be beyond question.

Christian magistrates

Unfortunately, there have always been many governments that have been unwilling to do what God says. In the Old Testament this was a frequent problem and the solution was in theory straightforward: Israel was God's chosen nation on earth and the solution was to get a godly magistrate instead of an ungodly one. In the New Testament era, our era, the problem of bad government has not disappeared, but the solution is less straightforward. Israel is now God's church, scattered among the nations. All governments are God's governments but no nation is God's chosen nation.

Christians have responded to this situation in a variety of ways. Some have rejected all civil government, often advocating a unique blend of Christian sect and society. For what it is worth, each one of these has, to date, descended into anarchy and gross immorality. One only needs to think of the city of Münster in the sixteenth century, or the so-called Lord's Resistance Army in Uganda, or the strange cults that tend to thrive in Utah or appear in places such as Texas. A second option, popular among most followers of the sixteenth-century Anabaptists, is to make peace with civil governments but refuse to participate personally in that government as rulers, law-enforcement agents, or military personnel. A third position is to participate in government insofar as a country or political party calls itself Christian.

Really, none of these options is satisfactory. All of them, in differing degrees, miss the thrust of Romans 13, which informs us that 'there is no authority except from God'. Paul goes so far as to say that the civil magistrate is a 'minister from God'. And in the book of Proverbs God says, 'By me kings reign, and rulers decree justice. By me princes rule, and nobles, all who judge rightly' (*Prov.* 8:15, 16). Now if God calls people to this task, surely Christians ought to see that it is probably desirable and definitely 'lawful for Christians to accept and execute the office of a magistrate, when called thereunto'. After all, God tells civil magistrates how to live. If anyone is called to a public office under God, they need to manage their tasks while maintaining 'piety, justice, and peace', and this must especially be true of Christians. It is not without divine threats that Psalm 2 urges judges to be wise and instructed (*Psa.* 2:10-12).

So, God appoints rulers. God also tells them how to live. And God tells us to pray 'for kings, and all who are in authority' (*1 Tim.* 2:2). We pray that they will abide by the 'wholesome laws of each commonwealth' or country, so 'that we may lead a quiet and peaceable life in all godliness and honesty' (*1 Tim.* 2:2). We can pray in the words of Psalm 82 and ask that God will use our governors to 'vindicate the weak and fatherless', 'do justice to the afflicted and destitute', 'rescue the weak and needy' and 'deliver them out of the hand of the wicked' (*Psa.* 82:3, 4).

Essentially, we want leaders like our God, magistrates who rule justly in the fear of the Lord (*2 Sam.* 23:3), and citizens who submit themselves to human institutions for the Lord's sake (*1 Pet.* 2:13). If the leaders and citizens are gifted Christians fully equipped for the task, this is no problem for the Christian church, only a blessing.

Just war

It should also be said that magistrates under God can at times wield weapons not simply to police a nation but to wage war. In the Old Testament Israel waged war by the direct command of God, carrying out his divine justice on the nations. In the New Testament no nation or church may claim the same authority. And yet there is such a thing as a just war and a subset of those just wars are actually necessary. In such circumstances a nation may engage in war.

In some respects, just wars are a pale reflection of the great spiritual battles which will rage until our Lord returns, as we see in the book of Revelation (*e.g., Rev.* 17:14-16). The evil in our world is real. There are some wars where Satan is more at work on one side than on the other. Any kind of positive warrant for war, however, comes not from possible biblical analogies, but from positive biblical comment about soldiers in the New Testament—for it is a striking fact that even the occupying Roman soldiers in Judea and Galilee are spared from occupational criticism by Jesus and the apostles. It has seemed to Christians in the tradition of the Reformation that we can infer from these comments that terrible as war is, there is nothing inherently wrong with warriors. When John the Baptist spoke to soldiers he told them to reform their ways but he did not tell them to leave their vocations (*Luke* 3:14). Paul tells us that magistrates bear the sword, and there is every reason to think that he has soldiers in view as much as executioners (*Rom.* 13:4).

In a sense, some soldiers appear in a privileged light in the New Testament. Jesus announced that a Roman centurion had more faith than any Israelite (*Matt.* 8:9, 10), and the gospel of God first broke through into the Gentile world in the home of Cornelius, another military leader (*Acts* 10:1, 2). At the same time, wars and rumours of wars remain one of the great calamities that come from a world fallen in sin, and must continue until Christ returns. Let us pray that he would return quickly, and that he would give us righteous civil magistrates while we wait for him.

🕊

Historic Text	*RCF (1788) Text*	*Modern Version*
23.3 The civil magistrate may not assume to himself the administration of the Word and sacraments, or the power of the keys of the kingdom of heaven:ᶜ yet, he has authority, and it is his duty, to take order, that unity and peace be preserved in the church, that the truth of God be kept pure, and entire; that all blasphemies and heresies be suppressed; all corruptions and abuses in worship and discipline prevented, or reformed; and all the ordinances of God duly settled, administered, and observed.ᶠ For the better effecting whereof, he has power to call synods, to be present at them, and to provide that whatsoever is transacted in them, be according to the mind of God.ᵍ	**23.3** Civil magistrates may not assume to themselves the administration of the Word and sacraments; or the power of the keys of the kingdom of heaven;¹ or, in the least, interfere in matters of faith.² Yet as nursing fathers, it is the duty of civil magistrates to protect the church of our common Lord, without giving the preference to any denomination of Christians above the rest, in such a manner, that all ecclesiastical persons whatever shall enjoy the full, free, and unquestioned liberty of discharging every part of their sacred functions, without violence or danger.³ And, as Jesus Christ has appointed a regular government and discipline in his church, no law of any commonwealth, should interfere with, let, or hinder, the due exercise thereof, among the voluntary members of any denomination of Christians, according	**23.3** Civil authorities may not assume to themselves the administration of the Word and sacraments, or the power of the keys of the kingdom of heaven, nor should they interfere in any way in matters of faith. Yet, as caring fathers, it is the duty of civil authorities to protect the church of our common Lord without giving preference to any denomination of Christians above the rest—doing so in such a way that all church authorities shall enjoy the full, free, and unquestioned liberty of carrying out every part of their sacred functions without violence or danger. As Jesus Christ has appointed a regular government and discipline in his church, no law of any commonwealth should interfere with, prevent, or hinder their proper exercise among the voluntary members of any denomination of Christians, according to their own profession and belief. It is

to their own profession and belief.[4] It is the duty of civil magistrates to protect the person and good name of all their people, in such an effectual manner as that no person be suffered, either upon pretence of religion or infidelity, to offer any indignity, violence, abuse, or injury to any other person whatsoever: and to take order, that all religious and ecclesiastical assemblies be held without molestation or disturbance.[5]

the duty of civil authorities to protect the person and good name of all their people in such an effective manner that no person be allowed, either in the name of religion or of unbelief, to offer any indignity, violence, abuse, or injury to any other person whatever. They should also take care that all religious and ecclesiastical assemblies be held without interference or disturbance.

Scripture Proofs (WCF)

23.3 [e] 2 Chron. 26:18, with Matt. 18:17, and Matt. 16:19; 1 Cor. 12:28,29; Eph. 4:11,12; 1 Cor. 4:1,2; Rom. 10:15; Heb. 5:4. [f] Isa. 49:23; Psa. 122:9; Ezra 7:23,25-28; Lev. 24:16; Deut. 13:5,6,10; 2 Kings 18:4; 1 Chron. 13:1-9; 2 Kings 23:1-26; 2 Chron. 34:33; 2 Chron. 15:12,13. [g] 2 Chron. 19:8-11; 2 Chron., chapters 29,30; Matt. 2:4,5.

Scripture Proofs (RCF)

23.3 [1] 2 Chron. 26:18 with Matt. 18:17 and Matt. 16:19; 1 Cor. 12:28-29; Eph. 4:11-12; 1 Cor. 4:1-2; Rom. 10:15; Heb. 5:4; [2] John 18:36; Acts 5:29; Eph. 4:11-12; [3] Isa. 49:23; Rom. 13:1-6; [4] Psa. 105:15; [5] Rom. 13:4; 1 Tim. 2:2.

Limits to authority

Chapter 23 paragraph 3 begins by announcing a limitation to the powers of the magistrate. Magistrates are appointed by God, and called to serve in his name, but they are ministers in the civil sphere only, and not the spiritual. Thus magistrates are not to do the work of the minister of the gospel: they are not to preach or administer the sacraments. Nor are they to do the work of an elder, for it is not their place to administer church discipline.

Interestingly, this distinction between spiritual and civil service can be seen in the Old Testament. Even during the centuries when church and state were one, monarchs were not permitted to assume the ministry of priests. This was a lesson that Uzziah had to learn when he entered the temple to offer incense and later left the temple as a leper, for he had overstepped the rights and duties of kings (*2 Chron.* 26:18). Nor must this lesson be lost in the New Testament era; Paul tells us that ministers of Christ are 'stewards of the mysteries of God' (*1 Cor.* 4:1, 2), but the same is never said of the civil magistrate.

If even the highest of magistrates had to remember their place when it came to worship, the same must be true when it comes to the matter of church discipline. In the Gospel of Matthew Christians are specifically instructed to take their most challenging spiritual problems to the church (*Matt.* 18:17), for it is to the elders of the church that Christ gave 'the keys of the kingdom', symbolic of entry into the church, and even heaven (*Matt.* 16:19). Indeed Paul reminds us that God set people in the church with gifts of government (*1 Cor.* 12:28, 29). No wise man, including a political leader from a category of potentially wise men, takes this honour of ruling God's church on himself. Even Jesus Christ did not take the honour of the high priesthood to himself; he was called to this responsibility by his Father (*Heb.* 5:4). Surely there is a lesson here for all politicians who crave influence over the church.

The magistrate as promoter of the church?

This opening statement of what the magistrate is *not* to do seems both clear and convincing. When the eighteenth-century American Presbyterian Church, under the leadership of the Scottish minister John Witherspoon, decided to revise a few paragraphs of the confession, it saw no need to change this first line of chapter 23 paragraph 3. However, the remainder of the original paragraph was, they judged, inconsistent with all that has been said about the civil magistrate so far in chapter 23. The following two ideas, expressed in the original paragraph, are particularly problematic.

The first idea is that the civil magistrate has a duty to defend and promote gospel truth; that 'he has authority, and it is his duty, to take order, that unity and peace be preserved in the church, that the truth of God be kept pure and entire, that all blasphemies and heresies be suppressed, all corruptions and abuses in worship and discipline prevented or reformed, and all the ordinances of God duly settled, administered, and observed'.

To support this idea the Westminster assembly cited a battery of Old Testament passages showing civil governors motivated by godly zeal in reforming worship, and priests motivated by godly zeal in reforming civil society (see *Isa.* 49:23; *Psa.* 122:9; *Ezra* 7:23, 25-28; *Lev.* 24:16; *Deut.* 13:5, 6, 10; *2 Kings* 18:4; 23:1-26; *1 Chron.* 13:1-9; *2 Chron.* 15:12, 13; 34:33). Most importantly, these Old Testament passages seem to show that although Israelite kings were not to carry out the work of the priests or Levites, they could make sure that priests and Levites were carrying out their proper work, including their tasks as teachers, leaders in worship, and spiritual elders.

The problem with these parallels is that what is good for the old covenant people of God is not always good for the new. In the Old Testament, Israel was the assembly or church of God *and* God's chosen nation. And so rulers in the nation also carried some responsibility for the church. In the New Testament the assembly or church of God is Israel, but there is no chosen political nation (*e.g., Gal.* 6:16; *Eph.* 2:11-16). The church is scattered among the nations (*1 Pet.* 1:1). Neither is any ruler in any nation responsible for the church.

The magistrate as a guide to the church?

The second idea in this original paragraph which American Presbyterians considered problematic is the thought that civil magistrates in the New Testament can exercise godly control by calling synods or councils, and even guide the work of those synods to ensure that they do what is 'according to the mind of God'. Here the Westminster divines cite the example of good kings such as Jehoshaphat and Hezekiah, and even a wicked king like Herod, all of whom called religious leaders to their sides to give them information or advice (*2 Chron.* 19:8-11; 29 and 30; *Matt.* 2:4, 5).

Of course this is just what the House of Lords and House of Commons did with the Westminster assembly itself. Parliament called them to advise its members on doctrinal matters. So who is surprised that they penned these lines? At least one historian is. The assembly's persistent commitment to civil involvement in the affairs of the church is ironic precisely because the members of the Westminster assembly discovered by bitter experience that the guidance of the civil magistrate could be deeply flawed. Sharp conflict between assembly and Parliament characterized many months in 1645 and 1646, with the assembly eventually stating that they could not accept the changes made to their texts by the House of Commons, and the Commons charging the assembly with breaking the law.

In the end, it still seems that there is a big difference between a government asking for the advice of godly church leaders and a government assuming that they have a right to such advice. There is a difference, too, between informally seeking counsel from the church, and seeking to govern the councils of the church.

The 1788 revisions

Long before the Westminster Confession of Faith was revised in 1788 (revised in large part to address perceived weaknesses with respect to the relationship between the church and the state), American Presbyterians had qualms about the original third paragraph of chapter 23. Obviously there were authorities which had blessed, or legalized, or even established one church or religion as the church or religion of a state or nation. And Christian people in those churches sometimes insisted that, in spite of the so-called 'establishment' of the church by the state, the state was not to interfere in the life of the church. Nonetheless, over time an increasing number of Christians, including many (but not all) Reformed Christians, were left with a lingering concern about the 'establishment' of a church in a state. Indeed, the idea of establishing one church in a nation—an idea embraced by the majority of people in the sixteenth and seventeenth centuries—was recognized by many in the eighteenth century to be a confusion of the two governments under God, the one churchly, the other civil. Although Christ is King of all, there is a very real sense in which he can say that his church, his spiritual kingdom, is not from this world, and that is a fact that the world's leaders need to respect.

It is because God has established governments in two distinct spheres that American Presbyterians, meeting in Philadelphia, concluded that the civil government should not 'in the least, interfere in matters of faith'. While it can be a great gift to Christians to experience the rule of a good magistrate, no magistrate should think that he is to use his gifts to rule the church. Christ's kingdom is not of this world as civil governments are (*John* 18:36). Obviously the church should 'obey God rather than men' if there is a contest between the two. But more than that, the church should recognize that when Christ ascended into heaven, he showered his church with all the necessary gifts for the perfecting of the saints, for the work of the ministry and for the edifying of the body of Christ. Those gifts included the special ministries of the New Testament apostles and prophets. They included evangelists, pastors and teachers. But they did not include civil magistrates (*Eph.* 4:11, 12). Civil governors are gifts, but not gifts to the church.

The magistrate as protector of the church?

The Philadelphia assembly did think that civil governors could function 'as nursing fathers' to the church, to use a remarkable mixed metaphor (and a poor translation) of Isaiah 49:23. Indeed, under the umbrella of a governing authority's duty to sanction 'good conduct' and approve 'what is good' (*Rom.* 13:3; see 13:1-6), the revised confession concludes that it is 'the duty of civil magistrates to protect the church of our common Lord', while not 'giving the preference to any denomination of Christians above the rest, in such a manner that all ecclesiastical persons whatever shall enjoy the full, free, and unquestioned liberty of discharging every part of their sacred functions, without violence or danger'. The state must protect the church. This is an idea not incompatible with the Bible; it is not, as far as I can see, an idea from the Bible.

The revised third paragraph also states that 'as Jesus Christ has appointed a regular government and discipline in his church, no law of any commonwealth, should interfere with, let, or hinder, the due exercise thereof, among the voluntary members of any denomination of Christians, according to their own profession and belief'. The state should not only 'do his prophets no harm', but it should not even 'touch' the Lord's people, his 'anointed ones' (*Psa.* 105:15). The state should ensure the church's freedom to govern itself.

Finally, the revised text of the Philadelphia assembly states that 'it is the duty of civil magistrates to protect the person and good name of all their people, in such an effectual manner as that no person be suffered, either upon pretence of religion or infidelity, to offer any indignity, violence, abuse, or injury to any other person whatsoever: and to take order, that all religious and ecclesiastical assemblies be held without molestation or disturbance'. The state should permit freedom of religion and freedom of assembly.

For this final assertion, too, it would be profitable to reflect upon the twin assertions in Romans and 1 Timothy that God's servants, his civil servants, are established for our good, and that we ought not to be afraid if we have done no wrong (*Rom.* 13:4). In fact, we pray for our rulers with the hope that they will permit us to 'lead a peaceful and quiet life' (*1 Tim.* 2:2). Texts of Scripture can be added to the revised paragraph, and have been added by subsequent generations of Presbyterians, to support the central claims given here. Nonetheless, in limiting the power of the state, the Philadelphia assembly was, fundamentally, thinking theologically and logically about the fact that God has established a civil government apart from and distinct from an ecclesiastical government, and each of the concerns expressed here, warnings issued, and boundaries demarcated, are intended to flow from this general biblical distinction. And in arguing for the protection and freedom of the church, the Philadelphia assembly was also articulating themes and phrases which would be echoed at the First United States Congress and in the American Bill of Rights.

The magistrate as protector of religion?

In leaving this discussion we should note that in introducing the words 'religion' and 'religious' here, in addition to the previous reference to Christians and the church, American Presbyterians were unlikely to have been intentionally broadening their viewpoint to include protection and freedom for non-Christian religions. The major influx of cults and pagan religions did not reach any kind of prominence in America until the nineteenth century, especially toward its end. However, the interesting question remains: does this confession permit the protection and freedom of professing Christians only, or of all religions?

In seeking to offer a conjectural answer to this frequently asked question we may usefully recall that, although the major American cults had not yet been born, there was very considerable diversity in the late eighteenth century among adherents to Christianity so called, including Catholics, Calvinists, Arminians and Quakers. The Philadelphia assembly was aware of this fact and made no effort to limit or qualify its definition to exclude anti-Trinitarians, biblical sceptics, and self-made prophets. For that reason, they may have under other circumstances also advocated civil protection and freedom for other religions, some of them not more significantly deviant or heterodox than Socinians or Deists. Only further research and study of that assembly will enable us to make more informed comment or conjecture.

Historic Text	*Modern Version*
23.4 It is the duty of people to pray for magistrates,[h] to honour their persons,[i] to pay them tribute and other dues,[k] to obey their lawful commands, and to be subject to their authority, for conscience sake.[l] Infidelity, or difference in religion does not make void the magistrate's just and legal authority, nor free the people from their due obedience to him:[m] from which, ecclesiastical persons are not exempted;[n] much less has the Pope any power and jurisdiction over them, in their dominions, or over any of their people; and, least of all, to deprive them of their dominions, or lives, if he shall judge them to be heretics, or upon any other pretence whatsoever.[o]	**23.4** It is the duty of people to pray for those in authority, to honour them, to pay them taxes or other revenue, to obey their lawful commands, and to be subject to their authority for the sake of conscience. Neither unbelief nor difference in religion makes void the just and legal authority of officeholders nor frees the people—church authorities included—from their due obedience to them. Much less does the Pope have any power or jurisdiction over civil authorities in their domains or over any of their people, nor can he deprive them of their domains or lives if he shall judge them to be heretics or on any other pretence whatever.

Scripture Proofs

23.4 [h] 1 Tim. 2:1,2. i 1 Pet. 2:17. [k] Rom. 13:6,7. [l] Rom. 13:5; Titus 3:1. [m] 1 Pet. 2:13,14,16. [n] Rom. 13:1; 1 Kings 2:35; Acts 25:9-11; 2 Pet. 2:1,10,11; Jude v. 8-11. [o] 2 Thess. 2.4; Rev. 13:15-17

The duties of subjects

If God has given us governments, we must learn how to live as those who are governed. Here, as in all other crucial questions for Christians, Scripture is not silent. In the first place, the Word of God tells us that we are to pray for our governors. We are to give 'supplications, prayers, intercessions, and thanksgivings . . . for all people', and that includes kings or anyone in 'high positions' (*1 Tim.* 2:1, 2).

Second, we are to honour our leaders. Readers of the Bible will know that while we are to 'love the brotherhood' we are at least to 'honour everyone'. This obligation is intensified when it comes to those who are in authority. We are to 'fear God' but special mention is also made of our responsibility to 'honour the emperor' (*1 Pet.* 2:17). There is something wrong if we view authority as a negative thing. Governments are given to guide, defend and restrain. We should desire government and, far from rebelling against it, we should respect and honour it.

Third, we are 'to pay them tribute and other dues'. As Paul told Christians in the capital city of the empire, we are to pay taxes and 'all what is owed to them'—taxes, revenue, respect, and honour (*Rom.* 13:6, 7). This tax money was not always well spent. Nonetheless, it had to be paid.

Fourth, we are 'to obey their lawful commands, and to be subject to their authority', as Paul says, 'for conscience sake' (*Rom.* 13:5; *cf. Titus* 3:1). We should not permit our consciences to grow accustomed to disobedience.

Unbelieving leaders

Christians must realize that these four areas of obedience are to extend to unbelieving leaders and not simply to Christian brothers or sisters in office. The Apostle Peter urged Christians to 'be subject for the Lord's sake to every human institution', by which he meant 'the emperor as supreme', or 'governors who are sent by him' to do his will (*1 Pet.* 2:13, 14).

Imagine what it took for Peter to say this. Glance for a moment at the end of his first letter (*1 Pet.* 5:13). Where is Peter writing from? He calls his location 'Babylon' but he was not in Iraq. 'Babylon' was code among early Christians for the pagan city of Rome. The earliest records indicate that Peter was there as the prisoner of the Emperor Nero, one of the most blood-thirsty, reckless tyrants of the ancient world, and a terrible ruler. Honour the emperor, Peter said. That emperor would one day take Peter's life.

Sometimes we are called to be subject to human beings who treat justice like a game to be played instead of a life to be lived. This was true of the ruler in Rome. It was also true of a ruler in Jerusalem three decades before Peter wrote this letter, and yet Jesus submitted to him. Nonetheless, 'infidelity, or difference in religion does not make void the magistrate's just and legal authority, nor free the people from their due obedience to him'. It is before all people that we are to 'live as people who are free' while not employing our 'freedom as a cover-up for evil, but living as servants of God' (*1 Pet.* 2:16).

Ministers of religion and the government of the state

When it comes to obedience to the magistrate, even 'ecclesiastical persons are not exempted', in spite of long medieval practice, and in spite of continuing papal claims to the contrary. As Paul told the Romans, '*every person*' is to be 'subject to the governing authorities' (*Rom.* 13:1). The Apostle Paul himself, surely one of the greatest church leaders of all time, still submitted to a ruler named Festus, and then to Caesar himself (*Acts* 25:9-11). What is more, when we read 2 Peter in context, it appears that another eminent apostle of the New Testament considered it a denial of our Master, and mark of decline among God's people, to despise authority. Most of us could take a few lessons from the angels, who, great as they are, are more respectful of powers—even evil powers—than some people are of legitimate authorities appointed by God (*2 Pet.* 2:1, 10, 11; see also *Jude* 8-11).[1]

If Peter and Paul under the inspiration of the Holy Spirit urge obedience to leaders, then surely the Pope should recommend this standard of obedience as well, rather than undermining it both in practice and in theory. For while New Testament warnings about the antichrist do

---

[1] The assembly also cites in support of this statement Solomon's appointment of priests in a variety of capacities. The problem with this example is that Israel was a theocratic nation, which no state today can legitimately claim to be (*1 Kings* 2:35).

not refer to the institution of the papacy or any one Pope in particular, many of the schemes, treacheries, and wars of various Popes have been eerily reminiscent of the megalomaniac featured in Paul's warnings and John's visions (*e.g., 2 Thess.* 2:4; *Rev.* 13:15-17). Contrary to past behaviour and to persistent assertions today, the Pope really must submit to civil authorities and not count himself among them. He is especially not to claim 'power and jurisdiction' over civil governments in their respective 'dominions' around the world. In effect, he is not to lay claim to any temporal authority 'over any of their people; and, least of all, to deprive them of their dominions, or' as has been done in the past, to deprive them of their 'lives, if he shall judge them to be heretics, or upon any other pretence whatsoever'.

Obviously to make these statements today may seem like a quaint exercise in early-modern apologetics, given the actual size of the current papal state. But the truth is that papal attempts to wield political power during the twentieth century, for example, have continued to set up both Christians and non-Christians for a profound confusion of categories with respect to spiritual and temporal authority. At best Rome muddles the distinct purpose of the church in the world. At worst, it has brought the testimony of the Christian church into disrepute, and undermined the authority which God has delegated to civil governments and not to the church.

CHAPTER 24:

OF MARRIAGE, AND DIVORCE

Historic Text

24.1 Marriage is to be between one man and one woman: neither is it lawful for any man to have more than one wife, nor for any woman to have more than one husband; at the same time.[a]

24.2 Marriage was ordained for the mutual help of husband and wife,[b] for the increase of mankind with a legitimate issue, and of the church with an holy seed;[c] and, for preventing of uncleanness.[d]

24.3 It is lawful for all sorts of people to marry, who are able with judgment, to give their consent.[e] Yet, is it the duty of Christians to marry only in the Lord:[f] and therefore such as profess the true reformed religion, should not marry with infidels, papists, or other idolaters: neither should such as are godly, be unequally yoked, by marrying with such as are notoriously wicked in their life, or maintain damnable heresies.[g]

Modern Version

24.1 Marriage is to be between one man and one woman. It is not lawful for any man to have more than one wife, or for any woman to have more than one husband, at the same time.

24.2 Marriage was ordained for the mutual help of husband and wife, for the increase of mankind with legitimate offspring and of the church with godly children, and for the prevention of sexual immorality.

24.3 It is lawful for all sorts of people to marry who are able to give their intelligent consent. Yet it is the duty of Christians to marry only in the Lord. Therefore, those who profess the true reformed religion should not marry unbelievers, Roman Catholics, or other idolaters; nor should Christians be unequally yoked by marrying those who are notoriously wicked in their way of living or hold to damnable heresies.

Scripture Proofs

24.1 [a] Gen. 2:24; Matt. 19:5,6; Prov. 2:17.

24.2 [b] Gen. 2:18. [c] Mal. 2:15. [d] 1 Cor. 7:2,9.

24.3 [e] Heb. 13:4; 1 Tim. 4:3; 1 Cor. 7:36-38; Gen. 24:57,58. [f] 1 Cor. 7:39.

[g] Gen. 34:14; Exod. 34:16; Deut. 7:3,4; 1 Kings 11:4; Neh. 13:25-27; Mal. 2:11,12; 2 Cor. 6:14.

Defining marriage: one man and one woman

When God instructed Adam about the basics of life, he stressed the importance of a man leaving his father and mother and cleaving to his wife. The words chosen by God are significant, for they twice emphasize the proper gender and number for a marriage: a parental pair is to consist of a father and a mother. Marriage is ordained to be between a husband and a wife (*Gen.* 2:24).

Every believer knows that even a hint of God's revealed will should be considered with the utmost seriousness, so eager should we be to please him. In Genesis 2 God gave much more than a hint that it is his will for a man to have one wife, and for a woman to have one husband, and neither to have 'more than one at the same time'. Obviously this was not a command just for Adam and Eve only, or even for them in particular; after all, they were the only human beings around. No, it was meant as a command for all future generations, although it was rarely kept with any faithfulness. God's people engaged in polygamy for centuries; other cultures experimented with polyandry.

The book of Proverbs had good reason to warn against temptations to adultery (*Prov.* 2:17). Long before the time of the New Testament, religious leaders had promoted ridiculous reasons for serial divorce and remarriage. Little wonder that our Lord Jesus Christ preached about God's pattern for marriage 'in the beginning' in Genesis 2. Little wonder that we need to do the same today, repeating the additional warning of our Lord, that what God has put together we must not divide asunder.

What is the purpose of marriage?

Genesis 2 teaches us how to identify a real marriage in God's sight. It also teaches us about the purpose of marriage. At its most basic level, and there is far more that could be said, marriage is for mutual support, reproduction of the human race, church growth, and sexual purity.

God paraded every kind of animal in front of Adam not only so that he could help rule the world by naming the animals, but also so that it would be crystal clear to him that no animal could give him the help and support he needed. For that, a wife was necessary. Together they were to work in this world.

It was also together that they were to be fruitful and to multiply the human race. We see this in God's command in Genesis 1, which helps us to understand the importance of parenting. Sometimes Christians cannot have children. But there needs to be a truly extraordinary reason for them to refuse to have children.

God wants men and women to have children but, in particular, God wants his people to have godly children. We can learn this in a variety of places in the Bible, including the message of the prophet Malachi. There the Lord God Almighty sends a clear message that means one of two things. Either the Lord says directly: 'I hate divorce' (NIV). Or he announces that he is opposed to the one who himself 'hates and [thus] divorces' (ESV note). Either way, one reason for his opposition to divorce, one reason why God rebukes men who reject the partners of their youth, is that they are breaking a marriage covenant. The second reason is that God is 'seeking a godly offspring' or 'seed', and this can be additionally challenging to achieve in the context of divorce (*Mal.* 2:13-16, esp. 15). We could tally many reasons to guard ourselves and our marriages, but the need to produce godly families should be high on the list. God sees Christian families as an important part of church growth.

However God also provides marriage as the normative context for sexual purity. About this Paul could not be clearer in 1 Corinthians 7. Marriage was created at a time when there was no immorality, but it continues in a time where every kind of sexual sin abounds. In this world some have the gift of purity. Most do not, and they should make it their ambition to marry (*1 Cor.* 7:2, 9).

Whom should Christians marry?

As people look for a spouse, they should, understandably, know what to look for. In general, any single adult can be married. One does not need to be a Christian to make promises approximating to what Malachi calls a marriage covenant. 'Marriage should be honoured by all', including those who are already married, the letter to the Hebrews tells us (*Heb.* 13:4). And Paul warns against those who 'forbid people to marry' (*1 Tim.* 4:3). We ought to encourage people to choose the most visible, most committed, form of marriage that a culture has. Christians need to be marriage maximalists, and not marriage minimalists, as is the trend in modern Western society.

Nonetheless, in commending marriage we should not carelessly accept the conventions of any age or place, including those of other cultures or older societies. For example, we ought only to encourage people to marry so long as both parties have the maturity and wisdom to make this decision or consent to an arrangement. In the 1640s the English Parliament rejected the idea that people should marry only if they are able to exercise proper 'judgment' and give their own 'consent'. Today many religions and cultures would also object to these provisos.

And yet there are hints in both the Old and New Testaments that a freedom of choice in marriage is a good thing. Paul discusses the possible options facing an engaged couple in 1 Corinthians 7:36-38 and it is not clear that he is discussing a parental arrangement; it seems as if he is teaching involved parties how to make informed judgments about a betrothal or engagement. If we turn to the Old Testament, it is hard to escape the sense that part of the beauty of the story of Isaac and Rebecca is that she was given a choice to marry this son of Abraham and bravely decided to do so (*Gen.* 24:57, 58).

Marrying in the Lord

As complicated as the matter of consent might be, there is complete clarity when it comes to a most basic requirement for God's people. Christians must assure themselves that they are marrying Christians, and they must have the best grounds for such a conclusion. This is the plain teaching of the Bible. After Paul discusses marriage and remarriage in 1 Corinthians 7, he assures his readers that they are free to marry anyone, as long as he or she belongs to the Lord (*1 Cor.* 7:39). All other arrangements, no matter what the motive, are forbidden.

It is obvious, then, that Christians ought not to marry those who are not Christians. If you are a Reformed Christian, you should not marry an unreformed person of any kind—a Roman Catholic, an infidel,[1] or anyone that flirts with idolatry of one kind or another. We should find our life-partner in a church that loves and preaches the gospel. This is

---

[1] Probably referring to Muslims or pagans.

illustrated in the Scriptures: although they hatched a devilish plan in their hearts, Jacob's sons spoke truth in spite of themselves when they said that they could not let their sister marry an uncircumcised man, a man who did not even conform to the outward ceremonies of God's people (*Gen.* 34:14). Indeed God warned repeatedly that marriage between his children and the children of idol-worshippers would lead to spiritual prostitution (*Exod.* 34:16; *Deut.* 7:3, 4). The danger of marrying unbelievers is just what Solomon ignored (*1 Kings* 11:4), Nehemiah fought (*Neh.* 13:25-27) and Malachi mourned (*Mal.* 2:11, 12).

Undoubtedly, we should not marry anyone who might profess to be a Christian, but lives a wicked life (perhaps a 'notoriously wicked' life), or clings to error (perhaps even 'damnable heresies'). Certainly it has relevance for Christian marriage when Paul warns us not to 'be yoked with unbelievers' (*2 Cor.* 6:14). Christians need to remember that in marriage we share all that we are and all that we hold most deeply. In that context 'righteousness and wickedness' cannot have much in common, nor can light and darkness find any deep fellowship. Let us put Jesus Christ first in our lives, and then we will find guidance in our engagements and a model for our marriages.

Historic Text	*RCF (1887) Text*	*Modern Version*
24.4 Marriage ought not to be within the degrees of consanguinity or affinity forbidden in the Word;[h] nor can such incestuous marriages ever be made lawful by any law of man or consent of parties, so as those persons may live together as man and wife.[i] The man may not marry any of his wive's kindred, nearer in blood, than he may of his own; nor, the woman, of her husband's kindred, nearer in blood, then of her own.[k]	**24.4** Marriage ought not to be within the degrees of consanguinity or affinity forbidden by the Word.[1] Nor can such incestuous marriages ever be made lawful by any law of man or consent of parties, so as those persons may live together as man and wife.[2]	**24.4** Marriage ought not to take place between persons who are within the degrees of close relationship by blood or by marriage forbidden by the Word. Such incestuous marriages can never be made lawful—so that such persons may live together as man and wife—by any law of man or by the consent of the parties involved.

24.5 Adultery, or fornication committed after a contract, being detected before marriage, gives just occasion to the innocent party to dissolve that contract.[l] In the case of adultery after marriage, it is lawful for the innocent party to sue out a divorce:[m] and, after the divorce, to marry another, as if the offending party were dead.[n]

24.5 Adultery or fornication committed after engagement, if detected before marriage, gives valid reason to the innocent party to break the engagement. In the case of adultery after marriage it is lawful for the innocent party to seek a divorce and after the divorce to remarry just as if the offending party were dead.

24.6 Although the corruption of man be such as is apt to study arguments, unduly to put asunder those whom God has joined together in marriage: yet, nothing but adultery, or such wilful desertion as can no way be remedied, by the church, or civil magistrate, is cause sufficient of dissolving the bond of marriage:[o] wherein, a public, and orderly course of proceeding, is to be observed; and, the persons concerned in it, not left to their own wills and discretion, in their own case.[p]

24.6 Although the corruption of mankind is such that people are apt to seek arguments to justify unwarranted separation of those whom God has joined together in marriage, nothing but adultery or such wilful desertion as cannot be remedied by the church or the civil authorities is sufficient cause to dissolve the bond of marriage. In such cases a public and orderly procedure is to be observed, and the persons concerned are not to be left to their own wills and discretion in their own case.

Scripture Proofs (WCF)

24.4 [h] Lev. 18:1-30; 1 Cor. 5:1; Amos 2:7. [i] Mark 6:18; Lev. 18:24-28. [k] Lev. 20:19-21.

24.5 [l] Matt. 1:18-20. [m] Matt. 5:31,32. [n] Matt. 19:9; Rom. 7:2,3.

24.6 [o] Matt. 19:8,9; 1 Cor. 7:15; Matt. 19:6. [p] Deut. 24:1-4.

Scripture Proofs (RCF)

24.4 [1] Lev. 18; 1 Cor. 5:1; Amos 2:7; [2] Mark 6:18; Lev. 18:24-28.

Consanguinity or affinity

When paragraph 4 speaks about 'consanguinity or affinity' it is referring to relationships by bloodline or by marriage. The basic idea, taught here, is that we should go to the Bible to define both marriage and any deviations from marriage. A listing of deviant sexual relations, and thus deviant marital relations, is provided in Leviticus 18. One of the most awful deviations is incest, especially the sort that Amos bemoaned in his rural context (*Amos* 2:7), Paul rebuked in an urban setting (*1 Cor.* 5:1) and John the Baptist denounced in the royal court (*Mark* 6:18). No one can make these kinds of relationship lawful.[1]

This chapter in the confession was penned at a time in which there was still some institutional memory of King Henry VIII's famous use of consanguinity in affinity to justify an annulment,[2] and when there was an ever-growing list of marriage prohibitions in English law. Here the members of the assembly attempt to restrain the civil law by using the Scriptures to define incest; this seems useful, although the list of incestual relationships in Scripture is not exhaustive.

Problematically, Leviticus 20 was employed in the original version of paragraph 4 to prohibit a marital arrangement that the biblical chapter does not actually discuss: marrying a deceased spouse's sibling. Indeed, Leviticus chapters 18 and 20 do not mention remarriage after death at all and appear only to mention a spouse's siblings in the context of forbidden adultery and forbidden polygamy. What is more, marrying a deceased spouse's sibling seems fairly natural, proved to be a fairly common occurrence, and appears to be commanded in some instances in Deuteronomy 25.

Nonetheless, perhaps because it gave too much freedom, for it permitted marriage with more distant relatives, the Long Parliament in the 1640s struck out the last line of the fourth paragraph,[3] an action which the Scottish Kirk ignored—indeed, the Church of Scotland ignored all of the revisions to the confession of faith imposed by the English Parliament. Because American Presbyterians derived the text of their confession from Scotch-Irish immigrants and avoided the bowdlerized version printed by the English Parliament, they were forced to reckon with the final line in paragraph 4. Eventually, in the eighteenth and nineteenth centuries, this final line came to be seen as too restrictive, and so the Americans removed it from their confession.[4]

---

[1] For a discussion of consanguinity and affinity, see Gillespie, *A Treatise of Miscellany Questions*, pp. 242-43.

[2] Henry argued for an annulment on the grounds that there was too close a bloodline between himself and his brother (consanguinity) to permit a biblical marriage to his brother's widow (affinity).

[3] The final clause was voted down by Parliament, 71 to 40 (*Commons Journals* 5:467-468, 18 February 1648).

[4] Excised by American Presbyterians in late nineteenth century. For the story of

Adultery

It is one thing to delineate deviations in the definition of marriage. It is another to discuss deviations within an actual marriage or an engagement, which is what we see in paragraph 5.

One reason for divorce will always be adultery. The Scriptures consider sexual activity in the context of a betrothal to be fornication or adultery, and judged that it is permissible to end a relationship on that basis. A betrothal was an agreement and a season of time which required both the commitment of marriage and the purity of an engagement. We see a breakup of a betrothal being premeditated by Joseph when he found Mary pregnant and suspected that she had had a relationship with another man (*Matt.* 1:18-20). Here the Westminster assembly continues that tradition of advocating rigorous sexual purity when it states that 'adultery or fornication committed after a contract, being detected before marriage, gives just occasion to the innocent party to dissolve that contract'.

On the other hand, Jesus spoke strong words on more than one occasion to the effect that nothing less than adultery should be used as a pretext for divorce in a marriage (*Matt.* 5:31, 32; 19:9). Divorce and remarriage must have a cause as strong as adultery in its defence. Adultery is often a mortal wound for a marriage. Illicit sexual activity does not necessitate divorce; it does not even make divorce recommended; but it certainly justifies it (*Matt.* 19:9; *Rom.* 7:2, 3). As the conclusion of paragraph 5 states, 'it is lawful for the innocent party to sue out a divorce: and, after the divorce, to marry another, as if the offending party were dead'.

Adultery or desertion and the efforts of others

Unfortunately men and women (until recently, and in many cultures, especially men) have studied ways of ending marriages. Our corrupt natures find inappropriate reasons to separate people whom God has joined.

Christians ought to be clear about how to promote marriage, and we should be equally clear in our minds that 'nothing but adultery'

its decline, see B. G. Waugh, 'The History of a Confessional Sentence', Ph.D. diss., Westminster Theological Seminary, 2002.

(*Matt.* 19:6, 8, 9), or, Paul adds, the 'desertion' of a spouse (*1 Cor.* 7:15), may be accepted as grounds to divorce.[1]

In any event, we can see even from Old Testament case laws that there is profound wisdom in requiring 'a public and orderly course of proceeding' in the consideration of divorce (*Deut.* 24:1-4). The general equity of that Old Testament law suggests that since marriage is such an intimate thing, and the breakdown of marriage such a destructive thing, the husband and wife should not be left to make the decision themselves. They ought to seek wise counsel from both the church and the magistrate, and then they ought to pay attention to it. Furthermore, since marriage is an orderly public declaration, there should be an orderly public attempt to mend marriages by church and civil governments. If such remedial action fails, only then should we consider there is sufficient cause to dissolve the strong bond of marriage.

For obvious reasons, as we seek counsel, we ought to seek God most earnestly of all. Adultery and desertion are some of the sorest trials ever to be endured by human beings. In such cases Christians need to find the wisdom, the comfort, and the example of forgiving mercy that resides in the One who is always faithful.

---

[1] Paul specifically mentions the desertion of an unbelieving spouse. Is there a particular case in Corinth he has in view? Or a likely scenario he envisaged or frequently encountered? Or is he limiting the 'desertion grounds' for divorce to desertion by an unbelieving spouse only? The latter option is difficult to accept simply because it is hard to imagine, in the parallel case, that the Scripture would limit the 'adultery grounds' for divorce to adultery by an unbelieving spouse only.

THE CHURCH

CHAPTER 25:

OF THE CHURCH

Historic Text

25.1 The catholic or universal church which is invisible, consists of the whole number of the elect, that have been, are, or shall be gathered into one, under Christ the head thereof; and is, the spouse, the body, the fullness of him that fills all in all.[a]

Modern Version

25.1 The catholic (that is, universal) church, which is invisible, consists of all the elect who have been, are, or shall be gathered into one, under Christ its head. This church is his bride, his body, and the fullness of him who fills all in all.

Scripture Proofs
25.1 [a] Eph. 1:10,22,23; Eph. 5:23,27,32; Col. 1:18.

An 'invisible' church

Most broadly conceived, the 'catholic' church, which means the 'universal' church, consists of all God's people—all whom he has chosen or elected to save. It includes those that 'have been, are, or shall be gathered' as one, under Christ. One only needs to look at the New Testament to see that there has been a church. One has only to be involved with a faithful local fellowship of Christian members and elders to see that there is still a church. One has only to read Ephesians 5 to see that there will be a church—for there the Apostle Paul eagerly anticipates the day when Christ will 'present to himself a glorious church' without detracting spot, wrinkle or blemish of any kind (*Eph.* 5:27).

Since this universal aspect of the church cannot be witnessed at one time, some theologians have spoken about the 'invisible church'. This label, employed by the Westminster assembly, must always be deficient as a definition of the church. Nonetheless, it suffices as a phrase to capture one aspect of the existence of the church. We cannot now see the whole church in its depth across the years or its breadth across the continents. There is an aspect of the church that is not visible to us from any one vantage point in time or space.[1]

The head of the church

However the church is described it must always be defined in relationship to Jesus Christ, and in this opening statement on the church the Westminster divines enlist a couple of metaphors that Paul employs in order to illustrate the relation of the church to Jesus Christ. God's people are gathered under Christ who is 'the head' of the body, to use a physical image for the church (*Eph.* 1:22; *Col.* 1:18), or head of the spouse, to use a relational image (*Eph.* 5:23-32).

Christ is head over all things and, in a special way, he is head over his church. All rule in the church is under his leadership. Every ministry is given by Christ. Every office is of his design. Every servant is to do his will. Every law is to be his creation. Every gift has been purchased by his own blood. The church is his. If we are to learn anything about the subject of the church, we are to learn it in Christ's school.

It is because he is the head that pastors must minister in his name, that elders rule under his oversight, that deacons serve under his care. Christ is the sole head of the church as much as he is its sole Saviour.

[1] As one example of the equating of the elect with the church of Christ the Westminster assembly pointed to Ephesians 1:10, which speaks of 'all things'—both in heaven and earth—becoming one in Christ. During the Reformation and post-Reformation periods the oneness in Christ, in the context of Ephesians 1, was understood to refer to the oneness of the church. 'All things' was commonly taken to mean either all elect people (both in heaven and on earth), or all elect beings (both angels in heaven and people on earth). The latter interpretation was adopted by Calvin in his Ephesians commentary; the former by the Geneva Bible; both interpretations are mentioned in *Annotations upon All the Books of the Old and New Testament, sub loc.*, and in *The Dutch Annotations upon the Whole Bible* (London, 1657), *sub loc.* The assembly obviously follows the interpretation of the Geneva Bible, but another interpretive possibility, suggested by the early Church Father, Irenaeus, is that the union of 'all things' refers to the whole cosmos (perhaps Irenaeus, *Against Heresies*, ANF 1:443). With the latter interpretation orthodox Christians understand that 'in him' does not teach a universal salvation (all united to Christ redemptively) but a universal dominion (all under Christ's authority).

Christ is the head and the church is his 'body'—a body with no significance or importance outside of Christ, and with every blessing and privilege and treasure of grace in Christ. Little wonder that Paul praises Christ and delights in his supremacy in the church. Little wonder that in the opening sentence of this confession's chapter on the church Christ's headship is affirmed.

The fullness of Christ

Nonetheless, the confession mentions not only Christ's headship in the church, but also, in faithfulness to Scripture, Paul's astonishing comment on the church: for in a surprising turn at the end of Ephesians 1, the apostle calls the church 'the fullness of him that fills all in all' (*Eph.* 1:23).

Naturally the triune God in his eternal perfections is complete and has no need of us. His church cannot be filling any lack in God himself. But when we think of Christ the king reigning over all, as Paul does in the context of Ephesians 1; when we think of Christ as head of the church, as Paul does in Ephesians 1; when we think of Christ as mediator, as Paul does in 1 Timothy 2:5, then we must affirm what Scripture says here. For what is a king without his kingdom? What is a head without a body? What is a mediator without all his people? In John Calvin's *Sermons on Ephesians,* first translated into English in 1577, he suggested that it is 'as if a father should say, my house seems empty to me when I do not see my child in it. A husband will say, I seem to be only half a man when my wife is not with me. After the same manner God says that he does not consider himself full and perfect, except by gathering us to himself and by making us all one with himself.'[1] There is a very real sense in which the church is the fullness of the one who in himself fills all in all, as the confession, and earlier Calvin, captures so clearly.

For the purpose of understanding the theology of the Westminster Confession of Faith, it is sufficient to see that the scriptural passages selected here do nothing to diminish the importance of the church. Far from it. This opening sentence offers an unembarrassed ecclesiology that eagerly employs verses which traditional opponents, such as the Roman

---

[1] John Calvin, *Sermons on the Epistle to the Ephesians* (1562; Edinburgh, 1998), p. 123.

Catholic Church, claimed for themselves. The church is Christ's 'spouse', his 'body', even his 'fullness'. Certainly the church and its ordering are topics that deserve biblical analysis and thoughtful discussion, and deserve a pride of place among other leading Christian doctrines.

Historic Text	*Modern Version*
25.2 The visible church, which is also catholic or universal, under the gospel (not confined to one nation, as before, under the law) consists of all those, throughout the world, that profess the true religion;[b] and, of their children:[c] and is, the kingdom of the Lord Jesus Christ,[d] the house and family of God,[e] out of which, there is no ordinary possibility of salvation.[f]	**25.2** The visible church, which is also catholic (that is, universal) under the gospel (that is, not confined to one nation, as it was before under the law), consists of all those throughout the world who profess the true religion, together with their children. It is the kingdom of the Lord Jesus Christ, the house and family of God, outside of which there is no ordinary possibility of salvation.

Scripture Proofs

   25.2   [b] 1 Cor. 1:2; 1 Cor. 12:12,13; Psa. 2:8; Rev. 7:9; Rom. 15:9-12.   [c] 1 Cor. 7:14; Acts 2:39; Ezek. 16:20,21; Rom. 11:16; Gen. 3:15; Gen. 17:7.   [d] Matt. 13:47; Isa. 9:7. [e] Eph. 2:19; Eph. 3:15. [f] Acts 2:47.

Universal and visible

The 'universal' or 'catholic' church can be contemplated, in some aspects, as invisible. It is more obviously the case that the church is a 'visible' entity. Paul wrote 'to the church of God at Corinth' because there was a visible body of believers who had been called and organized to serve God in Corinth (*1 Cor.* 1:2). He could write in the same way to any number of local churches.

However, the visible church is not only local. It too is 'catholic' or 'universal'. In fact, referring to the New Testament and the Old Testament, this section in the confession once again reminds us that under the gospel the church is 'not confined to one nation' as it was with Israel. Individual Christians are members of the church, whether they are

Jewish or Gentile, slave or free (*1 Cor.* 12:12, 13). Indeed, Christ's inheritance of those who were once unbelievers, ushered into the church from all nations, is a major focus of the Scriptures. It was promised by psalmists (*Psa.* 2:8), pledged by prophets (*2 Sam.* 22:50; *Psa.* 18:49; *Deut.* 32:43; *Psa.* 117:1; *Isa.* 11:10),[1] preached by apostles (*Rom.* 15:9-12), and will supply reason for thunderous praise in the new paradise, where a multitude which no man can number will be gathered together from all nations (*Rev.* 7:9). The fulfilment of this covenanted promise, first given to the patriarchs, is used in Scripture as sufficient reason for God's people to 'sing', 'rejoice', 'praise', and 'extol', and for the Gentiles to 'hope' (*Rom.* 15:9-13).

Professors and 'their children'

The church 'consists of all those throughout the world that profess the true religion'. But they must profess this faith. Today true Christians are often called 'believers'. In the seventeenth century true Christians were commonly called 'professors'. The more basic reason why Paul was willing to call the body of believers at Corinth a church was that they not only believed, but also acknowledged and owned the one true Redeemer. They assembled in Christ's name and in doing so joined those in every place who 'call on the name of Jesus Christ our Lord' (*1 Cor.* 1:2).

The church consists of 'professors'. It also consists 'of their children'. Being part of a Christian household, whether a household with one Christian parent or two, is a great privilege. God sets apart both the children and even the spouse of someone who is closely tied to him. They do not automatically become Christians by virtue of this relationship. The Apostle Paul, when he mentions this topic in passing, straightforwardly calls an unbelieving spouse of a Christian an unbeliever. Nonetheless, Paul says they are 'sanctified' and 'holy' compared to other unbelieving spouses, or other children without a Christian parent (*1 Cor.* 7:14) whether they like it or not. Perhaps a useful analogy is found in Romans 11:16, where Scripture says that 'if the dough . . . is holy, so is the whole lump, and if the root is holy, so are the branches'.

---

[1] All of these references are captured by the assembly in the citation of Romans 15:9-12.

The reason for the inclusion of children in the church finds its roots in the Old Testament, and it is a truth which God himself expressed passionately in the face of denial: children of professing Christians are God's before they are ours. In a dark chapter of Israel's history people took their sons and daughters and offered them as burned offerings to pagan gods. This was an outrage by any account, but the Lord describes it as an intense personal offence: the children which they considered theirs were 'born for me'; they were 'my children' (*Ezek.* 16:20, 21).

God takes ownership of covenant children. At the beginning of biblical revelation God promised to direct the future of Adam and Eve's 'seed' or descendants (*Gen.* 3:15). It is for that reason that he placed his covenantal ownership sign on all those who were under the instruction and authority of godly householders, especially their children (*Gen.* 17:7). It is for that reason, as the church was initiated into a new age at Pentecost, that Peter not only stressed that the promise of the gospel was for all those 'who are far off' (meaning, the Gentiles), but also for 'your children' (meaning, our children!, *Acts* 2:39).

The church as kingdom, house, and family

The church is visible, universal, and covenantal. It includes believing parents and their children. This church is further described in this second paragraph as 'the kingdom of the Lord Jesus Christ' and 'the house and family of God'. One of the greatest benefits that comes from being members of Christ's body is incorporation into 'the household of God', being accepted as one part of his 'whole family' (*Eph.* 2:19; 3:15). Christians have experienced this joy through the ages when they have come to faith, or moved to a new town, or travelled to another country, and found the Father's family waiting for them.

However, the church is more than a family. It is a kingdom. Now, it would be a mistake to woodenly equate the kingdom of God with the church, and members and contemporaries of the Westminster assembly did not see every reference to the kingdom of God as a reference to the church. They identified the kingdom of God with the proclamation of the gospel, with the coming of Jesus Christ, and with whatever else the passage and context might demand.[1] Nonetheless, while the kingdom of God is not the church, the church is certainly the kingdom of Jesus Christ. He is a king and he will never be dispossessed of what belongs to him. As the Prophet Isaiah foretold, Jesus Christ has a government that must increase. He has a throne. He rules with justice and righteousness. He has his hosts who will do his bidding (*Isa.* 9:7). His kingdom is bigger than the church, but it certainly includes the church, and God will cast a wide net to draw every kind of person into that church, into the kingdom of heaven, until his purposes are accomplished (*Matt.* 13:47).

Inside and outside the church

Having mentioned who is in the church, paragraph 2 ends by discussing those who are out of the church. And following Cyprian, Augustine, the medieval church, and the Protestant Reformers, the confession concludes that outside the church 'there is no ordinary possibility of salvation'. A family, a household, a kingdom—each of these requires something like membership, belonging, identity with the larger group.

A repentant thief on a cross, a Muslim convert to Christianity who has not yet discovered other believers, or a man stranded on the desert island with only a Bible, each has plausible reasons for not being a part of the church. But people who claim to be believers and refuse to join the church in the face of clear biblical instruction and providential opportunity to do so, should deeply worry us. They are like people who say they are in love but refuse to get married. Usually they want the privileges of the relationship without the accompanying responsibilities. Their refusal to publicly commit to Christ's church casts doubt on the genuineness of their devotion to him, as does a refusal to publicly commit to marriage.

The pattern of the New Testament is clear: when people were joined to Christ they were joined to his church. People devoted themselves to the best teaching, to fellowship, breaking bread, prayer, helping those in need, and praising God (*Acts* 2:42-47). And this was not done in the context of random or disassociated groups of believers. Luke tells us that 'the Lord added to the church those who were being saved' (*Acts* 2:47). May he continue to do so today.

[1] *E.g., Annotations upon All the Books of the Old and New Testament*, see Luke 17:21.

Historic Text	*Modern Version*
25.3 Unto this catholic visible church, Christ has given the ministry, oracles, and ordinances of God, for the gathering, and perfecting of the saints, in this life, to the end of the world: and does by his own presence and Spirit, according to his promise, make them effectual thereunto.[g]	**25.3** To this universal, visible church Christ has given the ministry, oracles, and ordinances of God for the gathering and perfecting of the saints, in this life, to the end of the age. For this purpose he makes these means effectual by his own presence and Spirit, according to his promise.

Scripture Proofs

25.3 [g] I Cor. 12:28; Eph. 4:11-13; Matt. 28:19,20; Isa. 59:21.

The ministry, oracles, and ordinances

To whom does the ministry belong? To individual believers? To any group of Christians? And what about Christian gifts, and ordinances?

When the Apostle Paul spoke about God's gifts of apostles, prophets, and teachers; and when he mentioned prophecy (oracle), miracles, healing and tongues; and when he talked about ordinances such as helping and governing, he had in view gifts which were to be used in the church (*I Cor.* 12:28). The God-ordained context for ministry is a churchly context. The church is a unique institution of which Christ is the head and it is the repository for special gifts related to the gospel. The government of Christians, and ordinances like preaching and the sacraments are reserved for the church.

Paragraph 3 of this chapter says as much, but also points out that these gifts are given to the visible church considered universally—not the 'invisible church' considered universally, or merely the visible church considered locally. When Paul brought up the subject of ministry and gifts he made it clear that they were not for use only in the local church to which he was writing (in Corinth), but for 'the church' in general (*I Cor.* 12:28). These gifts are for the catholic, visible, church—for the church of Christ as a whole, as it is visibly organized by God for his purposes.

Gathering and perfecting

The main purpose of all these gifts is for 'perfecting' saints, as Paul explained to the Ephesian Christians (*Eph.* 4:11). Paul knows that God's design is to make us more like the perfect man—the Lord Jesus Christ. The gifts that God has given to the church are not redundant until that goal is reached. Teachers are not temporary necessities, like Old Testament ceremonial laws. Ministers are not mere tutors for children. They are gifts that will be used until the church itself and every Christian becomes like Christ.

When a person is brought to Christ the church's work is not done; it has only just begun. So long as Christians are immature, so long as they are satisfied with the emptiness of this world instead of the fullness of Christ, so long as we see members wobble with every wave of error that comes our way, so long as these conditions exist, we have equipping to do, a ministry on the agenda, a body to build up. Actually, if anything is clear from these verses, it is that the gifts of the church are not merely given for the sake of the ministers, and not even for the members, but also for others. Paul assumes the mission of the church in Ephesians 4. Saints need to be gathered so they can be perfected. The confession makes this explicit, and points readers to the Great Commission at the end of the Gospel of Matthew, where the good work of spreading the gospel is required of the church's leaders.

To the end of the world

These gifts are needed in our own lifetime. They are useful to the ends of the earth and to the end of the world. The first truth is explicit in Jesus's command to teach and baptize all nations. The second is implicit in Christ's assurance that he would be with his preachers and teachers until the end of time (*Matt.* 28:19, 20).

Christ promised his presence before he ascended to heaven. He promised his Spirit long before he came to earth. It was by the terms of his covenant with his people that his Spirit was to come to them, and never leave them: 'My Spirit that is upon you, and my words that I have put in your mouth, shall not depart out of your mouth, or out of the mouth of your offspring, or out of the mouth of your children's offspring', promised the covenant Lord, 'from this time forth and forevermore' (*Isa.* 59:21). It is with such promises ringing in our ears that we trust that God will make 'the ministry, oracles, and ordinances' that he has given to us, effectual for us.

Historic Text	*Modern Version*
25.4 This catholic church has been sometimes more, sometimes less visible.[h] And particular churches, which are members thereof, are more or less pure, according as the doctrine of the gospel is taught and embraced, ordinances administered, and public worship performed more or less purely in them.[i]	**25.4** This universal church has been sometimes more and sometimes less visible. Particular churches, which are members of this universal church, are more or less pure to the extent to which the doctrine of the gospel is taught and embraced, the ordinances are administered, and public worship is performed more or less purely in them.
25.5 The purest churches under heaven are subject both to mixture, and error:[k] and some have so degenerated, as to become no churches of Christ, but synagogues of Satan.[l] Nevertheless, there shall be always a church on earth, to worship God according to his will.[m]	**25.5** The purest churches on earth are subject to both mixture and error, and some have so degenerated that they have become no churches of Christ at all, but rather synagogues of Satan. Nevertheless, there shall always be a church on earth to worship God according to his will.

Historic Text	*RCF (1936) Text*	*Modern Text*
25.6 There is no other head of the church, but the Lord Jesus Christ;[n] nor can the Pope of Rome, in any sense, be head thereof: but is, that antichrist, that man of sin, and son of perdition, that exalts himself, in the church, against Christ, and all that is called God.[o]	**25.6** There is no other head of the Church but the Lord Jesus Christ.[1] Nor can the Pope of Rome, in any sense, be head thereof.[2]	**25.6** There is no other head of the church but the Lord Jesus Christ. Nor can the Pope of Rome be its head in any sense.

The visibility of the church, and the marks of the church

When the confession says, in the opening line of chapter 25, paragraph 4, that the 'catholic church has been sometimes more, sometimes less visible', it simply means that the universal church is more or less evident. There have been periods, both under the law and under the gospel, when it proved very hard to see the church surviving at all. Certainly the existence of a faithful body of believing people was not evident to Elijah—he had no idea that the Lord had reserved seven thousand men who had not bowed their knees to an image of Baal (*Rom.* 11:3, 4). The same ambiguity about the wellbeing of the church might be pictured in the flight of the woman—perhaps the church—mentioned in Revelation 12:6, 14.

What is true of the universal church is also sometimes true of local congregations. 'Particular churches', which are members of the universal church, are more or less pure depending on the relative purity of the gospel 'taught and embraced' in those churches, the way in which they dispense the sacraments, and the manner and conduct of their public worship. In fact, the Westminster assembly was willing to calibrate the purity of a church based on the relative purity of these three marks of a church.

That the proper administration of the sacraments also includes church discipline is evident from the fact that the assembly here cites two scriptural passages that treat the subject of sin in churches. One passage, 1 Corinthians 5:6, 7, is a classic text for church discipline where the Apostle Paul urges the Corinthian church to expel a person from the church for sexual misconduct. The other text, Revelation 2-3, shows the necessity of discipline, since churches frequently tolerated error to their eventual detriment or demise, as in the case of some of the seven churches in Asia Minor.

Mixed churches

In spite of all efforts towards purity, even 'the purest churches under heaven are subject both to mixture and error'. We are subject to error because we are sinners and because 'now we see in a mirror, dimly' (*1 Cor.* 13:12). Christ's church contains some unbelievers amid the body of believers. The gospel's wide net not only attracts all kinds of people from various nations but also all kinds of people for various reasons (*Matt.* 13:24-30).

Sadly some churches have 'so degenerated', and in them the truth is so poisoned by error, that they have 'become no churches of Christ' but 'synagogues of Satan'. Here the assembly has in view the fallen Babylon of the book of Revelation (*Rev.* 18:2), the old Israel mourned in the letter to the Romans (*Rom.* 11:18-22), and a group of people, perhaps a rival 'church', troubling the church of Philadelphia (*Rev.* 3:9).

Sorry as this affair surely is, 'nevertheless, there shall be always a church on earth, to worship God according to his will'. Perhaps we can infer the permanence of God's worship and his people from the Psalms, which assure us that God's 'name shall endure for ever' (*Psa.* 72:17) and that God's children shall remain 'established' (*Psa.* 102:28). Undoubtedly we can derive this assurance from the enduring task of the Great Commission, from the promise that Christ will be with his disciples 'to the end of the world', and from Jesus' own promise that even 'the gates of hell will not prevail' against his church (*Matt.* 16:18; 28:19, 20).

The only head of the church

In the final section of this chapter the Westminster assembly returned to where it started: the headship of the Lord Jesus Christ over the church. It is fitting that in 'all things' Christ will 'have the preeminence', especially in his church (*Col.* 1:18). 'All things' are 'under his feet', and 'to his church' he is 'head over all things' (*Eph.* 1:22).

It is because he is the sole head of all by right that our Lord Jesus Christ brooks no rivals. Thus the 'Pope of Rome', in spite of his claims, cannot 'in any sense' be head of the church. Here the Westminster assembly cites Jesus' command that we call no man master, teacher, or father (*Matt.* 23:8-10). That is not to say Christian leaders should not rule in the church, or teach, or be gentle in a fatherly way. It is to say that no one should supplant the Lord God himself in these roles. Christ is our Master, and we should never set ourselves up as people who must be obeyed—our authority is merely derivative and representative. There is only one 'Chief Shepherd' and his name is Jesus (*1 Pet.* 5:2-4). The Holy Spirit is the authoritative Teacher and all other teachers must only pass on what he has taught us. God is our Father, and leaders in the church should never cultivate a dependency on them akin to that of a father with his children.

The pope as the antichrist?

In a controversial conclusion to the chapter, the Westminster assembly not only prohibited Christians from permitting the Pope to heap these titles upon himself, but also provided labels for the Pope: the 'antichrist', 'man of sin', and 'son of perdition'.

In using these labels for the Pope, the assembly was offering a particular interpretation of New Testament passages. Two of these names, here ascribed to the Pope, are from 2 Thessalonians 2, as is the following reason, also mentioned by the assembly: that he 'exalts himself above all that is called God'—which is probably not the best translation of that phrase, but in the context of the verse clearly means that he sets himself up as a rival to God (*2 Thess.* 2:3, 4; see also verses 8, 9). The name 'antichrist' is used by the Apostle John, perhaps referring to the same phenomenon as that described by Paul in 2 Thessalonians (see *1 John* 2:18; 4:3; *2 John* 7).

The Word of God does not identify the Pope as the antichrist, nor does it conclusively suggest that there is one person or position that the antichrist occupies, nor does the Apostle John consider the antichrist to be merely a person or position of the future. Furthermore, the papacy was a creation of the future: certainly the papacy as it existed in the post-Reformation period was an institution which had taken centuries to develop (as assembly members themselves were quick to argue) and did not even emerge as a dominant force in the earliest church for two centuries.

Although subsequent Presbyterians were in full sympathy with the assembly's dismay at the blasphemous claims of the papacy, agreed with the assembly that such departures from the truth of Scripture are predicted in Scripture, and heard in them dangerous echoes of the devil's own deceptions (*Rev.* 13:6), many were not willing to interpret these passages and these names as references to the papacy, and so for many decades permission was granted for church officers to take exception to this final line of chapter 25 paragraph 6. It was finally removed from mainstream American editions of the confession in 1903, and a similar revision of the sixth paragraph has been adopted by subsequent confessional American Presbyterians. Confessional standards need to reflect the clearest, and not the most controversial, interpretations of Scripture.

CHAPTER 26:

OF THE COMMUNION OF SAINTS

Historic Text

26.1 All Saints, that are united to Jesus Christ their head, by his Spirit, and by faith, have fellowship with him in his graces, sufferings, death, resurrection, and glory:[a] and, being united to one another in love, they have communion in each other's gifts and graces,[b] and are obliged to the performance of such duties, public and private, as do conduce to their mutual good, both in the inward and outward man.[c]

Modern Version

26.1 All saints—who are united to Jesus Christ their head by his Spirit and by faith—have fellowship with him in his graces, sufferings, death, resurrection, and glory. And, being united to one another in love, they participate in each other's gifts and graces and are obligated to perform those public and private duties which lead to their mutual good, both inwardly and outwardly.

Scripture Proofs

26.1 [a] 1 John 1:3; Eph. 3:16-19; John 1:16; Eph. 2:5,6; Phil. 3:10; Rom. 6:5,6; 2 Tim. 2:12. [b] Eph. 4:15,16; 1 Cor. 12:7; 1 Cor. 3:21-23; Col. 2:19. [c] 1 Thess. 5:11,14; Rom. 1:11,12,14; 1 John 3:16-18; Gal. 6:10.

Union with Christ

In moving from chapter 25 to chapter 26 the Westminster Confession of Faith shifts from the topic of the headship of Christ with his whole church to the union of Christ with every Christian. The first paragraph states how we are united to Christ, in what way we fellowship with him, and how we are to find communion with the saints. The second paragraph explains how we are told to hold communion with one another in and out of the boundaries of corporate worship. The final paragraph clarifies the limits of union and communion with Christ and his people. The chapter offers a useful treatment of a major Christian doctrine. It pushes the communion of the saints back into the theological spotlight after a long time in the shadows.

The first observation made in paragraph 1 is that all saints *are* in fact savingly 'united to Jesus Christ'. This is stated with some stylistic ambiguity in the opening line of this chapter. Nonetheless it is stated everywhere in the New Testament epistles and elsewhere in this confession. Christians are always united to Christ. They are 'in Christ', Christ is in them, and they are joined to him by Spirit-worked faith. As the letter to the Ephesians tells us, God the Father strengthens us 'with power through his Spirit' in our 'inner beings' so that Christ may 'dwell' in our 'hearts by faith' and fill us 'with all the fullness of God' (*Eph.* 3:16-19).

Once united to Christ, we cannot but 'have fellowship with him'. 'Truly', as the Apostle John wrote, 'our fellowship is with the Father and with his Son Jesus Christ' (*1 John* 1:3). Fellowship with Christ involves knowing his love and loving him in return. Fellowship with Christ involves learning from him and speaking to him. Amazingly, fellowship with Christ also involves sharing in his graces.[1] John tells us that from the overflow of Christ's fullness we receive 'grace upon grace'—and surely we do. Jesus came not only to bring much-needed truth, but also to bring much-needed grace (*John* 1:16, 17). This is what sinners, including sinful Christians, must always keep before them: 'by grace you are saved' (*Eph.* 2:5).

However, we not only share in the grace of Christ, but we share in his grace by sharing in his sufferings, his death, resurrection, and glory. We share in the 'fellowship of his sufferings', as Paul puts it, 'becoming like him in his death' (*Phil.* 3:10). Indeed, while 'we were dead in sins, we were made alive together with Christ' (*Eph.* 2:5). It is not too strong a phrase to say that we were 'crucified with him' (*Rom.* 6:6). And 'if we have been united with him in a death like his, we shall certainly

---

[1] The phrase 'fellowship with him in his graces' could refer either to saving graces or to Christ-likeness in life. The proof-texts offered by the assembly at this point (*John* 1:16 and *Eph.* 2:5) suggest that the gathering intended the former. A similar reference by Obadiah Sedgwick to 'communion with Christ in his graces' refers clearly to the birth or growth of holiness in a Christian, and thus the latter interpretation. Obadiah Sedgwick, *The Bowels of Tender Mercy Sealed in the Everlasting Covenant* (London, 1661), p. 132.

be united in a resurrection like his' (*Rom.* 6:5). Thus it is that God 'has raised us up . . . and made us sit together in heavenly places in Christ Jesus' (*Eph.* 2:6). Indeed, if we were to compress the range of these realities into a few words, we would say what Paul said to Timothy, 'if we suffer, we shall also reign with him' (*2 Tim.* 2:12).

Communion with the saints

Now, if all Christians are united to Christ, we must also recognize that in Christ we are united to one another. Are we united to Christ in love? Then we are 'united to one another in love'. Do we share in the grace of Christ? Then we must also have 'communion in each other's gifts and graces'.

This is the clear teaching of Paul's epistles. Christians together 'grow up in every way into him who is the head, into Christ'. It is in him that we are joined and held together, and together we speak the truth in love and are built up in love (*Eph.* 4:15, 16). This communion of the saints in gifts and graces is so important that the Holy Spirit is given 'for the common good' (*1 Cor.* 12:7). For that reason Christians are called to stop competing with each other, and recall instead that we belong to each other and that we have been knit together and to Christ (*1 Cor.* 3:21-23; *Col.* 2:19).

Because we are in union with Christ and in communion with each other, we are obliged to perform 'public and private' duties for our 'mutual good'—taking care of the Christians around us. Paul exhorted the Thessalonians to 'encourage one another and build one another up' as they were already doing. The apostle also wanted them to 'admonish the idle, encourage the fainthearted, help the weak', and 'be patient with them all' (*1 Thess.* 5:11, 14). Paul himself longed to see other Christians so that he could be of 'some spiritual' benefit to them. He in turn hoped to be comforted by them (*Rom.* 1:11, 12, 14).

Christian communion is not simply occupied with the inner man. It also cares about the outer man. In fact the sharing of physical, in additional to spiritual, goods is one indication that we know the love that comes from union with Christ. After all, as the Apostle John asks, 'if anyone has the world's goods and sees his brother in need, yet closes his heart against him, how does God's love abide in him?' Ultimately this love for each other cannot be restricted to what we have; it needs to encompass who we are. Here too, it is our communion with Christ that informs our communion with each other. He shared his life so that we could live. 'He laid down his life for us, and we ought to lay down our lives for the brothers.' So 'little children, let us not love in word or talk but in deed and in truth' (*1 John* 3:16-18). 'So then, as we have opportunity, let us do good to everyone, and especially to those who are of the household of faith' (*Gal.* 6:10).

Historic Text

26.2 Saints by profession, are bound to maintain an holy fellowship and communion in the worship of God, and in performing such other spiritual services as tend to their mutual edification;[d] as also, in relieving each other in outward things, according to their several abilities, and necessities. Which communion, as God offers opportunity, is to be extended unto all those, who, in every place, call upon the name of the Lord Jesus.[e]

26.3 This communion which the saints have with Christ, does not make them, in any wise, partakers of the substance of his Godhead; or, to be equal with Christ, in any respect: either of which to affirm, is impious, and blasphemous.[f] Nor does their communion one with another, as saints, take away, or infringe the title, or propriety which each man has in his goods and possessions.[g]

Modern Version

26.2 It is the duty of professing saints to maintain a holy fellowship and communion in the worship of God and in performing such other spiritual services as help them to edify one another. It is their duty also to come to the aid of one another in material things according to their various abilities and necessities. As God affords opportunity, this communion is to be extended to all those in every place who call on the name of the Lord Jesus.

26.3 The communion which the saints have with Christ does not make them in any way partakers of the substance of his Godhead, or in any respect equal with Christ. To affirm either is irreverent and blasphemous. Nor does their fellowship with one another as saints take away or infringe upon any person's title to, or right to, his own goods and possessions.

Scripture Proofs
26.2 [d] Heb. 10:24,25; Acts 2:42,46; Isa. 2:3; 1 Cor. 11:20. [e] Acts 2:44,45; 1 John 3:17; 2 Cor., chapters 8,9; Acts 11:29,30.

26.3   ᶠ Col.1:18,19; 1 Cor. 8:6; Isa. 42:8; 1 Tim. 6:15,16; Psa. 45:7, with Heb. 1:8,9.
ᵍ Exod. 20:15; Eph. 4:28; Acts 5:4.

The worship of God

Part of our profession as Christians is to maintain fellowship and communion in all that we do and have and are. But we are especially bound to maintain a holy fellowship and a holy communion both with God and with each other.

From the earliest days of the church there have always been those who have 'devoted themselves' to God-appointed teaching and fellowship, to breaking bread and prayers, sharing 'food with glad and generous hearts' (*Acts* 2:42, 46). In fact the faithful worship of God's people, and the eagerness of 'many peoples' to be taught God's ways so that they can 'walk in his paths' provide yet further fulfilment of divine prophecy (*Isa.* 2:3).

In experience, many Christians can testify that worship on the Lord's day has been a foretaste of heaven, both in their communion with the triune God, and in their communion with each other. Nevertheless, it is also true that there has always been a drift in the Christian church away from active, corporate worship. The New Testament tells us that already in the days of the apostles it was 'the habit of some' to avoid meeting with the rest of the body (*Heb.* 10:25). Thus from the beginning, the Word of God has actively warned Christians against 'neglecting to meet together' and directs us instead to be always 'encouraging one another' to gather 'and all the more as you see the Day drawing near' (*Heb.* 10:25).

In all of these 'spiritual services' to God, there is a 'spiritual service' offered to each other. In fact 'mutual edification' should be one of our goals as we worship. The letter to the Hebrews encourages this sort of activity in a direct exhortation: 'let us consider how to stir up one another to love and good works' (*Heb.* 10:24). Paul, in the first letter to the Corinthians, challenged the church to abandon what appeared to be worship, but was really self-serving greed, which God did not accept as worship (*1 Cor.* 11:20).

The 'outward things'

One overflow of this communion in worship is a communion in goods: 'relieving each other in outward things', according to our various abilities and a brother's or sister's various necessities. In the account that he offers of the early worship of the church, this sharing and caring is intermingled with Luke's account of their worship (*Acts* 2:44, 45; *cf.* verses 42-47). John questioned whether people even know the love of God if they close their hearts against a brother in need (*1 John* 3:17). And one of the longest sections in Paul's second letter to the Corinthians has to do with his judicious and thoughtful fund-raising for the needs of the Judean church (*2 Cor.* 8, 9).

Paul's actions—indeed, the early church's actions—recorded in the letters and the book of Acts, indicate that this kind of communion, as God gives opportunity, is necessarily 'to be extended to all those who, in every place, call upon the name of the Lord Jesus' (*2 Cor.* 8, 9; *Acts* 11:29, 30). The communion of the saints extends beyond the confines of our church or locality. It is to be an expression of the overflow of Christ's love for all his people, among all his people.

Qualifiers about communion: no possibility of divinization

Having outlined the doctrine of the communion of saints with Christ, and with each other, the final section of this chapter explains what communion is not.

In the first place, the communion that we have with Christ is with Christ as our mediator, not with Christ in his being—in his substance as a member of the Trinity. Paul explained something like this to the Colossians. Christ is the head of the body. He is the firstborn of all who are raised from the dead. We have much in common with the one with whom we have union. But he remains the head. He is the firstborn. He is in everything preeminent. 'For in him all the fullness of God was pleased to dwell' (*Col.* 1:19). In the early church, at the Reformation, and today, there are those who devalue Jesus, or overvalue the rest of us. This is a great mistake.

There is 'one Lord, Jesus Christ, through whom are all things and through whom we exist' (*1 Cor.* 8:6). He is the one whom the Scriptures call 'the blessed and only Sovereign, the King of kings and Lord of lords, who alone has immortality, who dwells in unapproachable light, whom no one has ever seen or can see'. There is much that we gain and become in union with Jesus Christ. But the Bible ascribes 'to him' and not to us 'honour and eternal dominion' (*1 Tim.* 6:15, 16). God speaks in his Word about the thrones of the saints, our participation in the great judgment, the righteousness of which we partake, and the anointing of the Holy Spirit. But of the Son he says, 'Your throne, O God, is forever and ever, the sceptre of uprightness is the sceptre of your kingdom. You have loved righteousness and hated wickedness; therefore God, your God, has anointed you with the oil of gladness beyond your companions' (*Heb.* 1:8-9, quoting *Psa.* 45:7).

The same simply cannot be said of us. Surely we do not share in his divine qualities. Indeed, we are not 'equal with Christ in any respect'. We are clothed in his wisdom, his holiness, his righteousness, because we are united to him. But we are never as holy, as wise, as righteous as he is in himself. Truly it is not too much to say that any other teaching is both 'impious and blasphemous', however unintentional such an error in thinking might be. Certainly God spoke advisedly to the prophet Isaiah when he declared, 'my glory I give to no other' (*Isa.* 42:8). Needless to say, this is a demanding subject to understand in any depth. Nonetheless, careful limits must be placed on our understanding of the contours and extent of our union with Christ.

Qualifiers about communion: no requirement for communalism

In the second place, we must also understand the parameters of our communion with one another. The Scriptures both exhibit and require saints sharing with those who are in need. But beyond doubt, this does not mean that communion requires communalism. Generosity is not the same as collectivism. After all, as the scriptural references offered by the assembly point out, what sense would there be in commanding God's people not to steal—a command repeated in the New Testament—if they are required to give up their property and share everything they own? (*Exod.* 20:15; *Eph.* 4:28).

It may be implicit in Paul's command in Ephesians 4:28 that Christians own the things they share. In that passage we are called to work hard so that we 'may have something to share with anyone in need'. There can, however, be no question about the point made in Acts 5:4. The Apostle Peter's question to Ananias about his property contains its own answer: 'While it remained unsold, did it not remain your own? And after it was sold, was it not at your disposal?'(*Acts* 5:4). Even in what proved to be a radical period of intense property-sharing, neither the church, nor its leaders, nor individual Christians had the right to 'take away', trespass on, or infringe the title or right which people have to their own goods and possessions.

Nonetheless, in respecting these limits to communion, let us remember that if we are united to Christ, then we are raised with Christ, and must set our hearts on things above, where Christ is, and not on this world, and the things around us through which we journey only for a time.

CHAPTER 27:

OF THE SACRAMENTS

Historic Text

27.1 Sacraments are holy signs, and seals of the covenant of grace,[a] immediately instituted by God,[b] to represent Christ, and his benefits; and, to confirm our interest in him;[c] as also, to put a visible difference between those that belong unto the church, and the rest of the world;[d] and, solemnly to engage them to the service of God in Christ, according to his Word.[e]

27.2 There is in every sacrament a spiritual relation, or sacramental union, between the sign and the thing signified: whence it comes to pass, that the names, and effects of the one, are attributed to the other.[f]

Modern Version

27.1 Sacraments are holy signs and seals of the covenant of grace. They were directly instituted by God to represent Christ and his benefits and to confirm our relationship to him. They are also intended to make a visible distinction between those who belong to the church and the rest of the world, and solemnly to bind Christians to the service of God in Christ, according to his Word.

27.2 In every sacrament there is a spiritual relationship, or sacramental union, between the visible sign and the reality signified by it, and so it happens that the names and effects of the one are attributed to the other.

Scripture Proofs
    27.1 [a] Rom. 4:11; Gen. 17:7,10.   [b] Matt. 28:19; 1 Cor. 11:23.   [c] 1 Cor. 10.16; 1 Cor. 11:25,26; Gal. 3:27.   [d] Rom. 15:8; Exod. 12:48; Gen. 34:14.   [e] Rom. 6:3,4; 1 Cor. 10:16,21.
    27.2 [f] Gen. 17:10; Matt. 26:27,28; Titus 3:5.

Signs and seals of the covenant of grace

What are sacraments? Sacraments are both signs and seals of the gospel, or the covenant of grace.[1] We can glean this information, for example,

[1] See chapters 7, 14.2, and 17.2.

from the sacrament of circumcision. It is called a 'sign' in Scripture. Besides, it was a 'seal' of the righteousness that comes from God alone (*Rom.* 4:11). The sacrament of circumcision was gracious, representing God's undeserved favour to sinners who believed in the Son. Moreover, it was covenantal, cementing God's promises to his people (*Gen.* 17:7, 10).

Signing and sealing terminology had a particular meaning in the post-Reformation period—the period in which the Westminster Confession of Faith was written. In the seventeenth century 'seals' were understood to be confirming tokens or authenticating symbols. When that meaning was applied to the sacraments, a seal was understood to protect a promise, emphasize an obligation, or solidify a covenant. Most basically, a seal *validated* something.

'Signs' carried a much wider range of possible meanings in the seventeenth century than did seals. Generally a sign was a visible indicator, a tangible token of something else. A sign could have a symbolic reference to something that was not material or was in some way abstract. In any case, a sign was a visible action or material object which symbolized something else. When applied to the sacraments, signs were understood to be emblems or badges that established one's identity. A sign in this sense could indicate that the person marked belonged to God and was part of the church. Most basically, it *pointed* to something.

Thankfully seventeenth-century theologians did not take their contemporary meanings for 'signs' and 'seals', carelessly transfer those meanings to biblical words, and then insert them into this confession. The very opposite is the case. The Westminster assembly observed the biblical use and context of these words, and then drew conclusions about their meanings. Actually biblical meanings of sign and seal appear to be well-represented in their seventeenth-century usages, for in biblical usage a sign is a distinguishing mark that points to something which exists, and a seal confirms or authenticates the genuineness of something.[1] Indeed, these early-modern meanings were likely informed by the Bible, the most widely read and known text in English history.

[1] Grammatically, the 'seal' phrase in Romans 4:11 could mean to modify or define the 'sign', in which case 'sign' and 'seal' could be used interchangeably. Nonetheless, the general use of these terms in Scripture suggests otherwise.

Given by God

It is clear from the inspired writings of Moses, Matthew, and Paul that the sacramental signs and seals of the Old and New Testaments were given directly by God. We see this when the great covenant was made with Abraham, when the Great Commission was given to the apostles, and when our Lord, on the night of his betrayal, instituted a new sacrament for his disciples (*Gen.* 17:7, 10; *Matt.* 28:19; *1 Cor.* 11:23).

These sacraments were given by God. Of course they were. Who better than God could (and who other than God should!) institute emblems for each of the four purposes mentioned in this opening paragraph?

Four functions of sacraments

Sacraments were first instituted by God to 'represent Christ, and his benefits'. They point, above all else, to the Saviour and to the blessings which flow from a vital relationship with him. One New Testament sacrament is called 'a participation' in the body and blood of Christ (*1 Cor.* 10:16; *cf. 1 Cor.* 11:25); it proclaims Christ (*1 Cor.* 11:26). Sacraments point to Christ the mediator and his saving work. They confirm the genuineness of biblical testimony and the benefits that come to us under the terms of God's gracious covenant.

Second, the sacraments 'confirm our interest in' our Redeemer. They fortify, or give God's authority to, our interest in Christ. Here 'interest' is used in the old sense of the word: our 'interest' means 'our share in' or our 'title to' something or someone. In this section it refers to our share in or claim to Jesus Christ himself. Sacraments signify or point to our relationship with Jesus. And they seal or confirm that we belong to him by God's great grace. This is why the New Testament represents Christians, in the act of participating in a sacrament, as having 'put on Christ' (*Gal.* 3:27).

Third, the sacraments 'put a visible difference between those that belong unto the church and the rest of the world'. The Lord made it clear to the people he was saving from Egypt that when a new family began to move in Israelite circles, the head of that family was supposed to demonstrate his commitment to the Lord by having himself and all the males in his household circumcised (*Exod.* 12:48). We see hints of this teaching much earlier, in the second generation after Abraham (*Gen.* 34:14). But we see it most clearly in our Lord Jesus Christ, who was circumcised not only to 'confirm the promises given to the patriarchs', but to 'show God's truthfulness' to those around him: it was a testimony that set him apart. Sacraments signify or point to this difference. They seal or confirm it before the world.

Fourth, the sacraments 'solemnly . . . engage' us 'to the service of God in Christ, according to his Word'. Surely, serious battle against sin and for Christ is the dual message of the sacramental imagery used in Romans 6:3, 4. Perhaps there is also a double meaning in the idea of 'participating' in Christ—both union with him, and commitment to him (*1 Cor.* 10:16). In any case, the sacraments signify, or point to the need for devoted service. They seal, or confirm, that God's Word calls us to this service. They remind us that we cannot have it both ways: our commitment is either to Christ or to the devil, but not to both (*1 Cor.* 10:21).

Sacramental union

To say that sacraments sign, seal, and represent something—or someone—is to say that there is 'in every sacrament a spiritual relation, or sacramental union, between the sign and the thing signified'. In fact, sometimes when the Scriptures speak about the sacraments and salvation, occasionally 'the names and effects of the one are attributed to the other'. In the Old Testament God actually calls the sign of circumcision itself 'my covenant' (*Gen.* 17:10). In the New Testament the cup of wine is called 'the blood of the covenant' (*Matt.* 26:27, 28). The Apostle Paul, perhaps speaking of baptism, refers to 'the washing of regeneration' (*Titus* 3:5). And the Apostle Peter says that 'baptism . . . saves you' (*1 Pet.* 3:21).

In this second paragraph the confession is really offering a manual for the right reading of scriptural terminology. It is telling us how terms are sometimes used in the Bible. The fact is, God chose his sacramental signs so well that sometimes a saving reality and the thing that signifies it are spoken about interchangeably in his holy Word. Understanding this will help us to understand the Bible better, and it will keep us from building a grand sacramental system on a wrong foundation.

🔥

Historic Text

27.3 The grace which is exhibited in, or by the sacraments rightly used, is not conferred by any power in them: neither does the efficacy of a sacrament depend upon the piety, or intention of him that does administer it:[g] but, upon the work of the Spirit,[h] and the word of institution, which contains, together with a precept authorizing the use thereof, a promise of benefit to worthy receivers.[i]

27.4 There be only two sacraments ordained by Christ our Lord, in the gospel; that is to say, baptism and the supper of the Lord: neither of which may be dispensed by any, but by a minister of the Word lawfully ordained.[k]

27.5 The sacraments of the old testament, in regard of the spiritual things thereby signified, and exhibited, were, for substance, the same with those of the new.[l]

Modern Version

27.3 The grace which is exhibited in or by the sacraments, rightly used, is not conferred by any power in them. Neither does the efficacy of a sacrament depend on the piety or intention of him who administers it, but rather on the work of the Spirit and on the word of institution, which contains (together with a precept authorizing its use) a promise of benefit to worthy receivers.

27.4 There are only two sacraments ordained by Christ our Lord in the gospel: baptism and the Lord's supper. Neither sacrament may be administered by any person except a minister of the Word, lawfully ordained.

27.5 With regard to the spiritual realities signified and exhibited, the sacraments of the old testament were essentially the same as those of the new testament.

Scripture Proofs
27.3 [g] Rom. 2:28,29; 1 Pet. 3.21. [h] Matt. 3:11; 1 Cor. 12:13. [i] Matt. 26:27,28; Matt. 28:19,20.
27.4 [k] Matt. 28:19; 1 Cor. 11:20,23; 1 Cor. 4:1; Heb. 5:4.
27.5 [l] 1 Cor. 10:1-4.

Grace exhibited

The first paragraph of chapter 17 tells us that the sacraments have representing, confirming, differentiating, and engaging functions. The second paragraph mentions that there is a 'sacramental union' of sorts between the sign and what (or whom!) it signifies. The third paragraph opens by stating that grace is 'exhibited'—meaning 'presented'[1]—and 'conferred'[2] in or by the sacraments.

The grace that is presented or conferred is the saving grace of the gospel (see WCF 27.1), and the Westminster assembly states that this presentation or conferral happens when the sacraments are rightly used. What does this mean? Since sacraments are wrongly used when they are wrongly understood, the Westminster assembly begins by issuing some key limitations to the idea of 'presented' or 'conferred' grace. It first states the case negatively, and later positively.

On the one hand, no grace is conferred 'by any power in' the sacraments. After all, as Peter and Paul both note, Christians are not created by water 'removing dirt from the body' in the new covenant, or Jews by the 'outward and physical' act of circumcision in the old covenant (*1 Pet.* 3:21; *Rom.* 2:28, 29).

On the other hand, if it is not the action or the material of the sacrament that saves, neither does its efficacy 'depend on the piety or intention' of the person administering the sacrament. The assembly appears to have drawn this negative conclusion about piety and intention from two positive conclusions about the Holy Spirit and the word of institution.

First, any efficacy in the sacrament depends on the work of the Holy Spirit. John the Baptist pointed forward to the baptism of the Holy Spirit as the true power to which the crowds should look, and which baptism merely symbolized (*Matt.* 3:11). Paul pointed out that it is 'in one Spirit' that we are baptized and, perhaps looking to the Lord's supper, says that 'all were made to drink of one Spirit' (*1 Cor.* 12:13). The sacraments are constantly linked to the work and power of the Holy Spirit. Sacraments

[1] Obsolete and modern meanings of the verb 'exhibit' range from strong conveyance verbs such as 'grant', 'provide', and 'administer', to weak display verbs such as 'show' or 'set forth'. All of these meanings were employed in the 1640s. The assembly's own use of 'exhibit' was usually synonymous with the verbs 'offer' or 'present' (see Van Dixhoorn, ed., *The Minutes and Papers of the Westminster Assembly*, vol. 5, Docs 20, 29, 77, 88, 99, 119). Indeed, on one occasion the assembly complained that a minority report was seen by the gathering, but was not 'exhibited'—that is presented—'though often desired' (*Ibid.,* Doc 99).

[2] Here the conferral of grace is inferred from the opening line's negation. See WCF 28.6 for an explicit statement of conferral.

work 'by the Spirit', as Paul wrote to the Romans, speaking of circumcision (*Rom.* 2:29).

Second, the Holy Spirit, in turn, uses 'the word of institution'—the instruction which accompanies the sacraments. This word contains 'a precept authorizing the use' of the sacrament. Thus we see in Matthew 26, or Matthew 28, clear instructions to partake of, and to administer the sacraments (*Matt.* 26:27, 28; 28:19, 20). This word of institution also contains a clear 'promise of benefit to worthy receivers'. We see this, too, in the Gospel of Matthew. The wine symbolizing the blood of the covenant is poured out 'for the forgiveness of sins'. And baptism is to be joined with teaching, as we see in the wording of the Great Commission (*Matt.* 26:27, 28; 28:19, 20).

The sacraments are the work of the Holy Spirit, by the institution of Christ. Signifying and sealing God's promise, and also his judgment, they are God's signs. For that reason their usefulness does not rest on the holiness or the aims of the one who administers them.

A minister

Nonetheless, it does matter who administers the sacraments. The Corinthians administered the supper to themselves, each person grabbing what they wanted, when they wanted it. Paul deemed that this was not the Lord's supper at all (*1 Cor.* 11:20). Distributed decently and orderly, the sacraments are dispensed by the leader of the congregation. Properly administered, the teacher who gives the words of institution is the one commissioned to give the sacrament.

The Old Testament sacraments offer potentially significant parallels for the new covenant church, since the holy rites God commanded in the old covenant were committed only to those people whom God himself had appointed. People did not take these honours on themselves. They performed those special actions 'only when called by God, just as Aaron was' (*Heb.* 5:4).

If the sacraments are properly termed gospel 'mysteries', it may be that the New Testament teaches that the sacraments are for ministers to administer, for the Apostle Paul says, 'this is how one should regard us, as servants of Christ and stewards of the mysteries of God' (*1 Cor.* 4:1).[1] Certainly, when considering the persons who should administer the sacraments, it is important to note that Jesus commissioned his chosen disciples to go into all the world with word and sacrament—it was a charge deliberately given to the church's teachers (*Matt.* 28:19).

Two sacraments

Obviously the Lord issued many commands during the time when he established his church, but a search through the four Gospels—or even the gospel broadly considered as the whole New Testament—turns up 'only two sacraments ordained by Christ our Lord'. Only two signs are given special significance and are commanded not merely by example, but by precept; not once, but repeatedly. Only two signs and seals were subsequently understood by the first generation of Christians to be an enduring part of the life of the church: baptism and the Lord's supper.

These signs were not merely local practices. Baptism, for example, was required of converts 'of all nations' (*Matt.* 28:19). These signs were not merely examples of the sort of symbols that Christians are permitted to invent for themselves. On the contrary they were to be administered just as the Lord Jesus instructed. Without a doubt, the apostle considered the Lord's supper to have been abused by the Corinthians, and they were rebuked by him, precisely because they did not celebrate it as it was 'received from the Lord' and 'delivered to' the church (*1 Cor.* 11:20, 23).

In substance the same

It remains to be said, in this prefatory chapter on the sacraments, that 'the sacraments of the old testament' with respect to 'the spiritual things thereby signified and exhibited, were, for substance, the same with those of the new'. That is one reason why Paul could refer to the Exodus as a baptism, because the substance of the two are the same—Jesus Christ and his glorious gospel (*1 Cor.* 10:1-4).

---

[1] *E.g., Annotations upon All the Books of the Old and New Testament, sub loc.*

CHAPTER 28:

OF BAPTISM

Historic Text

28.1 Baptism is a sacrament of the new testament, ordained by Jesus Christ,[a] not only for the solemn admission of the party baptized, into the visible church;[b] but also, to be unto him a sign, and seal of the covenant of grace,[c] of his engrafting into Christ,[d] of regeneration,[e] of remission of sins,[f] and of his giving up unto God through Jesus Christ, to walk in newness of life.[g] Which sacrament is, by Christ's own appointment, to be continued in his church until the end of the world.[h]

Modern Version

28.1 Baptism is a sacrament of the new testament, ordained by Jesus Christ, by which the person baptized is solemnly admitted into the visible church. Baptism is also for him a sign and seal of the covenant of grace, of his engrafting into Christ, of regeneration, of forgiveness of sins, and of his surrender to God through Jesus Christ to walk in newness of life. By Christ's own appointment, this sacrament is to be continued in his church until the end of the age.

Scripture Proofs
28.1 [a] Matt. 28:19. [b] 1 Cor. 12:13. [c] Rom. 4:11, with Col. 2:11,12. [d] Gal. 3:27; Rom. 6:5. [e] Titus 3:5. [f] Mark 1:4. [g] Rom. 6:3,4. [h] Matt. 28:19,20.

The baptism of the Christian church

The last paragraph of the previous chapter emphasizes that New Testament sacraments have their roots in the Old Testament. Christian baptism finds its background in Old Testament water ordeals, events symbolizing salvation and judgment such as the flood and the Red Sea (*1 Pet.* 3:18-22; *1 Cor.* 10:1-5). But it is uniquely 'a sacrament of the new testament' and it was 'ordained', both ordered and established, 'by Jesus Christ'. It is a core part of the church's commission given by our Lord (*Matt.* 28:19).

New Testament baptism is the baptism of the Christian church because it is a symbol given to the church, and because it marks a 'solemn admission of the party baptized'—either an individual Christian or a whole family—into the visible church. We are baptized into one body of Christians, as Paul explained to the Corinthians. Water baptism marks Jews and Greeks, slave and free, as members of one community united not by ethnic background or economic status, but by a spiritual thirst satisfied only by the Holy Spirit (*1 Cor.* 12:13). When it comes to defining an emblem for entry into the church, or a badge of belonging, we have no right to make up our own symbol or ceremony. God has given us baptism.

A five-fold spiritual significance

Baptism is a marker for entry into the church, but it is not only that. As the chapter on the sacraments in general would lead us to expect, baptism has gracious significance, and the Westminster assembly mentions five facets of that significance here.

The first thing that baptism points to and validates is God's gospel. To the person being baptized, and to all who witness or experience the event, or to all who even consider the symbol, baptism testifies to the truth of an enduring promise which God himself made, which he continues to proclaim, and which he continues to honour: it is the promise of redemption for all who trust in Christ alone for their righteousness.

As the previous chapter stated, the action or event of baptism does not contain 'power in itself' (WCF 27.3). Nonetheless, by the Holy Spirit, and with the interpretive word of institution which explains what baptism means and which sets it apart from being an unusual shower or bath, this sacrament is a powerful, 'sign and seal of the covenant of grace'.

Baptism preaches to Christians in the same way that circumcision preached to the patriarchs: it is a sign and seal of a righteousness that is ours by faith, to paraphrase Paul in Romans (*Rom.* 4:11). But in fact Romans should be read alongside Colossians, because in the latter Paul explains that baptism pictures salvation in a way similar to circumcision. Circumcision's cutting off of the flesh symbolized the removal of our sin by Christ, who was himself completely cut off in the flesh: he was killed.

And Paul says we benefit from this work of Christ because we are 'in him' (*Col.* 2:11). Baptism's washing with water symbolizes the removal of our sin by Christ, who was completely covered by our sin and then cleansed in his resurrection: he was buried and raised again to new life. And Paul says we benefit from this work of Christ because we are 'with him' (*Col.* 2:12).

Every sacrament has a primary reference to that which is always true, and a secondary reference to that which is often true—a reference to that which is, and a reference to that which ought to be. Baptism is most basically and universally—just as circumcision was—about the works and the righteousness of Another, and not about the righteousness of ourselves. It is primarily about the person, promises and actions of God and not about us—not even about the righteousness which we have in Christ as Christians. The enduring importance of baptism rests in what it *always* says about God and his gospel, and not what it *sometimes* says about the person who is baptized.

Nonetheless, baptism is, in the second place, a sign and seal not only of redemption promised, and redemption accomplished, but of redemption applied. It signifies and seals a person's 'engrafting into Christ'. It is because baptism points to and validates a vital connection to the Saviour that in Romans 6 Paul employs a baptismal analogy, and in Galatians 3 states that 'as many of you as were baptized into Christ have put on Christ' (*Rom.* 6:5; *Gal.* 3:27).[1] The Westminster assembly aims in this paragraph to simply set forth biblical teaching rather than to qualify these statements. The assembly explains neither why some baptized people do not appear to be united to Christ nor why some people are to be baptized before they are united to Christ. The Scriptures present a strong connection between baptism and union with Christ, so that is what is presented here.

---

[1] With Paul's words ringing in our ears, Christians also know that not all baptized people have in fact been savingly united to Christ. Just as not all who were of the circumcision were truly circumcised in heart (*Rom.* 2:28, 29), so too not all who are baptized are baptized in heart. The functions of a sacrament (WCF 27.1)—the 'spiritual relation, or sacramental union, between the sign and the thing signified' (WCF 27.2), the 'engrafting into Christ'—these are not events guaranteed by God, let alone events worked by the power of the sacrament.

So too, in the third and the fourth places, the Scriptures draw baptism into close proximity to regeneration and the remission of sins—it points and testifies to these saving realities too. When Paul speaks of the washing of regeneration he may be referring to baptism (*Titus* 3:5). And if the baptism of John and his disciples can illustrate aspects of the baptism of Christ and his disciples, then there is also such a thing as 'a baptism of repentance for the forgiveness of sin' (*Mark* 1:4).

Lastly, and most familiar to evangelical Christians today, baptism is a sign and seal of a life given up to God, through Jesus Christ. It points to, and testifies to, a dedication to God, and a 'walk in newness of life' (*Rom.* 6:3-4). Baptism preaches the gospel promised and accomplished. But because it also depicts that gospel applied, it includes a call to be what we are in Christ: it calls us to surrender our lives to God, through Christ. After all, 'Do you not know that all of us who have been baptized into Christ Jesus were baptized into his death? We were buried therefore with him by baptism into death, in order that, just as Christ was raised from the dead by the glory of the Father, we too might walk in newness of life' (*Rom.* 6:3, 4).

It is no doubt because baptism is so rich in its significance and is so clearly a pointer to Christ himself, that our Lord appointed it to be continued in his church until the end of the world. And by his Spirit, and in our teaching and in our baptisms, he will be with us 'always, to the end of the age' (*Matt.* 28:19, 20).

Historic Text	*Modern Version*
28.2 The outward element to be used in this sacrament is water, wherewith the party is to be baptized, in the name of the Father, and of the Son, and of the Holy Ghost, by a minister of the gospel, lawfully called thereunto.[i]	**28.2** The outward element to be used in this sacrament is water, with which the person is to be baptized in the name of the Father, and of the Son, and of the Holy Spirit. Baptism is to be performed by a minister of the gospel, lawfully called to that office.
28.3 Dipping of the person into the water, is not necessary: but, baptism	**28.3** Dipping of the person into the water is not necessary. Baptism is rightly

is rightly administered, by pouring, or sprinkling water upon the person.[k]   administered by pouring or sprinkling water on the person.

Scripture proofs

  28.2 [i] Matt. 3:11; John 1:33; Matt. 28:19,20.
  28.3 [k] Heb. 9:10,19-22; Acts 2:41; Acts 16:33; Mark 7:4.

Water

Baptisms in the medieval church, following the developments in the early church, were elaborate affairs. As it slowly began to attribute too much power to the sacrament of baptism, and as it sought to compete with the elaborate rituals of rival religions, the church felt obliged to 'improve' on the simple baptismal formula of the New Testament. Already in the early centuries of Christianity consecrating oil had been added to the symbol of water baptism, for Christians had forgotten that water alone can symbolize the giving of the Holy Spirit (*Matt.* 3:11; *John* 1:33). By the late medieval period, the baptismal formula included multiple exorcisms—indeed, it appeared to have more to do with getting rid of the devil than getting the grace of God.

The Reformers had opposed these medieval innovations, and by the time of the Westminster assembly theologians could offer, without argument, a return to the simple instruction of the New Testament: the 'outward element to be used' in the sacrament of baptism 'is water', administered in the name of the triune God by a properly appointed minister.

The basic element of water is one of the points of continuity between the sacraments of John and Jesus and their disciples: John the Baptist was sent by God to baptize with water, and subsequent Christian baptisms never varied from this (*Matt.* 3:11; *John* 1:33). What did change was that Jesus, rather than John, began to appoint servants to baptize; that the baptismal message became that of Jesus' full-orbed gospel and not John's prophetic warnings; and that Christians were to administer baptism in the name of the three persons of the Godhead, rather than in the promise of a more powerful Spirit to come (*Matt.* 3:11; *John* 1:33; *Matt.* 28:19, 20).

The conviction that baptism is to be administered in the name of Father, Son and Holy Spirit, and 'by a minister of the gospel, lawfully called' rather than self-appointed, is established in the Great Commission. It was, after all, a commission: Jesus' instruction to baptize was given to men whom he had called to ministry. And what made this commission great, was not so much the magnitude of the task, but the name of the Father, Son and Holy Spirit who would carry the work forward (*Matt.* 28:19, 20). Given Jesus' command that baptism be administered in the name of the triune God, we should not consider the baptism practised by today's Trinity-denying cults a true baptism, any more than seventeenth-century Christians considered baptism as practised by Socinians, or others who denied the Trinity, true baptism.

Dipping, pouring, and sprinkling

A sacrament involves an element (such as water), words of institution ('I baptize you . . .'), and an action. While most Protestants agree on the use of water for baptism and the need for words of institution, they disagree about the mode of baptism: how should the water of baptism be applied to the person being baptized? Should a person be dipped or immersed under the water, or should the water be put on him, either by pouring or by sprinkling? Baptist story-Bibles picture John or Philip immersing new converts; Reformed story-Bibles picture them scooping up water and pouring or sprinkling it on their heads.

Clearly many Christians today believe that in Christian baptism a person must be dipped into the water. The Westminster assembly did not want to exclude this mode of baptism, or to deny that those who have been immersed have a valid form of baptism. Nonetheless, the assembly's summary of biblical teaching is clear, both when it says that 'dipping of the person into the water is not necessary', and when it states that 'baptism is rightly administered by pouring, or sprinkling water upon the person'.

As it happens, the word 'baptism' does not imply any one kind of mode. It simply means 'washing' and washing can be symbolic (with a little liquid), or real (with a lot of it). There are, in fact, scriptural indications that baptismal washing often involved a little water, rather than a lot, and the Westminster assembly, in the scriptural passages it cites, presents four places where this appears to be the case.

That baptismal washing sometimes referred to water poured on a part of the body, or sprinkled on something, is suggested, in the first place, by the everyday use of the term in New Testament times. The Gospel of Mark explains how Jews did not eat after being in the market place unless they had baptized (or washed). In fact Mark 7:4 adds that they also baptized 'cups, pots, copper vessels and dining couches'. There is no body of evidence to suggest that Jews immersed themselves before meals, or immersed their furniture. They probably washed their hands and possessions with some water.

Second, there were times when too many people were baptized to permit immersion. Acts 2:41 tells us that 3,000 people were baptized on one day in Jerusalem. It is hardly possible that in such a dry climate the Jews would allow Christians to use and to pollute the amount of water necessary for so many baptismal immersions.

Third, there were times when baptism happened too quickly, it seems, to have involved immersion. The Philippian prison warden came to faith in the middle of the night and 'he was baptized at once, he and all his family' (*Acts* 16:33). The language of immediate baptism does not suggest that they went through the city and were baptized at the river, or a pool. Paul probably reached for a jug or a bowl and, after explaining baptism, poured or sprinkled water on these new converts.

Fourth, baptismal washing also has an important background in Old Testament washings. The New Testament calls these ceremonies where sacrificial blood was sprinkled 'baptisms'. We see this in Hebrews 9:10. In that verse the Bible speaks of various baptisms (or washings), and then in subsequent verses lists some of the bloody baptisms of the Old Testament, and tells us that they symbolized the forgiveness of sins (*Heb.* 9:19-22). Thus not only does the Greek word for baptismal washings frequently not refer to immersion, it usually refers in the Bible to something else—namely, sprinkling or pouring.

Nonetheless, what is most significant to note is that the actions of sprinkling and pouring repeatedly symbolize the divine work of salvation in the Bible in a way that immersion simply does not. The coming of the Holy Spirit is symbolized by anointing, by being poured out. Forgiveness is symbolized by sprinkling (*Heb.* 9:19-22). So too is sanctification, for we are told to 'draw near with a true heart in full assurance of faith, with our hearts sprinkled clean from an evil conscience and our bodies washed with pure water' (*Heb.* 10:22). The only plausible picture of immersion in baptism is that of Romans 6 or Colossians 2, but arguably it is plausible to us because we think of burials vertically, six feet under the ground, whereas in hard Palestinian soil burials were often effected horizontally, behind a rock in a cave. It is for that reason that we find the weight of biblical testimony tilting us consistently toward the Westminster assembly's conclusion: 'dipping of the person into the water is not necessary; but baptism is rightly administered by pouring, or sprinkling water upon the person'.

Historic Text	*Modern Version*
28.4 Not only those that do actually profess faith in, and obedience unto Christ,[1] but also the infants of one, or both believing parents, are to be baptized.[m]	**28.4** Not only those who personally profess faith in and obedience to Christ, but also the infants of one or both believing parents, are to be baptized.

Scripture Proofs

28.4 [1] Mark 16:15,16; Acts 8:37,38. [m] Gen. 17:7,9, with Gal. 3:9,14, and Col. 2:11,12, and Acts 2:38,39, and Rom. 4:11,12; 1 Cor. 7:14; Matt. 28:19; Mark 10:13-16; Luke 18:15.

Baptizing believers

In paragraph 4, the assembly discusses one point that no Christian disputes and one point that many Christians dispute: we all agree that baptism is for those who believe; we do not all agree that baptism is also for believers' children.

In the book of Acts we see that when people received the Word of God, when they believed the preaching about the kingdom of God, when their hearts were opened to attend to what God was saying to them, then those unbaptized people were baptized (*Acts* 2:41; 8:12, 13; 16:14, 15).[1] The

---

[1] It is ironic that one of the least controversial of all the confession's statements (that believers are to be baptized) leans on the most doubtful pair of all the confession's

emphasis in all of these passages is on faith before baptism, and so the Westminster assembly here refers to the 'believing' (WCF 28.4) and later refers simply to 'believers' (WCF 29.1, 29.7).

Explicit in all of these New Testament episodes is a requirement of faith in Jesus as the Saviour. It is also true that implicit in each of these episodes is a commitment to Jesus as the Lord. Certainly it is hard to imagine a New Testament baptism taking place where a new convert was willing to trust Jesus as the Christ, but not submit to him as the King.

And yet it is worth noting that these passages, and others which could be cited, can only confirm by biblical example a doctrine of *adult* baptism. There are no explicit examples of children being baptized in the New Testament. All identified persons baptized in the New Testament are adults, perhaps none of them under the age of thirty. We are not told that the Philippian jailor had a college-aged daughter who was baptized with him, or that Lydia had twin ten-year olds who came to faith. The fact is that Philip did not meet a couple of teenage joggers along the road; he met a diplomat in a chariot. We see adults coming to faith and being baptized. We see adults asking about baptism and being told about Jesus Christ. And that is all.

If we are to build our theology on explicit proof texts, we must stop with adult believers' baptism. It takes additional work to arrive even at a principle of all believers' baptism. Thankfully no one does stop with adult baptism. First, Christians assume that in the five mass baptisms and four household baptisms mentioned in the New Testament younger people came to faith and were baptized. Second, and more significantly, Christians make a theological judgment—we make a theological inference that goes beyond the raw data of the New Testament—in order to arrive at the very sensible conclusion that all unbaptized believers ought to be baptized, no matter what their age. The practice of baptizing children of *any* age is a doctrinal deduction from scriptural examples, rather than the explicit teaching of Scripture.

proof texts: *Mark* 16:15, 16 and *Acts* 8:37, 38. In no other footnote in the confession is every scriptural support derived from weak manuscript evidence. As is always the case, rare questions about isolated biblical texts never result in real questions about Christian doctrine, and the point made with the assembly's choice of texts is easily established elsewhere, such as in *Acts* 2:41; 8:12, 13; 16:14, 15.

Covenantal continuity

There are no stories of children or teens being baptized in the New Testament, or toddlers or babies for that matter. So what are we to do about all the children in our churches? The Westminster assembly, following the ancient understanding of God's people, concluded that children of believers are to receive sacramental signs as well as the believers themselves. 'Not only' the faithful, 'but also'—to take what was originally the most common and now the more controversial case among Protestants—'the infants of one, or both believing parents, are to be baptized' too.

In drawing this conclusion the assembly again employs theological reasoning, although it is reasoning that involves both Testaments of the Bible and makes a much stronger case than the argument for believers' baptism from New Testament examples only. Rather than turn to the mass baptisms or household baptisms of the New Testament, the assembly's footnote here draws together five texts of Scripture in order to make a basic argument about baptism, beginning with Genesis 17.

It is in Genesis 17 that the covenant Lord established a relationship with Abraham, the head of his family, and through Abraham with his 'offspring'. The bond between God and Abraham is described as an 'everlasting covenant', a God-initiated multi-generational arrangement (*Gen.* 17:7, 9). Remarkably, as we read from Genesis to Galatians, we discover that the blessing God offered to Abraham is not restricted to his biological family. As the Apostle Paul explains, 'those who are of faith are blessed along with Abraham, the man of faith'. Actually, 'in Christ Jesus the blessing of Abraham' is to 'come to the Gentiles' (*Gal.* 3:9, 14). Paul's inclusion of new covenant people in the old covenant community provides the theological skeleton on which our doctrine of church membership and sacraments is to be fleshed out. It is because we are inheriting a family-centred covenant rather than an individual-centred covenant that we continue to apply the covenantal entry-sign of baptism much as we applied the covenantal entry-sign of circumcision.

Little surprise, then, that the next stop along the assembly's whistle-stop Bible tour is Colossians 2:11, 12, where a parallel between circumcision and baptism is explicitly made by the Apostle Paul. In this passage

Paul preaches the inadequacy of the world, the sufficiency of Christ, and the Christian's union with Christ. Along the way Paul speaks about Christ's sufficiency and our union with him in symbolic terms: in him we are circumcised, putting off the flesh by the circumcision of Christ; in him we are baptized, raised to new life. What makes this gracious parallel so significant is that both sacraments picture redemptive realities that come through Christ alone.

There is substantial biblical continuity both in the plan of redemption, and in the sacraments that emblemize that redemption (WCF 7.6 and 27.5). That is why Peter could both preach words of promise about repentance and baptism, forgiveness and the gift of the Holy Spirit— and 'promise' that the gospel and its symbolism 'is for you and for your children and for all who are far off, everyone whom the Lord our God calls to himself' (*Acts* 2:39).

Peter's words could easily have been addressed to Abraham or his descendants. Instead, at that most unusual of all Pentecosts, they were addressed to those who could become Abraham's descendants by faith. This wide-embracing view of the covenant was, as ever, according to plan. As Paul wrote to the Romans, God's 'purpose was to make [Abraham] the father of all who believe without being circumcised, so that righteousness would be counted to them as well, and to make him the father of the circumcised who are not merely circumcised but who also walk in the footsteps of the faith that our father Abraham had before he was circumcised' (*Rom.* 4:11, 12).

Baptizing infants

With that background in place, the assembly's footnote helps us to understand three further statements and actions which have a bearing on children as the recipients of God's blessing.

First, Paul states in 1 Corinthians 7:14 that there is a sense in which the children of even one believing parent are made holy—they are set apart from the world—by God.

Second, New Testament texts commanding baptism are always more, and not less, inclusive than circumcision. The assembly could have noted that in the New Testament (unlike the Old) females, and not only males, can receive the new covenant sign. Instead, it observes that in the Great Commission the disciples of all the nations, and not simply Jewish disciples, are to be baptized (*Matt.* 28:19). The only hard evidence that the Bible offers indicates an expansion of the set of all people who may be baptized. Why should some Christians insist on a contraction by removing children from the covenant?

Third, both Mark 10:13-16 and Luke 18:15 tell the story of Jesus' reaction to parents who brought their infants and children to be touched by him. The disciples thought that he would be too busy with adults to bother with children; too busy healing and teaching to make time for blessing them. That proved to be an error, for Jesus took 'them in his arms and blessed them, laying his hands on them' (*Mark* 10:16).

In deciding whether to include children, even infants, in household baptisms, Reformed Christians have always found sufficient evidence in the five realities seen in these biblical passages: (1) the continuity of the covenant of grace, (2) the parallels between baptism and circumcision, (3) the setting apart of believers and their children, (4) the expansion, rather than the contraction of that covenant, and (5) Jesus' willingness to richly bless children brought to him by parents who trusted in him. Those who are children of Abraham by faith, just like those who were once children of Abraham by birth, should give their children the sign and seal of the gospel, and pray that they will come to understand and believe the gospel their parents hold so dear.

Historic Text	*Modern Version*
28.5 Although it be a great sin, to contemn, or neglect this ordinance,[n] yet grace and salvation are not so inseparably annexed unto it, as that no person can be regenerated or saved, without it;[o] or, that all that are baptized, are undoubtedly regenerated.[p]	**28.5** Although it is a great sin to despise or neglect this ordinance, nevertheless, grace and salvation are not so inseparably connected with it that a person cannot be regenerated or saved without it. Neither is it true that all who are baptized are undoubtedly regenerated.
28.6 The efficacy of baptism is not tied to that moment of time, wherein it is	**28.6** The efficacy of baptism is not tied to that moment of time when it

administered;^q yet, notwithstanding, by the right use of this ordinance, the grace promised, is not only offered, but really exhibited, and conferred, by the Holy Ghost, to such (whether of age, or infants) as that grace belongs unto, according to the counsel of God's own will, in his appointed time.^r

is administered. Nevertheless, by the right use of this ordinance, the grace promised is not only offered but really exhibited and conferred by the Holy Spirit to all (whether adults or infants) to whom that grace belongs, according to the counsel of God's own will, in his appointed time.

28.7 The sacrament of baptism is but once to be administered unto any person.^s

28.7 The sacrament of baptism is to be administered only once to any person.

Scripture Proofs

28.5 ⁿ Luke 7:30, with Exod. 4:24-26.   ^o Rom. 4:11; Acts 10:2,4,22,31,45,47. ^p Acts 8:13,23.

  28.6 ^q John 3:5,8. ^r Gal. 3:27; Titus 3:5; Eph. 5:25,26; Acts 2:38,41.

  28.7 ^s Titus 3:5.

Neglecting baptism

The reasons for despising ('contemning') baptism are almost as varied as the persons who neglect the ordinance. In the medieval period, and even more so in the sixteenth century, there were those who thought it was more spiritual to abandon baptism than to partake of it. Today, carelessness about baptism often accompanies negligence about church membership. But whatever the reason, it is a great sin to neglect baptism, for the neglect of the sign is perilously close to the neglect of the reality which it represents.

Jesus had no words to commend the Pharisees and lawyers who snubbed the baptism of John. Indeed he said that they 'rejected the purpose of God for themselves' in rejecting the sign of baptism (*Luke* 7:30). Moses (or his son) was almost killed by God at a road-side camp for neglecting to circumcise his son (*Exod.* 4:24-26). In reflecting on episodes like these the Westminster assembly clearly concluded that it is wrong to disregard baptism either for adults or for children. It is no less problematic to neglect baptism in the New Testament era than it was to neglect circumcision in the Old.

An inseparable annex?

Baptism is so basic for believers and their children that it is a 'great sin' to neglect it, either by over-spiritualizing the sacrament, or by ignoring it, or by opposing infant baptism. Nevertheless, it is not so critical in its importance that 'grace and salvation are . . . inseparably annexed' or joined to it. In other words, it is possible to be 'regenerated or saved without it'.

Here the analogy between circumcision and baptism is once again useful. In Romans 4 the Apostle Paul makes a point of the fact that Abraham received circumcision as a Gentile (*Rom.* 4:11). Circumcision was a sacramental sign that sealed a righteousness which the patriarch already had, by faith, as an uncircumcised man. Obviously, then, one can be a believer without having the sign and seal of the promise, and there is every reason to think that what was true for the exemplar of old covenant believers is just as true for ordinary new covenant believers.[1]

In fact the assembly offers the case of Cornelius in Acts 10 as a good example of a person identified as a believer but not yet baptized. He is introduced to us as a godly Gentile. By the end of the chapter he had received Peter's praise, Peter's preaching, and the gift of the Holy Spirit. Only then did the Christians decide that they could not withhold the water of baptism from a man who had shared in all the blessings of baptized believers (*Acts* 10:2, 4, 22, 31, 45, 47). Clearly baptism was not required for salvation.

Baptismal regeneration?

Adults should not seek baptism unless they have sufficient evidence that they are born again. As argued earlier, this is not necessary for their children. Indeed, it is possible that the Holy Spirit could make elect infants new creatures even as the sign of new life is being applied to them. At least one member of the assembly thought that this would be the norm. However, it remains to be said in this corrective paragraph that not 'all

---

[1] Paul goes on to say in the second half of the verse that Abraham was made 'the father of all who believe without being circumcised', but as the apostle is referring to Christians who would presumably have been baptized, it is safe to conclude that it is the first half of the verse, and not the second, which is intended to support the assembly's point.

that are baptized are undoubtedly regenerated', and the assembly recalls the sad story of Simon Magus to demonstrate the truth of this assertion. Simon believed the gospel, and was baptized, before it became obvious that he had not truly believed the gospel at all, but simply wanted the power of the apostles for himself. Peter judged that Simon was in the 'gall of bitterness and in the bond of iniquity' (*Acts* 8, esp. verses 13 and 23). This is not the kind of description which the apostles reserved for the regenerate.

When is baptism useful?

In maintaining that those who are baptized are not always regenerated, the Westminster assembly also held that 'the efficacy of baptism is not tied to that moment of time wherein it is administered'. Christians have often wanted more consistency and predictability in God's gracious blessing of the sacraments than he is willing to give. In a sense, we have tried to tame the Spirit and to harness his work to baptism or to the Lord's supper. He will never permit this. Surely one of the lessons that Nicodemus was to have taken home with him from his evening encounter with Jesus was that the Holy Spirit was not to be scheduled. We need to be 'born of water and the Spirit' to 'enter the kingdom of God'. Nonetheless, the movement of the Spirit is as free as the wind: 'the wind blows where it wishes, and you hear its sound, but you do not know where it comes from or where it goes. So it is with everyone who is born of the Spirit' (*John* 3:5, 8). He will not tether his work to his sacraments.

'Yet, notwithstanding' all these qualifiers, the sacrament of baptism does have a purpose. It is a means of exhibiting or conferring 'the grace promised' (see WCF 27.3). As indicated previously, the ordinance needs to be properly used: it is not be used as a talisman or good luck charm; it is to be accompanied by an explanatory word of institution. Nonetheless, when a right use of baptism is made, God's promised grace 'is not only offered' but actually 'exhibited' (or presented) and 'conferred' by the Holy Spirit. It is conferred to adults (people 'of age') or infants. It is a means of grace. It is conferred to all people to whom 'grace belongs', 'according to the counsel of God's own will'. And it is conferred 'in his appointed time'.

Obviously the Westminster divines are shying away from any suggestion that baptism works invariably and automatically. It is a tool of the Holy Spirit and works when *he* chooses and not when *we* choose. But the assembly is calling Christians to recognize that baptism really is a tool, and that the Holy Spirit often chooses to use it—so much so that to the Galatians Paul could say that 'as many of you as were baptized into Christ have put on Christ' (*Gal.* 3:27); to Titus Paul could link 'the washing of regeneration and the renewal of the Holy Spirit' (*Titus* 3:5); to the Ephesians Paul could say that Christ sanctified his church, 'having cleansed her' not only 'with the word' but 'by the washing of water' (*Eph.* 5:25, 26); to a crowd drawn from many countries Peter could say, 'Repent and be baptized every one of you in the name of Jesus Christ for the forgiveness of your sins' (*Acts* 2:38); and to the church of all the ages Luke could say that 'those who received' Peter's preaching 'were baptized', and it was upon that reception and that baptism that the apostles were willing to conclude that souls were added to the church that day (*Acts* 2:41). The Holy Spirit can use the visible word to preach to us, just as he can use the audible word, and he has often done so.

Baptized once

It remains to be said that 'the sacrament of baptism is but once to be administered unto any person'. Just as the 'renewal of the Holy Spirit' is a one-time event, so is the 'washing of regeneration' that signifies this renewal (*Titus* 3:5). Nowhere in the New Testament do we see people being rebaptized, except for the people whom Paul found in Ephesus who had known only the baptism of John the Baptist.

Admittedly, it is puzzling to consider what baptism should mean to us when it was not used or intended rightly (as in the Roman Catholic Church), and yet the person baptized later becomes a believer. It is also troubling to think that some people falsely confess faith and are baptized as hypocrites, perhaps only later coming to true faith. Such cases remind us that the church is to labour to avoid both improper baptisms and the baptism of improper subjects. Nonetheless, if we understand the point of the previous paragraph, we will see that the Holy Spirit can use baptism—even deficient baptisms—as he wills. God's grace has a priority over the intention and manner of administration and over the truth or falsity of a profession. God's grace is displayed in baptism and needs to be displayed only once.

CHAPTER 29:

OF THE LORD'S SUPPER

Historic Text

29.1 Our Lord Jesus, in the night wherein he was betrayed, instituted the sacrament of his body and blood, called the Lord's supper, to be observed in his church, unto the end of the world, for the perpetual remembrance of the sacrifice of himself, in his death; the sealing all benefits thereof unto true believers, their spiritual nourishment and growth in him, their further engagement in, and to, all duties which they owe unto him; and, to be a bond, and pledge of their communion with him, and with each other, as members of his mystical body.[a]

Modern Version

29.1 Our Lord Jesus, on the night when he was betrayed, instituted the sacrament of his body and blood, called the Lord's supper. It is to be observed in his church until the end of the age for the perpetual remembrance of the sacrifice of himself in his death, for the sealing of all the benefits of that death unto true believers, for their spiritual nourishment and growth in him, for their increased commitment to perform all the duties which they owe to him, and for a bond and pledge of their fellowship with him and with each other as members of his mystical body.

Scripture Proofs

29.1 [a] 1 Cor. 11:23-26; 1 Cor. 10:16,17,21; 1 Cor. 12:13.

The sacrament of body and blood

One reason for the particular poignancy of the Lord's supper in the life of the Christian church is its birthdate: this sacrament came into being the night Jesus was betrayed. The Gospel histories highlight this fact. The Apostle Paul recalls this context again in his letter to the Corinthians. And Paul in turn was only delivering what he had received from the Lord himself. Here, in a paragraph which paraphrases a passage from Paul's Epistle to the Corinthians, the Westminster assembly brings us back once again to the night of the betrayal. In returning to that scene, we are reminded of all the cardinal truths about this supper and what it represents.

First, it was our Lord Jesus who instituted this new sacrament. No one less than Jesus could and did replace the Passover meal with another meal. No one less than Jesus could and did command the Christian church to celebrate a meal that centred completely on himself. As Paul explained to the Corinthians, this meal is 'the table of the Lord' and 'the cup of the Lord'; it is 'the Lord's supper' and we are to observe the meal as he requires (*1 Cor.* 10:21; 11:20).

Second, it was on that night that Jesus instituted a sacrament of 'his body and blood'. This is a striking phrase, not popular in Protestant churches today, but historically very accurate in its emphasis. When Jesus instituted the Lord's supper, he showed, he ate, and he drank the elements of bread and wine. But his words emphasized not the elements of the supper, but the reality they represented. For what did Jesus say? 'This is my body which is for you.' 'This cup is the new covenant in my blood' (*1 Cor.* 11:24, 25; *cf. Matt.* 26:26-28; *Mark* 14:22-24; *Luke* 22:19, 20).

Third, the sacrament of Christ's body and blood is 'to be observed in his church'. This is a point which paragraph three will take up in greater detail, but it is evident enough in the very context in which the Lord's supper was originally delivered. This meal was not given to Peter, James, and John—a few favourite friends of Jesus. It was given to all the disciples (*Matt.* 26:20; *Mark* 14:17; *Luke* 22:14, 15). It is to be observed, or performed, in the church.

Fourth, this supper is to be observed until 'the end of the world'. Christians have always understood that when Jesus twice told his disciples to remember him, that he intended a 'perpetual remembrance of the sacrifice of himself in his death'. This is why the Apostle Paul repeated both of Jesus' calls to remembrance, and then concluded by saying that 'as often as you eat this bread and drink the cup, you proclaim the Lord's death until he comes' (*1 Cor.* 11:24-26). It is unthinkable that Christians would forget Christ's sacrifice. On the contrary, we proclaim his death until he returns, not only with our words, but also with his supper.

Fifth, a return to the events of that dark night helps us to see that Jesus was promising benefits to true believers. We celebrate the supper not only in remembrance of Christ's sacrifice of himself, but also in remembrance that Jesus promised his body for us, and that his bloody covenant is with us (*1 Cor.* 11:24, 25). Jesus gave himself in our place, and for our sake, and the supper was designed to keep this glorious fact before our eyes. It is because the supper serves as a seal of the benefits and treasures of redemption that Paul refers to the wine as 'the cup of blessing' (*1 Cor.* 10:16; for 'sealing' see WCF 27.1).

Sixth, this supper is to be observed for our 'spiritual nourishment and growth' in Christ. We can see from the Gospels that the Lord's supper was, at least in part, a ceremonial addition to an existing meal. It was not a normal meal. It was not intended for bodily nourishment and growth. Paul had to remind the Corinthians of this because they were hurrying to serve themselves so that they would have enough to eat (*1 Cor.* 11:17-22). That is one reason why we need to remember that Jesus took the symbolic cup and used it as an emblem of his own sacrifice '*after* supper' (*Luke* 22:20; *1 Cor.* 11:25). The Lord's supper is like a good sermon: it is intended as food for the soul.

Seventh, we are to celebrate the Lord's supper for our 'further engagement in, and to, all duties' which we owe to him. In saying this the Westminster assembly is not drawing on a particular passage in Scripture. The gathering is simply noting the gratitude that guilty Christians show in response to grace. In realizing that Jesus not only gave us himself, but also gave us this abiding reminder of his gospel, we are moved to thought and action. We are renewed in our commitment to Christ and in the service that we owe him. These are reasons enough to observe the supper; nonetheless, participation in this meal is also a profession of exclusive loyalty to Jesus Christ that implies submission to his lordship alone. After all, as Paul warned the Corinthians, 'You cannot drink the cup of the Lord and the cup of demons. You cannot partake of the table of the Lord and the table of demons' (*1 Cor.* 10:21).

Eighth, the Lord's supper is to be observed in the church as a powerful symbol of our communion with Christ, by his Holy Spirit. We can see that this meal is communal by thinking about its first participants: the disciples were there communing with Jesus. Naturally, Jesus was there with those disciples in a way that he is not with later disciples. Nonetheless, Jesus Christ is present with us by his Spirit in this supper (see WCF 29.7), a fact which is central to one of the proof-texts proffered by the authors of this confession. In fact Paul speaks of Christians partaking of the cup as those who 'drink of one Spirit' (*1 Cor.* 12:13). He also refers to the act of drinking the cup as 'a participation' or 'fellowship in the blood of Christ', and the act of breaking bread as 'a participation' or 'fellowship in the body of Christ' (*1 Cor.* 10:16).

Ninth, recollection of that first supper and reflection on 1 Corinthians 10 are clearly calculated by God to underscore the closeness of our communion not only with Christ, but with Christians. The disciples communed with Christ at the last supper, but they also communed with one another. And while 1 Corinthians 10:16 stresses our union with Christ in this supper, 1 Corinthians 10:17 stresses our union with other believers in this same supper: 'Because there is one bread, we who are many are one body, for we all partake of the one bread'. This unity with one another in Christ, reinforced in this supper, is also a unity with one another in the Spirit. Just as 'in one Spirit we were all baptized into one body' so also, now with reference to the Lord's supper, 'all were made to drink of one Spirit' (*1 Cor.* 12:13). No wonder that the assembly concluded that the sacrament of Christ's body and blood is to be observed as 'a bond and pledge of their communion with him, and with each other, as members of his mystical body'. The meal so often called the last supper was really the first supper.

Historic Text	*Modern Version*
29.2 In this sacrament Christ is not offered up to his Father; nor, any real sacrifice made at all, for remission of sins of the quick or dead;[b] but only a commemoration of that one offering up of himself, by himself, upon the cross, once for all: and, a spiritual oblation of all possible praise unto God, for the same:[c] So that, the popish sacrifice of the mass (as they call it) is most abominably injurious to Christ's one, only sac-	**29.2** In this sacrament Christ is not offered up to his Father, nor is any real sacrifice made at all for the forgiveness of the sins of the living or the dead. Instead, this sacrament is only a commemoration of that one sacrifice by which Christ offered himself on the cross once for all. The sacrament is a spiritual offering of the highest praise to God for that sacrifice. So, the Roman Catholic sacrifice of the mass (as they

rifice, the alone propitiation for all the sins of his elect.[d]

call it) is a detestable insult to Christ's one and only sacrifice, which is the only propitiation for all the sins of his elect.

Scripture Proofs

29.2 [b] Heb. 9:22,25,26,28. [c] 1 Cor. 11:24-26; Matt. 26:26,27. [d] Heb. 7:23,24,27; Heb. 10:11,12,14,18.

Not an offering, not a sacrifice

Having once charted out what the Lord's supper is, the confession now adds comments about what it is not. It is not, in the first place, an offering. 'In this sacrament Christ is not offered up to his Father'. In fact, in the ceremony of the supper, there is not 'any real sacrifice made at all'. Jesus is not given up once more either for the forgiveness of the sins of the living, or of the dead, or for any other purposes.

As students of history will know, the Westminster assembly is here refuting the notion of a 'sacrifice of the mass'. As students of world religions should know, this continues to be an abiding error in the sacramental theory of the Roman Catholic Church. As students of the Bible surely know, that Christ can ever be sacrificed again is denied in the most emphatic terms in the New Testament, especially in Hebrews 9.

First, in contrast to the old covenant regime, Jesus has no intention to 'offer himself repeatedly', or to 'suffer repeatedly'. The very thought is absurd to the author of Hebrews. We see this in Hebrews 9:25, 26.

Second, there is no way of improving or adding to a finished work. Jesus 'has appeared once for all at the end of the ages to put away sin by the sacrifice of himself'. Nothing more will ever be needed. There is only one Christian sacrifice and it is seen on the cross and not in a supper. We see this in Hebrews 9:26.

Third, the so-called bloodless 'sacrifice' that is supposedly offered in the Roman Catholic mass can have no merit because 'without the shedding of blood there is no forgiveness of sins'. We see this in Hebrews 9:22.

A commemorative offering or a commemoration of an offering?

The second point made in this second paragraph is that this sacrament is not a commemorative offering but a 'commemoration' of an offering. Roman Catholics under siege will describe the mass merely as a commemorative offering of Jesus—a memorial offering. Given the stern statements of Hebrews 9, the Westminster assembly is right to see the supper instead as a commemoration of an offering—the one offering up of Jesus himself, by himself, upon his cross, once in history for all time. That is why Jesus kept saying that Christians are to observe the supper in his remembrance (*1 Cor.* 11:24-26): because it is that important, and because it will not be repeated.

By its very nature the Lord's supper is the kind of commemoration which is also a 'spiritual oblation'. Christians engage in this supper, like Christ, by blessing God and giving thanks (*Matt.* 26:26, 27). As it is a meal which offers spiritual rather than physical benefit, in doing so we are giving thanks for Jesus more than we are giving thanks for wheat or wine. We are offering a heartfelt sacrifice of praise to God for Jesus. We are publicly proclaiming the good news of what Jesus has done, which is yet another way of offering praise (*1 Cor.* 11:26). Nonetheless, it is praise that we offer again and again in the supper, not Jesus. The meal remains a commemoration.

It is for that reason that Reformation-era theologians protested effectively against what some major medieval theologians had earlier protested *in*effectively: the 'popish sacrifice of the mass'. And for those reasons it is not an exaggeration to say that the mass 'is most abominably injurious to Christ's one, only sacrifice, the alone propitiation for all the sins of his elect'. The 'sacrifice' of the mass requires the return to a temporary priesthood, while we have priests enough in the one permanent priest who is Christ (*Heb.* 7:23, 24). The 'sacrifice' of the mass calls for continued offerings when Christ has 'once for all . . . offered up himself' (*Heb.* 7:27).

So let us listen to the Scriptures! They tell us that Jesus 'offered for all time a single sacrifice for sins'. Let us trust the Word of God, which tells us that after Jesus offered himself and completed his work, 'he sat down at the right hand of God' (*Heb.* 10:11, 12). Let us never drift into a church that ceremonially re-sacrifices Christ when 'by a single offering he has perfected for all time those who are being sanctified' (*Heb.* 10:14). Let us not look for grace or forgiveness mediated through the mass when we find it directly from Christ himself.

After writing eloquently about the end of daily sacrifices in the final sacrifice of Christ, the author of the letter to the Hebrews reflected on what this means for Christians who will one day be summoned to meet God. By the inspiration of the Spirit, he was brought to recall two promises of God in Jeremiah 31:33 and 34. In the first, God promised to put his law on our hearts and write it on our minds. In the second, he added, 'I will remember their sins and their lawless deeds no more.'

If that is the essence of God's gracious covenant with us, then, as Hebrews 10:18 rightly states, 'where there is forgiveness of these, there is no longer any offering for sin'. The Lord's supper witnesses to what Christ has already done—the one who is the only propitiation, the only wrath-remover, for all God's chosen ones.

Historic Text	*Modern Version*
29.3 The Lord Jesus has, in this ordinance, appointed his ministers to declare his word of institution to the people; to pray, and bless the elements of bread and wine, and thereby to set them apart from a common to an holy use; and, to take, and break the bread, to take the cup, and (they communicating also themselves) to give both to the communicants;[e] but, to none who are not then present in the congregation.[f]	**29.3** In this ordinance the Lord Jesus has appointed his ministers to declare his word of institution to the people; to pray and consecrate the elements of bread and wine, and so set them apart from a common to a holy use; and to take and break the bread, take the cup, and give both to the communicants, and to partake with the congregation. But they are not to give the elements to any who are not then present in the congregation.
29.4 Private masses or receiving this sacrament by a priest or any other, alone;[g] as likewise, the denial of the cup to the people,[h] worshipping the elements, the lifting them up or carrying them about for adoration, and the reserving them	**29.4** Private masses—or receiving this sacrament from a priest or anyone else, alone—are contrary to the nature of the sacrament and to the institution of Christ. For the same reasons it is forbidden to deny the cup to the members

for any pretended religious use, are all contrary to the nature of this sacrament, and to the institution of Christ.[i]

of the congregation, to worship the elements, to lift them up or carry them around for adoration, or to reserve them for any supposedly religious use.

Scripture Proofs

29.3 [e] Matt. 26:26-28, and Mark 14:22-24, and Luke 22:19-20, with 1 Cor. 11:23-26. [f] Acts 20:7; 1 Cor. 11:20.

29.4 [g] 1 Cor. 10:16. [h] Mark 14:23; 1 Cor. 11:25-29. [i] Matt. 15:9.

Celebrating the supper

Having defined the essence of the supper in paragraphs 1 and 2, the confession gives directions for its celebration in paragraphs 3 and 4. The assembly's teaching is drawn from the fourfold summary of the first supper recorded in the Gospels of Matthew, Mark and Luke, and in Paul's First Epistle to the Corinthians (*Matt.* 26:26-28; *Mark* 14:22-24; *Luke* 22:19, 20; *1 Cor.* 11:23-26). In these passages we find three key features.

First, Jesus, serving as the prime minister of the new covenant, declared his word of institution—he directed the disciples, telling them what to do and when, and explaining what the elements and actions meant. His disciples then passed the Lord's instructions on to other disciples, although the subject of the supper was important enough for the Apostle Paul to have received instructions on the supper directly from the risen Christ (*1 Cor.* 11:23).

Second, an essential element in the celebration of the supper is prayer, as we can see from Jesus' own example. Our prayers are to include a petition for the blessing of the elements, that God would set apart what is common for a holy purpose. We are to ask that God would take the ordinary bread and ordinary wine and bless it by his Holy Spirit for extraordinary good.

Third, the minister is 'to take and break' the bread, and 'to take the cup' and, not forgetting to partake of the meal himself, he is to give the supper to all those who are communing with Christ and his people at the supper, just as Christ did on the night when he was betrayed.

Private communion

The last line of the third paragraph specifies that the Lord's supper is not to be received privately. One reason why the Westminster assembly frowned on bringing the bread and wine to persons not present in the worship service, was presented in paragraph 1: this meal is intended to celebrate communion not with Christ only, but also with fellow Christians.

A second related reason why the assembly disapproved of private communion is drawn from the dysfunctional Corinthian church: not only did the individualistic approach of the Corinthian believers earn an apostolic rebuke (*1 Cor.* 11:20; *cf.* 17-22), it also seems to have been the settled pattern of the first Christians to 'gather together to break bread' rather than to eat in isolation (*e.g., Acts* 20:7).

A third reason why the assembly worked to banish the still-popular practice of private communion is suggested in paragraph 2 and clarified in the opening line of paragraph 4: the Roman Catholic Church had long taught the saving efficacy of the mass; priests offered private Masses as a kind of life-line to grace. The assembly considered the continuation of private communion a poor example, even in churches where the theology of the Lord's supper had been corrected. Like the Israelites who were to remember the rebels of the wilderness days, Protestants were to remember the Romanists of the theological wilderness and avoid their ways (*1 Cor.* 10:6).[1]

Pretended religion

Having forbidden private communion, the assembly proceeded to tackle other ceremonial abuses too. The most egregious was the Roman Catholic practice of forbidding people to drink of the cup, lest they should accidentally spill the blood of Christ on the floor of the church. Suffice to say that when Jesus gave the cup, he gave it to all his disciples, both the coordinated and the clumsy (*Mark* 14:23; *1 Cor.* 11:25-29). The practice

---

[1] There may be some cases where a pastor will find it wise to minister to the infirm by bringing bread, wine, and a part of the leadership and membership of the church, to celebrate the supper within the context of a special, small (and usually brief) worship service.

of withholding the cup from the laity was a gradual, natural, and tragic development from the idea that the wine miraculously becomes blood when blessed by the priest—a theory which the assembly confronts in paragraphs 5 and 6.

Actually, any additional ceremonies attached to the supper and required either of those who administer or of those who receive the supper are an offence to God. Bowing down to the elements, lifting up the elements, parading the elements, adoring the elements, storing them for later religious purposes—all of these activities oppose the true nature of the sacrament and subvert the simple institution of Christ. It is vain worship—empty and useless. Yet all of these practices were commanded by the Roman Catholic Church, with penalties for non-conformity. Some of these practices were commanded by the Church of England, with penalties for nonconformity too. Both the Reformation and post-Reformation histories vividly illustrate the drift and the danger to leaders in the church who 'teach as doctrines the commandments of men' (*Matt.* 15:9).

Historic Text	*Modern Version*
29.5 The outward elements, in this sacrament, duly set apart, to the uses ordained by Christ, have such relation to him crucified, as that, truly, yet sacramentally only, they are sometimes called by the name of the things they represent, to wit, the body and blood of Christ;[k] albeit, in substance and nature, they still remain, truly, and only bread and wine, as they were before.[l]	**29.5** The visible elements in this sacrament, when they are properly set apart for the uses ordained by Christ, have such a relationship to Christ crucified that they are sometimes called—truly, but only sacramentally—by the name of the things they represent, namely, the body and blood of Christ. This is true even though in substance and nature they still remain truly and only bread and wine, as they were before.
29.6 That doctrine which maintains a change of the substance of bread and wine, into the substance of Christ's body and blood (commonly called transubstantiation) by consecration of a priest,	**29.6** The doctrine which teaches that the substance of the bread and wine is changed into the substance of Christ's body and blood (commonly called transubstantiation) by the consecration of

or by any other way, is repugnant, not to Scripture alone, but even to common sense and reason; overthrows the nature of the sacrament, and has been, and is, the cause of manifold superstitions; yea, of gross idolatries.ᵐ

a priest, or in any other way, is repugnant not only to Scripture but even to common sense and reason. It overthrows the nature of the sacrament and has been and is the cause of many superstitions and gross idolatries.

Scripture Proofs
 29.5 ᵏ Matt. 26:26-28. ˡ 1 Cor. 11:26-28; Matt. 26:29.
 29.6 ᵐ Acts 3:21, with 1 Cor. 11:24-26; Luke 24:6,39.

A reader's guide to the sacraments

The fifth paragraph of this chapter offers a condensed reader's guide to the sacramental sections of the Bible, one of a number of such guides to Bible readers found in the confession. It is designed to explain the vivid language used in Scripture to describe the Lord's supper: 'The outward elements in this sacrament', the bread and the wine, when 'duly set apart to the uses ordained by Christ', have such a close 'relation to him crucified' that 'they are sometimes called by the name of the things they represent'.

We see this kind of language, for example, in Matthew 26:26-28. There 'Jesus took bread, and after blessing it broke it and gave it to the disciples, and said, "Take, eat; this is my body." And he took a cup, and when he had given thanks he gave it to them, saying, "Drink of it, all of you, for this is my blood of the covenant"'. The Westminster assembly's observation here is that Jesus did not say that the bread was like his body. He did not say that the wine was like his blood. He effectively, and shockingly, told his disciples to eat his body and drink his blood. The Westminster assembly's conclusion here is that what Jesus spoke, he spoke 'truly'. That is to say, there is nothing inappropriate or problematic about this kind of talk. It is just as acceptable for us to use this language today as it was for Jesus to use that language himself. He substituted the reality for the symbol, instead of the symbol for the reality. And so can we.

Evidently Jesus spoke this way because his sacrament and his sacrifice are so closely related; because the symbol chosen by Christ is so perfectly suited to represent himself. Nonetheless Christ's statement (made by a saviour of flesh and blood) was true in a sacramental sense only. That is to say, the bread is a true symbol of Christ's flesh. In 'substance', in 'nature', the bread is bread and the wine is wine.

The interchange between symbol and substance is amply illustrated in 1 Corinthians 11, where Paul moves back and forth between mentioning 'the body and blood of the Lord' (once, referring to the crucifixion and the supper), and eating the bread and drinking the cup (three times, referring to the supper). Since the apostle continues to speak of the bread and cup, this guides our understanding of his references to 'the body and blood of the Lord'. His usage implies that even after these common elements are properly set apart for holy use, 'they still remain truly and only bread and wine, as they were before'.

The trouble with transubstantiation

If the fifth paragraph's instructions on reading biblical language is correct, then the truth of the sixth paragraph carries real force. The Roman Catholic 'doctrine which maintains a change of the substance of bread and wine into the substance of Christ's body and blood (commonly called transubstantiation)' is simply incorrect. The doctrine of transubstantiation teaches that when the elements of bread and wine are consecrated, or ceremonially set apart by a priest, the real substance of the bread and wine changes into flesh and blood even though all the apparent characteristics of the bread and wine do not change. The bread still looks and feels and smells and tastes (and if you drop enough of it on the floor it still sounds) like bread. The wine still tingles on the tongue and smells like the South of France or Napa Valley. But Roman Catholics are taught that it is really Christ's flesh and blood.

Transubstantiation was the dominant theory, but by no means the only theory, employed to explain how the elements of the supper could become the body and blood of the Lord. Here the Westminster assembly is rejecting not just transubstantiation, but any theory that attempted to justify a doctrine of the real physical presence of Christ. Neither the 'consecration of a priest', nor any other special words or actions, are capable of changing the substance of the elements of the Lord's supper. The idea of transubstantiation or any similar theory really is 'repugnant, not to

Scripture alone, but even to common sense and reason'. Without doubt it is contrary to Scripture. After all, as the resurrected Jesus explained to his disciples, he has normal 'flesh and blood' (*Luke* 24:39). As Peter told the 'Men of Israel' in Solomon's portico, heaven has received Jesus and will keep him until all things are restored at the last day (*Acts* 3:21). We celebrate the supper 'in remembrance' of Jesus, but 'remembering' is certainly an odd thing to do if Jesus is actually present with us bodily, first on the table, and then in our mouths (*1 Cor.* 11:24-26). Angels once had to tell people standing around an empty tomb, 'He is not here, but has risen' (*Luke* 24:6). We sometimes need to tell people standing around the Lord's table, 'He is not here, but has ascended.'

Transubstantiation and the family of associated theories are also contrary to common sense. We should not require a simile in order to identify a metaphor. When Jesus stated that the bread or wine was his body or blood, we should not need for him to spell out that he means that the bread or wine 'is like' his body or blood. It is no exaggeration to say that the idea of a physical presence of our Lord in the Lord's supper theologically and linguistically 'overthrows the nature of the sacrament' but also, historically, has been the cause of many superstitions—yes even obscene idolatries.

Historic Text	**Modern Version**
29.7 Worthy receivers outwardly partaking of the visible elements, in this sacrament,[n] do then also, inwardly by faith, really and indeed, yet not carnally and corporally, but spiritually, receive, and feed upon Christ crucified, and all benefits of his death: the body and blood of Christ being then, not corporally or carnally, in, with, or under the bread and wine; yet, as really, but spiritually, present to the faith of believers in that ordinance, as the elements themselves are to their outward senses.[o]	**29.7** Worthy receivers of this sacrament, outwardly partaking of its visible elements, also inwardly by faith—really and indeed, yet not physically but spiritually—receive and feed upon Christ crucified and all the benefits of his death. The body and blood of Christ are not physically in, with, or under the bread and wine; yet in this ordinance the body and blood of Christ are present to the faith of believers in as real a spiritual sense as the bread and wine are to their physical senses.

29.8 Although ignorant, and wicked men receive the outward elements, in this sacrament: yet, they receive not the thing signified thereby; but by their unworthy coming thereunto, are guilty of the body and blood of the Lord to their own damnation. Wherefore, all ignorant, and ungodly persons, as they are unfit to enjoy communion with him, so are they unworthy of the Lord's table; and, cannot without great sin against Christ while they remain such, partake of these holy mysteries,[p] or be admitted thereunto.[q]

29.8 Even if ignorant and wicked men receive the outward elements in this sacrament, yet they do not receive that which is signified by the elements. Rather, by their unworthy coming to the sacrament, they are guilty of the body and blood of the Lord, to their own damnation. Therefore, all ignorant and ungodly people, because they are unfit to enjoy fellowship with the Lord, are also unworthy to participate in the Lord's supper. As long as they remain unworthy, they cannot be admitted to the Lord's table or partake of the holy mysteries without great sin against Christ.

Scripture Proofs
29.7   [n] 1 Cor. 11:28.   [o] 1 Cor. 10:16.
29.8   [p] 1 Cor. 11:27-29; 2 Cor. 6:14-16.   [q] 1 Cor. 5:6,7,13; 2 Thess. 3:6,14,15; Matt. 7:6.

The spiritual presence of Christ in the supper

The remedy to a doctrine of the real physical presence of Christ is not a doctrine of real absence, but a doctrine of spiritual presence, and paragraph 7 presents that old Calvinistic doctrine of the spiritual presence of Christ in the supper. When we are properly receiving the supper (including an examination of ourselves, *1 Cor.* 11:28), we are 'inwardly' partaking of Christ while 'outwardly partaking of the visible elements'. The Apostle Paul calls this 'participating' or 'fellowshipping' in the blood and in the body of Christ (*1 Cor.* 10:16)—a concept which usefully challenges conventional assumptions in evangelicalism that the Lord's supper is merely a memorial moment to remember Jesus.

This participation in Christ in the supper is 'by faith' and 'spiritually'. That is to say, when we come to the supper, trusting afresh in Christ and the triumph of his cross, we find Christ present by his Holy Spirit in the supper. And through this meal we by faith receive him, with all the benefits of his death which are reserved for believers. We feed upon him.

We are nourished by him. And although that receiving and feeding is not carnal or corporal, it is nevertheless real and actual.

To state it a different way, and even more emphatically, 'the body and blood of Christ' is not during the supper 'corporally or carnally, in, with, or under the bread and wine'. Christ is not present in the body or in the flesh. No Catholic, or Lutheran, or 'high Anglican' formula of real presence in the sense of physical presence is correct.[1] Nor are these doctrines necessary! Spiritual does not mean artificial. Spiritual realities are true realities. And so this confession rightly insists that Christ is present 'really but spiritually' in the supper. He is as 'present to the faith of believers in that ordinance, as the elements themselves' are present 'to their outward senses'.

Eating and drinking damnation

Along with the theory that Christ is physically present in the supper, came the puzzle of unworthy participants eating the bread of the supper. Did they partake of Christ in the supper? The early medieval answer to the question was yes, but without benefit. Later theories argued that any participation in the mass had almost automatic benefit. Medieval sceptics about the physical presence, and the Protestant Reformers with them, parodied the theory by asking about the mice. Did mice eating the crumbs that had fallen on the cathedral floor also partake of Christ's body? Unlikely, it seemed. But how could the conclusion be avoided?

The Westminster assembly, like the Reformers before them, concluded that 'ignorant and wicked men receive the outward elements in this sacrament' but 'not the thing signified thereby'. They get food and drink. They do not get the Saviour or any benefit from him.

Nevertheless, not only is there no positive benefit in coming to the table, there is also real harm. As Scripture states clearly, by unworthy participation in the supper, people become 'guilty of the body and blood of the Lord' (*1 Cor.* 11:27; *cf.* verses 27-29). That is to say, they drink to their own damnation. 'Ignorant and ungodly persons . . . are unfit

---

[1] The Roman Catholic understanding of the physical presence of Christ affirms transubstantiation, where the substance of the elements changes, even though their physical properties do not. Anglicans and Lutherans reject transubstantiation, but a subset of them allow for some other kind of physical presence of Christ in his supper.

to enjoy communion with' the Lord and 'so are they unworthy of the Lord's table'. The problem is not simply that unbelievers should not hide in the ranks of believers. It is much deeper than that. This meal speaks of Christian partnership and fellowship and, as Paul asks, 'what partnership has righteousness with lawlessness? Or what fellowship has light with darkness? Christ with Belial? God with idolatry?' (*2 Cor.* 6:14-16). Partaking of 'these holy mysteries' while remaining an unbeliever is not merely a mistake, it is a 'great sin against Christ'. Ministers need to speak words that force a serious rethink for non-Christians who assume they are entitled to partake of Christ's supper.

But why does coming to the table unworthily involve eating and drinking damnation? Why is it a great sin? What is so dangerous about a pretended communion with Christ and his church? The answer is found in the great privilege of partaking of a meal which so perfectly pictures our participation in Christ. It is intended to nourish Christian faith. To come to the table without that Holy-Spirit-worked faith in the Saviour is to try to seize a gift which can only be given. Coming to the table then becomes the personal symbol of a man or a woman's presumption. The supper becomes an emblem of the arrogance of someone who fancies he or she can fellowship with the Father, without coming through his Son.

Out of concern for unbelievers themselves, we warn them not to partake of the table. We also refuse to invite them to the table because those who reject Christ and his church must not be admitted to the fellowship meal designed for those accept him and his people. Here, what is true of the membership of the church is true for the sacrament of the church. What Paul says in 1 Corinthians 5 applies to his discussion in 1 Corinthians 11. 'Do you not know that a little leaven leavens the whole lump? Cleanse out the old leaven that you may be a new lump, as you really are unleavened. For Christ, our Passover lamb, has been sacrificed' (*1 Cor.* 5:6, 7). The church and the table need to be 'purged' (*1 Cor.* 5:13). We must, in the strong words of Jesus for those who reject truth, not 'give dogs what is holy' or 'throw pearls before pigs' (*Matt.* 7:6). As a serious warning to those who are erring, we must avoid fellowship and warn 'any brother' who is idle and unwilling to be instructed—surely a command which sometimes justifies suspending a member of the church from the communion table of the church, and always justifies insisting that those who come to the table be members in good standing with a church that loves and preaches the gospel of the triune God (2 *Thess.* 3:6, 14, 15).

CHAPTER 30:

OF CHURCH CENSURES

Historic Text

30.1 The Lord Jesus, as king and head of his church, has therein appointed a government, in the hand of church officers, distinct from the civil magistrate.[a]

30.2 To these officers, the keys of the kingdom of heaven are committed: by virtue whereof, they have power, respectively, to retain, and remit sins; to shut that kingdom against the impenitent, both by the Word, and censures; and to open it unto penitent sinners, by the ministry of the gospel, and by absolution from censures, as occasion shall require.[b]

Modern Version

30.1 The Lord Jesus, as king and head of his church, has appointed a government in it, to be administered by church officers, distinct from the civil authorities.

30.2 To these church officers he has committed the keys of the kingdom of heaven. For this reason they have authority to retain and to remit sins, to shut the kingdom against the unrepentant both by the Word and by censures, and to open it to repentant sinners by the ministry of the gospel and by releasing from censures, as the occasion requires.

Scripture Proofs

   30.1 [a] Isa. 9:6,7; 1 Tim. 5:17; 1 Thess 5:12; Acts 20:17,28; Heb. 13:7,17,24; 1 Cor. 12:28; Matt. 28:18-20.

   30.2 [b] Matt. 16:19; Matt. 18:17,18; John 20:20-23; 2 Cor. 2:6-8.

The government of the church

The first port of call for a chapter on church censures is the subject of church government. Thus the first paragraph of chapter 30 begins by identifying the governor himself: the Lord, whose name is Jesus.

In his verses about the coming servant king, Isaiah wrote about one who would carry on his shoulders a government, the increase of which would know no end (*Isa.* 9:6, 7). This governor is the 'king and head of his church', the one with 'all authority in heaven and on earth'. He issues the commands, as he did in the Great Commission (*Matt.* 28:18-20). He is the one who appointed New Testament governors and government under himself. It should not need to be said that no mere mortal should seek for himself the title of head of the church, when the actions of our Lord, and the praise of his apostles, give this title to him alone (*Eph.* 1:22; 5:23; *Col.* 1:18).

The governors that Jesus Christ appoints under him are called 'elders' (*1 Tim.* 5:17; *Acts* 20:17, 18) or 'leaders' (*Heb.* 13:7, 17, 24). Here they are simply called 'church officers'. They have the gift of 'governing' or 'administering' (*1 Cor.* 12:28). The Christian church knows them as those who 'labour among' us and 'over' us. They are the people who sometimes 'admonish' us (*1 Thess.* 5:12). These are the hands used by the head of the church.

Christ's government is administered by church officers, distinct from civil magistrates. Historically, the very fact of the independence of church government was resisted by both King and Parliament, for leaders in the state did not want to be accountable to a leadership in the church. Nonetheless, there is no doubt that in the New Testament Christ established a government that was churchly, or ecclesiastical, over Christians, and that government was separate from the civil government.

We know this, historically, because the Roman civil government that was over Christians was opposed to the church, its message, and its work; and biblically, because only the government of the church would do the kind of work God commands elders to do: not just ruling, but preaching and teaching, speaking to us the Word of God, and 'keeping watch over' our souls (*1 Tim.* 5:17, *Heb.* 13:7, 17). The church is not the religious arm of the state; it is an institution distinct from the state and has its own unique purpose.

The keys of the kingdom

The focal point of church government is the power and exercise of what Jesus called 'the keys of the kingdom of heaven'. Here the confession is picking up language used in Matthew 16, where the keys of the kingdom are mentioned in the context of the pre-eminence of Christ. Before all the disciples Peter confessed Jesus as 'the Christ, the Son of the living God'. Our Lord commended him, and with a word play on Peter's name (which means 'rock') he promised, 'on this rock I will build my church, and the gates of Hades will not overcome it' (*Matt.* 16:13-18).

It is a passage that underlines the government of Christ, his power, and rule over the church. Famously it is also the passage where Jesus goes on to declare to his disciples that they would be given 'the keys of the kingdom of heaven': 'whatever you bind on earth', Jesus says, 'will be bound in heaven, and whatever you loose on earth will be loosed in heaven' (*Matt.* 16:19). Jesus gave these keys in Matthew 16 to his disciples, and in them to the governors or officers who rule his church. Church officers are given the task of binding and loosing, or retaining and remitting sins—making judgments as to whether sinners are impenitent, unrepentant, and bound by Satan, or penitent, repentant, and freed for Christ.

The same truth was taught again by our Lord, recorded only two chapters distant, in Matthew 18. There Jesus was again speaking with his disciples, this time giving instruction about church discipline. At the end of the discussion Jesus announced, 'I tell you the truth, whatever you bind on earth will be bound in heaven, and whatever you loose on earth will be loosed in heaven' (*Matt.* 18:17, 18). On yet another occasion, recorded in John 20:23, Jesus told his disciples, 'If you forgive the sins of any, they are forgiven them; if you withhold forgiveness from any, it is withheld' (*John* 20:23).

The message of these three passages is astonishing. It seems to be the plain point of these pronouncements in Matthew 16, 18, and John 20 that it is the responsibility of church officers to judge by the Word of God, as far as is possible, who is going to heaven and who is not. Church governors have power from Christ, 'respectively, to retain and remit sins'. The elders of the church guide the body of Christ in determining whether someone is to be treated as a brother, as an erring brother, or as what Jesus called a Gentile or a tax collector. The elders 'shut that kingdom against the impenitent, both by the Word and censures; and to open it unto penitent sinners, by the ministry of the gospel'. Sometimes, 'as occasion shall require', we leaders must preach stern words, and exercise real discipline. Sometimes, 'as occasion shall require', we must open wide the kingdom by preaching the gospel and offering release from correction. Officers offer what the Westminster assembly calls 'absolution from censures', and what the Apostle Paul calls a turning 'to forgive and comfort' (*2 Cor.* 2:7; *cf.* verses 6-8). Even the most godly church officers are by no means perfect, as we all know, but they are appointed as gatekeepers who, 'as occasion shall require', sometimes shut the kingdom on Christ's behalf.

They do this 'by the Word and by censures'. The preaching of the Word alone lets some people know where they stand before God. The reading and preaching of the Word is the most commonly applied tool of discipline, for it convicts us of sin and drives us to repentance. Usually this is enough for us. Sometimes we need the censures of the church to have matters further clarified for us. Practically, this means that when the officers of a church examine a person for membership in the church, they are making an extremely important decision. They need to decide whether or not they will give someone the assurance that, in their opinion, all is well with their soul. And when the elders travel a long way down the road of church discipline they often have to ask hard questions: does this person's life and testimony so contradict the Word of God that they must be put outside of the church and excluded from a present hope of heaven?

This should carry real significance for the members of the church. If you are a member in good standing in the church of Christ, then this is material for encouragement. Those whom Christ has appointed to look after your eternal welfare have come to the conclusion that there is sufficient reason to think that you are on the narrow road of God's kingdom. And if on the other hand the eldership of a church admonishes a member, or suspends them, disciplines them, or excommunicates them, that member should consider the reasons for such actions with the utmost gravity, and once the matter is made public, every other member must be in prayer for that person incessantly.

Historic Text

30.3 Church censures are necessary, for the reclaiming and gaining of offending brethren, for deterring of others from the like offences, for purging out of that leaven which might infect the whole lump, for vindicating the honour of Christ, and the holy profession of the gospel, and for preventing the wrath of God, which might justly fall upon the church, if they should suffer his covenant, and the seals thereof to be profaned by notorious and obstinate offenders.ᶜ

30.4 For the better attaining of these ends, the officers of the church are to proceed by admonition; suspension from the sacrament of the Lord's supper for a season; and, by excommunication from the church; according to the nature of the crime, and demerit of the person.ᵈ

Modern Version

30.3 Church discipline is necessary for reclaiming and gaining fellow Christians who are guilty of offences, for deterring others from committing similar offences, for purging the leaven which might infect the whole lump, for vindicating the honour of Christ and the holy profession of the gospel, and for averting the wrath of God which might justly fall on the church if it should allow his covenant and its seals to be profaned by notorious and obstinate offenders.

30.4 For the better attaining of these purposes, the officers of the church are to proceed by admonition, by suspension from the sacrament of the Lord's supper for a time, and by excommunication from the church, according to the nature of the offence and the degree of the person's guilt.

Scripture Proofs

30.3   ᶜ 1 Cor. 5:1-13; 1 Tim. 5:20; Matt. 7:6; 1 Tim. 1:20; 1 Cor. 11:27-34, with Jude v. 23.

30.4   ᵈ 1 Thess. 5:12; 2 Thess. 3:6,14,15; 1 Cor. 5:4,5,13; Matt. 18:17; Titus 3:10.

What are church censures for?

Christ has a government in his church and it is called to administer discipline. But what are these censures for? Paragraph 3 summarizes five reasons why church discipline is necessary.

First, it is necessary 'for reclaiming and gaining' the offender. Discipline is intended to help sinners, to draw them back to the Lord. Jude urged Christians to save people 'by snatching them out of the fire' (*Jude* 23). The Apostle Paul told Timothy that Hymenaeus and Alexander were 'handed over to Satan'. Why? So 'that they may learn not to blaspheme' (*1 Tim.* 1:20). The apostle urged the Corinthians to correct a man. Why? 'So that his spirit may be saved in the day of the Lord' (*1 Cor.* 5:5). He warned them about their sinful conduct at what they called the Lord's supper. Why? Because he did not want them to 'eat and drink judgment' on themselves (*1 Cor.* 11:29). He later reminded them that 'when we are judged by the Lord, we are disciplined'. Why? 'So that we may not be condemned along with the world' (*1 Cor.* 11:32).

Second, the chastisements of the church are necessary as a deterrent. Discipline is alarming. It focuses the minds of disciples and often discourages them from following the pattern of an offender. Paul told Timothy that when it came to people 'who persist in sin, rebuke them in the presence of all, so that the rest may stand in fear' (*1 Tim.* 5:20). Censures help us avoid following the wrong people down the wrong path. God has a preventative purpose to discipline.

Third, God-ordained ecclesiastical punishments, such as those mentioned in paragraph 4, are necessary for keeping the germ of sin already present in the church from infecting the whole body. When Paul chided the Corinthians, who were reluctant to correct one of their own members, he used this third argument for church discipline with great force: 'Do you not know that a little leaven leavens the whole lump? Cleanse out the old leaven that you may be a new lump, as you really are unleavened' (*1 Cor.* 5:6, 7). Discipline purifies the church.

Fourth, church censures are necessary 'for vindicating the honour of Christ and the holy profession of the gospel'. What Christ offers to us is holy; it is a pearl of great price. We are to keep what is holy from those who act like dogs and pigs in the church (*Matt.* 7:6). Furthermore, God's people are called to be godly. Jude says we are to hate 'even the garment stained by the flesh' (*Jude* 23). We discipline for Christ's sake.

Finally, discipline is also sometimes necessary 'for preventing the wrath of God, which might justly fall upon the church, if they should suffer his covenant and the seals thereof, to be profaned by notorious and obstinate offenders'. Paul's admonitions about the Lord's supper, his mysterious comment in 1 Corinthians 11 about some offenders being weak, ill and dead—these are warnings about God's displeasure against those who disrespected the seals of the covenant (the sacraments) or the covenant itself (the gospel). God is displeased with churches that tolerate sin—for example, allowing unrepentant sinners to partake of the supper or baptize their children. To avoid God's displeasure, we must deal with sin faithfully, and that sometimes entails discipline. If only we judged more faithfully in the church, and more truly, the apostle tells us that we would not have to be judged by the Lord (*1 Cor.* 11:27-34).

Degrees of discipline

It remains to be said that there are different kinds and degrees of censure to be carried out by the church's officers (rather than the church's congregation) for the attaining of any of these five ends. The method of discipline pursued, and the lengths to which it is pursued, should always take into consideration the nature of the wrong itself, the faults of the person, their response to correction and, we might add, God's great grace to us.

Sometimes all that may be needed is 'admonition'. This is the kind of rebuke that Paul urged the Thessalonians to accept from their leaders (*1 Thess.* 5:12).

Sometimes what may be required is suspension from the sacrament of the supper, at least for a time. This may be what Paul meant when he wrote to the Thessalonians about keeping away from disobedient brothers and sisters—that they might be ashamed and heed the warning, but still be treated as brethren (*2 Thess.* 3:6, 14, 15).

Sometimes someone may need to be cut off from communion with the saints altogether: 'excommunication from the church'. This is the severe treatment that Paul advocated for a member of the Corinthian church; it is also what Jesus commanded for those who refuse to listen to the church, and what Paul called Titus to do with divisive people who ignored multiple warnings (*1 Cor.* 5:4, 5, 13; *Matt.* 18:17; *Titus* 3:10). Yet even here, it is our hope that the sinner will be restored (*1 Cor.* 5:5). And as the church can testify with joy . . . they sometimes are!

CHAPTER 31:

OF SYNODS AND COUNCILS

Historic Text

31.1 For the better government, and further edification of the church, there ought to be such assemblies, as are commonly called synods or councils.[a]

31.2 As magistrates may lawfully call a synod of ministers, and other fit persons, to consult and advise with, about matters of religion;[b] so, if magistates be open enemies to the church,

RCF (1788) Text

31.1 For the better government and further edification of the church, there ought to be such assemblies as are commonly called synods or councils:[1] and it belongs to the overseers and other rulers of the particular churches, by virtue of their office, and the power which Christ has given them for edification, and not for destruction, to appoint such assemblies;[2] and to convene together in them, as often as they shall judge it expedient for the good of the church.[3]

Modern Version

31.1 For the better governing and further edifying of the church, there ought to be such assemblies as are commonly called synods or councils. Overseers and other rulers of particular churches, by virtue of their office and the power which Christ has given them for edification and not for destruction, have authority to appoint such assemblies and to convene together in them as often as they judge it expedient for the good of the church.

the ministers of Christ,
of themselves, by virtue
of their office; or, they,
with other fit persons,
upon delegation from
their churches, may
meet together in such
assemblies.[c]

Scripture Proofs (WCF)
    31.1 [a] Acts 15:2,4,6.
    31.2 [b] Isa. 49:23; 1 Tim. 2;1,2; 2 Chron. 19:8-11; 2 Chron., chapters 29,30; Matt.
2:4,5; Prov. 11:14. [c] Acts 15:2, 4, 22-23, 25.

Scripture Proofs (RCF)
    31.1 [1] Acts 15:2,4,6; [2] Acts 15:1-35; [3] Acts 15:1-35; 20:17.

A case for councils

Chapter 30 announced that church government is needed to administer
requisite discipline. Chapter 31 offers additional reasons for authoritative management and direction in the church. Church government has
many purposes besides discipline, and 'for the better government, and
further edification of the church, there ought to be such assemblies as are
commonly called synods or councils'.

The case for councils can easily be made from Scripture, for we see at
least one ecclesiastical assembly or synod in the early days of the church:
the council of Jerusalem, where, following a dispute in Antioch, leaders
gathered in Jerusalem and discussed what they should do (*Acts* 15:2-4;
see also *Acts* 6:1-7). What makes the council of Jerusalem so significant
for later generations of Christians is that it was held at a time when the
apostles were active and yet chose to call a gathering of elders. Time and
again the fact that the elders joined with the apostles in the deliberative
process is highlighted in the account provided by Luke (*Acts* 15:2, 4, 6).
This fact, among others, has signalled to later generations that the apostles were not pulling rank and speaking at the council in their office as
apostles, but in their office as elders.

Who can call a synod? Historic British and American perspectives

Presbyterians, and other Christians with them, are agreed that synods should be part of the regular life and government of the church. Questions remain, however, about the body or bodies that can call a council or summon a synod. The Westminster assembly itself was called by the Long Parliament, a revolutionary political body engaged in a civil war with forces loyal to King Charles I. Thus it is no surprise that members of the Westminster assembly held that 'magistrates may lawfully call a synod of ministers, and other fit persons, to consult and advise with about matters of religion'. After all, did not Isaiah promise Israel, 'Kings shall be your foster fathers, and queens your nursing mothers'? (*Isa.* 49:23). Is there not a good reason why the church is to pray for 'kings and all in high positions' especially? (*1 Tim.* 2:1, 2). Did not the godly king Jehoshaphat appoint both religious and civil leaders over his people, and the honourable Hezekiah take it in hand to reform religion in his own day? (*2 Chron.* 19:8-11; *2 Chron.* 29-30). Even King Herod knew enough to assemble religious leaders, and they knew enough to comply (*Matt.* 2:4, 5). The old proverb good for the Israelites seemed good for the church too: 'Where there is no guidance, a people fall, but in an abundance of counsellors there is safety' (*Prov.* 11:14).

The Westminster assembly was convinced that godly civil authorities could summon a synod and that there was wisdom in many counsellors. Nonetheless, 'if magistrates' proved to 'be open enemies to the church, the ministers of Christ, of themselves, by virtue of their office, or they, with other fit persons upon delegation from their churches, may meet together in such assemblies'. The events recorded in Acts 15 persuaded the assembly that by virtue of their teaching and ruling office alone, or by delegation from local churches, synods could meet without the approval of Christian magistrates (*Acts* 15:2, 4, 22, 23, 25).

The first body to indicate discomfort with the second paragraph was the Church of Scotland, which in officially adopting the confession for its use in 1647, qualified some parts of paragraph 2 to apply only to churches which had not yet settled a church government. The qualifying declaration had the effect of supporting the existence of the Westminster assembly and validating the Church of Scotland's part in it. It also suggested that a magistrate's involvement in calling a synod would be the exception and not the rule.

Following its Declaration and War of Independence from Britain, American Presbyterians revisited this chapter and found themselves unable to concur with its opening two paragraphs as originally framed, and they determined to revise the text that had stood for more than a century. In the spring of 1788, the synod of New York and Philadelphia, meeting in Philadelphia and functioning as the national assembly of the American Presbyterian Church, expanded the first paragraph of the original chapter and deleted the second, reflecting seven points of divergence between the old and the new chapters.

In the first place, the Philadelphia assembly disagreed with the Westminster assembly's assumption that synods summoned by civil authorities could be considered a norm for the church of Christ. Indeed, none of the scriptural passages cited by the Westminster assembly proved that the state could direct the church in any way. The prophecy of Isaiah showed at most that God could lead civil authorities to be well-disposed and supportive of God's old covenant people. Certainly it did not indicate that the state could guide the church. Paul's call to the church to pray for kings and for all in authority was a long way from a declaration of the state's direct involvement in the life of the church. The examples of Jehoshaphat, Hezekiah, and their officials were understood in the context of Israel as a theocratic state—a body which was at once a nation and a church. The church, as the New Israel, is more analogous to Israel in exile than Israel in Canaan: the church is scattered among the nations but not identified with any one of them (1 Pet. 1:1). It is not a political entity and cannot be led by political entities. The example of Herod is hardly applicable to the church: he was motivated by a greedy lust for power, and those who attended by a desire not to lose their heads. Certainly, 'Where there is no guidance, a people falls', but the 'abundance of counsellors' recommended in the book of Proverbs can be found in the officers of the church itself, and not only in officers of the state.

Second, the 1788 revisions allowed for a different mechanism for triggering the call of a synod. It is not the need or the wisdom of the magistrate that justifies summoning an assembly, but the 'good of the church'.

Thus an assembly should meet as frequently as expedient. Again, this reflects the priorities of the New Testament. The synod at Jerusalem was needed, therefore it was called.

In the third place, American Presbyterians disagreed that, within the church, only ministers should call synods, presumably by virtue of their office of teaching. 'It belongs to overseers and other rulers' to call synods, they said, 'by virtue of their office' of government. Indeed, Acts 15 repeatedly mentions the role of 'elders' (*Acts* 15:2, 4, 6, *etc.*).

In the fourth place, the revised confession states that elders are to attend the synod as overseers and rulers 'of the particular churches'. The normative role of an elder as a representative is highlighted by the mention of local congregations—a principle apparent in Acts 15, but not in the Westminster assembly's original paragraphs on synods.

Fifth, the American revision omitted all references to additional 'fit persons' being summoned to an assembly. At the Westminster assembly, these 'fit persons' were Members of Parliament. No doubt that assembly either meant to allow members of the government to attend future assemblies of the church, or intended to include theologians who could advise assemblies, as had been done in the past. The Philadelphia assembly, however, concluded that the only 'fit persons' to attend an assembly are the persons already appointed by Christ to govern his church, such as the elders and ministers who attended the assembly of Acts 15.

The sixth distinguishing mark between the first British paragraphs and the later American ones is the way in which the latter explicitly highlighted the fact that the power to appoint an assembly is a benevolent one. Church councils had often abused their power, passing rules which oppressed the people of God, and even put some of them to death. Here the American Presbyterian Church reminded itself that it had a power 'for edification, and not for destruction'.

The final difference between the first two paragraphs originally penned and the later revision is the clear statement that the authority given to an assembly is a 'power which Christ has given'. This declaration of the derived, or passed-on, power of the church is a truth fully in accord with statements of Christ's headship already mentioned in the opening lines of the chapters on the church (WCF 25.1) and on church censures (WCF 31.1). It is a truth well worth repeating here too: councils, and the members of councils, must minister in Christ's name alone.

Historic Text	*RCF (1788) Text*	*Modern Version*
31.3 It belongs to synods and councils, ministerially to determine controversies of faith, and cases of conscience, to set down rules and directions for the better ordering of the public worship of God, and government of his church; to receive complaints, in cases of maladministration, and, authoritatively, to determine the same: which decrees, and determinations, if consonant to the Word of God, are to be received with reverence, and submission; not only, for their agreement with the Word, but also for the power, whereby they are made, as being an ordinance of God appointed thereunto in his Word.[d]	**31.2** It belongs to synods and councils, ministerially to determine controversies of faith, and cases of conscience; to set down rules and directions for the better ordering of the public worship of God, and government of his church; to receive complaints in cases of maladministration, and authoritatively to determine the same: which decrees and determinations, if consonant to the Word of God, are to be received with reverence and submission; not only for their agreement with the Word, but also for the power whereby they are made, as being an ordinance of God appointed thereunto in his Word.[1]	**31.2** Synods and councils have authority ministerially to decide controversies of faith and cases of conscience, to set down rules and directions for the better ordering of the public worship of God and the government of his church, and to receive and authoritatively act on complaints of maladministration in the church. If the decrees and decisions of these synods and councils are in accordance with the Word of God, they are to be received with reverence and submission, not only because of their agreement with the Word, but also because of the authority by which they are decided, as being an ordinance that God has appointed in his Word.

Scripture Proofs (WCF)

31.3   [d] Acts 15:15,19,24,27-31; Acts 16:4; Matt. 18:17-20.

Scripture Proofs (RCF)

31.2   [1] Acts 15:15,19,24,27-31; Acts 16:4; Matt. 18:17-20.

The threefold task of synods and councils

Synods and councils, whether small and local, or large and international, are called to serve the Master of the church. They are to offer verdicts based on his revealed will, as did the apostles (as ministers) and elders (as governors) in Acts 15 when they made a judgment based on the words of the prophets recorded in Scripture (*Acts* 15:15). In this way, these bodies serve 'ministerially', or minister as Christ's servants. And they do so in three principal ways.

First, assemblies are to 'determine controversies of faith' and make judgments about ethical and theological issues (what used to be called 'cases of conscience'). Councils can help settle troubled minds, and sort out troubling disagreements. This is just what James and others with him did at the council of Jerusalem in their debate about the treatment of the Gentiles (*Acts* 15:19, 24, 27-31).

Second, synods or councils can 'set down rules and directions' to better order both public worship and church governance. In the first chapter of this confession the Westminster assembly argued 'that there are some circumstances concerning the worship of God, and government of the church, common to human actions and societies, which are to be ordered by the light of nature, and Christian prudence, according to the general rules of the Word' (WCF 1.6). Examples of wisdom applied to worship and government can be found in directories for worship, which include instructions about the order of a worship service, or in directories for church government, which include various steps taken in ecclesiastical discipline, or toward the training and ordination of ministers. In this thirty-first chapter the Westminster assembly is simply asserting that synods and councils can play a part in ordering and directing these secondary matters.

Third, synods and councils are 'to receive complaints' (including appeals) and make determinations about them. It seemed to the Presbyterians at the Westminster assembly that it was a principle of the light of nature, a seemingly intuitive truth revealed by God, that synods and councils were needed as courts of appeal for accusations of administrative injustice—procedural faults or unfairness in the hearing of a case at a local church. Just as Jesus directed people to make an appeal to the church (*Matt.* 18:17-20), so, by way of analogy, people should be able to make an appeal within the church as we see, again, in Acts 15.

Ministerial and *authoritative*

In the cases of controversies and complaints, a synod must serve Christ and his church ministerially. But it cannot be forgotten that a synod also serves 'authoritatively'. The entities we call 'church councils' (in the case of controversies), or could call 'church courts' (in the case of appeals or complaints), are 'authoritatively, to determine' what is brought before them. It is because Christ gives his power and because we follow his Word that assemblies have limited power: Christians are to receive 'decrees and determinations, if consonant to the Word of God'. And it is because Christ gives his power and because we follow his Word that assemblies have real power: Christians are to receive decrees and determinations with 'reverence and submission'.

The authority of church assemblies is twofold. First, their decisions are to be received with reverence and submission 'for their agreement with the Word'. The Word of God is always to bind the consciences of Christians, and those who speak truly from it should be heeded.

Second, 'decrees and determinations' of councils are to be received because of the 'power whereby they are made, as being an ordinance of God appointed thereunto in his Word'. God has given power to the church, and it is a significant fault if someone 'refuses to listen even to the church' (*Matt.* 18:17; *cf.* 17-20). God has employed synods in his service as one instrument to be used in government, and we are to heed their determinations not just as we would another Christian speaking truth to us, but as a duly appointed assembly of the church of Christ speaking truth to us.

In fact, this kind of contrast, the difference between the private opinions of some people and the confirmed decisions of councils, is seen in Acts 15. People had initially gone out from the Jerusalem church but had 'no instructions' from the council, and therefore could be ignored, not simply because they were wrong, but because they had no real authority (*Acts* 15:24).[1] This is the very opposite of how the council in Acts

---

[1] Since the 'from us' of Acts 15:24 refers to the 'apostles and elders' of the council and not to the 'apostles' or to the Jerusalem church, it suggests that the council may

intended its decrees to be taken. They refer to their decisions as 'requirements' (*Acts* 15:28), as 'decisions . . . reached by the apostles and elders' to be 'delivered' and observed (*Acts* 16:4).

Strikingly, the council went so far as to say that its rulings seemed 'good to the Holy Spirit and to us' (*Acts* 15:28). Perhaps it said this because of the extraordinary working of the Spirit. It may be because of the presence of the apostles that the council could have this kind of confidence. But it was not because of the presence of the apostles that the council carried force. In fact, first the apostles and elders in their decree, and then Luke in his record of the events, carefully excluded any possible interpretation that the council was authoritative only because the apostles were a part of it. They did this, again, by stressing repeatedly that their ruling came from the 'apostles and elders' and not from the apostles alone (*Acts* 15:2, 4, 6, 22, 23; 16:4).

Although Presbyterian churches, and some other Reformed churches, still maintain this practice in the use of presbyteries and general assemblies, the current of modern Christianity has drifted away from a respect for councils, their creeds, and their rulings on controversies. It seems that not only this confession, but the Word of God itself is calling us to heed councils not less, but more. The Westminster assembly did not overstep its bounds in calling Christians to receive the decisions of councils, at least those consonant with the Word of God, with 'reverence and submission'.

have met previously, and was perhaps a recognized feature of the Jerusalem-centred Palestinian church.

Historic Text	*RCF (1788) Text*	*Modern Version*
31.4 All synods or councils, since the apostles' times, whether general, or particular, may err; and, many have erred. Therefore, they are not to be made the rule of faith, or practice; but, to be used as an help in both.^e	**31.3** All synods or councils, since the apostles' times, whether general or particular, may err; and many have erred. Therefore they are not to be made the rule of faith, or practice; but to be used as a help in both.¹	**31.3** Since apostolic times, all synods and councils, whether general or particular, may err, and many have erred. Therefore, they are not to be made the rule of faith or practice, but are to be used as a help in regard to both.
31.5 Synods and councils are to handle, or conclude nothing, but that which is ecclesiastical: and are not to intermeddle with civil affairs which concern the commonwealth; unless by way of humble petition, in cases extraordinary; or, by way of advice, for satisfaction of conscience, if they be thereunto required by the civil magistrate.^f	**31.4** Synods and councils are to handle, or conclude nothing, but what which is ecclesiastical: and are not to intermeddle with civil affairs which concern the commonwealth; unless by way of humble petition, in cases extraordinary; or, by way of advice, for satisfaction of conscience, if they be thereunto required by the civil magistrate.¹	**31.4** Synods and councils are to handle or conclude nothing but what pertains to the church. They are not to intermeddle in civil affairs which concern the state, except by way of humble petition in extraordinary cases, or by way of advice, for satisfaction of conscience, if they are required to do so by the civil authority.

Scripture Proofs (WCF)

31.4 ^e Eph. 2:20; Acts 17:11; 1 Cor. 2:5; 2 Cor. 1:24.
31.5 ^f Luke 12:13,14; John 18:36.

Scripture Proofs (RCF)

31.3 ¹ Eph. 2:20; Acts 17:11; 1 Cor. 2:5; 2 Cor. 1:24.
31.4 ¹ Luke 12:13-14; John 18:36.

A doctrinal declaration

In paragraph 4 of this original chapter 31, or paragraph 3 of this revised chapter, the assembly makes a doctrinal declaration, an historical observation, and two biblically balanced directives.

The doctrinal declaration is that 'all synods or councils, since the apostles' times', whether general assemblies or particular ones, really '*may* err'. The apostles, working in concert, were kept from error in guiding the church.[1] But since that time, any gathering of rulers, from ecumenical councils to congregational elderships, may err. Only by the inspiration and miraculous guidance of the Holy Spirit can we be kept from fault. And while the Holy Spirit still guides his church, his inspired guidance ended with the completion of the New Testament. The Christian church and its teachings are 'built on the foundation of the apostles and prophets, Christ Jesus himself being the cornerstone' (*Eph.* 2:20). The church is not to look for an expanded foundation in the pretended apostolic succession offered by popes, or the supposed apostolic restoration offered by Mormons. Regardless of the claims of Roman Catholics or the contentions of any number of cults, there is no human leadership, either individual or collective, that can be kept from error. The sixteenth-century Protestant apologist William Whitaker was often quoted on the floor of the Westminster assembly. It was his judgment that Roman Catholics cannot 'possibly prevail against us by the scriptures; and therefore they press us as closely as they can with the authority of the fathers'.[2] But church fathers, though useful, are not second-generation apostles.

An historical observation

This is all the more apparent when we join the assembly in making an historical observation: that when one considers the decisions of 'synods or councils since the apostles' times, whether general or particular . . . many have erred'. Whether deemed ecumenical councils or local synods, we know that these councils must have erred, since they sometimes contradict one another, and truly opposing opinions cannot both be correct.[3]

We also know that they have erred because they contradict the teaching of Scripture. One only has to think of the Fourth Lateran Council in 1213 which helpfully clarified the doctrine of the Trinity, but also formally

---

[1] The apostles, working alone, sometimes erred, as Peter did with respect to the Gentiles and circumcision.

[2] William Whitaker, *A Disputation on Holy Scripture* (Geneva, 1610; Cambridge, 1849), p. 565.

[3] *E.g.,* Calvin's examples in *Institutes,* IV.ix.9.

adopted the flawed doctrine of transubstantiation (see WCF 29.6); or the Council of Trent meeting in phases between 1545 and 1563, which ruthlessly attacked the biblical doctrine of justification (see WCF 11.1).

Biblical directives

It is because councils may err, and have erred, that the assembly gives its two biblical directives. On the one hand, councils and synods 'are not to be made the rule of faith, or practice'. This follows from the teaching of Scripture itself. If the church is founded on the 'apostles and prophets, Christ Jesus himself being the cornerstone' (*Eph.* 2:20), then we need to look to the record of their teachings preserved in the Scriptures. If the examination of even apostolic teaching is commended by God, in the case of the noble Berean Christians who compared the words of Paul's preaching with the Word of God (*Acts* 17:11), then we cannot make any other text our norm for doctrine or duty. The best councils have summoned many wise men, but if we are warned in Scripture that our faith should not 'rest in the wisdom of men but in the power of God' (*1 Cor.* 2:5), then we cannot make the determination of ecumenical assemblies or local leaders a rule for our faith and practice. If the apostles themselves refused to 'lord' their position over the faith of believers, and called Christians to stand firm in their faith (*2 Cor.* 1:24), then it is not the place of any council to command our consciences on its own authority. The limits of conciliar power are established, Scripture being our supreme guide. In true wisdom the Westminster assembly acknowledged this limitation and redirected its readers to Holy Scripture (*cf.* WCF 1.4, 1.5, 1.10).

On the other hand, councils and synods are 'to be used as a help in both' faith and practice. We see this in Scripture itself, certainly in Acts 15, and probably also in Acts 6. Hopefully, we can see the wisdom of listening to, and learning the Christian faith from, gatherings of learned leaders who are well-versed in the Bible and fluent in theology. Hopefully, as we re-examine our Christian practice, we will never be so focused on what the Holy Spirit is teaching us that we will have no interest in what he has taught others. Certainly the Westminster assembly was hoping that others would learn from its discussions (which is perhaps why scribes were hired to record its debates). But they also expected that people would learn from their decisions, which is why the divines came to Westminster and subsequently submitted their confession to the English and Scottish Parliaments for use in the churches.

Synods, councils, and civil affairs

The last paragraph of the chapter is a reflection on two sayings of Jesus. The first saying was issued to a jealous brother before a watching crowd. A man demanded that Jesus come to his aid in an inheritance dispute. Jesus, having just been identified as a 'teacher' of God's people, refused to participate: 'who made me a judge or arbitrator over you?' (*Luke* 12:13). Jesus had the authority and capacity as the new Moses to rule over every aspect of Israel's existence, both religious and civil. Nonetheless, in the last days of Israel as a holy nation, Jesus chose to distinguish the sphere in which he would serve. And as the teacher of his people, the one to whom all other teachers ought to conform, he kept his distance from this spat between brothers about an estate. This, the assembly could not but help think, has real ramifications for the role of the church generally, *vis-à-vis* the state.

The second saying was issued to Pilate on the day Jesus was crucified. Pilate was interrogating Jesus about his authority and kingship. Jesus, in response, three times emphasized that his kingdom was not of this world (*John* 18:36). This assertion, too, seemed to have clear implications about the spirituality, rather than the worldliness, of the church and its mission.

Jesus the teacher was not interested in settling civil disputes. Jesus the king insisted before a ruler that his authority was distinct from that of the magistrate. And so the assembly concluded that the church's officers, in keeping with the unique sphere of the church, should only make decisions about 'that which is ecclesiastical'. The church is 'not'—even in its highest assemblies—'to intermeddle with civil affairs which concern the commonwealth'. This was a conclusion that no known civil government would resist. However, it was a conclusion which would directly contradict the aspirations of the Roman Catholic Church which later sought, and still pretends to, an authority over this world.

Petitions and advice

The assembly offered two exceptions to this general rule. First of all, in 'cases extraordinary', churches can make 'humble petition'. They cannot command civil authorities, but they can make requests. Second, they can give 'advice' to the civil magistrate, to settle cases of conscience (ethical matters), *if* they are required to do so. When asked what we believe and do, we should have an answer. When required to answer, we should do that too—as our Saviour, the king and head of the church, did before Pilate (*John* 18:33-38).

These were provisions that the assembly exercised often. They considered their own times and responsibilities to be 'extraordinary', and sent many an 'humble petition' to the House of Commons and the House of Lords. They did indeed have an unusual relationship with the English Parliament and were often *required* to give their 'humble advice' to the civil magistrate. In fact this confession of faith was first entitled, *The humble advice of the Assembly of divines, now by authority of Parliament sitting at Westminster, concerning a Confession of Faith.*

THE LAST THINGS

CHAPTER 32:

OF THE STATE OF MEN AFTER DEATH, AND OF THE RESURRECTION OF THE DEAD

Historic Text

32.1 The bodies of men, after death, return to dust, and see corruption:[a] but, their souls (which neither die, nor sleep) having an immortal subsistence, immediately return to God who gave them:[b] the souls of the righteous, being then made perfect in holiness, are received into the highest heavens, where they behold the face of God, in light and glory, waiting for the full redemption of their bodies.[c] And the souls of the wicked are cast into hell, where they remain in torments and utter darkness, reserved to the judgment of the great day.[d] Beside these two places, for souls separated from their bodies, the Scripture acknowledges none.

Modern Version

32.1 After death, the bodies of men decay and return to dust, but their souls, which neither die nor sleep, having an immortal existence, return immediately to God, who gave them. The souls of the righteous are then made perfect in holiness and received into the highest heavens, where they behold the face of God in light and glory as they wait for the full redemption of their bodies. The souls of the wicked are cast into hell, where they remain in torments and utter darkness as they are kept for the judgment of the great day. Scripture recognizes no other place except these two for the souls which have been separated from their bodies.

Scripture Proofs

32.1 [a] Gen. 3:19; Acts 13:36. [b] Luke 23:43; Eccles. 12:7. [c] Heb. 12:23; 2 Cor. 5:1,6,8; Phil. 1:23, with Acts 3:21, and Eph. 4:10. [d] Luke 16:23,24; Acts 1:25; Jude v. 6,7; 1 Pet. 3:19.

Dust to dust

Chapter 32 begins its discussion of the state of human beings after death with a grim reality, echoing a key phrase from the wretched curse recorded in Genesis 3. For Adam and Eve the crushing reality of death as a result of sin was first experienced in the loss of their own child. From that day to this, we have never really become accustomed to living alongside death. At the same time, we have become accustomed to the *fact* of death. The fact of death, on which our news media report every day, is hardly a ground-breaking story.

Nonetheless, human beings were not made to die. Actually, it was only when evil invaded this world that God explained the full ramifications of sin and death to the first sinners: 'By the sweat of your face you shall eat bread, till you return to the ground, for out of it you were taken; for you are dust, and to dust you shall return' (*Gen.* 3:19). At our end, we are brought back to our beginning. We 'return to the ground'. Adam was composed of the dirt of the ground and, after our demise, it is dirt that our decomposed bodies become. Our bodies, even the bodies of kings, 'see decay', as Paul reminded people in Pisidian Antioch. Indeed, there is only one person who has ever died who was kept from corruption (*Acts* 13:36, 37).

Immortal subsistence

Ominously (for unbelievers) and wonderfully (for believers) while the human body disintegrates for a time, the human soul does not. A fully conscious aspect of every one of us never dies—in fact, never even sleeps.[1] We have at our core what might be called 'an immortal subsistence' which continues to exist, and is never annihilated.

However, we must believe in something more than the mere immortality of the human soul. We must also confess that the soul has a destination. In speaking of the continued life and clear destination of our souls the confession echoes the language of an inspired pundit. Near the end of Ecclesiastes, the wise man describes the decline of life and concludes that 'the dust [shall] return to the earth as it was: and the spirit shall return unto God who gave it' (*Eccles.* 12:7). Here the poet adds information to what the Lord reveals in Genesis 3. We as dust will indeed return to the earth. But we are not merely absorbed by the

---

[1] The doctrine of soul sleep was reasserted at the time of the Reformation. For an early refutation, see John Calvin, *An Excellent Treatise of the Immortalytie of the Soule* (London, 1581); the book was written in 1534, first printed in 1542.

earth, becoming one with the world. No, our spirit returns to God. Like homing pigeons, our souls always wing their way back to our Creator. It is this truth which underlay a promise to a dying thief, on the day that Jesus re-opened paradise. When the man died—as when every woman, man, and child dies—his body was left on this earth, but his soul went to meet the God-man (*Luke* 23:43).

In our natural or native state we are souls with bodies. Only in the period between death and resurrection does a human being exist, temporarily, as a soul without a body.[1] It is essential to understand the soul in its native state. Nonetheless, if some description of who we are must stand for the whole, it is appropriate to think of who we are as souls, lost souls, or saved souls. In attempting to understand this 'immortal subsistence' and existence—man as soul—we need to pay careful attention to the way in which Jesus used his pronouns when speaking to a dying thief: '*you*', he said, 'will be with *me* in paradise'. In saying this, Jesus was not speaking about an embodied existence, either for the thief, or for himself. The thief would be thrown on a heap or into a pit. Jesus would be buried in a borrowed tomb. So Jesus was speaking about the presence of their souls in heaven, which means that humanity as soul represents and encapsulates so much of what we are that the soul alone can be considered a 'me' or a 'you'. Jesus did not need to say, 'I'll meet your soul

---

[1] The human soul is not the sum total of who we are. Nor is it the 'best' part of what we are, as some philosophers and theologians have thought. We are, after all, deliberately embodied souls, and the separation of soul and body is temporary and not eternal; an unnatural distortion of what should be and will be, only made possible by the miraculous power of God himself in the window of time between death and resurrection. If we are embodied souls, the severance of the body from the soul at death can only be understood as a consequence of humanity as fallen, and not as a consequence of humanity as created. That also means that the resurrection of our bodies at the last day, and the reunion of the whole man, soul with body, on that day, is not one of many different possible modes of existence for the human soul. It is the restoration of the only proper form of existence. One reason why Christians reject the *re*incarnation of the soul is that we reject, properly speaking, even the incarnation of the soul. The soul is not an eternal or pre-existent thing that happens to be blessed with a human body. A careful reading of Genesis 2:7 indicates that the soul is man, and except in death, the soul is embodied man. It is for that reason that we also deny that the soul can inhabit a human body in one cycle of life and inherit some other life-form in another cycle.

later today.' Although it is difficult for us to imagine how, it was entirely appropriate—it was most accurate and true—for Jesus to say, I will see 'you' in heaven, later today, when my work on earth is done.

Waiting for redemption

What Jesus Christ said to this new Christian on the cross next to his was meant, of course, to comfort him. For those who have looked for their righteousness in Christ, meeting 'God, the judge of all' constitutes a quantum leap in happiness, because the souls of those who are declared righteous actually become perfected in holiness. 'The spirits of the right-eous' are 'made perfect' (*Heb.* 12:23).

Jesus was received in heaven, and the great blessing of that saved soul on the cross, as with any saved soul, was to be received in the place where Jesus is (*Acts* 3:21). That is why a man like Paul was so 'hard pressed' in trying to decide between embodied service on earth and an immediate presence with Christ. In the end his desire was 'to depart and be with Christ, for that is far better', even though Paul's work on earth was still needful (*Phil.* 1:23).

From the moment that we become Christians we are 'enrolled in heaven' (*Heb.* 12:23). It is our privilege to be admitted where Christ is, and he is in the highest place. As Paul told the Ephesians, the one who once 'descended is the one who also ascended far above all the heavens' (*Eph.* 4:10) and it is by far our highest privilege to be with him—our highest privilege even when we are reduced to being souls awaiting the full redemption from the curse, the full deliverance of our bodies from the power of death and decay, the full reconstruction of the 'tent that is currently our earthly home' (*2 Cor.* 5:1).[1]

For Christians there is always a sense 'that while we are at home in the body we are away from the Lord' (*2 Cor.* 5:6). At home in the body, we are still in some sense homeless. It does not always feel this way

---

[1] It appears that the Westminster assembly concluded that 2 Corinthians 5:1 referred to the destruction of our current bodies and, in Paul's reference to 'a build-ing from God, a house not made with hands, eternal in the heavens', a reference to our glorified bodies. This is a plausible interpretation of the text. Some interpreters disagree, and see here a reference to Christ's resurrected body and the shelter we find in him.

when a friend or family member dies. Our home feels empty without them. But the truth is that we have lost a travelling companion. *They are already home.* The point is that our current temporary distance from God should help us to think clearly about our future temporary absence from our bodies.

In thinking about our absence from God, we gain perspective. However, in thinking about the presence of God, we gain courage. It is true, that when we die we will have to wait for 'the redemption of our bodies'. This can be discouraging, even frightening, to think about. But when we consider the beginning of an eternal life with our Saviour, it really is possible to conclude with Paul that 'we would rather be away from the body and at home with the Lord' (*2 Cor.* 5:8). To be home with the Lord is to 'behold the face of God'. To be home with the Lord is to bask in his 'light and glory'.

Reserved for judgment

And yet in the confession's scriptural footnote that directs us to Luke 23 and the two thieves on the cross, we are reminded also of the two destinies of mankind. One thief, having trusted in Christ and repented of his crimes, headed to heaven (*Luke* 23:43). The other, for all that the Bible tells us, did not.

The Scriptures teach that those who are merely remorseful, rather than truly repentant, end up in their own place—a place different from the place to which believers are gathered (*Acts* 1:25). That place has a name: it is called hell. The souls of unredeemed people remain there; they may be those whom Peter has in mind when he speaks of 'spirits in prison' (*1 Pet.* 3:19), awaiting the day when they will be taken before the judge for the final declaration about their everlasting state. They are like the rebellious angels whom Jude mentions, 'kept in eternal chains under gloomy darkness until the judgment of the great day' (*Jude* 6).

The place where they are kept is described in the Word of God in the darkest terms. Lost creatures awaiting the final judgment day are already 'undergoing a punishment of eternal fire' (*Jude* 7). The misery of lost people is so vividly pictured by Jesus in the story of the lost rich man, who oppressed Lazarus in his lifetime and then was oppressed by God after death, that we are surely to take warning (*Luke* 16:23, 24).

The story of the rich man and Lazarus, much like the history of the two thieves, reminds us that the Word of God does not mention any third location for the souls of the departed. Purgatory and *Limbus Patrum* do not feature in the Bible.[1] There is no other place mentioned besides heaven and hell, and 'beside these two places, for souls separated from their bodies, the Scripture acknowledges none'. As there is also no other name under heaven given for our salvation, let us acknowledge the Lord and Saviour of mankind and seek salvation in him and from his judgment.

### *Historic Text*	### *Modern Version*
32.2 At the last day, such as are found alive, shall not die, but be changed:[e] and, all the dead shall be raised up, with the selfsame bodies, and none other, although with different qualities, which shall be united again to their souls forever.[f]	**32.2** At the last day those who are alive shall not die but shall be changed. All the dead shall be raised up with their selfsame bodies, and no other (although with different qualities), which shall be united again with their souls forever.
32.3 The bodies of the unjust, shall, by the power of Christ, be raised to dishonour: the bodies of the just by his Spirit, unto honour; and, be made conformable to his own glorious body.[g]	**32.3** By the power of Christ the bodies of the unjust shall be raised to dishonour. The bodies of the just shall be raised to honour by his Spirit and brought into conformity with Christ's own glorious body.

Scripture Proofs

    32.2 [e] 1 Thess. 4:17; 1 Cor. 15:51,52. [f] Job 19:26,27; 1 Cor. 15:42-44.

    32.3 [g] Acts 24:15; John 5:28,29; 1 Cor. 15:43; Phil. 3:21.

---

[1] According to Roman Catholic teaching, purgatory is the place where sinners, after death, continue to make satisfaction to God for their sins. *Limbus Patrum,* an incorrect but less objectionable doctrine, is the place where Old Covenant believers were supposed to have slept while awaiting the accomplishment of redemption by Christ, at which point they were awakened and their souls translated to heaven. The doctrine of *Limbus Patrum* is of much greater antiquity than that of Purgatory.

Never to die

World history has an end point. As there was a first day, so there will be a last day. The 'day' of the Lord's return need not be conceived of as a literal twenty-four hour period. The term refers to an event more than a unit of time. Indeed, the events surrounding our Lord's return are in Scripture also referred to as an 'hour', as well as a 'day' (*e.g., John* 5:25).

On that last day there will be people, perhaps very many people, who will be left alive. It is surprisingly hard to know whether unbelievers still living when Christ returns will remain alive, or will be crushed before him, only to be quickly raised to face him at the judgment. While there is some question about the sequence of events for living unbelievers, there can be no doubt, however, about what will happen to living believers on that great day. The Apostle Paul knew that first-century Christians in Thessalonica were wondering what would happen if Christ should return in their lifetime, and so the apostle gave them this teaching: 'we who are alive' (the 'we' referring to believers), 'who are left, will be caught up together with them in the clouds to meet the Lord in the air, and so we will always be with the Lord' (*1 Thess.* 4:17). In other words, believers found alive by Christ will never experience death. They will begin an eternity of communion with Christ at that moment.

Nonetheless, as Paul told the Corinthians, although 'we shall not all sleep', it is still the case that 'we shall all be changed'. The change shall be instantaneous. It will come 'in a moment, in the twinkling of an eye, at the last trumpet'. When the trumpet sounds, and as the dead are 'raised imperishable', those who are alive, like those who were dead, 'shall be changed' (*1 Cor.* 15:52).

Ever to live

As Paul implied in the passage from 1 Corinthians just quoted, and in the verse prior to the citation from 1 Thessalonians, the last day will also be a redefining, and reconstituting, moment for those who have died. 'The dead shall be raised up, with the selfsame bodies' that they had while alive. It is challenging to comprehend how this can be the case for bodies that have been ravaged and destroyed, first in this life, and then completely in the grave.

It is because we baulk at this possibility that God gave us the book of Job. There we see Job's incredible confidence, uttered even as his heart fainted within him. For what could be a clearer expression of confidence in a future resurrection and reconstitution of the body, than his assurance to his friends, that even 'after my skin has been . . . destroyed, yet in my flesh I shall see God'. The deliberate phrasing of his confession emphasizes his expectation of seeing God in his own body. And lest anyone should miss this point, the patriarch went on to say that he would see God 'for myself'. Yes 'my eyes shall behold, and not another' (*Job* 19:26, 27).

For those Christians who have died, and will die, before the return of their Lord, they will on that day be raised with their own bodies, although the promise of 'change' in the Scriptures indicates that their bodies will have 'different qualities'. The Scriptures assure us that at the resurrection of the dead we shall be raised 'imperishable', with bodies characterized by 'glory' and 'power'. These will be real physical bodies even though they are 'spiritual bodies'—that is, bodies characterized by the glory and power of the spiritual realm (*1 Cor.* 15:42-44).

And lest we forget, the confession reminds us that this reunion of soul and body is permanent. It is a union that will last 'forever'. All people will in some sense live forever, although for those who are isolated from God their eternal existence will be experienced as an eternal death.

Dishonour and *honour*

In fact the horror of this reality is the first point in the final paragraph of this chapter. Yes, the resurrection will be a resurrection 'of both the just and the unjust' (*Acts* 24:15). Yes, 'an hour is coming when all who are in the tombs will hear his voice and come out' (*John* 5:28, 29). Yes, by the power of Christ the bodies of those who are unrighteous shall be brought to life. But there is no promise of power, of glory, or anything good for those resurrected and reunited people. The Scriptures say nothing about the resurrected bodies of the wicked. Suffice it to say that they will 'be raised to dishonour'.

The bodies of the just, or the righteous, on the other hand, will have an entirely different experience and existence. 'The bodies of the just by his Spirit' will be raised to 'honour; and be made conformable' to the 'glorious body' of Jesus Christ. We shall be remade after his pattern.

Astonishingly, for those who look to Christ, the dishonour and the weakness that characterize us now will be gone forever (*1 Cor.* 15:43). The life-long process of being made more Christlike shall be in that moment totally complete. United to the resurrected Saviour, at our resurrection we shall finally be like him. By the agency of his Spirit (a fact not emphasized with respect to the resurrection of the unjust),[1] and by the immense 'power that enables him . . . to subject all things to himself', Christ 'will transform our lowly bodies to be like his glorious body' (*Phil.* 3:21).

Our first honour on the last day will be greater than every honour granted on any day. And yet it remains the case that this is a 'mystery' (*1 Cor.* 15:51). We do not know what imperishable bodies will be like: how our bodies will be the same, yet different; what stage of development our bodies will be in or whether there will be such a thing. But we do know that at the last day perfected souls will be given perfect and honourable bodies, and wicked persons be clothed with imperishably dishonourable bodies. Given what we do not know, and especially what we do, let us seek first the kingdom of God, and everything else will fall into place.

---

[1] Beattie, *The Presbyterian Standards* (Richmond, 1896), pp. 394-395.

CHAPTER 33:

OF THE LAST JUDGMENT

Historic Text

33.1 God has appointed a day, wherein he will judge the world, in righteousness, by Jesus Christ,[a] to whom, all power and judgment is given of the Father.[b] In which day, not only the apostate angels shall be judged,[c] but likewise all persons that have lived upon earth, shall appear before the tribunal of Christ, to give an account of their thoughts, words, and deeds; and, to receive according to what they have done in the body, whether good or evil.[d]

Modern Version

33.1 God has appointed a day in which he will judge the world in righteousness by Jesus Christ, to whom all power and judgment has been given by the Father. In that day not only shall the apostate angels be judged, but also shall all people who have ever lived on earth appear before the judgment seat of Christ in order to give an account of their thoughts, words, and deeds, and to receive judgment according to what they have done in the body, whether good or evil.

Scripture Proofs

33.1 [a] Acts 17:31. [b] John 5:22,27. [c] 1 Cor. 6:3; Jude v. 6; 2 Pet. 2:4. [d] 2 Cor. 5:10; Eccles. 12:14; Rom. 2:16; Rom. 14:10,12; Matt. 12:36,37.

The Judge

The last chapter of the confession is an extended reflection on Paul's promise to the people of Athens long ago, that God 'has fixed a day on which he will judge the world in righteousness by a man whom he has appointed' (*Acts* 17:31). The 'day' of judgment emphasizes the certainty of the coming event, 'the world' its scope, and 'righteousness' the true goodness and justice of the judge himself. It stands to reason that the man who will judge is Jesus Christ, the one to whom the 'Father . . . has given all judgment'. In fact, as Jesus made clear when speaking about himself, he has been given 'authority to execute judgment, because he is the Son of Man' (*John* 5:22, 27).

The choice of biblical texts offered here by the Westminster assembly is very significant. The self-reference of Jesus in the Gospel of John as the promised Son of Man brings us back to the first man. God made a man in Genesis and appointed him to rule the world, a task at which he failed miserably. Later in the Old Testament the book of Daniel spoke of a coming ruler, the Son of Man, who would bring in a kingdom and rule the world (*Dan.* 7:13, 14). Here and elsewhere Jesus identified himself as that man, as the perfect governor the world looks for and groans for. And his ultimate act as ruler will be the judgment of the whole world.

Angels

In that day of judgment 'not only the apostate angels shall be judged, but likewise all persons that have lived upon earth shall appear before the tribunal of Christ'. In the New Testament the final judgment of angels is announced, twice as a warning and once as an encouragement. God did not spare 'the angels who did not stay within their own position of authority' and they now wait 'in eternal chains under gloomy darkness until the judgment of the great day' (*Jude* 6). And 'if God did not spare angels when they sinned, but cast them into hell and committed them to chains of gloomy darkness to be kept until the judgment', then he knows both how to punish the unrighteous and to 'rescue the godly' (*2 Pet.* 2:4, 9).

In the New Testament the final judgment of angels is also mentioned in the context of our judgments of one another. In 1 Corinthians 6 Paul rebukes litigious Christians at Corinth for daring to take their problems before unbelievers: 'Do you not know that the saints will judge the world? And if the world is to be judged by you, are you incompetent to try trivial cases?' For that matter, 'Do you not know that we are to judge angels? How much more, then, matters pertaining to this life!' (*1 Cor.* 6:2, 3). If Christ is the final judge, Christians compose a kind of final jury. Thus the apostle sees suits between believers as ludicrous given that we will one day join Jesus in judging much greater matters. In 1 Corinthians 6 there is no distinction between the judgment of good angels or of bad, but Jude 6 clarifies that it is the fallen angels who are to be judged.

Human beings

The Scriptures remind us that this judgment is to include angelic beings, but it is also to include human beings. Actually, there is no indication in Scripture that all angels will come before God in the same way that all people will come before him. The only race which we know will be fully judged is the human one.

In expanding on the reality of human judgment, the Scriptures emphasize the certainty and breadth of the judgment: 'We will all stand before the judgment seat of God'; 'each of us will give an account of himself to God' (*Rom.* 14:10, 12). Sometimes, the Scriptures also stress the depth of that judgment: 'God judges the secrets of men by Jesus Christ' (*Rom.* 14:10; 2:16).

The judgment of God will in every way be comprehensive, and buried in the middle of this section about judgment is a reminder that 'all persons that have lived upon earth shall appear before the tribunal of Christ, to give an account' of nothing less than our 'thoughts, words, and deeds'. This truth is stressed in the Old Testament and in the New Testament. The book of Ecclesiastes concludes with a warning: 'God will bring every deed into judgment, with every secret thing, whether good or evil' (*Eccles.* 12:14). And as Jesus once said, 'on the day of judgment people will give account for every careless word they speak, for by your words you will be justified, and by your words you will be condemned' (*Matt.* 12:36-37).

The thoroughness of this judgment inevitably reflects biblical teaching on sin and righteousness. For those who are apart from Christ, this is a damning verdict, for God hates any and all sin. Indeed, the thought of our every dark reflection, careless word, and loveless action being replayed before God's throne should make any sane person tremble with a heightened awareness of the solemnity of judgment. And yet Christian believers must take courage in their special standing with Jesus Christ. God, as the believers' good Father, is delighted with the righteous thoughts, words and deeds of his children. Admittedly, they are far too few, and even our best efforts are tarnished in so many ways. What is worse, God will not tolerate our sins. But thankfully, for those found in Christ, our unworthy efforts will be accepted in Christ along with our unworthy persons, and our evil deeds will be covered over by Christ's spotless righteousness. It is in this righteousness of Christ that we will stand. We will find no real reason to be proud of ourselves before the judgment seat of God. Nor will we find reason to fear.

In speaking about the judgment, the final phrase of this section is unmistakably a paraphrase of 2 Corinthians 5:10: 'For we must all appear before the judgment seat of Christ, so that each one may receive what is due for what he has done in the body, whether good or evil.' Paul's reference here to the body is not easy to understand. Is this passage emphasizing that we will be judged bodily (as the Bible teaches elsewhere)? Or that we are going to be judged for sins done in the body (that is, actual sins committed in our lifetime)?[1] Whatever the answer, it is clear from other portions of Scripture that we shall be raised bodily and judged bodily for all our deeds, whether good or bad, and whether done in thought, word, or deed.

There are, as one might expect, wide implications to the day of judgment. It is clearly the case in Scripture, for example, that the coming judgment is closely connected to ethical imperatives. In Matthew 12 we are told that we should be sensitive about what we say because we will give account for every idle word. In Romans 14 we are told that we should not make a brother stumble because by our words we shall be justified or condemned. 'Every one of us shall give account of himself to God'. Clearly, as Scripture consistently teaches and as this confession ably summarizes that teaching, we will only stand in the judgment by the righteousness of Christ. Nonetheless, while reflecting on the coming judgment, it is necessary for each of us to ponder our present way of life.

---

[1] Both meanings are suggested in *Annotations upon All the Books of the Old and New Testament, sub loc.*

Historic Text	*Modern Version*
33.2 The end of God's appointing this day, is, for the manifestation of the glory, of his mercy, in the eternal salvation of the elect; and, of his justice, in the damnation of the reprobate, who are wicked, and disobedient. For, then, shall the righteous go into everlasting life, and receive that fullness of joy and refreshing, which shall come from the presence of the Lord: but, the wicked, who know not God, and obey not the gospel of Jesus Christ, shall be cast into eternal torments, and be punished with everlasting destruction from the presence of the Lord, and from the glory of his power.ᵉ	**33.2** God's purpose in appointing this day is to manifest the glory of his mercy in the eternal salvation of the elect, and the glory of his justice in the damnation of the reprobate, who are wicked and disobedient. On that day the righteous shall go into everlasting life and receive that fullness of joy and refreshing which shall come from the presence of the Lord; but the wicked, who do not know God and who do not obey the gospel of Jesus Christ, shall be cast into eternal torments and be punished with everlasting destruction from the presence of the Lord and from the glory of his power.

Scripture Proofs

33.2 ᵉ Matt. 25:31-46; Rom. 2:5,6; Rom. 9:22,23; Matt. 25:21; Acts 3:19; 2 Thess. 1:7-10.

The purposes of God's judgment

In one of Jesus' best known pictures of the judgment day, he speaks of the separation of the sheep and the goats. The sheep are blessed by the Father, and ushered into their eternal inheritance. The goats are cursed, commanded to depart from God and to enter the eternal fire first prepared for the devil and his angels (*Matt.* 25:31-46).

The most surprising aspect to Jesus' account of the day is that both groups contest what they deserve. Believers are told that they satisfied their Lord's hunger, slaked his thirst, welcomed him, clothed him, identified with him even in his suffering. In other words, they loved him. When they deny that they were so good, they are assured that in loving the Lord's people, they also loved him. With the unbelievers, the story is a total reversal. Jesus judges that they ignored his hunger and thirst; refused to welcome, clothe, or minister to him in prison. In other words, they did not care for him. Naturally they protest: they are better than he thinks. But the Lord confirms his judgment, for in despising his people, they despised him too.

Both reactions are striking in their own way. On the one hand, it is plain that God's people are finally, on the judgment day, at their wisest. They see no good in themselves. Faced with the awesome holiness of God, the imagined holiness which we parade during this life completely disappears. For Christians, this last day is a display of God's grace, a 'manifestation of the glory of his mercy' in their 'eternal salvation'. They will be saved because they are objects of electing love, and for no other reason.

On the other hand, it is painfully evident that on the same day God's enemies are at their most foolish. Face to face with the judge, they are more brazen in their declarations of worthiness than ever before; they lived their lives in their own sufficiency and they stick to their lines to the bitter end. They will not understand it, but for them, this day is a display of 'his justice', resulting in 'the damnation of the reprobate, who are wicked and disobedient'. They will be judged both because they are reprobate, and because they are 'wicked and disobedient'.

God, not man

Although great throngs will stand before the seat of judgment, the first focus on the final day will be on God, not man. On the day of judgment the world will finally know for sure who are God's elect, and who are the reprobate. Nonetheless the chief event will be the presentation of *God's* character, as his glory is seen in his unfailing mercy and in his true justice. This is the 'end' or the purpose in 'God's appointing this day'. It is to manifest something glorious about his mercy, about his justice, ultimately about himself.

In this judgment God's mercy will be amply exhibited. It will be seen in his endurance, 'with much patience', of those who were destined for destruction (*Rom.* 9:22). It will be seen in the way in which he fashioned 'vessels of mercy, which he . . . prepared beforehand for glory' (*Rom.* 9:23). It will be seen in his over-generous assessment of his 'good and faithful' servants, who were 'faithful over a little' but are now set 'over much' and 'enter into the joy' of their master (*Matt.* 25:21). In short, 'the righteous' enter 'everlasting life, and receive that fullness of joy and refreshing' which comes from the 'presence of the Lord'.

In this judgment, God's justice will also be on display, a grim spectacle that all will see. There are those with a 'hard and impenitent heart' who are 'storing up wrath . . . when God's righteous judgment will be revealed'. They will be judged 'each one according to his works' (*Rom.* 2:5, 6). These are the people who will be shown wrath; people 'prepared for destruction' (*Rom.* 9:22). These are the people who should dread the day 'when the Lord Jesus is revealed from heaven with his mighty angels in flaming fire, inflicting vengeance on those who do not know God and on those who do not obey the gospel of our Lord Jesus' (2 *Thess.* 1:8). And as the righteous are blessed by entering God's presence, the wicked are cursed by being cast from it. 'They will suffer the punishment of eternal destruction, away from the presence of the Lord and from the glory of his might' (2 *Thess.* 1:9).

The judgment day is primarily a declaration about the Lord. But it is an event that should inject urgency into Christian conversations with the unconverted. Given the glory of the eternal state for believers, and the horror of the eternal state for the lost, the Bible's message to all unbelievers is not only clear, but also emphatic: 'repent therefore, and turn back, that your sins may be blotted out' (*Acts* 3:19).

Historic Text	*Modern Version*
33.3 As Christ would have us to be certainly persuaded, that there shall be a day of judgment, both to deter all men from sin, and for the greater consolation of the godly in their adversity;^f so, will he have that day unknown to men, that they may shake off all carnal security, and be always watchful, because they know not at what hour the Lord will come; and, may be ever prepared to say, come Lord Jesus, come quickly, amen.^g	**33.3** As Christ would have us to be absolutely convinced that there will be a day of judgment, both to deter all men from sin and to give greater consolation to the godly in their adversity, so will he have that day unknown to men, that they may shake off all carnal security, may always be watchful—because they do not know at what hour the Lord will come—and may always be prepared to say, 'Come, Lord Jesus. Come quickly. Amen.'

Scripture Proofs

33.3 ^f 2 Pet. 3:11,14; 2 Cor. 5:10,11; 2 Thess. 1:5,6,7; Luke 21:27,28; Rom. 8:23,24,25.
^g Matt. 24:36,42-44; Mark 13:35-37; Luke 12:35,36; Rev. 22:20.

A certain day

The focus of this chapter, to the end, is personal, rather than cosmological. What will happen to this planet when the curtain rises on eternity? Will it become a suburb of heaven? A slum of hell? Will it experience a glorious transformation? Will it exist at all? These are among the questions that the confession does not seek to answer—to which could be added theories of millennial rule and the destiny of the Jews. Instead of speculation, the final note in this confession of faith is one of persuasion. For two different reasons, the Lord Jesus Christ wants us to be 'certainly persuaded that there shall be a day of judgment'. There must be no attempt to escape this fact because there can be no successful attempt to escape this day. 'We must all appear before the judgment seat of Christ' (2 Cor. 5:10).

We need to be persuaded of this fact—and 'knowing the fear of the Lord, we persuade others' (2 Cor. 5:11)—because the judgment day is designed, in part, 'to deter us from sin'. The Apostle Peter tells his readers that 'all things are to be dissolved', and since this is the case, we must mind 'what sort of people' we ought to be with respect to holiness and godliness (2 Pet. 3:11). In other words, since we are waiting for his return we must 'be diligent to be found by him without spot or blemish, and at peace' (2 Pet. 3:14). A reminder of the return of Christ is a call to careful thinking and living.

Like the Lord's first disciples, we also want to keep the return of the Lord in mind so that we can find comfort in adversity. We want to be persuaded of Christ's return because when the 'Son of Man' comes 'with power and great glory', we can 'straighten up and raise' our heads, because our 'redemption is drawing near' (Luke 21:27, 28). There are persecutors from whom many Christian people long to be delivered. Yes, Christians pray first for the salvation of their enemies. But we also take comfort in the fact that we can leave justice to God. Paul states this plainly: 'God considers it just to repay with affliction those who afflict you, and to grant relief to you who are afflicted as well as to us, when the Lord Jesus is revealed from heaven with his mighty angels' (2 Thess. 1:5-7). We live in hope. We 'who have the firstfruits of the Spirit, groan inwardly as we wait' for all the blessings that will be ours in fullness, which are now ours in part. We wait 'eagerly' and 'we wait for it with patience' (*Rom.* 8:23-25).[1]

An unknown date

The day is certain. It is set in the calendar of God. But 'concerning that day and hour no one knows, not even the angels of heaven, nor the Son, but the Father only' (*Matt.* 24:36). Just 'as Christ would have us to be certainly persuaded that there shall be a day of judgment . . . so will he have that day unknown to men'.

Here too, just as in the revelation of the fact of the day, so also in the mystery of the timing of that day, God surely has a purpose. And from what we can gather, one major purpose is to help us to 'shake off all' false sense of human security and carelessness in which we so easily rest. It was precisely because they did not know when he would return that Jesus urged his followers once and again to 'stay awake', to 'be ready', to be 'dressed for action', to have their 'lamps burning', to be 'waiting' for the Master (*Matt.* 24:42-44; *Mark* 13:35-37; *Luke* 12:35, 36).

It is also because the return of the king marks the end of all opportunity to repent, that the Lord urges us to consider his second coming. As understood by the Westminster assembly, the coming of the Lord, the resurrection, and the judgment, are all distinct but closely related aspects of one great event; there is no gap in 'time' between them. In the recollection of the return of Christ, Christians and non-Christians are called away from their constant drift towards carelessness. When Jesus returns, every rebel should want to have made his peace with God already. When Jesus returns, every Christian should want to be found awake and serving, rather than awash in sin.

---

[1] The citation of these passages is the closest that the assembly comes to emphasizing a 'realized eschatology'—the fact that heaven and hell have already, to some extent, broken through into this world, and that there is a sense in which the blessings or curses of eternity are at once already, and not yet, a reality for God's people *and* God's enemies (see, *e.g., Col.* 3:1-4, which describes believers 'in the heavens' already, although they are living in Colosse; one could add to that specific text events pregnant with typology, such as the flood, the destruction of Sodom and Gomorrah; or places resonant of the new creation, such as the land of Canaan, or the city of Jerusalem).

Come Lord Jesus!

Nonetheless, well beyond the healthy desire to break free from destructive habits, better than the hope that we will not bring shame to his name when he returns for the final time, we want to *welcome* our Lord. There is a note of joyful expectation in the final line of this confession that reflects the joyful and blessed hope of the Scriptures. Christians are not braced for the coming of the Lord, anxiously worrying about his arrival. We are eager for his coming, hoping to be the generation that will hold the door open for him (*Luke* 12:36). And since it is sure that he is coming momentarily, as God counts his moments, we always want to be praying, 'Come, Lord Jesus!' Come quickly (*Rev.* 22:20).

SCRIPTURE INDEX

GENERAL INDEX

adoption, 54, 171-75
adultery, 330-31
American Bill of Rights, 317
American Presbyterian Church, 313, 315-16, 329, 412-14
Ames, William, 245n
Anabaptists, 309
angels, 48-50, 279, 436-37
antichrist, 320, 347-48
Apocrypha, 9, 11-12
Arminianism, 162, 168n
assurance, 14-15, 50, 55, 192, 225-35, 372
Augustine of Hippo, 138, 341
authorship, 11

baptism, 179, 188, 285, 364-85
Brooks, Thomas, 232
Burgess, Anthony, 79n, 186
Burroughs, Jeremiah, 97n, 186, 284-85

Calvin, John, 126n, 251n, 336n, 337
carnal Christian, 219

causation, 70-71
Cawdrey, Daniel, 246n
ceremonial law, 243-45, 261-62
Charles I, 411
Cheynell, Francis, 6
Christian communion, 351-56
Christian liberty, 259-72
church
censures of, 271-72, 401-7
councils of, 410-22
discipline in, 312-13, 405-7, 410, 415
governing of, 19-20, 401-4, 415
marks of, 345-46
membership in, 377
officers of, 402-4
ordinances of, 342-43
synods of, 410-22
Church of Scotland, 329, 411-12
circumcision, 251, 366-67, 374, 376, 379
civil disobedience, 319
civil government, 269-72, 421-22
civil magistrate, 307-21
communalism, 355-56

The Banner of Truth Trust originated in 1957 in London. The founders believed that much of the best literature of historic Christianity had been allowed to fall into oblivion and that, under God, its recovery could well lead not only to a strengthening of the church, but to true revival.

Inter-denominational in vision, this publishing work is now international, and our lists include a number of contemporary authors along with classics from the past. The translation of these books into many languages is encouraged.

A monthly magazine, *The Banner of Truth*, is also published. More information about this and all our publications can be found on our website or supplied by either of the offices below.

THE BANNER OF TRUTH TRUST

3 Murrayfield Road
Edinburgh, EH12 6EL
UK

PO Box 621, Carlisle,
Pennsylvania 17013,
USA

www.banneroftruth.co.uk